CISTERCIAN STUDIES SERIES: NUMBER THIRTY-EIGHT

ABBA

CISTERCIAN STUDIES SERIES: NUMBER THIRTY-EIGHT

ABBA

Guides to Wholeness and Holiness East and West

Papers presented at a Symposium on Spiritual
Fatherhood/Motherhood at the Abbey of New Clairvaux,
Vina, California, 12–16 June, 1978

EDITED BY
John R. Sommerfeldt

Cistercian Publications
Kalamazoo, Michigan
1982

© Copyright, Cistercian Publications, Inc., 1982

ISBN 0 87907 823 3

Library of Congress Cataloging
in Publication Data

Main entry under title:

Abba: guides to wholeness and holiness, East
    and West.

    (Cistercian studies series ; no. 38)
    1. Spiritual direction—Addresses, essays,
lectures. 2. Spiritual direction—Comparative
studies—Addresses, essays, lectures.
I. Sommerfeldt, John R. II. Institute of
Cistercian Studies (Vina, Calif.) III. Series.
BX2438.A22   248.4   81-1800
ISBN 0-87907-838-3   AACR2

Typeset by Gale Akins, Kalamazoo, Michigan
Printed in the United States of America

With respect and affection
the editors of Cistercian Publications
dedicate this volume to

Ambrose Southey
Archabbot of Citeaux

TABLE OF CONTENTS

INTRODUCTION

This volume presents the papers prepared for the Cistercian Symposium held at the Abbey of New Clairvaux, Vina, California, in June 1978. That was the fifth Cistercian Symposium, and this is the fifth volume to appear in this series within a series.[1]

The idea for the Vina Symposium was born on a casual stroll through the streets of Oxford, England, in June 1973. It was a sleepy Sunday morning in a town ordinarily bustling with academic—and other—activity. On that walk M. Basil Pennington, a monk of Saint Joseph's Abbey in Spencer, Massachusetts, and I were discussing the recently concluded—and very successful—Orthodox-Cistercian Symposium. Father Basil suggested that I, then the Executive Director of the Institute of Cistercian Studies at Western Michigan University, organize the next Symposium. He further suggested the topic: The Spiritual Master, East and West. In January of 1974, at the Cistercian novice masters meeting in Kalamazoo, Michigan, Father Basil repeated his request and told me of the generous offer of the abbot and community at Vina to act as our hosts.

I contacted our Vina host, Thomas X. Davis, Abbot of New Clairvaux and President of the American Region of Cistercian monasteries and requested that he join me in asking the advice of the abbots, abbesses, and other superiors of the cistercian monasteries in the United States and Canada[2] about the topic and date of the next Symposium. The results of this poll indicate the wide range of interests among Cistercians and may perhaps suggest the topic for the next Symposium:

1. The Spiritual Master, East and West;
2. The Cistercian Identity;

3. Poverty;
4. Authority and Obedience;
5. Prayer;
6. Liturgy;
7. Cistercian Art and Spirituality;
8. Scripture;
9. Communication;
10. Spiritual Direction;
11. *Ascesis;*
12. Ecumenism; and
13. Christology in Cistercian Spirituality.

The titles are mine and do not reflect the complexity and sophistication of the responses. For example, what I have called 'Cistercian Identity' was variously described as:

1. New Trends in Contemplative Searching and Living;
2. The Cistercians and Technology:
   A Counter Culture?;
3. The Cistercian Charism;
4. The Equilibrium of Cistercian Life:
   The Fathers and Today;
5. Future Shock and Cistercian Spirituality;
6. The Relation of Cistercians to Culture;
7. The Cistercians of Today and the Cultural
   Revolution; and
8. Monastic Life and Prophecy.

The responses did, however, justify the interest of Abbot Thomas and Father Basil in the topic, The Spiritual Master, East and West. I began a long and laborious process of discovering and inviting oriental masters who could enlighten us on the spiritual traditions of the Far East. Finding monks and nuns to do the same for the western spiritual heritage seemed much easier for someone with contacts among cistercian abbeys. Yet the number of Cistercians, Benedictines, secular clergy, and laymen who knew both traditions and could provide comparative studies surprised me.

I invited these *periti* to submit the papers collected in this volume, and I asked the cistercian monasteries of the Region to share community reports on their experience in this area. These papers were distributed to the Symposium participants —in America North and South, Asia, and Europe—and these participants gathered in California to discuss the papers in a four-day series of intense, though informal, sessions. Roman Catholics, Anglicans, Protestants, Jews and Buddhists helped us understand the existential reality of their spiritual traditions.

What emerged from the papers and discussions was a deeper realization of the fact that the master-disciple relationship of the Far East complemented, but did not reflect, the Western understanding of growth toward spiritual maturity through personal relationships. We spent less time speaking of masters and disciples than of fathers and sons, mothers and daughters, and spiritual friendship.

This fact is reflected in the title of this collection. Our topic was no longer 'Spiritual Masters, East and West', but 'Guides to Wholeness and Holiness, East and West'. Guidance toward spiritual self-realization and maturity takes different forms in the East and West. We profited much from understanding that difference and found ourselves enriched by it. Moreover, we discovered—or rediscovered—much about our own tradition and thus about ourselves. This self-knowledge is the true humility which the Cistercian Fathers taught. I hope that this volume will help the reader achieve similar knowledge and understanding.

Of course, the Symposium and this volume would have been impossible without the splendid hospitality of Abbot Thomas and the community of New Clairvaux. They generously welcomed all, Abbot–General and guru, nuns and laity, into their midst as Saint Benedict would have them do.[3] They tolerated willingly the interruption of their monastic schedule in a way which assured the guests that their life was one of deep spirituality and not mere comfortable routine. For that witness to their Father, Master, and Brother we can all be grateful.

John R. Sommerfeldt
The University of Dallas

NOTES TO INTRODUCTION

1. The papers from these symposia have been published in *The Cistercian Spirit: A Symposium in Memory of Thomas Merton* (CS 3; 1970); *Rule and Life: An Interdisciplinary Symposium* (CS 12; 1971); *Contemplative Community: An Interdisciplinary Symposium* (CS 21; 1972); and *One Yet Two: Monastic Tradition East and West* (CS 29; 1976), all edited by M. Basil Pennington, OCSO.

2. Superiors of both cistercian observances, the Order of Cistercians of Strict Observance (OCSO, commonly called Trappists) and the Order of Cistercians (O. Cist.) were polled.

3. The *Rule* of Saint Benedict urges (in chapter 53): 'All who arrive as guests are to be welcomed like Christ . . . ' . See David Parry, OSB, *Households of God: The Rule of St. Benedict with Explanations for Monks and Lay-people Today* (CS 39; 1980), pp. 140-43.

THE WESTERN TRADITION

THE SPIRITUAL FATHER IN THE SCRIPTURES

Felix Donahue, o c s o
Abbey of Gethsemani

W E CAN APPROACH our topic by taking a certain number of soundings. The ones which occured to me are: the use of the word 'father' in the Old and New Testaments (sections 1 and 2), then priest, prophet, and wisdom teacher as spiritual father (3-5), and finally Jesus and St Paul as spiritual fathers (6 and 7). These explorations should give us a sense of spiritual fatherhood as understood by the Judeo-Christian Scriptures.[1]

THE WORD 'FATHER' IN THE OLD TESTAMENT

'Father' occurs over 1,300 times in the Old Testament. A Greek concordance for the Septuagint listed something like 1,390. Using a Hebrew concordance, and a Greek one for the books not in the Hebrew Bible, I have counted 1,310, more or less.

Of these 1,300 uses, some twenty-one refer to God as Father. The vast majority refer to the male parent or to ancestors, forefathers. Apart from these references to God or to the male parent or forefathers, 'father' is used twenty to twenty-five times in a variety of senses. Let us look at these.

'Father' can mean founder or originator or prototype. Thus in Gn 4:20f., Jabel is called the father of herdsmen, while Jubal is styled 'father of all who play the lyre and the pipe'. In Jr 35:6, 8, 10, 14, 16, 18, the Rechabites refer to their founder, Jonadab, as 'our father'. God chose to trace

3

the Aaronic line of priests through Phinehas and so Mattathias of Modein, himself a priest of this line, praises Phinehas as 'our father' (1 M 2:54).

A chief minister or other high ranking administrator may be entitled 'father'. Thus the patriarch Joseph speaks of himself as 'a father to Pharoah' (Gn 45:8). Eliakim, steward over the royal household, is described as 'a father to the inhabitants of Jerusalem and to the house of Judah' (Is 22:21), although there are indications that his administration was not all that paternal (see v. 25; also Esther 13:6 and 16:11).

'Father' could express respect or indebtedness. Naaman the Syrian's servants speak to him as 'my father' (2 K 5:13). David addressed his father-in-law, Saul, as 'my father' (1 S 24:11). A certain Raziz, for his kindness and good will, was called 'father of the Jews' (2 M 14:37). Lasthenes, governor of Coelesyria, had helped king Demetrius back to power. In grateful recognition, Demetrius wrote to him as 'Lasthenes his father' (1 M 11:32). Among the names given the ideal king described in Is 9:6 is 'Father forever'. Job claims to have been 'a father to the poor' (Jb 29:16; see also 31:18).

Priest (Jg 17:10; 18:19), prophet (2 K 2:12; 6:21; 13:14), or wisdom teacher (Pr 4:1; Si 3:1) might be referred to as 'father'.

G. Quell suggests these various uses of 'father' may be interdependent. Commenting on the title 'father' given to a priest (Jg 17:10; 18:19), he writes:

This remarkable term, used to denote priestly authority, is connected with a tradition whereby the discharge of priestly ministry is thus incumbent on the actual head of the family, so that whoever functions in his place acquires the dignity of father. The young man was called 'father' because he did what the father was required to do.[2]

Quell notes that the head of the house functions as priest at the passover meal according to Ex 12:1-14, 21-28. According to the Yahwist and Elohist sources, in patriarchal times and into the period of the monarchy, every man of Israel, but especially the head of the family, was entitled to offer sacrifice

4

on altars other than those connected with a temple. Examples are: Abraham (Gn 22), Jacob (Gn 31:54; 46:1), Moses (Ex 17:15; 24:4-8, but Moses did belong to the tribe of Levi as did Aaron, his brother), Gideon (Jg 6:20-28), Manoah (Jg 13:15-23), Adonijah (1 K 1:9), Elijah (1 K 18:30-38).

Quell continues:

This priestly head of the house transfers his dignity as father to priestly officials who do not belong to the tribe, then to the prophets, who are called 'father' by their pupils (1 K 2:12) or by the king (1 K 6:21), and finally to administrators (Gn 45:8, Joseph; Is 22:21, Eliakim; I M 11:32, Lasthenes), those who bear trustworthy authority, or benefactores, the 'fathers of the poor' (Jb 29:16) . . . . Thus the figure of the father is a kind of ideal when it represents the side of the priestly office which should evoke respect, or when it stands for the even higher authority of the prophet with its demand for unconditional acknowledgement. It would also appear that supreme family rank was freely and spontaneously accorded, not merely in address but in official language, especially to the highranking administrator as one who discharges his office by commanding with loving concern.[3]

In these diverse instances, various aspects of the father-image operative in Israel are brought to the fore. At times, the accent is on the authority of the father and the honor and obedience due him. At other times, the love, care, concern, and wisdom with which this authority is exercised are stressed. The very terms 'father-son' suggest a communication and nurturing of life, but this is not made very explicit in the extended uses we have considered. On the other hand, the priestly, mediatorial, intercessory role of the father, as well as his role in the handing on of religious knowledge and practice, of tradition, take us into the realm of spiritual parenthood, in a sense. In other words, being parent in the Jewish tradition involved being spiritual parent, as many of the wisdom sayings illustrate.

Fathers, in the sense of forefathers, ancestors, the patriarchs, and other holy forebears, were considered as abiding sources of God's blessing and favor, that is, of life and everything required to sustain and prosper it. God looked upon Abraham, Isaac, Jacob, or David, and lavished his gifts and forgiveness on their descendants out of regard for them (see 2 K 13:23; Ex 32:13; Dt 9:27).

THE WORD 'FATHER' IN THE NEW TESTAMENT

The Greek word for father, *patēr,* occurs 415 times in the New Testament, while the Aramaic, *abba,* occurs three times. Of these 418 occurrences, some 255 refer to God, either as the Father or Jesus' Father or our Father. Compare this with the Old Testament in which the word 'father' occurs some 1,300 times, but refers to God in only some twenty cases.

In seventy-six instances, 'father' in the New Testament refers to the patriarchs or ancestors of the Jewish people. Abraham, Isaac, Jacob, Moses, and David are still vital forces, not only by the example of their lives, but also because the promise made to them is being fulfilled for us. We are heirs to the covenant God struck with them. Their descendants— according to the flesh and according to the Spirit—are still loved by God for the sake of the patriarchs (see Rm 4:1, 11-18; 9:4-8; 11:28; Ac 3:25; 13:32f.). Despite this, we may note that Jesus as presented by the gospel, when speaking in his own name, never refers to the patriarchs or to anyone else save God as his father. (However, see Jn 7:22 for 'father*s*'.)

Apart from the actual male parent or ancestors, do any other humans receive the title 'father' in the New Testament? In Ac 7:2, Stephen addresses the Jewish council as 'brethren and fathers'. Paul uses the same address when speaking to the Jews in Jerusalem (Ac 22:1). 1 Jn 2:13f. is directed to 'fathers,' presumably the older members of the community. Paul asserts that he is the father who begot the Corinthians in Christ Jesus through the gospel (1 Co 4:15). With the Thessalonians, Paul exhorted, encouraged, affirmed as a father would his children (1 Th 2:12). He wrote the Philippians that Timothy served with him as a son with his father (Ph 2:22). We shall reserve our treatment of Paul for later. The other instances can be

6

seen as customary forms of respectful address.

This gives the overwhelming impression that to the early Christians 'father' meant God. According to Mt 23:9, Jesus' disciples are to 'call no man on earth your father, for you have one Father, who is in heaven'. Mt 23 is part of the evangelist's polemic against the scribes and Pharisees (but also against those Christians in his community inclined to imitate the abuses ascribed to the scribes and Pharisees). The scribes or rabbis, teachers of the Jewish law, were called 'father' by their disciples. The rabbi was considered to have begotten his pupils by means of the Torah, the law.[4] Jesus is here depicted as rejecting this custom. While Mt alone records this saying, there is something to be said for its substantial authenticity. That Jesus might say something like ' "Father" means God, your heavenly Father,' seems well within the realm of plausibility. If Paul refers to himself as 'father' on occasion, he may have been unaware of Jesus' prohibition and followed his rabbinic training while making an important point with the help of father imagery.

So far as we can tell from the gospel, Jesus himself called no man on earth his father. Nor was he himself ever called father, a striking fact in view of the rabbinic practice and the number of times he is addressed as teacher or master or rabbi. The title 'Father forever' given the ideal king in Is 9:6 must have been tempting, but nowhere does the New Testament employ it of Jesus.

The absence of 'father' is eloquent in Jesus' saying that 'Whoever does the will of God is my brother and sister and mother' (Mk 3:35; see also 10:30). Notice the careful wording of Jn 1:12f.: 'But to all who received him—the Word, the true light—who believe in his name, he gave power to become children of God; who were born, not of blood nor of the will of the flesh nor of the will of man, but of God'. The Word gives the capability of becoming children of God, but these children are born of God, are God's children. In Jn 20:17, the risen Lord says to Mary Magdalen: 'Go to my brethren and say to them, I am ascending to my Father and your

Father'. Jesus is brother, son of the same Father though in a different way. Paul is equally exact: God is the Father who predestined us 'to be conformed to the image of his Son, in order that he might be the firstborn among many brethren' (Rm 8:29; see also Eph 1:5).

The closest the Bible comes to the actual term 'spiritual father' seems to be Heb 12:9 where God is referred to as 'the Father of spirits'. The *New English* Bible is justified in translating this as 'Spiritual Father'. Runner-up would be Paul's beautiful 'father in Christ' (1 Co 4:15).

THE PRIEST AS SPIRITUAL FATHER

When tracing the word 'father' through the Old Testament, we found it was used on occasion of priest, prophet, and wise man. Let us follow these leads to see if the roles of priest, prophet, wisdom teacher contain elements suggestive of spiritual fatherhood.

A few texts may help us situate these three functions in relation to each other. Jeremiah presents his opponents as denying the threatening, negative side of his message: 'Come, let us make plots against Jeremiah, for the law [torah] shall not perish from the priest, nor council from the wise, nor the word from the prophet' (Jr 18:18). Similarly, in describing the punishment about to befall Israel, Ezekiel laments: 'They seek a vision from the prophet, but the law [torah] perishes from the priest, and counsel from the elders' (Ezk 7:26). Just as the word of God or vision characterizes the prophet, and counsel the wise men and elders, so torah (law or instruction) is linked with the priests.

The Israelite priests had a variety of functions, including the offering of sacrifices, blessing the people in the name of God, transporting the ark of the covenant, burning incense on the altar inside the veil, consulting the Lord through Urim and Thummim or sacred lots, conducting ordeals to resolve doubtful cases, treating ritual impurities, for example, those connected with various diseases or from contact with the dead, judging the people, teaching them torah.

We have already looked at the suggestion that the young and presumably unmarried Levite in Judges (17:10; 18:19) was addressed as a 'father and a priest' because he was stepping into a ministry and authority held and exercised formerly by the head of the family. Upon questioning, an Israelite might have responded that all the functions of the priesthood just listed led him to look upon the priest as father. On reflection, he might affirm that all of them were life-giving in one way or another. Our interest, however, is especially attracted to his function as teacher of torah.

Let us single out this teaching for closer attention. In his final blessing of the twelve tribes, Moses is pictured as saying of the tribe of Levi: 'They shall teach Jacob thine ordinances, and Israel thy law' (Dt 33:10). In Leviticus (10:10f.), the Lord commissioned Aaron, saying: 'You are to distinguish between the holy and the common, and between the unclean and the clean; and you are to teach the people of Israel all the statutes which the Lord has spoken to them by Moses'. M. Haran synthesizes thus:

The priests' instruction of the people did not exist as a special institution but was generally a by-product of their other activities. Thus *torah* followed from the legal discussions held before the priests (Dt 17:11; 33:10). *Torah* was also taught by the way of guidance given by the priests to the people in matters of impurities and diseases (Dt 24:8; Hg 2:11ff.). Indeed, the various types of laws of impurity were called *torah* (Lv 11:46; 13:59, *et al.*) and were to be learned by the public (Lv 10:10f). The various cultic customs were also called *torah* (Lv 6:2, 7, *et al.*), and many of the sections dealing with laws and rebukes interspersed throughout the Pentateuch actually constitute scrolls of *torah*. Books of law were preserved mainly by the priests.[5]

This priestly torah or instruction dealt with both cultic and moral precepts. It encompassed the whole of Israel's life and her relations with God. This inclusiveness is evident when the prophet Malachi paints an ideal picture of the priest in contrast with the priests of his own day:

True instruction was in his [Levi's, ancestor of the levitical tribe of priests] mouth, and no wrong was found on his lips. He walked with me in peace and uprightness, and he turned many from iniquity. For the lips of the priest should guard knowledge, and men should seek instruction from his mouth, for he is the messenger of the Lord of hosts. But you have turned aside from the way; you have caused many to stumble by your instruction; you have corrupted the covenant of Levi, says the Lord of hosts, and so I make you despised and abased before all the people, inasmuch as you have not kept my ways but have shown partiality in your instruction (Ml 2:6-9). (The word 'instruction' which occurs four times in this text could also be translated 'law' or simply transliterated as 'torah'). On this teaching function of priests, see also 2 K 17: 26ff.; 2 Ch 15:3; 17:7ff.; Jr 2:8; Ho 4:6.

Many texts place a heavy share of the blame for the spiritual ruin of Israel on the priests, implying that a major share in the responsibility for the spiritual welfare of God's people was theirs. This spiritual influence of the priests waned with the rise of the Pharisaic doctors of the law toward the time of Christ. It may be the nature of our biblical sources which prevents us from seeing how this priestly torah was carried out in day-to-day living. Vignettes like the exchanges between the priest Eli and Samuel's mother, Hannah, (1 S 1) are hard to come by.

If the address 'father' occurs only in the one passage from Judges, I cannot think of any other titles by which the priests were addressed.

THE PROPHET AS SPIRITUAL FATHER

As the prophet Elijah was being caught up into heaven by the whirlwind, Elisha, his chosen disciple, cried out: 'My father, my father! The chariots of Israel and its horsemen!' (2 K 2:12). Elisha had been appointed by God to be prophet in Elijah's place. Elijah symbolized this by casting his mantle over Elisha at their first meeting. Thereafter Elisha followed Elijah and ministered to him (1 K 19:16-21). Unfortunately,

Elisha drops out of sight until it is time for Elijah's departure, so we are given little insight into what his cry 'Father!' meant to him. Elijah invited Elisha to make some parting request. Elisha took him up on this by saying, 'I pray you, let me inherit a double portion of your spirit' (2 K 2:9). In fact, Elisha did inherit the spirit of his master, signified by the mantle Elijah left him (v. 13). Thereafter Elisha functioned as worthy successor to his spiritual father. Whatever Elijah may have taught his follower by word or example, the crucial thing seems to have been the communication of the prophetic spirit, seen partly as an inheritance but mostly as a gift of God which Elijah might or might not have been able to gain for his spiritual heir.

A few chapters later, an unnamed king of Israel speaks to Elisha as 'my father' (2 K 6:21). The only other information the Bible gives about the relationship of this king with the prophet is that Elisha sometimes used his gifts of clairvoyance and miracle-working to help the king against the hostile Syrians. Finally, as Elisha lay dying, Joash, king of Israel, wept over him crying: 'My father! My father! The chariots of Israel and its horsemen' (2 K 13:14). Before dying, Elisha had Joash perform symbolic actions which turned out to signify victories the king would gain over Syria. Not only did the prophet foretell victory but he was instrumental in bringing it about. In this context, both 'my father' and 'The chariots of Israel and its horsemen' would have meant that real power and victory and protection lay with God and his spokesman.

Another promising lead is the 'bands of prophets' or 'sons of prophets' that occur in 1 S 10 and 19, and in the Books of Kings. They seem to have had some connection with Samuel but especially with Elisha. In 2 K 6:1f., one such group says to Elisha: 'See, the place where we dwell *under your charge* is too small for us'. They went on to ask if they could build something larger near the Jordan. They address Elisha as 'master' and refer to themselves as 'your servants' (2 K 6:3, 5). Elisha sends one of them to anoint Jehu as king of Israel (2 K 9:1ff.). 2 K 4:38-41 shows Elisha at table with the

11

'sons of the prophets' located at Gilgal. Unfortunately, the account goes no deeper than this into the relations between the master and these prophets gathered in community.

The prophet was a person who received from the Lord a word or vision which he, or she, was supposed to hand on to God's people. 'Go, prophesy to my people Israel', Amos is told (Am 7:15). Over and over in the accounts of the prophets' vocation or in particular messages they are given to pass on, it is stated that they are sent to the people. Their warning, their promises, their demands are directed to the people or, at least, to some segment of the people or its leaders. The prophet might receive a word from the Lord for the nation or the king or some prominent official or the oppressive wealthy or the exiles. These were offered as calls to conversion, to trust in God. They might pointedly condemn this or that crime and show the way to justice and a healthy relationship with God.

A recognized characteristic of the prophet was intercession, prayer for the needs of the people, needs of which the prophets were especially aware. (*Abraham,* Gn 18; 20:7; *Moses,* Ex 32:11-14; Nb 11:2; 12:13; 14:13-19; 21:7, 25-29; *Samuel,* 1 S 7:5, 8f.; 12:19, 23; 15:11; *Jeremiah,* Jr 4:10; 7:16; 11:14; 14:11f.; 15:11; 18:20; 42:2-9; *Ezekiel,* Ezk 9:8; 11:13). Through the word of life they mediated, through their prayer, through the concern expressed in the way they fulfilled their mission, the prophets might well be called fathers of the people, though the people were usually too irritated with them to regard them in such terms.

Elijah and Elisha worked miracles for the benefit of individuals, and prophets sometimes served as oracles available to anyone and everyone; for example, Samuel in 1 S 9. But one faces a long and disappointing search to come up with any word the prophet might have, say, for one of his disciples or a next door neighbor or someone who took him in. It is hard to assess this. Were the prophets commissioned, given words only at the national or international levels? Were they consulted only about such things as stray asses (1 S 9:9) or whether a

12

sick child would recover (1 K 14:1-5) or how a battle would turn out (1 K 22:5-17)? So far as I know, in all the writings of the prophets there are only two instances of a prophet being given a word to communicate to an ordinary individual. Ebedmelech, the Ethiopian, saved Jeremiah's life (Jr 38:7-13). Later, the word of the Lord came to Jeremiah that Ebedmelech's life would be spared when destruction overtook Jerusalem (Jr 39:15-18). In the other instance, Jeremiah received a word for his faithful secretary Baruch, that he would survive a catastrophe but should not expect much more than survival while the people were afflicted (Jr 45).

This is intriguing. What has come down to us from the prophets attests that they were men very close to God, with a deep sense of who God is, of his presence and action in the life of his people. They try to share this experience with the people as a whole. Yet there seems to be no evidence of their trying to lead individuals into this experience, this vision, into a life completely attentive and surrendered to the work of God. Someone must have gathered and cherished their sayings (and, often, reapplied them to new situations). Is 8:16, 18, in one reading, speaks of such disciples. But this is as far as the Bible takes us. Is it that the prophets did not engage in one-to-one guidance? Or is it that the nature and purpose of the writings in question led them to focus on the prophets' public activity and message while filtering out other aspects of their life?

THE WISDOM TEACHER AS SPIRITUAL FATHER

Recall once more the texts of Jeremiah and Ezekiel which joined prophet, priest, and wise man. While instruction or torah is sought from the priest and a word or vision from the prophet, what the wise man has to offer is counsel. Counsel about what? About how to live, how to act.

To get a feeling for this counsel, let us look at some samples from the typical wisdom book, Proverbs.

> Hatred stirs up strife, but love covers all offenses (10:12).
> Better a man of humble standing who works for himself

> than one who plays the great man but lacks bread
> (12:9).
> A wise son hears his father's instruction, but a scoffer
> does not listen to rebuke (13:1).
> The teaching of the wise is a fountain of life, that one
> may avoid the snares of death (13:14).
> He who spares the rod hates his son, but he who loves
> him is diligent to discipline him (13:24).
> The simple believes everything, but the prudent looks
> where he is going (14:15).

Perhaps most of the sayings in Proverbs and Sirach are just such earthy, common sense aphorisms as these. They include numerous admonitions to heed one's father and mother. Twice the teacher refers to himself as 'father' (Pr 4:1; Si 3:1), and he frequently addresses his hearer(s) as 'sons' or 'children'.

In all probability, the original setting of many proverbs would have been the instruction for life a parent gave his child or the advice drawn from experience that parents or reflective friends shared with each other. Some of the proverbs, however, call for a different setting, that of the court. They might have to do with the king or behavior around him (Pr 16:10-15; 20:8, 26, 28; 25:2-7). Pr 25:1 gives us a clue. It introduces one of the several collections of proverbs in this book with, 'These are the proverbs of Solomon which the men of Hezekiah copied'. Already in the time of David, a scribe, that is, a professional writer or secretary, is mentioned among his officers. Seemingly he modeled his administration on that of Egypt, which featured a large body of scribes. They were needed to keep records, handle correspondence, and produce and copy literature, whether religious, scientific, or historical. The only schools in the ancient Near East were scribal schools. While learning their craft, students were also educated to make their way in the world they were entering.

Here seems to be the source of the wisdom *literature*—and there are striking, earlier parallels to it in Egypt and Meso-

14

potamia—a professional guidebook wherein the budding
scribe learned the practical wisdom which would shape his
conduct and further his advancement.[6]

A further development took place during the exile. The
monarchy might disappear, but the scribes grew in influence
to become, with the priests, the custodians of Jewish religious
traditions. This is illustrated by the great post-exilic leader,
Ezra, both priest and scribe.

Therefore, biblical wisdom might have been adequately
described by these words of R. Scott as 'a way of thinking
and an attitude to life that emphasized experience, reasoning,
morality and the concerns of man as man rather than an
Israelite. Its interest was in the individual and his social
relationships rather than in the distinctive national religion
and its cult. A generalized religious element was present from
the first in wisdom's recognition of the rightness of a certain
order of life.'[7] The editors of the *Jerusalem Bible* calculate
that, even in the two primitive collections contained in the
Book of Proverbs, one proverb in seven is religious in theme.
The dominant tone, however, is that of human, worldly
wisdom, and the great Old Testament motifs of law, covenant,
election, salvation are absent. Absent, too, is reflection on
the past or future of the nation. Instead, the emphasis is on
the individual and his destiny.[8]

During and after the exile, the study of torah, the law,
the expression of what was most special and distinctive in
Israel's religion, blended with the wisdom stream. In fact, the
scribes had a hand in the final shaping of the Pentateuch,
which fused the various traditions of torah. Again, Ezra
exemplifies this trend. He is described as a 'scribe skilled in
the law of Moses' (Ezr 7:6), as having 'set his heart to study
the law of the Lord, and to do it, and to teach his statutes
and ordinances to Israel' (Ezr 7:10). The torah, the law God
had given to his people, was now seen as supreme wisdom
(Ba 4:1-4; Ps 19:7-11; Si 24:23-27). Still there remained
much room in day to day living for the practical, experiential
kind of wisdom.

In the Wisdom Books, some of this evolving wisdom was garnered. Something of the climate in which it was handed on has been crystalized as well. The scribe, obviously, experiences himself here as spiritual father, educating his spiritual son in the art of living well, wisely, according to God. Generally, the matter is phrased in a way that is intriguing, easy to catch and retain. The tone is personal, even affectionate, more that of persuasion than of commandment. The appeal is to experience, common sense, and filial piety rather than to abstract reason. The authority invoked is that of experience, of life lived with awareness and reflection. The Lord gives wisdom (Pr 2:6; 1 K 3:9-12; Jb 28:12-28; Si 1:1; Ws 7:7, 15-17, 22, 25-27; 8:21; 9:1-6, 9-18), but teacher and student evidently can help the process along (Ws 7:7). The scribe may have been instructing a class, but his words are directed to individuals. He offers them a chance to grow in wisdom and desires to teach them (Si 51:23-26).

One can only guess how much the scribe dealt with individuals apart from the class, but the content of the wisdom literature would have served well in a counselling situation. According to a tradition going back at least to Origen (d. 254), *Proverbs, Ecclesiastes,* and the *Song of Songs* provide step-by-step guidance to perfect communion with God. *Proverbs* teaches us to amend our behavior and to keep God's commandments; *Ecclesiastes* shows the emptiness of the world and fragility of transitory things; the *Song of Songs* leads to the contemplation of God with pure and spiritual love.[9]

These spiritual fathers were aware that their words were 'life to him who finds them' (Pr 4:20-22; 13:14). Even in its earliest form, the wisdom literature would have helped make the whole of one's life an expression of the fear of the Lord for 'the fear of the Lord is instruction in wisdom [or, the foundation of wisdom]' (Pr 15:33; 1:7; 9:10).

JESUS AS SPIRITUAL FATHER
Instead of lamenting the dearth of material in the gospel expressly referring to spiritual fatherhood, let us take a different

16

tack for this section. Let us ask what it would have been like to be one of Jesus' disciples. What would it have been like to share his life, to witness his miracles, to hear his teaching to the crowds, to have a share in the intimate give and take within the circle of disciples, to receive his special instruction, to have him share something of his own mission, to follow him through his death and resurrection, and afterwards? How would he have trained us, instructed us, educated us?

Let us try to enter imaginatively into the gospel. Lest our treatment become overcomplicated, let us work with the gospels as they stand, Jesus' own words and deeds, but also the experience and witness of the early christian communities and of the evangelists.

'Come follow me' (Mk 1:17; 2:14; Jn 1:43; Mk 10:21). In one way or another, we would have heard this invitation of the Master, heard it as addressed to us. In one way or another, we would have known this was the pearl of great price we had been searching for. Gladly we would have sold all to buy it (Mt 13:45f.). Somehow, the observance of the commandments, a good and upright life, had left us feeling we lacked something, the one thing necessary (Mk 10:17-22). Something clicked, and we knew that 'we have found him' (Jn 1:45). We chose him, but, more profoundly, he chose us (Jn 15:16).

And we followed him. That says it all. The main element in our formation was simply staying close to him. 'And he appointed twelve, to be with him . . . ' (Mk 3:14). 'Have I been with you so long, and yet you do not know me?' he asked (Jn 14:9; see Mt 10:29; Lk 22:28; Ac 1:21; Jn 15:27). To be around him was to absorb his words, his actions, his ways of doing things, of viewing things, his attitudes. To be around him was to want to be as he was, to want to be as he wanted us to be. To be around him was to realize one's need of repentance, but it was also to realize one's worth and possibilities. Unbelievably, sinners were attracted to him and were able to bring their need for healing to him (Mk 2:15-17; Lk 15:1-2). The taunt was perfectly true; he *was* 'a friend of sinners' (Mt 11:19)—and they knew it. To stay near such a

17

friend is to be transformed.

Think of some of the things Jesus did and how they would have affected us. He welcomed, even sought out, all kinds of people, even those regarded as outcasts from religious society. He gave himself to them through his preaching, teaching, healing, listening. He had time for tax-collectors, sinners, Samaritans, women, children, the aged, diseased, dull. Instead of repelling them by his purity, he so attracted crowds that he was hard-pressed to find time to eat (Mk 3:20; 6:31). The paralytic had to be lowered through a breach in the roof to get to him (Mk 2:4). On occasion, he would slip away to have time for prayer or to reach other audiences (Mk 1:35-38; 6:46; 7:24; Lk 3:21; 5:16; 6:12; 9:18; 28f.; 11:1). Once, when things were hectic, Jesus said to his apostles: ' "Come away by yourselves to a lonely place, and rest a while." For many were coming and going, and they had no leisure even to eat . . . . Now many saw them going, and they ran there on foot from all the towns, and got there ahead of them.' What was Jesus' reaction? 'He had compassion on them, because they were like sheep without a shepherd; and he began to teach them many things' (Mk 6:31-34).

Imagine the impression it would have made on the disciples to be present at miracles worked out of this same compassion (Mt 14:14; Mk 1:41; 8:2; Lk 7:13). Often Jesus would touch the ones to be healed or lay hands on them or take their hand. This was a sign of the healing power that went out from him, but it was also a very human gesture. How much it must have meant to the untouchable leper (Mk 1:41). Authority over unclean spirits and the power to heal were so much his that he could share them with the twelve (Mk 3:15; 6:7; 13).

If we had been followers of Jesus, we would have heard his public preaching, and this would have been a major factor in our transformation. Imagine standing among the crowd in the synagogue of Capernaum, on the shore of the lake, in the Jerusalem temple. We too would have been swept by the general astonishment 'at his teaching, for he taught as one who had authority' (Mk 1:22). 'No man ever spoke like this

18

man' (Jn 7:46). 'Where did he get all this? What is the wisdom
given to him?' (Mk 6:2; here astonishment issued in incre-
dulity).

His message was 'the good news' (Mt 4:23; Mk 1:14f.; 8:35;
Lk 4:43). The core of this good news could be expressed in a
variety of ways: God's reign has begun. God is our Abba. We
are called and enabled to love as he loves.

'The kingdom of God has come upon you' (Mt 12:28). 'The
time is fulfilled, and the kingdom of God is at hand . . . '
(Mk 1:15). Tax collectors and harlots are entering it (Mt 21:31).
'Behold, the kingdom of God is in the midst of you' (Lk 17:21).
We can receive it if only we repent, turn back to him, believe,
become like children, allowing God to rule our lives and world
(Mk 1:15; 10:14f.). More accurately—and this is important—
God's rule *has* begun, has come upon us, is in our midst and
this enables us to repent, turn back, believe, sell all as our
response to his gift of the kingdom. God's kingdom comes as
the grace that sets our hearts on him and his will. God himself
is the kingdom, the reign offered to us in Jesus and his ministry. In his parables, Jesus brought home different aspects of
this kingdom. These parables would have intrigued us, got us
thinking, drawn us into Jesus' own experience and vision.

Another way in which Jesus would have led us into this
same reality was his manner of being toward, and speaking
about, God as his and our Father. If we understand the words
in their full biblical sense, Jesus' whole mission was to reveal
the Father, to make him known as Father, as the Son himself
knows him. Here revelation involves transformation: Jesus
must make us sons as he is that we may know the Father as
he does (see Mt 11:25-27). Jesus taught his followers to
pray to God as Father, even by the term of endearment *abbā,*
'Poppa'. His will must become our desire. To please him must
be the motivation of all we do. He knows our needs and has a
care for them, so we can leave them in his hands without
anxiety. Yet we should pray to him, ask, seek, knock, confident he will give us his good gifts. Since we are his children,
we are to love all as he does. The Sermon on the Mount (Mt 5-7)

amounts to guidance and encouragement to live as God's children and, consequently, as brothers and sisters to each other.

A third view of the heart of Jesus' message is the two-fold commandment of love, in Matthew's version: You shall love the Lord your God with all your heart, and with all your soul, and with all your mind. This is the great and first commandment. And a second is like it. You shall love your neighbor as yourself. On these two commandments depend all the law and the prophets (Mt 22:37-40). Love of God first. But then—and also essential—love of neighbor. Would it be so obvious that God wants our love without this commandment? What kind of a God is it who commands us to love him? What kind of a God is he who inseparably links love of neighbor with love of himself? St John spells out what is clearly implied in the whole of Jesus' life: 'This is my commandment, that you love one another as I have loved you' (Jn 15:12; see 13:34).

When the two commandments are fulfilled, God's reign has arrived and we know him as Abba. We can fulfill them because the kingdom is here and we have experienced him as our Father. His rule and his being our Father are gift, then, but so is our fulfillment of his commandment.

Notice that Jesus does not seem to have talked much about God directly. He concentrates more on what God offers us and does for us and asks of us.

One other point about Jesus' preaching seems worth bringing out. Try to put yourself in the place of the first hearers, Jews, when Jesus made statements like: 'Moses said to you . . . but I say to you . . . ', again and again pushing the frontiers of God's demands all the way into our hearts (Mt 5:20-48). The congruity of what he said with the God who had made himself known to this people carried conviction; it gave his words authority. God really was the way Jesus said he was, and the new demands Jesus made in his name really fitted this God. Jesus' skill as a parable teller would also have allowed him to communicate his own experience intact and to convince us that things were as he told us.

If we had been among Jesus' disciples, then, a good part of our training would have come from living close to him and listening to his preaching. But we would also have been with him when some of the religious leaders harassed him. Often this was the occasion of precious teaching and clarification. Do they object that he has to do with sinners? He tells them: 'Those who are well have no need of a physician, but those who are sick; I came not to call the righteous, but sinners' (Mk 2:17). What of the parables of lost sheep, the lost coin, and the lost son (Lk 15)? Do they object that Jesus' disciples do not fast? But they have the Bridegroom with them; how could they fast? (Mk 2:18-20). Do they cavil that the disciples do not wash their hands before eating? Jesus points out that his monitors disobey basic commandments of God under the pretext of observing traditions they have built up around God's commandments. What defiles a person is what comes out of his heart, not anything outside of him (Mk 7:1-23). Do they complain that Jesus heals on the Sabbath or his followers pluck and eat grain on the Sabbath? 'The Sabbath was made for man, not man for the Sabbath', he responds (Mk 2:23-3:6). Do they seek to know the times and signs of the coming of the kingdom? 'Behold, the kingdom of God is in your midst' (Lk 17:21).

Jesus teaches that the law is fulfilled in the twofold love. He pushes the demands of the law all the way into man's heart (Mt 5:21-48). He calls for a righteousness exceeding that of the scribes and Pharisees, the professional religious (Mt 5:20). He can be adamant about getting rid of anything that causes us to sin (Mt 5:29-30; Mk 9:43-48). He can be utterly demanding when charity is at stake (Mt 5:21-26, 38-48; 18:21-22). He can reverence the temple with such zeal that he drives out those who do business there (Mk 11:15-17). He can even acknowledge the scribes and Pharisees as successors of Moses. Hence, what they teach but not what they do is to be practised and observed (Mt 23:2-3). So Jesus' obedience to the Father's will, sometimes expressed in command-

ments, and the obedience he expected of those who would
come after him, was total and demanding. Precisely because
of his radical commitment to the Father and his will, Jesus
could be utterly free with observances and traditions which
did not embody that will or which ran counter to it. Let
traditions of human origin get in the way of charity and
Jesus departs from them without further ado. Something
important was at stake: behind the different views of
observance lay different images of God. The God Jesus knew
was not worried about munching grain to satisfy hunger on
the Sabbath or eating with unwashed hands or healing on
the Sabbath (Mk 2:18-3:5; 7:1-23). Through their participation in such disputes, the disciples would have caught something of Jesus' searching and delicate dedication to the
Father's will, as well as something of his freedom, balance,
and common sense.

Apart from such public preaching and discussion, Jesus
seems to have given special teaching to those he was training
to carry on his mission. He might clear up some difficulties
regarding a parable (Mk 4:10-20; 7:17-23). He might warn
them against the influence and spirit of the Pharisees (Mk
8:14-21). He might embarass them by asking: 'What were you
discussing on the way?' when they had been debating who
was the greatest (Mk 9:33-35). He might rebuke them for
their lack of faith and understanding (Mk 4:40; 8:17, 21, 33),
for their proneness to use violence (Lk 9:55; 26:52). He might
challenge them to take a leap forward in faith with a question
like: 'But who do you say that I am?' (Mk 8:29; see Jn 6:67).
When sending them out on mission, he gave them instructions
(Mk 6:6-13). He may well have done something to prepare his
own for his impending rejection, failure, and death, though it
is improbable he went into the detail of the passion predic-
tions as they stand in the written gospels (Mk 8:31; 9:31;
10:32-34).He kept the last passover and instituted the
Eucharist with his disciples (Mk 14:14, 22-25).

Because they saw him pray, the disciples asked Jesus to
teach them to pray (Lk 11:1-4). We have seen that intercessory

prayer was a mark of the Old Testament prophets. Jesus at prayer is a theme especially prominent in Luke, but so paralleled in the other gospels and re-enforced by his repeated commands to pray as to make it clear Luke does not overstate (Lk 3:21; 5:16; 6:12; 9:18; 28-29; 22:32, 40-46; Mk 1:35; 6:46; 14:32-39). Jesus, on the rare occasions when the content of his prayer can be glimpsed, prayed to his Father about the Father's will, plan, working (Mt 11:25-27; Jn 11:41; 12: 27-28; 17; Mk 14:36; Lk 23:34, 46). He prayed for his disciples, thanking the Father for having chosen to reveal himself to them, for making them a part of the achievement of his plan, asking the Father to protect them and keep them faithful (Mt 11:25-27; Lk 22:32; Jn 17; see also Lk 6:12). He interceded for his own, asking God's grace and their capacity to receive it. By example and instruction, he drew his disciples into this mediation. The *Our Father* reflects a twofold focus on the Father's glory, kingdom, will, and our need to be nourished, sustained, preserved. 'Give *us* this day *our* daily bread and forgive *us our* trespasses . . . . Lead *us* not into temptation but deliver *us* from evil'. Our needs, experienced in faith, reveal those of our neighbor and *vice versa.*

How did Jesus compare with the Jewish spiritual leaders and teachers, the scribes, the rabbis, the doctors of the law? Both by his disciples and by others, Jesus is called 'rabbi' or its equivalent 'teacher', more than any other title. Like the others, he was regarded as a teacher of the law, of the Scriptures. Like them, he gathered disciples. If he taught with authority and not as the scribes (Mk 1:22), his teaching frequently did take Scripture as its starting point.[10] The relationship between Jesus and his disciples was not entirely the same as that of the rabbi and his disciples. Jesus demanded a more complete personal surrender to himself than did the rabbis. His disciple must be willing to abandon father and mother, son and daughter, and to take up his cross and lose his life in following Jesus (Mt 10:37-39) . . . . The disciples of Jesus differed from the disciples of the rabbis also because they could not hope to attain his dignity; their entire life

23

was to be spent in discipleship.[11] He did, however, share his mission of preaching and teaching with them (Mk 3:13-15; 6:7-12; Lk 10:1; Mt 28:19-20; Mk 16:15).

We have already noted that, though 'Father' was a title of respect commonly used in addressing the rabbis, it was never used of Jesus, by himself or by his disciples or by anyone else, as the gospel tells it. The good news, the experience, the consciousness Jesus labors to instill is that God is our Abba, our dear Father—with the fullness of content which Jesus' teaching, prayer, life, self give to 'Abba'. Jesus himself is the 'beloved Son' (Mk 1:11; 9:7). His person and function are carefully distinguished from those of the Father.

In a variety of ways, we have seen, Jesus brought his followers to life and maturity as children of the Father. If we choose to employ the term 'spiritual father', he merits it more than anyone else. Yet we have found that he avoided the title, and have noted why.

The followers of Jesus were most often called 'disciples'. In the Acts of the Apostles, the term is broadened to include all Christians, not just those who followed Jesus during his ministry. While John the Baptist and the rabbis were said to have disciples, only once is this said of any of the apostles. Indeed, according to Matthew 23:8 and 10, Jesus had told his disciples: 'You are not to be called rabbi, for you have one teacher . . . . Neither be called masters, for you have one master, the Christ'. The unique exception is Ac 9:25 where 'his [Paul's] disciples' helped him escape from Damascus. This rings so strange among the two hundred and sixty-one occurences of 'disciple' in the New Testament that perhaps the gist is: the disciples of Jesus made by Paul, Christians converted by him. Of course, Paul's careful schooling as a Pharisee may have surfaced here for a moment.

We have just said the followers of Christ were most often called 'disciples'. This needs to be qualified. *All* two hundred and sixty-one instances of 'disciple' occur in the gospels and Acts (between 6:1 and 21:16 only). What replaced it? Mainly 'brothers' and 'sisters', which turn up over two hundred times and are solidly rooted in the gospels (Mk 3:34f.; Mt 23:8; 25:40; 28:10; Jn 20:17; 21:23).[12] This agrees with Mt 23:8: 'But you are not to be called rabbi, for you have one teacher, and you are all brethren'. We might note that, while Jesus speaks of his disciples as brothers and sisters, he never directly addresses any of them as brother, nor does anyone call him brother.

Jesus' careful reservation of the name 'father' for the Father, the equally careful use of 'master', 'teacher', 'disciple', 'brother', the pointed words of Jesus about not being called 'rabbi', 'father', or 'master' more than suggest that spiritual fatherhood should be an exercise of spiritual brotherhood and service.

Moments before his death, Jesus said to one described only as 'the beloved disciple', 'Behold, your Mother' (Jn 19:26). Mary highlights several aspects of spiritual motherhood.

Her charism was not to preach, to exercise pastoral ministry, to give direction or counsel in any official way. Above all, she was the handmaid of the Lord, the ideal disciple, the one who waited and received all from him. As such, she draws us into a like following of her Son. One who is open to receive God's gift, the gift of his Son, as fully as Mary, enlivens all who come into contact with her. What such a one does, says, is, becomes a channel, a sacrament of God's gift of life. How many persons have been sources of life for us simply by being who they are? Spiritual parenthood extends far beyond 'spiritual direction'.

In the Johannine writings, Mary and the Church coalesce in the symbol of the Woman, the new Eve, Mother of all the living. Similarly, the spiritual father/mother must so stand in the lifestream of the Church, so identify with it as to embody it, to be 'church' for their charges. Technique, personal endowments, experience have their place, but the main function of the spiritual parent is to communicate the life, the gifts, the ways Christ has bestowed on his Church.

Mary reminds us that spiritual parenthood is to foster, not just any type of fulfillment, but the life of Christ within us.

Abba, *The Spiritual Guide*

The most significant content of history (and of our personal histories) is Christ coming to birth and growing to maturity in our world and our lives. Such life is a fully human life, *the* fully human life, in the sense of being a life as God intended it to be. Manifestly, this Christ-life can be engendered only by the Holy Spirit. Yet the Spirit often works through human persons in such a way that life is given through them.

The fact that Mary/Church was given as Mother to the representative disciple at the hour of Christ's death suggests not only that her fecundity is one of the fruits of the Paschal Mystery but also that her spiritual parenthood is a prolongation or modality of Christ's own.

SAINT PAUL AS SPIRITUAL FATHER

With St Paul, we come to a number of explicit references, not only to his spiritual fatherhood, but also to his spiritual maternity. He considers himself father, first of all, to those whom he has begotten in the faith through his preaching of the gospel. They may have many guardians in Christ, but he is the one who first brought them to life in Christ. His fathering does not stop there. He has an ardent love and affection for his children and calls upon them to reciprocate. Urged by this love, he can exhort and encourage, but admonish and command as well. Repeatedly, he calls his correspondents to imitate him as he does Christ.

Notice some of the pertinent texts: I write this . . . to admonish you as my beloved children. For though you have countless guides in Christ, you do not have many fathers. For I became your father in Christ Jesus through the gospel. I urge you then to be imitators of me. Therefore, I sent you Timothy, my beloved and faithful child in the Lord, to remind you of my ways in Christ, as I teach them everywhere in every church (I Co 4:14-17). The Greek word here translated 'guide' is *paidagogos,* meaning custodian, tutor, guardian. The term is not flattering. Paul is referring to the troublesome, arrogant persons who stirred up divisions and factions under the guise of imparting a higher wisdom. It is

26

also worth noting that the Greek for 'I became your father in Christ Jesus' is rather more dynamic and concrete: 'I *begot* you in Christ Jesus . . . '.

Not only Timothy, but Titus and the slave Onesimus were considered Paul's children because he called them to the faith. Paul could write to Philemon, master of Onesimus, 'I appeal to you for my child, Onesimus, whose father I have become in my imprisonment' (Phm 10). Here again, the Greek has 'whom I begot' or even 'whom I bore'. (On Timothy, see I co 4:17; Ph 2:22; 1 Tm 1:2, 18; 2 Tm 1:2; 2:1. On Titus, see Tt 1:4.) There is a chance that Paul did not always restrict 'father' and 'son' to those whom he had personally converted, depending on the interpretation given Acts 16:1 (but Paul had already visited Systra twice, Ac 14:6, 21; 2 Tm 1:5; 3:15, concerning Timothy). Both Timothy and Titus were sons also in the sense of being Paul's protegees and invaluable helpers: 'Timothy's worth you know, how as a son with a father he has served with me in the gospel' (Ph 2:22).

At least six times in his letters Paul exhorts his followers to an imitation of himself. In 1 Co 4:16, quoted above, Paul explicitly connects this imitation with the fact he has begotten these Corinthians in Christ Jesus. 'I appeal to you [urge, exhort, encourage you] *therefore,* become imitators of me'. Until this point in his letter, Paul has been admonishing the Corinthians for their pride in their wisdom and in being partisans of Peter or Christ or Apollos or Paul. He appeals to them to imitate especially his humility: 'We are fools for Christ's sake, but you are wise in Christ' (1 Co 4:10). Factionalism has led Paul to insist on his being the father of the Corinthian church, the one who first evangelized it, led it to faith in Christ.

There is more to it than this. He really cares for these people. His concern is such that he could hardly help thinking in terms of father/child relationship. 'Our heart is wide open to you. In return—I speak as to [my] children—widen your hearts also' (2 Co 6:11, 13). These words were written to a congregation which gave him a good deal of trouble. He

stresses that he is their father and has a father's affection for
them because he must energetically correct flagrant abuses.
He is obliged to do this because he has a father's responsibility and care. He appeals to them to return his love and to
show it by heeding his warnings, by imitating his example.
He capitalizes on his position as father to provide motivation,
to evoke a change of heart and conduct.

Let us look rapidly at other instances where Paul calls his
flock to imitate his way of life. 'Be imitators of me as I am of
Christ' by living in such a way that others will be saved instead
of scandalized (1 Co 11:1). 'You became imitators of us and
of the Lord' in that you received and held to the word despite
opposition and persecution (1 Th 1:6). 'You yourselves know
how you ought to imitate us' in that we worked to earn our
living in order not to burden any of you (2 Th 3:7). 'Brethren,
I beseech you, become as I am, for I also have become as you
are', that is, become as I am in rejecting those who would
make you observe the Jewish law (Ga 4:12). 'Brethren, join
in imitating me, and mark those who live as you have an
example in us'—imitate me in placing all your trust in Christ,
not in fulfilling the law (Ph 3:17).

This insistence on imitation reminds us of the advantage
the spiritual father has in being able to teach us by his life
and not merely by his words. Some of the desert fathers
carried this so far as to refuse giving advice or commands to
their disciples: 'Let him do as I do if he wants'. The father so
manifests the life of Christ that to imitate him is to imitate
Christ. The life thus transmitted is the life of Christ in us
(see Ga 4:19).

Paul could conceive of his whole ministry in terms of a
father carefully, lovingly raising his children: ' . . . You know
how, like a father with his children, we exhorted each one of
you and encouraged you and charged you to lead a life
worthy of God, who calls you into his own kingdom and
glory' (1 Th 2:11-12). In this way Paul voiced God's call,
re-enforced it, kept his charges mindful of it, thereby participating in God's own fatherly initiative. (Note the 'each one

of you', suggesting individual relationships).

When Paul protests the selflessness of his love for the Corinthians, the image of parenthood again comes to his mind and pen: 'I will not be a burden, for I seek not what is yours, but you; for children ought not to lay up for their parents, but parents for their children. I will most gladly spend and be spent for your souls. If I love you the more, am I to be loved the less?' (2 Co 12:14-15). Paul seeks them for Christ. Recalling and rekindling their affection for himself is part of Paul's strategy for healing the divisions and self-seeking within this difficult community.

Apparently, Paul had been accused of evangelizing the Thessalonians out of self-interest (1 Th 2:3-6). He recalls his conduct and true motivations in terms of mothering: But we were gentle among you, like a nurse taking care of her children. [Actually, the comparison is with a nursing mother fondly caring for her own children.] So, being affectionately desirous of you, we were ready to share with you not only the gospel of God but also our own selves, because you had become very dear to us (1 Th 2:7-8). Not desire for gain or glory or power, but love, affection, were behind his preaching of the gospel. It is this he sees as a mothering, a warming and a nourishing to life and maturity.

One of the ways in which Paul met the conceit of his Corinthian problem children was by pointing out how he had deliberately avoided any show of worldly wisdom in presenting the gospel so that their faith might rest, not on his wisdom and eloquence, but on the power of God. Yet there is a wisdom of God, an insight into the gifts bestowed on us by God. This wisdom can be taught only by the Spirit of God and communicated only when speaker and hearer possess this Spirit. Such a wisdom Paul claims to impart to the mature. Then comes the ego-deflating line: 'But, brethren, I could not address you as spiritual men, but as men of the flesh, as babes [infants, immature] in Christ. I fed you with milk, not with solid food, for you were not ready for it; and even yet you are not ready' (1 Co 3:1-2). His words carry the negative connotation that they are immature when they should have been mature (see also 1 Co 14:20). Far from being wise, they are not yet ready to receive God's wisdom. Paul likens himself to a mother, ready to provide appropriate nourishment for her children, anxious to bring them to maturity.

This citation of 1 Co brings out the strong sense in which 'spiritual' should be understood in 'spiritual fatherhood'. Spiritual fatherhood/motherhood can be viewed from many angles. One angle from which Paul views it is as an imparting of God's own wisdom. To know and appreciate God's gifts as God himself does is to enter into possession of them. Much more than a communication of information, of ideas, is involved. God himself must reveal to us what he has given to us, has in store for us, and he does this through his Spirit. Often, even normally, human agents will have a part to play in this communication: 'Faith comes from what is heard' (Rm 10:17). Yet both speaker and hearer must be in the Spirit or no communication can take place. The spirit must reveal to the speaker the thoughts of God as well as provide him with words apt to express them. But the hearer too must be in possession of the Spirit or he will not be able to pick up the content. 'We impart this in words not taught by human wisdom but taught by the Spirit, interpreting spiritual truths to those who possess the Spirit. The unspiritual man does not receive the gifts of the Spirit of God, for they are folly to him, and he is not able to understand them because they are spiritually discerned' (1 Co 2:13-14). The spiritual man, the one who has received the Spirit and lives according to that Spirit, is enabled to judge, discern all things from the viewpoint of the Lord, of Christ (15-16).

To some, the Spirit gives the charism of discernment of spirits in an eminent way (1 Co 12:10). Yet Paul prayed for all the Philippians that their 'love may abound more and more with knowledge and discernment, so that you may approve what is excellent . . . ' (Ph 1:9-10).[13] Obviously, Paul wished this latter sort of discernment for his not-yet-mature Corinthians.

30

Here and there Paul gives criteria by which the working of the Holy Spirit may be recognized within a person. Does the person acknowledge Jesus as Lord (1 Co 12:3)? Does his way of living acknowledge him as Lord? The works of the flesh and the fruit of the Spirit differ vastly, and the signs enable one to tell whether he is being led by the Spirit (Ga 5:16-23). The various lists of charisms and ministries and gifts (1 Co 12:4-11; Rm 12:6-8; Eph 4:11-16) give a sense of how the Spirit is liable to work in the community and in our lives. This discernment is vital because the whole christian life is a walking in the Spirit, a being led by the Spirit (Ga 5:16, 18, 25; Rm 8:14). The freedom Christ has won for us is freedom from the flesh, from the law, from sin, that we may be led by God's own Spirit, no longer slaves but sons and daughters (Rm 8:1-17; Ga 5:13-25). In a sense, the Spirit of God becomes our deepest self—or deeper within us than our self—so that love and all the virtues into which love is orchestrated are the fruit of the Spirit (Ga 5:22-23). Paul's role is to explain what this freedom is and is not, how one can tell desires arising from the Spirit from those of the flesh. He forcefully calls his spiritual charges to this life in the Spirit, this freedom, this maturity (Ga 5:1, 13, 25; Rm 8:2, 12-17; 2 Co 3:17).

All of this surely amounts to an exercise of spiritual fatherhood. But note what happens in those great chapters where God's fatherhood is very much to the fore (Rm 8 and Ga 5): Paul consistently addresses the Roman and Galatian communities as 'brethren'. Let us make several points in this connection. In every one of his letters, Paul explicitly refers to God as 'Father' or 'our Father'—over forty times in all. If Paul thought of his ministry in terms of spiritual fatherhood or motherhood, this was not at all to the detriment of God's fatherhood. According to Eph 3:14-15, God is 'the Father from whom every family in heaven and on earth is named' (or 'from whom every family, whether spiritual or natural, takes its name'—*Jerusalem Bible*). While the Greek word for child (*teknon*) is used in the pauline letters some fourteen times of Paul's spiritual children—compared to some six times

31

of God's children—the word for son (*huios*) is used only of God's sons (about thirteen times).

A second point: as we just noted, Paul refers to individuals or the members of communities as his children (*tekna*) about fourteen times. He addresses or refers to them as 'brothers' or 'sisters' (*adelphoi, adelphai*) one hundred forty times, more or less. Thus, Timothy, Titus, Philemon are all referred to as 'son' or 'child' (both *teknon:* Timothy in 1 Co 4:17; Ph 2:22; 1 Tm 1:2, 18; 2 Tm 1:2; 2:1; Titus in Tt 1:4; Philemon in Phm 10). Yet they are also spoken of as 'brothers' (Timothy in 1 Th 3:2; 2 Co 1:1; Phm 1; Titus in 2 Co 2:13; Philemon in Phm 16). Christ himself is 'the firstborn among many brethren' (Rm 8:29). 1 Tm 5:1-2 accurately expresses Paul's spirit: 'Do not rebuke an older man but exhort him as you would a father; treat younger men like brothers, older women like mothers, younger women like sisters, in all purity'. The charisms are ministries, varieties of service, and gifts bestowed for the upbuilding of the body of Christ (1 Co 12, especially vv. 5 and 7). If Paul considers himself the servant of God and of Jesus Christ, he also thinks of himself as servant or slave of all for Jesus' sake (2 Co 4:5; 1 Co 9:19; Ga 5:15). In fact, the Lord he serves and imitates and urges his faithful to imitate 'took the form of a servant' and 'became obedient unto death . . . ' (Ph 2:7-8).

Paul's taking of the stance of brother and servant by no means involved an abdication of the authority conferred by his call and by the tradition from which he spoke. Much of 1 and 2 Co and Ga amounts to a defence of his authority (see 2 Co 3:5-6; 5:18-20; 10:8; 13:10). This authority being preserved, we could speak of Paul exercising a spiritual brotherhood or *diakonia* (ministry), as well as spiritual motherhood or fatherhood. Each term has its advantages. The father image lends itself to notions of begetting, educating, correcting; the mother image to child-bearing, gentleness, nurturing. Both imply a tender affection. Brotherhood is a reminder that God is the father and we are all equally his children. *Diakonia,* ministry, reminds us that spiritual parenthood is service to, rather than lordship over, others. That Paul seems equally at home with spiritual motherhood or fatherhood invites us to broaden our ways of thinking and speaking.

As with the prophets and Jesus, an important dimension of Paul's spiritual motherhood was prayer. For examples, see 1 Th 1:2-3; 2 Th 1:11; 2 Co 13:7-9; Rm 1:9; Ph 1:3-11; Eph 1:16-23; Col 1:3, 9-12; Phm 4-6; 2 Tm 1:3. We should note, however, that none of these texts speaks of prayer as an exercise of spiritual parenthood. What Paul has in mind when he speaks of spiritual fatherhood is begetting children in Christ through the preaching of the gospel, then raising them to maturity through instruction, exhortation, admonition, and example, and the love behind this care.

CONCLUSION

Here is how Fr Hervé Briand summed up his survey of the Old Testament wisdom literature and St Paul: spiritual **paternity** is rooted in the subsoil, common, but solid and fundamental, of physical paternity by which a man engenders another to natural life: his son! This physical paternity is prolonged and finds its full meaning in a 'sapiential' paternity by which the father initiates his son into the art of living. In ideal cases, this sapiential paternity becomes 'religious paternity' which initiates into 'life with God'. Sapiential and religious paternity may be fulfilled by the same person as physical paternity, but often, in part at least, they are taken up by another person who thus fulfills a genuinely paternal role . . . . ' [With St Paul, we arrive at a] 'spiritual paternity' which, in its first degree, gives birth to the life of the Spirit and, in its second degree, causes this life of the Spirit to grow, blossom, fructify.[14]

The wisdom teachers, the rabbis, and St Paul readily thought and spoke of themselves as (spiritual) fathers. The gospels carefully avoid any such thing. The use of the term can convey that life is truly communicated and fostered in a spirit of love. The avoidance, even prohibition, of this term can serve as a reminder that it is God's life which is being shared, a life of which he is the unique source. God is so much Father and Mother that humans do well to be wary of thinking about themselves in such terms. We are brothers, sisters, servants of God and of each other, through whom God sometimes enlivens and graces his other sons and daughters.[15]

In the Scriptures

NOTES

1. Scriptural quotations are taken from the *Revised Standard Version.*
2. *'Patēr'* in G. Kittel (ed.), *Theological Dictionary of the New Testament* (Grand Rapids, 1968) 5:962.
3. *Ibid.,* p. 963.
4. *Ibid,* p. 1006; see also 977 (G. Schrenk).
5. 'Priests and Priesthood' in *Encyclopaedia Judaica* (New York, 1971) 13:1080.
6. See J. McKenzie, SJ, article 'Scribe' in his *Dictionary of the Bible* (Milwaukee, 1965) 779-81.
7. 'Wisdom; Wisdom Literature' in *Encyclopaedia Judaica,* 16:558.
8. 'Introduction to *The Proverbs*' and 'Introduction to the Wisdom Books' in *The Jerusalem Bible* (Garden City, New York, 1966) pp. 932 and 723.
9. Origen, *Commentary on the Song of Songs,* Prologue 3. See also Jerome, *Letter to Laeta* (Letter 107), 12; and Bernard of Clairvaux, *On the Song of Songs,* Sermon 1:2-3.
10. See McKenzie, 'Rabbi' and 'Teacher, Teaching,' *Dictionary of the Bible,* 718, 869-71.
11. McKenzie, 'Disciple,' *Dictionary,* 199-200.
12. For this suggestion, I am indebted to Dr Bernard Scott, Professor of New Testament at St Meinrad's School of Theology. Other designations for Christians in the New Testament are: 'saints' (55 times), 'sons of God' (22), 'children of God' (13), 'heirs', 'co-heirs' (8), 'members' of the Body of Christ (5), 'Christians' (3), 'Nazarenes' (1).
13. 'Discernment' in this quotation from Ph is *aisthesis,* insight, perception, rather than the *anakrinein* and *diakrisis* of the preceding quotations from 1 Co 2 and 12.
14. H. Briand, OCSO, 'La Paternité Spirituelle: Enracinements Bibliques' in *La paternité spirituelle.* Mimeographed notes of a seminar for Cistercian novice mistresses held at Laval in September 1974, pp. 13-49. Wisely, Père Hervé concentrated his commendable

35

study on the Wisdom literature and St Paul. He traces the development of Israelite wisdom from the family circle, through the scribes of the king to the scribes of the law of the Lord, and he emphasizes that life was transmitted at each stage. He carefully analyzes the relevant pauline texts, both those concerning birth to life in the Spirit and those concerning the growth of that life. Along the way, he offers helpful treatments of the nature of the wise man's 'counsel', aspects of 'education for life' according to the Old Testament and St Paul, the ways in which man is the origin and God is the origin of life in its various levels, the Word of God as life-giving. Particularly valuable is Briand's locating spiritual paternity/maternity within the wisdom tradition. He brings out the strong affinities with this tradition in contexts where Paul employs the terminology of spiritual parenthood. Despite this continuity, Briand discerns a leap from the sapiential paternity of the Old Testament to the spiritual paternity of the New. The life of union with God into which the two lead is significantly different. Unfortunately, Père Hervé's article became available to me only after I had completed my own.

15. Among the reasons our explorations have not yielded more satisfying results may be the following. By and large, the biblical writings are addressed to communities, if not to the whole people. The people of the Bible were less given to introversion and psychologizing than we. When there is a strong, supportive community, clear about its ideals and the basic means for achieving them, members feel less need for direction and support on a one-to-one basis. This may be a reaction against certain customs current in Jewish religion or pagan mystery cults. (The mystagogue who initiated newcomers into the mysteries was sometimes entitled 'father'.) A very great part was played by the father himself in the religious, moral, social upbringing of his children in a less sophisticated society. In the New Testament there is the overpowering sense that God was Father, alone capable of originating a life which was a share in his own. It is tantalizing that spiritual paternity draws its wherewithal so largely from the Scriptures, and can even be viewed as a mediation of the scriptural word, yet is not one of the key categories in which biblical thought flows.

SPIRITUAL FATHERHOOD IN THE LITERATURE
OF THE DESERT

André Louf, OCSO
Abbaye Sainte-Marie-du-Mont

WE CAN ALMOST SAY that the literature of the desert identifies itself with the exercise of spiritual fatherhood. The *Apophthegmata,* its master work, for example, is entirely constructed on a question-answer scheme, a monk asking an elder: 'Abba, tell me a word so that I may be saved.'

This form appears in written literature only on the eve of the fourth century, but its semitic aspect attests to a distant origin rooted in primitive Judaic-Christian traditions. *Abba* was kept as it was in Aramaic, though Coptic inflection changed its pronunciation to *apa.* The custom of naming 'father' whoever transmitted life in the Spirit was soon established among christian communities in spite of Jesus' admonition: 'Call no one on earth your father' (Mt 23:9). Moreover Jesus used the word himself in referring to those who had preceded his listeners in their faith in God: 'they are their fathers' (Lk 1:55; Jn 6:31, 49; 1 Cor 10:1). The expression had long been accepted when monastic tradition adopted it, and any reference to Mt 23:9—inspired by the desire to be free from one's father's tutelage—was immediately stigmatized as the fruit of diabolic illusion and an evident sign of pride. We recall here the sad account Palladius gives of a proud monk named Heron, 'filled with rebellious thoughts against the fathers' (*The Lausiac History,* 26, 1).[1] The fatherhood known to monastic tradition is not the one rejected by Jesus. Another was substituted for it, one entirely transparent to him, to the fatherly image he came to earth to reflect.

Abba finds its synonym in 'old man' or 'elder', a biblical term which implies not age but rather a ministry of wisdom at the center of any christian community. (Ac 11:30; 14:23; 15:2, 4, 6, 22; 20:17; 1 Tim 5:17; Tt 1:5; 1 P 5:17). In a well known instance the name became *kalogiros* or 'handsome elder', an epithet Pachomius used to greet the great Macarius, whom he had discovered hidden among the postulants of his monastery (*The Lausiac History,* 28, 6).

The questioner's aim is expressed by 'so that I may be saved' or 'so that I may live'. Here again the primitive aramaic idiom, which by one root expresses both concepts, is quite evident.

THE WORD

The object of the request is the *rhema* or 'word'. At first, questioners sought not a teaching, but rather an active word charged with mysterious power which, well received, touches the heart and opens a way by which new life may burst forth. Thus described, the *rhema* appears very close to the Word of God as we know it in the Bible. In the same way, the word of the fathers needs to be meditated on, that is, to be repeated over and over again within the heart, before it comes to fruition. By his word the true abba soon stands out among his brothers. He may be very young, as was Agathon, whom the great Poemen daringly called 'father' and then explained to his inquiring disciples: 'All that comes from his lips entitles him to that name' (Poemen, 61).[2]

A father's word is weighty. He does not speak idly. That is why he is listened to attentively and his word scrutinized: 'The fathers say nothing in vain, but everything they utter is for the salvation of the soul' (Barsanuphius, *Letter 652*).[3] Even seemingly meaningless pronouncements must be respected as having a meaning which may escape us at first: 'If the fathers tell you that darkness is light, try to believe it is so; for they do not speak without God's approval' (Barsanuphius, *Letter 842*). The effectiveness of the fathers' word is

also considerable. It produces an undeniable effect even if we
do not understand it, even if we forget it. A monk tempted to
give up questioning his father, on the grounds that he keeps
forgetting what he has learned, is instructed: 'Just as a jug
filled regularly with water or oil is cleaner than one remaining
empty, even if the liquids do not remain, so it is with the soul
persevering in questioning the fathers even if the answers are
forgotten' (*Anonymous Series,* 91).[4] Though demons will exert
themselves to sow seeds of trouble in the soul, inducing it to
error as to what the fathers have said, the confusion will be
only momentary, and in the end the power of the word will
triumph: If you question the fathers and, even for a moment,
demons trouble you with regard to their words, never stop
your inquiry, for they ordain nothing that might be harmful
or oppressive; the fathers are in fact disciples of him who said:
'My yoke is easy, and my burden light' (Mt 11:30). Later on
we will discover the fruit of their assistance and exclaim with
the Psalmist: 'You have changed my sorrow into joy'. (Ps
30:12).

The word's aim is not primarily to teach a precept or a
method, moreover. Reduced to its simplest expression, it
proclaims and grants salvation, and it does so with such a
sovereign might that it seems to come from God himself. If
the disciple asks the father questions in order to receive from
him a saving word, the most direct answer he can hope for is
to hear him proclaim salvation as if he were passing judgment:
be saved! This very word John the Theban waited in vain to
hear from his abba Ammoe as he nursed him patiently during
his illness. At the time of his death, however, the elder
rewarded his faithful disciple. He took his hand in the presence
of all the other elders and pronounced three times the phrase
which resounded like a verdict: 'Be saved, be saved, be saved . . .
He is an angel, not a man' (John the Theban, 1).

This word, coming after a long wait, could not have been
uttered without that waiting, for the word takes effect only to the
extent to which it has been sought by the disciple with the
proper attitude. The father's wisdom or experience is not

enough. The inner preparation of the disciple does much to release the word within his heart and on the father's lips. If the petitioner's intent is self-interest, the father remains silent. We recall a brother who badgered Abba Theodore for three days, hoping to obtain a *rhema.* The elder did not give it. When the importunate guest had left, Theodore explained to the disciple who lived with him: 'I did not speak, for he is a peddler seeking self-glory from someone else's speech' (Theodore of Pherme, 3). It is useless to seek any gain from the word except its inherent good. To do otherwise would reduce the word to naught.

If the intention of the petitioner is truly to know God's will, however, then somehow, somewhere, in the most un-expected manner, God will provide a father. Here is what Dorotheos of Gaza said to a brother who complained of not finding a sound spiritual father: If anyone truly seeks God's will with his whole heart, God will never abandon him but will guide him according to his will. Yes, it is true, if anyone directs his heart toward the divine will, God will enlighten even a little child to make his will known. But, if someone who does not sincerely seek God's will goes to consult a prophet, God will provide the prophet with an answer consistent with the perversity of the inquirer's heart' (Dorotheos of Gaza, *Discourses* 5, 68).[5]

This means that the charism of spiritual fatherhood dwells within the son's as well as the father's heart. If, at some time, the fathers have no more to say, this is, first of all, because there are no longer hearts disposed as sons to receive (Felix, 1). In approaching his father, a son will therefore pray God to enlighten his father, and he will surrender completely to the word of God which comes through his father's answer: 'If you go to ask a father questions about your thoughts, first pray to God and say:"Lord, put on the elder's lips what you will, so he may tell me. And I will receive from you, Lord, what will come from him. Strengthen him, Lord, in your truth so that I may learn, through him, your will"' (Nau, 592/58).[6]

40

The role of the father, answering, is formidable. From weakness and unworthiness he bends under the weight of the word he is to deliver, for he knows he has no sure grasp of the word. Witness John the Prophet's answer to a brother who insisted on getting advice: 'You write me again, senseless and ignorant as I am? . . . So I tell you the truth. I am nothing and know nothing. But out of obedience, I tell you what is in my heart. And I do not pretend that it is exactly so, but it is what I have. I tell . . . unworthy though I am' (Barsanuphius, 212).

The word of the fathers is not intended to dazzle the great and the wise of this world. It is rough and unwavering. It does not have polish. Abba Theodore of Pherme stood before a visiting count frankly and without artifice: 'His tunic was torn, his chest exposed, and his hood was hanging in front.' To his disciple who reproached him for his lack of decorum, Theodore gave the following answer: 'Are we still slaves of men? We have done what is necessary; the rest is superfluous. He who would be edified, let him be edified; he who would be scandalized, let him be scandalized. As for me, I meet people as I am.' The fathers' word does not need human affectation.

Thus, if the word is clear and rough, it has the advantage of brevity and needs to be followed by a silence as meaningful as the word itself. The truly enlightening word is self-sufficient; it has no need of prolix commentary. It would drown in a flow of words. When Abba Ammoes went to church, he did not allow his disciple to walk near him, but kept him at some distance. Whenever the latter would come closer to question his father on his thoughts, Ammoes would answer him and move away quickly, 'for fear that strange conversation slip in' (Ammoes, 1).

The saving word springs forth from the depth of the rapport between father and son, at once rough and stripped down, yet very profound in faith. The two bring to dialogue the same lack of restraint, each at his own level. Each needs the other, the father the son as much as the son the father for

41

something to occur. Saint Anthony ends an exhortation to his sons by giving a definition, before its time, of the true spiritual dialogue: 'It is good to exhort one another mutually in faith and to become animated through discourses. You, my sons, bring to your father what you know; I, your elder, deliver you what experience has taught me' (*The Life of St Anthony,* 16).[7] And as it is on both sides that giving and receiving take place, it is easy to understand Ammonas' words as he writes to a community of his disciples: 'Wherever the fathers receive their sons, God is present on both sides' (Ammonas, *Letter 6,* 2).[8] The word shared in fraternal joy can only be God's Word.

BECOMING A FATHER

Through the fathers, God's word continues to echo in ears willing to ask them questions. Such inquiry, addressed by a younger member to one more experienced, is one of the fundamental observances of the desert. Dorotheos of Gaza has preserved for us a manuscript, still unpublished, attributed to the great Poemen: 'The fathers say that staying in a cell is half [of monastic observance], and to see the elders the other half' (Dorotheos of Gaza, *Letter 1;* see MS Paris grec, 1598, fo 73). This is an indispensable guarantee against all forms of illusion entertained by secret pride. St Anthony and others after him call on a text of the Scripture borrowed from wisdom literature: 'I know monks who, after having borne many labors, fell into pride of the spirit because they placed their hope in their good works and neglected the precept of the one who said "Question your father and he will teach you" ' (Pr 4:1ff; Anthony, 37).

But how does one find a father according to God, and how does one become someday the father of one's brothers? We have already seen the essential attitudes expected of anyone looking for a father: a sincere desire to know God's will and the beginning of detachment from all selfish desire. He who will be chosen as father must not side with the disciple's desires. The anonymous series of apophthegmata has

42

preserved the story of a young man who addresses an elder thus: 'Abba, I would like to find an elder conformed to my will, and die with him.' The elder pretends to accept his request, but soon lets him know that the peace he seeks in this manner would be vain and superficial: 'Perhaps it is not for you to follow the elder's will, but for him to follow yours so that you may have peace' (*Anonymous Series,* 113).

Ordinarily, the father will not fall into such an obvious trap. He is supposed to be experienced in the ways of obedience. This, according to St John Cassian, is an absolutely indispensable condition. Gallic monasticism, for which Cassian composed his tales of monastic pilgrimage in the Near East, he reproached with being overcrowded with young abbots lacking experience, having acceded to their ministry without a chance to immerse themselves first in playing to its limit the role of disciple: 'Without the experience of the elders' teaching, we dare to take the first place in the monasteries, and, passing ourselves off as "abba" before having been disciples, we do as we please, more inclined to demand the observance we invented than to keep the doctrine tested by the elders' (*Instit.,* II, 3, 5).[9] This attitude leads to the ruin of any tradition of rules faithfully transmitted. But the necessity of experience is even more true in the spiritual domain. The same John Cassian warns that one can teach the *scientia spiritualis* to others only to the degree of one's own learning, not by reading or studying, but by 'the sweat of experience' (*Coll.,* XIV, 17).[10]

This experience does not only come from exceptional graces. It first comes from a familiarity with temptation and trial. A father not himself purified by fire could easily lead others to despair (see *Anonymous Series,* 85). He would even be incapable of understanding the questions being asked. 'What you ask me,' writes Barsanuphius to one of his correspondents, no one can discern but the one who has reached in adequate level. The living man feels the warmth or coldness of objects presented to him, but a dead man has lost the ability to feel. So it is that we come to perfect knowledge

43

of letters by learning them; then we can distinguish them. But if they are not studied and effort is lacking, we cannot know their meaning even if we inquire and are told a thousand times what the letters are. So it is here: speak to someone as much as you wish; what is more necessary is the discernment of experience (Barsanuphius, 154).

Not every experienced monk is called to transmit his experience to another brother. Ancient texts imply a more direct manifestation of God's will concerning the new abbot. The most famous example is perhaps Abbot Zacharias. The first three apophthegms devoted to him allude to such an event, and we find it again slightly amplified in an apophthegm from the Ethiopian Collection (Zacharias, 1-3; *Eth. Coll.,* 14, 34).[11] Moses questions young Zacharias, who is still his disciple (in Zacharias, 1, it is Macarius); the latter asks why. The answers given by various texts are convergent. Moses, who questions one still his son, feels compelled to do so. 'Zacharias, my son, I am confident about you. It is God, in fact, who spurs me on.' Or better yet: 'Believe me, Zacharias, my son, I have seen the Holy Spirit come down upon you, and since then I am compelled to ask you questions.' This last confidence is confirmed by Apophthegm 2: 'Abba Moses, on his way to fetch water one day, found Abba Zacharias praying by the well and God's Spirit was over him.'

In other circumstances it is a saying, markedly enlightened, which reveals the true father: 'His tongue marks him as abba,' said Poemen of a very young monk (Poemen, 61). Or, more strikingly, a miracle reveals the spiritual quality of a brother previously held in contempt. Such is the case of the monk 'who took upon himself all the wrongs done by his brothers, going so far as to accuse himself of fornication'. But while the others are muttering, a miracle saves his work from fire and burns that of the others. 'On witnessing that,' continues the apophthegm, 'the brothers were afraid; they bowed profoundly to the brother and from then on looked upon him as a father' (Nau, 328).

Still more significant: a test patiently borne by the son

44

shows complete credence in the word pronounced by the
father. Such was the case of Abba Joseph of Aframet, sent
away by his abbot on a retreat of forty days in solitude after
confessing a serious temptation against chastity. When he
came back, calmed and joyous, his Abba kissed him several
times on the lips and head and then said: 'Today you have
become my son' (*Eth. Coll.,* 14, 27).

Is it necessary to add that no abba ever wishes to be one?
In most instances a genuine terror seizes him when the offer
is made. Witness again Abba Zacharias who, when asked his
first spiritual question by Abba Moses, 'laid himself on the
ground, beat his face on the earth, sprayed ashes over his
head and cried' (*Eth. Coll.,* 14, 34)—expressive signs of grief
and anguish.

UNVEILING THOUGHTS

We must now examine in depth the relationship which
almost always began with a question on salvation. First let us
take a closer look at the question itself. Its aim is very seldom
of an abstract or theological nature, except on extremely rare
occasions when the orthodox faith is in danger. Abba Joseph
admits his ignorance when a difficult passage of the Scriptures
is submitted to him (Anthony, 17), as does Abba Arsenius
(Arsenius, 42). Abba Poemen advises against discussing the
Scripture: it is better to discuss the elders' sentences (Amoun,
2), which proves that those elders did not venture often in this
domain. Moreover, Poemen imposed this rule on himself.
Questioned about the Scriptures, he turned away and remained
silent. It was left to his disciples to explain to the discon-
certed visitor: 'The elder does not speak willingly of the
Scriptures, but if he is queried about the soul's passions he
answers' (Poemen, 8).

The favorite topic for dialogue was indeed the passions
and the sicknesses which affect the soul and which the elder's
word must reveal and heal. Inasmuch as passions appear to
the conscience as desires, they are called either *logismoi*
(thoughts) or *thelēmata* (will, desires). A blasphemous thought

45

occurs to a brother who is ashamed to reveal it to his abba,
Poemen. He tries to do so several times with no success: 'He
left without having said anything to the elder.' Poemen, however, aware of his attitude and guessing the truth, encourages
him to open up, all the while dispensing sound advice, and
'the devil, seeing his suggestion uncovered, left him, thanks to
Christ's grace' (*Collection systématique grecque,* X, 63).[12]
One of the aims of the unveiling of thoughts is the bringing
to the surface of tendencies lurking deep in the heart where
they cause havoc because they are not shared with anyone.
Brought to light they often vanish. This is not, therefore, a
confession of faults which might have been committed. It is
no use to ask about a known weakness: 'Does he who knows
he is losing his soul need to inquire? Hidden thoughts are to
be questioned, and it is the elders' task to test them; as for
visible flaws, there is need not to inquire but to remove them
right away' (Poemen, 152).

 'Thought' or *logismos* is to be understood here in a dynamic sense. It has nothing to do with any random thought
coming to mind but rather a deep affective thought, seeking
understanding from a heart which listens. After a question
from one of his correspondents, the elder John makes the
point: 'You must not inquire about all the thoughts springing
from the heart, for many are transitory. But you must seek
advice about the thoughts that remain within and war with
man' (Barsanuphius, 165). It is not necessary to open up too
quickly or on any subject whatever. God may give light
directly, and Barsanuphius even gives criteria to help one
decide for oneself if recourse to the spiritual father is needed:
'When something comes to your mind, pray to God three
times on the matter, asking him that you may stay on the
right road. If your thought remains unchanged, then do as it
tells you, for it comes from God and not from you. If you are
still not sure, question the fathers' (Barsanuphius, 841).

 It is true that this advice was addressed to a layman, and
we wonder if it would be as valid for a monk when we witness
the insistence with which monks are sent out by a spiritual

father to seek discernment. The more exceptional the asceticism, the more perilous it is and the more it must be shared with an elder. This fact is verified by eremitic whimseys: 'A brother found a spot in the desert for a quiet retreat. He begged his father: "Order me to live there, and I hope that thanks to God and to your prayers I will practice mortification." His abba, however, would not allow it and said: "I know very well that you would mortify yourself, but, without an elder, you would put your trust in your own works, convinced that they are pleasing to God, and because of this confidence in your own work as a monk you would lose your caution and your reason" ' (Nau, 370). St Anthony had already remarked: 'Some have crushed their body through asceticism, but for lack of discernment, have become estranged from God' (Anthony, 8).

Discernment or acuteness of judgment, even in the humblest details, is necessary for the monk. Adds Anthony: 'In the measure it is possible, the monk must tell the elders the number of steps he walks in his cell and the number of drops of water he drinks to learn if, in so doing, he is mistaken' (Anthony, 38).

Demons' ruses creep in everywhere, as water seeps into a boat through the slightest crack and eventually sinks it. The spiritual father must be a vigilant captain, recommends the great Macarius, who left us this vivid image: 'The pilot is never free of worry for his craft; he examines its joints to see which ones let the water in . . . . So it is with him who is father over his brothers; he must always examine all the passions and evil thoughts within to determine which one . . . lets bad water into the soul, for fear . . . there would be danger and just complaint before God should the brothers be swallowed by the sea because he has not examined them' (Amélineau, 189, 6).[13]

Here it would be appropriate to paraphrase the long apophthegm of Nau 641. It tells the story of a monk from the Thebaïd 'who led fully a life of asceticism: he persevered in numerous vigils, prayers, supplications, lived in absolute

47

poverty, trying his body by fasts and difficult works'. For a long time he was a toy in the demons' hands, so much so that one day he asked God for the power to perform miracles. God suggested he submit his judgment to the discernment of a holy hermit. Our 'athlete' gave in and went, as had many others before him, to ask of the elder the ritual question, 'Teach me the way to salvation'. The holy man, knowing him well, simply sent him to the nearest town to buy supplies. The monk was so embarrassed he did not dare make the purchase himself, for fear of losing his reputation. Instead, he asked some laymen he knew to do it for him. When the monk returned with the provisions, the elder surprised him by saying: 'Take it all, go to your cell and while praying eat a loaf of bread and a pound of meat, drink a pint of wine each day—then come back in ten days.' Extremely vexed, the brother left whining, but he obeyed the elder's request. And God, heeding his repentance and humility, offered solace. The monk came to understand the motive which led him to live as he had—without good judgment. He thanked God and recognized the truth of the Prophet's sentence: 'All man's acts of justice are like a dirty cloth' (Is 64:5) (Nau, 641). A salutary conversation was granted in exchange for the mani- festation of inquiry and obedience to a spiritual father, for it is true, according to another apophthegm in the same collec- tion, that 'if anyone calls on God with all his heart and goes to seek advice from a man about his thoughts, the man answers—or rather God does—telling him what is right through this intermediary. For He who opened the jaw of Balaam's ass answers even if the inquirer is an unworthy sinner' (Nau, 592/50).

OBEYING THE WORD

The unveiling of thoughts is always teamed with obedience. Each calls for the other; they belong to the same movement, to the same method or spiritual therapy. As a first move, the disciple comes to show certain inclinations to his father; then, by renouncing them, in the conciliating—yet not frustrating—

light of fatherly judgment, he finds his own freedom. Then, someday, he in turn accedes to the charism of discernment.

In the East as well as in the West, the novice's initiation invariably begins with the renunciation of one's own will, that is, all desires, varied and contradictory, successfully called forth in one's heart. 'The concern and principal aim of the abba's teaching, when in charge of young novices,' writes John Cassian, 'a teaching which will allow the young monk to rise later to the highest summit of perfection, will be to teach him first of all to master his will' (*Instit.,* IV, 8). Dorotheos of Gaza echoes him from Palestine. In his admirable *Discourses* for beginners, he says: 'Each time we cling obstinately to our own will. . . while thinking everything is going beautifully, we set traps for ourselves and do not know that we are going to our ruination.'

It is evident that such obedience is but remotely related to the so-called sociological obedience which necessarily char-acterizes any relationship between a brother and his mentor within a human group. Whenever the elders speak of obedience, what is today called the 'common good' never appears on the horizon. They consider only the personal well-being of the brother who, facing his father, submits to training in obedi-ence as he would to spiritual therapy. It is, above all, a way to internal freedom and spiritual maturation. That is why this training demands a great deal and seems, at times, to go past the bounds of what we know to be reasonable within the normal relationships between inferior and superior in the service of the common good. This apparent excess can be understood only in the light of the psychological and spiri-tual development it was designed to set in motion. Some borderline cases simply set up a sort of shock-therapy that only a father can impose upon his own son, not only because he is supposed to know him better than anyone else, but above all because the son trusts him totally and feels loved, without limits, without hesitation, as only God can love his children. (We shall come back to this point later on.)

Obedience will therefore go to some excess. Even if the

abba appears unreasonable and tries his son's patience in a stupid way (Nau, 631), or if he orders dangerous feats, such as catching and binding a hyena. (John, 1), or a painful trial, such as putting one's hand into the fire (Chaine, 270),[14] the novice will try to obey the order given. The last example serves the father in testing the docility of a brother who has come to confide himself to the mercy of his fatherhood: 'Make me your son so that I may learn near you.' In other circumstances the disciple will even risk his life, for 'only obedience unto death allows recognition of the true monk' (J, 752).[15]

To obey is to be sure of acceding to God's will. In practice true obedience dispenses the brother from all concern about the commandments, because it guarantees conformity with God's wishes: 'If someone trusts an elder and obeys him, he must no longer be concerned with God's commandments, but abandon all his self-will to his spiritual father, for by always obeying him he will not expose himself to sin before God' (Nau, 290).

Obedience thus becoming the only norm, renunciation of one's own will causes God's will to appear in everything that happens. The one who obeys is free from all care and worry. He becomes *amerimnos,* without care. 'He who has a spiritual father is relieved through him of all worry' (Guy, p. 418, no. 8).[16] 'Be without care,' writes Barsanuphius to one of his correspondents, 'if you want to do God's work, and I will carry the burden' (Barsanuphius, 253).

The command given by the spiritual father is often called a 'blessing'. For the father's word which allows a son to act in one way or another brings at the same time the power to succeed. 'This is what you must remember until death: do not do the least or greatest thing without consulting the spiritual father who lives with you: do not leave your cell without his permission; do not drink water before he has uttered a prayer; do not eat a piece of fruit until he has made the sign of the cross over it; do not touch a meal until you have said: "Bless this, Father"; do not put water or oil into the pot without having said the same thing. At night, do not lay down

till you have bowed profoundly to him and taken leave'
(K, 298).[17] The entire life of the disciple is steeped in the
father's blessings and, through them, in God's strength. It
should not be surprising, then, that obedience succeeds in
accomplishing miracles. A special apophthegm has been preserved to tell of a resurrection attributed to obedience,
although another brother thought he had obtained it by his
asceticism: 'It is because of your brothers' obedience that
this man has been raised up' (Nau, 294).

Revealing one's thoughts to the father provokes a discerning response or word. This, in turn, must be accepted in total
obedience. The brother who renounces all his personal desires
to espouse the light springing from his elder's counsel unfail-
ingly espouses God's will contained in it. In so doing, he is
purified from his own wishes, liberated from their pull; he is
clothed with God's power which in turn allows him to act
effectively and to help others in their good judgment.

IN THE IMAGE OF GOD:
GENTLENESS AND TENDERNESS

The word of itself is not enough. As important, and perhaps
even more important, is the father's example which leaves its
imprint on the son. At worse, the word could come from an
acquired knowledge. It could also lead to a misunderstanding
if the disciple were naive or inexperienced. But example never
misleads. It is a *tupos,* and enough to imitate if one is to be
schooled in daily concrete practice.

The fathers often recall the necessity of example. Pachomius' disciples were anxious to do good works after listening
to him. But they remembered that 'even when silent, Pachomius made his actions a discourse' (Psenthaisios, 1). According
to others, the word always retains its ambiguity; example
alone is effective. So it seemed to Abba Sisoes, who answered
someone asking for a word: 'Why do you insist on my speaking
idly? Do what you see' (Sisoes, 46). There are also situations
in which the excessive attachment of a disciple to his father's
words become suspect to Abba Poemen: One day, Abbot

51

Serinus, accompanied by his disciple Isaac, went to see Poemen and asked: 'What must I do for Isaac who listens willingly to me?' Poemen answered: 'If you want to be helpful to him, you must show him virtue through your behavior, for he who depends on words alone does not profit from them. But if through your action you show him virtue, he will be marked' (PE, IV, 38, 3).[18]

In a letter to one of his charges, Barsanuphius underlines the importance of the son's attention to his father's behavior. A curious exegesis of Genesis 30:37-40, provides the opportunity. We must be bound securely to the holy fathers, and through their examples, their teachings, their sufferings, their beautiful life, we will be filled with compunction before God. Indeed Jacob's ewes saw the rods in the water and conceived lambs in the rods' likeness. If we imprint on our mind the fathers' examples in order to act in the same manner, it will not be long before we walk alongside them' (Barsanuphius, 393). From a father's way of life a mysterious influence emanates, an influence more powerful than what he says. 'Teach by deeds and by word what must be practised,' writes Dorotheos of Gaza to superiors in his monasteries, 'but most of all by your deeds, for examples are much more efficacious. Be their model even in physical works, if you are able, and if you are too weak, teach them by the goodness of your soul and the fruits of the Spirit listed by the Apostle [Gal 5:22-23]: love, joy, peace, patience, kindness, goodness, faithfulness, gentleness, and control over all passions' (Dorotheos of Gaza, *Letter 2,* 184).

The virtues mentioned by Dorotheos, following St Paul, are characteristic of the New Testament. They are already, through the father's example, outflowings of the world to come, secret but powerful energies which reshape the hearts confiding in him. These virtues can be summarized by gentleness and mercy, two concrete terms for love in God's image. Ancient monastic literature swarms with examples—all of great force. Forbearance sometimes comes close to being a weakness and can only be grasped and justified insofar as the image of God the Father in heaven is perceptible behind it.

Barsanuphius attests to this explicitly to a brother reluctant to importune him with his questions: 'If God were disturbed or bothered by the requests he receives, the saints would be too.' On the contrary, 'these latter, when they are questioned, rejoice, being perfect as their Father is perfect' (Barsanuphius, 484). There are even better examples, and their profusion attests that, as God bears with man patiently without punishing his negligence, so the father bears with and overlooks his son's thoughtlessness. 'After God I have spread my wings over you till this day,' writes Barsanuphius to a young brother, a scatter-brain. 'I bear your burdens and your misconduct, your scorn of my teachings and your thoughtlessness. I have seen and covered all that, just as God sees and overlooks our faults, waiting for you to do penance' (Barsanuphius, 239).

Applications are legion: forbearance and gentleness are the most striking signs of God's presence in the father. We would do well at this time to quote the little Directory composed by Dorotheos of Gaza to remind superiors how they must correct their brothers. Love always prevails, nothing must shock, for a 'severe heart' and the 'fruits of mercy' go together. Do not be angry about errors . . . . If reproach is necessary, take the right attitude and wait for a propitious time. Do not be overconcerned with little faults, as if you were a severe judge. Do not always reprimand; it is insufferable, and such a habit leads to insensitivity and contempt . . . . If a brother resists you and this troubles you at the time, hold your tongue so as not to say anything in anger . . . . May your own frailty make you sympathetic to your brother. Pray for the opportunity to forgive, so that you too may obtain God's forgiveness for more serious and numerous sins' (Dorotheos of Gaza, *Letter 2*, 184-85).

This text summarizes admirably a tradition which goes back to the origins of life in the desert. John Cassian relates the example of a father who, faced with the impudence of a disobedient son, did not snub him but was satisfied to grieve in his heart, pondering the word in Philippians 2:6 and 8, in which Jesus is represented as obedient till death (*Inst.,* XII, 28). Another brother who—as everyone knew—spent each night with a woman in a nearby village, was not immediately reprimanded by his father, in spite of the grumbling of the other disciples, unable to understand such a scandalous patience. The father intervened later at a very propitious time and brought about the conversion of the culprit. To those inquring about the unusually long delay, the father answered: 'I saw Satan holding our brother by the hand and leading him into the world, but I patiently held his other hand for fear that a reproach would drive him faster into the world where the devil was leading him. When God thought it right to save his creature, then we took our brother's other hand and brought him back safe and sound' (PE, IV, 48, 1-11).

Thus the father does not brutally oppose sin. His first reaction is akin to God's: sorrow, of course, but above all patience and mercy; he resorts to wiles to administer reproach in a discreet and round-about way, to spare the brother's feelings. If the father himself is involved and his own teaching has been scorned, his attitude does not vary. Abba Romanos, for instance, recalls at the time of his death that he never told any of the brothers to do something without first making up his mind not to get angry should his orders not be carried out (Romanos, 1). In another case, the father accompanies his son into sin, as it were, by pretending that he has experienced an identical temptation. The aim, as always, is to save the disciple by any means (Nau, 44).

Such condescension, however, is never weakness. It does not surrender to sin nor is it ever its ally. A strange apophthegm preserved by Amélineau in a coptic series unites in the same striking image the double demand of firmness and gentleness. The words are from the great Macarius. It is not possible, he asserts, 'to give birth to spiritual sons in the way Elijah begot Elisha or Paul begot Timothy and Onesimus', if the father is not in a state of 'kindness and gentleness'. He must be in his own person 'the image and likeness of the true shepherd, the real master, whose body is marked by blows, nails, and lance . . . all endured of his own volition and with great gentleness'. To be the true image of his father, the disciple must also 'bear on his cheeks the traces of the fingers of his master and *hegumenos* [abbot] . . . with great patience, without complaint' (Amélineau, 177, 11). The marks on the son's face could only be—if we interpret it correctly—those of the slap administered by the father, which in no way compromises the image of God's fatherhood if it results from a true love.

FRIENDSHIP
   All that has been said so far finds its full meaning in the light of love, the source of the relationship between father and son. Ancient monastic literature, we know, always remained reticent about any obvious intimacy between brothers, but Barsanuphius makes an explicit exception in the case of the friendship between a father and his son: The father's love for their children is one thing, the brothers' love for their brothers is another. The spiritual fathers' love for their children is not at all carnal or harmful, for they are secure in their spirituality and, by either deeds or words, they are always attentive to the young, whatever their needs may be. And while loving them, they do not hide their weaknesses. Since because of his love your father does not hide your faults, it appears that his love for you is of a spiritual nature (Barsanuphius, 342).
   Saint Anthony, in his letters often overflowing with tenderness, had already introduced an analogous distinction: 'My sons, my love is not of this earth, it is a spiritual love, according to God' (*Letter 3*, 1).[19] That his spiritual children may grasp the quality of his love for them is the very object of his prayer: 'O, my sons in the Lord, day and night I beg my Creator, through the Spirit poured into me, to open your heart that you may understand my love for you' (*Letter 4*, 12).
   Since the father knows and loves his children for what they are in the eyes of God, he does not have to know their

55

birthname. This is the case for Joseph of Panephysis, who did not bother to learn the name of a disciple who has been living with him for two years (Joseph of Panephysis, 9). St Anthony, too, frequently, let it be known in his letters that he greeted his disciples not by their 'mortal, passing, or ephemeral name,' but by their true spiritual name which he alone is likely to know, their name as Israel's sons according to the Spirit (3, 1; 4, 1-8; 5, 1; 6, 1.3; 7).

In the warmth of this paternal love, little by little, in the course of the years, a strong friendship develops between father and son. A touching example is given at the death of St Anthony whom 'everyone wanted for a father' (*Vita,* 81), in a description left by Saint Athanasius: 'When he was done speaking, his disciples kissed him. He stretched out his feet and, looking fondly at his companions rejoicing in their presence, he remained abed, happiness showing in his face' (*Vita,* 103). In the end, Anthony had no secret left to confide to his closest children. He was asked to speak of his ecstasies. He did not refuse. His biographer writes: 'He expressed himself as a father who cannot hide anything from his children' (*Vita,* 66). Graces received are not the only things the father shares; frequently he tells them of his own temptations so that he can comfort his sons. 'I, brothers, weak as I am, used to do that. You who are watchful will be under God's care' (Barsanuphius, 512). Such intimacy transcends death, as in the case of the father who shrouded his son and asked: 'Are you all right my child, or is there a little something left to do?' Thereupon the deceased answered, 'All is well, Father; you have fulfilled your promise' (Nau, 15).

The sons' love answers the father. 'Be your father's joy,' recommends Arsenius, 'so that when you are on your way to the Lord, he in turn can be your joy' (Arsenius, 35). In some cases this love is the best guarantee of monastic life, as in Amma Talis' monastery, where sixty young religious 'loved her so much that there was no need for a key at the gate, as was customary elsewhere, so taken were they by the amma's love' (*Lausiac History,* 138).

The son's love for his father requires judgment, however. Too great an assiduity might hide some secret ambition: 'Do not be too familiar with your abba and do not go see him too often because these encounters might bring a lack of constraint and you would begin to desire the first place' (Nau, 36). Moreover, this love must always be accompanied by fear, for it is not an easy and superficial tenderness which the son is entitled to expect from his father, but the firmness of intervention as well if the need arise. The priest Isidore says: 'The disciples must love as fathers those who are truly their masters, and fear them as leaders, that fear remains along with love, but their love is not shadowed by it' (Isidore the Priest, 5).

PRAYER

In this dialogue of love, the most effective word is the one pronounced before God by the father about the son he has borne to life in prayer. Intercession is the abba's task *par excellence.* A greek apophthegm of the Nau collection has retained an abbreviated but admirable specimen of this prayer: A holy abbot, father of a monastery, excelled in all the virtues, and above all in humility and kindness. He was also merciful, sympathetic, and surpassed many others in love. This man prayed to God as follows: 'Lord, I am a sinner, but I hope that in your mercy I shall be saved. In your goodness, Master, I beg you not to separate me from my community, not even in the world to come. But, in your goodness, grant them your kingdom along with me' (Nau, 449).

He who prays for a brother is the first to benefit from this prayer: A brother went to visit an elder gifted with discernment and asked: 'Pray for me, Father, because I am weak.' And the elder answered him: 'One of the fathers once said that whoever takes oil in his hand to rub a sick man is the first to benefit from the anointing performed by his own hand. So it is with whoever prays for a sorrowing brother; he benefits from it even before his brother because his intention was love' (Nau, 635). The first effect of prayer is not always to relieve a sorrowing brother. On the contrary, the

57

prayer and blessing of the spiritual father often sets in motion a test from which the son can profit. Ammonas is an ancient witness to this conviction (*Letters* IX, 1-2; XIII, 5). It is also attested to in an apophthegm of the coptic collection published by Amélineau; this apophthegm uses an eloquent image to teach us how effective for the son the father's prayer may be: A brother asked Abba Macarius: 'Teach me what it is to live in submission.' And he answered: 'Just as the wheel, when it grinds wheat, removes the chaff, and the wheat becomes pure bread, so it is with you my son. Your father is the wheel and you are the wheat. If you listen to him, he will pray to the Lord on your behalf; he will remove from your path Satan's chaff, and instead of being pure bread you shall become a son of God' (Amélineau, 126, 14).

It is in the heat of trial that the spiritual father's prayer becomes most effective. Macarius attests to this concerning his spiritual father's prayer: 'The remedies of my lord, Abba Anthony, are not carnal, but the Paraclete's power is at work in his prayer' (Amélineau, 120, 14). When tempted, the disciple in turning to God often claims the support of his father's prayers and leans on them in the form, we might say, of an ejaculatory prayer, well known in the monastic environment and famous for its efficacy: 'Because of my Father's prayer, deliver me!' (Nau, 293); 'God of virtues, by my Father's prayer, free me!' (Ammoun, 3).

The spiritual father never grows weary of the prayer. It pursues the son even into sin. On learning that his disciple Abraham had fallen, Abba Sisoes got up, stretched his hands toward heaven and said: 'God, whether you want it or not, I will leave you no rest until you heal him' (Sisoes, 12). This prayer might appear daring, but it springs spontaneously from the certainty that God will answer the spiritual father's prayer because it is the channel by which all graces come to the son.

This prayer accompanies the son even on his death bed: 'Abba, I see the powers of darkness coming to me but your prayers drive them back' (Nau, 23). And even after death, the father's prayers keep on helping his son. Blessed Paul the

Simple learned this in a vision when one of his recently
deceased disciples, whose life had not been a model of edifi-
cation, came joyously to meet him saying: 'Your prayers,
Father, have touched the holy Mother of God who loves you
very much. In turn she prevailed on the Saviour who has set
me free, for I was still bound in the chains of my sin' (Nau,
599). The father's prayer remains effective even when he
himself is dead. In Palestine, Abba Nicholas had predicted to
Antiochus, a disciple who was blind, that he would recover
his sight the week after his death. And it did happen while
Antiochus was seated grieving near Nicholas's tomb (K 187).

To conclude these testimonies on the spiritual father's
prayer, it would be appropriate to quote Barsanuphius' note
to one of his sons, Andrew, who had asked the father to pray
for him: I am letting you know that, even before you asked,
I had presented you to the holy, adorable, consubstantial,
and vivifying Trinity, without beginning, in a presentation
which will preserve you from all evil. But I do not want you
to be ignorant that there is another [presentation] more
formidable, more ineluctable and awesome, more desirable
and lovable, more honorable and glorious . . . . He is referring,
of course, to the Last Judgment, when each spiritual father
will be invited to speak and to present his sons: Each of the
saints, bringing to God the sons he has saved, will announce
with a resounding voice, with the greatest of ease, to the
astonishment of the holy angels and all the heavenly hosts:
'Here I am with all the little children God gave me' (Barsanuphius, 117). In this fashion, the father's prayer accompanies
the disciple from the time he is taken in charge until in
eternity he stands before the Judge's throne.

SONS BECOMING FATHERS
The father's fundamental role in the primitive monastic
experience must not allow us to forget that it was passing and
transitory. If it is essential to speak only to one spiritual
father and not to several at the same time (Amélineau, 127, 5),
it is just as important not to be so dazzled by one's father as to

forget Him in whose name the father speaks. When a brother asked to leave monastic life because the famous abba he sought did not take care of him, he was reproached as follows: 'It is just that God made me forget you, for you were depending not on Him but on me.' Any cult of personality is excluded in monastic life. The father is useless if he is not transparent to God's actions.

The relationship between father and son is expected to progress. The day comes when the son can break away from his father. It is the most evident result of this fatherhood. Moreover, the fathers recognize that a son is sometimes much more advanced than they are. Abba Carion admitted this: 'I took greater pains than my son Zacharias, yet I have not yet reached his level of humility or knowledge' (Carion, 1). Barsanuphius advised his son to pray for him that he might receive the Holy Spirit, for He is the 'Great Pilot' who can, in the end, really save and direct, and it would be wrong to reserve too much esteem for the spiritual father (Barsanuphius, 196).

In several well-known instances, the time came when roles were reversed: the son became the father of his spiritual father and vice-versa. New heights of love and humility are reached this way: An abba from Rome recalled that there was an elder who had a good disciple. Because of some narrowness of mind, he chased him out. The brother remained seated outside and, when the elder opened the door and found him still seated, he bowed to him saying: 'O, father, the humility of your patience has won over my narrowness of mind. Come in; from now on you are the elder and father and I shall be the younger and disciple' (An Abba of Rome, 2; see Nau, 451).

§

'To remain in submission to one's spiritual father, and to renounce one's own will' constitute a truly spiritual technique, an evangelical path embracing the total monastic experience. Ancient literature gives its conditions precisely and praises its advantages. The literature compares this way to other types of monastic life, but most of the time the comparison turns to its advantage. According to Abba Joseph the Theban: three actions are worthy in the eyes of the Lord: if, when a man is ill and temptations plague him, he welcomes them gratefully; second, if all pure works are done in God's presence and nothing human remains; third, when submission to one's spiritual father is present and all that is self-will is renounced. And the last of these holds an eminent crown (Joseph the Theban, 1).

An apophthegm by Abba Rufus contains an amplified version of this. It ends in a lyrical flight quite unusual in the language of the fathers, habitually so restrained: O obedience, mother of all virtues! O obedience that discovers the kingdom! O obedience that opens the heavens, which from earth allows men's ascent! O obedience, nourishment of all the saints who have suckled its milk and through it have become perfect! O obedience, living with the angels! (Rufus, 2; see Nau, 296).

A mysterious force springing from the relationship in which father and son face each other in a mutual casting off of all desires, obedience thus reveals God's will and gives new life to whoever, through his father's word, lets it mould him. And the father who, in his transparency, is the humble instrument of this mystery deserves indeed the name of *kalogiros,* since divine Beauty becomes fertile in him through the sons it gives him. This is a blessed ministry, thanks to which he comes to resemble God Himself.

Translated by Monique Coyne

NOTES

1. Palladius, *The Lausiac History* (trans. Robert T. Meyer; *Ancient Christian Writers,* 34; Washington, D.C.; London, 1965).
2. The names followed by a number refer to the alphabetic collection of apophthegmata edited by Cotelier and reproduced by Migne, PG 65.
3. Cited according to the French translation by the monks of Solesmes (1971), based on the edition of Nicodème l'Hagorite (2nd ed. by Scoina; Volo, 1960) and improved by reference to various manuscripts.
4. Ed. Nau in the *Revue de l'Orient Chrétien* (1907-1913), cited according to the French enumeration of J. C. Guy in *Textes de spiritualité orientale,* 1 (Abbaye de Bellefontaine, 1966).
5. Ed. Regnault in SCh 109 (Paris, 1963).
6. Anonymous Series (*Revue de l'Orient Chrétien,* 1907-1913) numbered according to J. C. Guy in *Recherches sur la tradition greque des Apophthegmata Patrum* (Bruxelles, 1962) reproduced by L. Regnault in *Sentences des Pères du Désert,* 2 (Solesmes, 1970).
7. PG 26:837-976.
8. *Ammonas* (ed. Nau) in *Patrologia Orientalis,* 10 (Paris, 1916) 567-616.
9. Ed. J. C. Guy, SCh 109 (Paris, 1965).
10. *Conférences* (ed. Pichery) in SCh 42, 54, and 64 (Paris, 1955-1959).
11. *Collection éthiopienne* (ed. V. Arras) in *Corpus scriptorum christianorum orientalium,* 238-39 (Louvain, 1963).
12. Ed. J. C. Guy in *Recherches sur la tradition grecque des Apophthegmata Patrum* (Bruxelles, 1962).
13. Apophthegmata translated from the Coptic by Amélineau, *Annales du Musée Guimet,* 25 (1894).
14. The manuscript of the Coptic version of the *Apophthegmata Patrum,* with a Greek Text and a French translation edited by

M. Chaine (Cairo, 1960).

15. Unedited manuscript Sinai 448, cited according to the French translation by L. Regnault in *Sentences des Pères du Désert,* 3 (Solesmes, 1976).

16. *Collection grecque anonyme,* edited by Guy in *Recherches de Sciences Religieuses,* 50 (1960), cited according to the pagination in *Textes de spiritualité orientale,* 1 (Bellefontaine, 1966).

17. Unedited manuscript Coislin 283, cited according to the French translation by L. Regnault in *Sentences des Pères du Désert,* 3.

18. *Pavlos Evergetinos,* ed. V. Matthaiov (Athens, 4 vols., 1957-1966).

19. *Letters de S. Antoine* (trans. A. Louf) in *Cahiers de spiritualité* (Bellefontaine, 1976). An English translation has been published as *The Letters of St Antony* (Oxford: Fairacres Press).

SPIRITUAL GUIDANCE AND COUNSELING
ACCORDING TO ST BERNARD

Jean Leclercq, OSB
Abbaye St.-Maurice, Clervaux

S T B E R N A R D has no specific teaching on spiritual
fatherhood. He devotes no treatise to the subject and
does not deal with it even in a sermon or letter. But he
does make allusions which reveal a certain *praxis.* Yet, it
is not easy to study this and to give an overall view of it. We
must avoid projecting ideas coming from other periods of
history, either before or after Bernard. What we have to do is
to try to guess, through the medium of numerous formulas,
whether or not something actually was done in the way of
'counselling' and, if so, what it consisted of and how it was
justified. Any order which we might put into Bernard's brief
allusions will necessarily be artificial, since it is not one which
he himself thought out, as he did when he formulated theoretical teaching. Here we must pay careful attention to words
because, generally, Bernard uses a dense and precise vocabulary, and we should ask ourselves whether he does so in this
field, too. The basic question is: how do the words which
Bernard uses to evoke the role of what we call today the
'spiritual father' reveal his conception of such a person?

THE ROLE OF SPIRITUAL PERSONS IN THE CHURCH ACCORDING TO ST PAUL

As always, St Bernard's inspiration comes from the Bible
and especially from the New Testament. In the letters of
St Paul there are two texts in which the word 'spiritual' is
applied to people. And in the works of St Bernard these texts

2

both recur several times in contexts where it is evident that
the men who are so called have a double role to play.

Discernment

The first of the pauline verses on which Bernard's teaching
is founded is in the First Letter to the Corinthians, chapter
two, verse fifteen, where we read what it means to be a
'spiritual' man and how such a person should act. We must
quote this text in Latin because St Bernard comments on the
words: *Spiritualis quippe omnia diiudicat, et ipse a nemine
iudicatur.* The 'spiritual' is that which comes from 'the Spirit
and the Bridegroom and from God in the Church', in opposition to all that is 'animal', 'of the flesh', 'secular', that is, all
that belongs to and is restricted to this 'present world' and is
in this sense 'temporal', sought after by those who 'love this
world'. All this is dangerous for the Christian because of the
prosperity which comes in its wake. In order to be free, the
Christian must cease living according to worldly intelligence,
he must give up being a *stultus saecularis* (a worldly fool), an
indoctus spiritualis (a spiritual ignoramus), and become a
really 'spiritual' man. He will then be able to judge everything
and not waver under the pressure of all that draws him in the
opposite direction. A man is spiritual because he is able to
discern. (Palm 1,1-2; 2,1-2).[1]

It is grace which allows a person to become 'spiritual' and
different from the 'animal man who does not see the things
of the Spirit of God, or at least, does not seek after them'.
Grace makes it possible for a Christian to use his reasoning
powers and his liberty in this 'judgement', this discernment
(Gra 4). Such discernment entails the consideration of three
criteria: 'What is permitted, what is fitting, what is useful'
(*an liceat, an deceat, an expediat*) (Csi 3, 15). Nor is this
judgement merely speculative; it is also practical: 'that is why
St Paul does not say "to judge" [*iudicare*] but "decide" to
[*diiudicare*], that is, to discern and then approve [*discernere
et probare*]', in other words to accept the implications of
one's discernment and prove that we conform to it (Div 34, 3).[2]

Bernard quotes this same verse elsewhere with the same variant, *diiudicare* for *iudicare,* and insists that each man is his own judge and that that is sufficient, because the reasoning power with which we were created is our major privilege as men. Combined with grace it allows us to consider ourselves objectively: How great is God's goodness to me! He has given me reason which judges [*iudicet*], in such a way that I am judged by no one . . . . I thank you, Lord Jesus, you who have given me to myself as a good judge, a judge who is favorable, a sufficient judge! Because the spiritual man judges and decides all [*omnia diiudicat*] and is judged by no one. If the spiritual man judges all that concerns him, that is sufficient; as Job says, 'God does not judge the same business twice.'[3] One could hardly proclaim more loudly the independence of the spiritual man who has no need of anyone else.

We see that all this is applied first to personal behavior: it is up to each individual to 'discuss himself, judge himself, and be lucid in his thoughts' (Ep 94, 2). Then, this process of discernment is applied to affairs for which one is responsible: if one is 'walking according to the Spirit', one is able to examine all the facts of a situation spiritually and objectively: *spiritualiter omnia examinare,* as St Bernard writes in the greetings which begin Ep 124, with a sure reminiscence of 1 Cor 2:15.

In all these texts inspired by or commenting on the verse from the First Letter to the Corinthians, we notice that Bernard speaks not of becoming *a* spiritual man, as though one belonged to some elite category of Christians, but of *being spiritual,* which is something required of all Christians, accessible to all and necessary for all.

Compassion

Another verse from St Paul to which Bernard frequently refers is Galatians 6:1: *vos qui spirituales estis, instruite huiusmodi in Spiritu caritatis, considerans teipsum, ne ipse tenteris.* In this text and in the commentaries Bernard gives, the word 'spiritual' is, in Latin, in the plural and means not a spiritual man, a select individual, but all Christians, who are supposed to be 'spiritual'. The whole context speaks of gentleness, compassion, pardon: we must have pity on those who are to be pitied, *miseri miserandi* (Pasc 2, 4). The way we can do them good (*instruere*) is to forgive them (*ignoscere*). We must show such compassion to those who are tempted and our compassion is to be the fruit of the 'consideration' of our own weakness (Pre 20).

This applies to every Christian with regard to everyone else: contrary to the 'spirit of fury', the spirit of gentleness leads us to 'help a sick brother' and to come to the aid of those who are still 'of the flesh', with the humility born of self-knowledge and self-consideration (Hum 13-14). This principle applies also to communities as a whole when they have to take in a fugitive: this should be done with the charity that excuses everything (Ep 101). It applies too to prelates, those whom we call superiors: 'Behave like mothers in being kind, like fathers by giving correction' (SC 23, 2). And lastly, this is fulfilled in every churchman (*vir ecclesiasticus*), in anyone who, having received the Spirit, can instruct kindly, heal, console, and correct like a 'spiritual physician' (SC 4, 2-3).

Other biblical references mentioning 'spirituals' are grouped round these two verses of St Paul. Such men are, according to St Bernard, responsible for their brothers who are still of the flesh: they must do good to them through the medium of the Word of God and by providing example (SC 29, 6). It is in this way that they go about the *eruditio spiritualis*, that is, formation which leads men out from the rough, the rude (*rudis*) state which is proper to primitive fleshly matter. This is the duty of fervent souls toward tepid ones: Bernard gives very realistic descriptions of both (Asc 6, 6-7). Thus, in a community, the spiritual masters (*spirituales eruditores*) do not form a distinct category, but are all those who are able to do good to others.

THE THEOLOGICAL FOUNDATIONS OF COUNSELLING

Such general spiritual aid becomes more specialized when

one person gives 'counsel' to another. In the Vulgate, the word designates one of the gifts of the Holy Spirit, *Spiritus consilii,* and is one of the prophetic names given to Christ: *Magni consilii Angelus.* The reality underlying these words is precisely discernment, which had come gradually to mean the same thing as 'counselling'.

St Bernard speaks of counselling in a very clear text, in a sermon about the seven gifts of the Holy Spirit (Div 14, 4). He there explains that experience of evil can create a habit which strengthens inclination to evil and heightens 'the fervor' of carnal desires. This is to be replaced by the 'fervor of the Spirit' in order that 'counsel be opposed to custom' in bad ways (*consuetudini consilium opponas*). It would be illusory to think that lust can be overcome by violence, that is, in chastising the body by excessive penance, because such inclination to evil has become second nature; in attempting to eradicate it by excessive penance, we risk wounding not only evil, but also the body itself. We must seek some other remedy: 'What is needed is counsel, either that given by the Angel of the Mighty Counsellor himself, or by some spiritual man [*ab homine aliquo spirituali*] who knows the thoughts of Satan and the way to heal them'. In this context St Bernard quotes the example of a hermit who in primitive monasticism was helped out of a temptation to fornication by the endeavors (*industria*) of a 'father', an 'elder'. This man did not go about 'counselling' with a lengthy speech, or even by 'saying a word', but simply by proving to the hermit, through someone who insulted him, that it is possible to bear difficulties.[4] This 'koan', so to speak, delivered with humor, illustrates 'counselling'.

But Bernard did even better: he has left us all the elements necessary to a true theology of *consilium.* He deals with this in his treatise *On Grace and Free Choice* and refers to his theory, or supposes that it is known, whenever he makes practical applications. His view is elaborated in a very theoretical context, and he uses subtle distinctions. On this subject his thought is inseparable from the corpus of his teaching on anthropology, Christology, pneumatology, and eschatology. We need consider here only what deals with the fact of being spiritual, of having the gift of counsel and therefore of being capable of dispensing it. We must notice that at the bottom of all Bernard's practice there is an authentic theology founded on the mystery of Christ and St Paul's interpretation of this mystery. We must notice too that St Bernard's theology on the matter is quite as plausible as the justification of counselling put forward by other religious traditions.

What Bernard says in a general way in the texts quoted above, he here says with more precision: *consilium* is one of the acts of free choice. This consists in *iudicium,* the discernment of what is permitted and what is not, and *consilium,* the confirmation, the fact of approving (*probare*) what should or should not be done. In other words, judgement is theoretical: it discerns; counsel is practical: it decides (Gra 11). Freedom of choice, a specific act of the human will (*librum arbitrium, id est humana voluntas,* 41), freedom of judgement, dependent on reason, is totally complete in every man. But freedom of counsel, the ability to decide freely, is proper to spirituals. And even so, it is never entirely possessed and partly only by a few among the spirituals (*paucis spiritualibus*). What are the characteristics of these few men? St Bernard describes them in a few sentences filled with pauline reminiscences: They have crucified their flesh with its vices and concupiscence, so that sin no longer reigns in their mortal bodies; that it should no longer reign is an effect of the freedom of counsel. When that which is perfect shall appear, that which is in part shall be done away with, and then freedom in counsel will be total . . . . However, each day, the Kingdom of God already comes little by little in them; from day to day it extends its boundaries further and further in those in whom the inner man, helped by God, is renewed daily. To the extent that the reign of graces increases, the power of sin decreases (Gra 12). This results in true wisdom (*verum sapere*) (Gra 20).

When man, in keeping with his ability to choose freely,

sinned freely, he lost, he loses, his freedom of counsel; he becomes the slave of sin. Christ alone can restore this to him: Man needs Christ, the power of wisdom of God; since he himself is wisdom, he can pour forth true wisdom, restoring free counsel', which will attain perfection in glory. 'Meanwhile, it is enough that in the body of this death, in this evil world, by reason of his freedom of counsel, man refrain from obeying sin by giving way to his own lust . . . . And this is already in itself no mediocre wisdom, to resist sin in this body of sin, in these evil days, even if we are not yet entirely free from it' (Gra 26). That will be the restoring in us of the image of God (Gra 27), but still imperfectly. 'Yes, indeed, here below we cannot be entirely without either sin or misery, but it is possible with the help of grace for us not to be dominated by sin and misery.' And as for the man to whom such a state is given, it is not so much that he no longer sins at all, but his sin is not imputed to him if it is punished by proportionate penance or covered by love in keeping with the text of Scripture which says that 'love covers a multitude of sins' (1 P 4:8), where we have proclaimed the beatitude of those whose sins have been covered up, and 'blessed is the man to whom is imputed no iniquity' (Ps 32:2). Thus, then, it is not given to us 'not to be without sin or misery, but only not to give way to them' (Gra 29).

How does this restoration come about? By the incarnation of Wisdom. With wonderful poetry Bernard here likens God to the woman who had lost a coin: in Christ, God, as it were, sets about looking for his own image, he finds it and restores it (Gra 32). Christ is the model, the form (*forma*) according to which the image of God in man must be re-formed, to which it must be conformed. He does this with strength and sweetness: he 'moves, orders, administers', 'he pacifies the will' (Gra 33). Bernard describes the psychological consequences of such governing of the freedom of choice on the body: It commands all the senses and every limb with so much power that he does not allow sin to hold sway in his mortal body, he does not give his members up to iniquity like weapons, but presses them into the service of justice . . . . And man then acts, no longer sadly or by necessity—which is only the beginning and not the fullness of wisdom—but with a prompt and winged will making sacrifice an acceptable thing: God loves a cheerful giver. Thus, in all, he can imitate wisdom when he resists sin strongly and his conscience is sweetly at rest (Gra 34).

It is in this way that the workings of grace and man's personal effort, love and humility, are conciliated. Because, adds Bernard with much realism, 'temptation continues to come from within or from without and the lust of the flesh and misery resist; thus the will feels itself to be less free, but it does not become bad as long as it does not consent to evil' (Gra 37).

The treatise ends on a note of joy, hope, and thanksgiving, with a discreet allusion to the Eucharist: 'I will take the cup of salvation, the cup of salvation is the blood of the Saviour' (Gra 48).

Such anthropology bears the stamp of an intensive dynamism, entirely directed towards the total consummation, the perfected restoration of the image of God. This work of restoration begins here below in the midst of daily *ascesis.* Bernard evokes the different forms which our ascetic effort may take, and it is here that the methods and disciplines offered by other traditions could fit in. What Bernard has to say holds good for every time and place: Such are our fastings, our watchings, continence, works of mercy, and the practices of the other virtues . . . : the intention, bowed downward, raises itself upward little by little; affectivity, languishing under pressure of fleshly desires, is gradually healed and turns towards the love of the Spirit; the memory, sullied by the remembrance of the shameful doings in the past, becomes all white and smiling under the influence of good actions. In these three things lies inner renewal: the rectification of the intention, the purification of the affectivity, the remembrance of acts of virtue through which the memory acquires a good conscience and becomes luminous (Gra 49).[5]

Though this programme may admit the use of non-christian

methods of unification, purification, and pacification, it is nevertheless specifically christian because essentially it is the work of Christ and his Spirit (Gra 50). This total change can, and must be operated in the person of every Christian. Is it possible to share it with others?

COUNSELLING IN PRACTICE

Bernard's theological concept of counselling is at the bottom of all he has to say on the manner in which one Christian can help another Christian, one monk another monk, in spiritual growth. This counsel, once it has been personally acquired, can be shared by other persons, people to whom Bernard gives different names. These names must be studied with precision for they are technical terms of the monastic vocabulary of the twelfth century. Such philological analyses may seem somewhat sterile, but they are indispensable if we wish to grasp the exact meaning of the texts.

Counsellors

The most precise of these terms is the one which derives directly from the word counsel: *consiliarius.* Christ is by far the greatest and the best counsellor, he of whom Isaiah foretold that he would be called, among other titles, 'wonderful counsellor' (Is 9:6). 'He is wonderful, converting our will, by a changing which can only be the work of the Most High. Then he is counsellor because he reveals his will to us, showing those whom he has converted what they must do' (Div 53, 1). In the works of St Bernard, the word 'counsel' is almost always associated with that of help given, as was the case in the formula of feudal law: *consilium et auxilium.*[6] It is with this compliment the word is applied to Christ, 'a friend full of sweetness, prudent counsellor, courageous helper' (SC 20, 3; Div 22, 5). 'As faithful counsellor, he is the educator, the wisdom of God, the one who instructs us when we must act' (Adv 7, 2). And as for the Holy Spirit, the very name 'Paraclete' means that he is the Counsellor (III Sent 110).

But this counselling, proper to Christ and to his Spirit, can also be done by humans: it is one of the charisms, 'given to us that we might be useful to others' (Div 88, 1). This is the grace of discernment (*discretio consilii,* Div 58, 1). It must always be followed by an efficacious help: 'The man who has counselled must also help, says God, seated among his attributes like a suzerain lord among his vassals in the course of this great counsel when the Incarnation was decided' (Ann 1, 14). This idea is also applied to the case in which the monk Humbert acted; Bernard describes him as giving 'faithful counsel, considerable help' (Humb 6). And it is also applied to the duties of the abbot towards his monks, and his monks towards him and among themselves: they are even supposed to give—even if only by example—'counsel so that ignorance be instructed, and help so that weakness be supported' (Adv 3, 5-6; SC 12, 5). We find the trilogy—most gentle friend, prudent counsellor, courageous helper—already quoted in connection with Christ, repeated for Humbert (Humb 1). We all have need of counsel, help, and support (*consilium, auxilium, praesidium*) (Adv 7, 1). 'When you are overcome by drowsiness, accidia, and boredom, look for a man who can help you, and ask him to draw you after him' (SC 21, 5). Everyone who is allowed by discipline—that is, who has authority—to speak must by 'his talks comfort the spiritual and physical infirmities of his brethren, and by his counsels form them and raise them up'.[7]

As explicit as Bernard was on the subject of what counsel is for each one, he is vague as to the manner of being a counsellor. He seems to consider this function a natural consequence for the person who has received the gift of counsel. It does not depend on a specific nomination and does not put the 'counsellor' into a special category. It is the normal overflow of the spiritual man—one of the normal ways for him to be charitable.

SPIRITUAL FATHERS AND BROTHERS

When St Bernard uses the noun 'father' or 'father of a family' (*paterfamilias*), or the adjective 'fatherly', 'paternal', these words are almost always attributed to God. When applied to

men they signify the patriarchs and the prophets of the Old
Testament or St Benedict.[8] Five times the name 'father' is
applied to the abbot, to the prelate, that is, the superior
(SC 53, 1; Abb 4 = Div 35, 4; III Sent 127; SC 19, 7). In this
last instance the use is dependent on the Rule of St Benedict
(Chap. 49). Bernard writes to a nun saying that her abbess is
her spiritual mother (Ep 115, 1).If St Malachy is considered a
spiritual 'son of Clairvaux', this is only because of the ties of
friendship which link him to this monastery (Mal 67).

The expression 'spiritual brother' is used twice. In the first
case it means those among the brothers who keep peace among
those members of a community who are generally at logger-
heads, namely, those who live inside enclosure and those who
live outside in the dependencies, the granges which were called
'obediences'. The majority of these monks living outside
enclosure were *conversi* (I Sent 26). In the second use of the
expression 'spiritual brother', Bernard refers to what he had
already taught in the preceding long sermon about the discerning of spirits (Div 23), and he adds that there are two
criteria by which a thought can be seen to be good: firstly, if
it is, as St James says, 'pure and peaceable' (Jm 3:17) and,
secondly, if it is approved by the judgement of the superior
and the spiritual brothers, 'because God would not do anything
without having revealed it to his servants' (Div 24, 1). These
two sermons are probably those in which Bernard is most explicit about discernment, not discernment in general but discernment between the good spirits in conformity with God and
those which do not conform.

Sometimes a word from a 'spiritual and perfect man' or
simply a glance at him, even recalling him to mind, is enough
to give us courage because unction, that is, the Spirit, only
comes to us through the mediation of a human person (SC
14, 6). But it does happen too that 'certain people pretend to
be spiritual in order to deceive all the more: they seduce by
their counsel whereas they themselves follow no one's counsel'
(Div 72, 3). In order to discern good and bad influence we
must see whether in those who exert such influence the inner

man has grown in the way explained in the treatise *On Grace and Free Choice.* From the theology of his two sermons on discernment of spirits, Bernard draws practical conclusions and psychological implications. But once again each one must discern, submitting afterwards if necessary to the approval of the superior and the 'spiritual brothers' (Div 23 and 24).

Thus we see that the notion of 'spiritual father' is not part of Bernard's teaching except when he speaks of the superior, and, even so, such mentions are rare and depend upon the Rule of St Benedict: it does not correspond to any spontaneous image in Bernard's mind. The allusion to 'spiritual brothers' is even less frequent. As for the subject of 'counsellors,' such allusions do suggest that the monks who are recognized as being spiritual can confirm to one another that their thoughts really come from God.

ELDERS

The words *senex* and *senior* are to be found in Bernard's writings, but not very frequently. If they are present, it is mainly because they are biblical words. In the works of St Bernard, as in Holy Scripture, these words do not designate the 'elderly' but those who, whatever their age, are wise—they may even be young. There are many texts in which Bernard explains this (Ep 42, 26; 77, 14; 146, 1) and some of them have been commented on elsewhere.[9] Here it will be enough to quote a single text. This one is all the more revealing in that it applies to cardinals and members of the Curia. Bernard advises Eugene III to take help from the elderly and not the young—a warning which was not superfluous in a time when noble families pushed forward, and even sometimes imposed for ecclesiastical honors, youngsters who were scarcely more than children, a practice which Bernard firmly and clearly denounces (Mor 25). In connection with cardinals he adds that 'they should be elders, but not so much in age as in their conduct; they should be among those who are recognized by the people as such, as says the Book of Numbers' (11:16) (Csi 4, 9).

This biblical conception of what it is to be an 'elder' was adopted in primitive monasticism and in the Rule of St Benedict—which explains the few allusions, about ten in all, three of which are in the treatise *On Precept and Dispensation* made by Bernard. In SC 19, 7 he distinguished between obeying 'an abbot and conforming to the counsel and example of the elders'. Further on, there is a distinction between 'the peace which is owed to the brothers and the obedience owed to the elders,' who here seem to be identified with the superiors (SC 46, 7). Letter 87, 8, has even more complex sequence of terms: there is mention of brothers (*conversare simpliciter inter fratres*), God (*devotus Deo*), the superior under whom one lives (*magistro subditus*), the elders whom one obeys (*senioribus oboedire*), the juniors to whom one must adapt (*iunioribus contemperans*), the angels whom one seeks to please (*angelis placens*), and all this by being useful through the words we speak (*verbo utilis*), humble of heart, and gentle towards everyone. This allusion to the useful word does not seem to be proper to the elders but applies in general to what any monk may have opportunity of saying to any other monk. Bernard's reference to elders would seem to be explained as being a reminiscence of the Rule of St Benedict (Chaps. 4, 50; 46, 5), without his giving them any other meaning than a certain undefined relationship with authority.

It is the same again in the treatise *On Precept,* where it is required of the monk that he should 'not discuss the orders of the elders' but 'obey them willingly' (*libenter oboedire*) (Pre 23), and where Bernard also mentions those 'various and innumerable things requested by the elders' (*in tam variis et innumeris quae a senioribus iudicuntur*) (Pre 30). There is also mention of the 'rule and the orders of superiors' (*regula vel praecepta maiorum*) (Pre 47). In this last text, and in other texts too, there does not seem to be any clear distinction between the *maior* and the *prior* (Pre 10).[10]

So, in general, the elders are superiors from whom we receive orders and whom we have to obey, but they are not monks to whom we go for counselling. There is only one,

very allusive exception in the text, where Bernard says in passing that we should "consult an elder" (*consultatio senioris*)
(Asspt 5, 12). This vocabulary seems to be inspired by that
of primitive monasticism. We have already seen in a text
quoted above that the words 'elder' (*senior*) and 'father' are
applied to those monks from whom one asks counsel.

A similar nuance is found in *Letter 7,* 12, which Bernard
wrote to a young monk, Adam of Morimond, in order to dis-
suade him from founding a new monastic group. Bernard was
shocked by the very idea that cistercian life, as it was then,
might possibly fail to satisfy everyone's spiritual needs. In
this matter his motives are not always very coherent.[11] In
order to exhort Adam to come back to his monastery, Bernard launches into a very beautiful but idealistic rhetorical
description of primitive monasticism. He compares Adam to a
modern Paul the Simple who had not, however, met another
Anthony. Bernard describes the myth in the following terms:
O you, you who are the Paul the Simple of our times, if only
you had met another Anthony! In this way everything which
his mouth uttered—even lightly [*vel leviter*] —you could accept without discussion and obey without delay, without
hesitation. Oh, the perfectly obedient monk who does not
lose one, even the slightest, word, not even a single iota, of his
elder [*O monachum oboedientissimum, cui ex quibuslibet
seniorum verbula, ne unum quidem iota praetervolet!*] He
does not heed what is commanded, being only too content
that he should be commanded something (*Non attendit quale
sit quod praecipitur, hoc solo contentus quia praecipitur*).

This text calls for several remarks. In the first place we
must remember that it recalls a time when there was no other
superior than the elder and the two functions were identified,
requiring obedience. Then we must remark that this describes
perfectly blind obedience, requiring neither information nor
control and founded solely on complete trust in the elder with
total dependence of one's own personal judgement to his.
Were all this to be taken literally, we should be far removed
from the free, intelligent obedience proposed by the New

Testament, by tradition, by Bernard himself, and by Vatican II
—even though there may have been in recent times a parenthe-
tical period, scarcely begun before the nineteenth century,
during which there was a different prevailing practice against
which ecclesiastical authority has so rightly reacted. Finally,
as we have already said, this text is set in a context from
which passion is not altogether absent. It is less vigorous than
other texts which Bernard did not write when under emotional
stress. Thus it is not very convincing. At the most, it confirms
that the seniorate was one of the fairly vague memories which
the twelfth century had of primitive monasticism. But the
elders did not form a separate category, nor did they have any
specific function.

THE SPIRITUAL PHYSICIAN

This image of the physician of souls was part of the patristic
tradition, and St Bernard is faithful to its total meaning. As
with the notion of counsellor and spiritual father, here again
God is the starting point for all his teaching: the spiritual
physician participates in one aspect of God's merciful intervention. The 'physician of souls' is then God himself (Hum
37) because it is indeed he who heals man from his sins (Div
107, 1). Here below on earth the first 'physician of man' was
Christ (Adv 1, 8)—and 'what a doctor' (*tantus medicus;* Adv
1, 10) he was. He was so by the very fact of his Incarnation:
'the doctor came to the sick' (V Nat 3, 1) full of kindness
and wisdom (*sed attende pium medicum, attende medicum
sapientem*) (V Nat 4, 2; 6, 1 etc.). He also fulfills this role by
his passion which was the medication we needed (Pasc 3, 1).

Here we recognize the idea, so often enlarged upon by
St Augustine, of Christ the physician.[12] Lastly, the Holy Spirit
who communicates to us the benefits of redemption is also
compared to a physician (III Sent 97).

This image had already been applied to the abbot by
St Benedict in his Rule (RB 27, 2; 28, 2), possibly in dependence upon stoic literature.[13] Yet we hardly ever find Bernard
making use of this application. He suggests in an allusion that

in the event of temptation 'the physician gives counsel and orders' (Conv 23; according to the short text in SBOp IV: 95, 20). Elsewhere he speaks briefly in the same sense in a text which I will quote shortly in connection with the next paragraph on confession (III Sent 92).

CONFESSION

We may wonder whether St Bernard considered the hearing of confession in the sacrament of penance as a form of spiritual fatherhood, as a relatively recent monastic tradition has accustomed us to think. Bernard applies the word *confessor* only to the holy confessors of the faith. And he uses the word *confessio* more often than not—in keeping with biblical and patristic use—for the praising of God;[14] then, sometimes, for the confession of the faith; and only in third place does he use it to mean an avowal of sins. In Bernard's works, this final practice is dealt with in few explicit texts and many allusions. It would be worth devoting a special and more developed study to the subject. Here, however, it is enough merely to recall the fact that Bernard hardly ever spoke of sacramental confession to a priest for anyone save seculars, and even this mention is rare. More frequently confession is the avowal to God in prayer. When one avows to another human, it is openness of conscience to a superior, without there being any question of absolution. But one may on such occasions receive advice which is a form of counselling (Circ 1, 5). When we go to the doctor we tell him everything (*totum exponat medico*), and we humiliate ourselves as does a guilty person before a judge; we obey his orders and make satisfaction (III Sent 92). 'We are given correction, exhortation, persuasion' (Div 104, 1), 'the help which comes to us from the compassion of the person to whom we confess' (Div 104, 2), and humility is fostered by humiliation (III Sent 16; 126, 2).

As we see, all this is not very explicit. Monastic confession is not considered to be what moderns call 'spiritual direction'. Above all, it is an occasion for humility in the presence of God and men, or one man in particular. This is said clearly in two texts concerning Bernard himself. In the first he describes what his monks tell him in private confessions: they do not accuse themselves of sins, but acknowledge their weaknesses and express their desire for God (SC 9, 3). The other text is William of Saint-Thierry's reconstruction of the confessions made by the monks of Clairvaux to St Bernard at the beginning of his abbacy. He heard them one after the other confessing to him and accusing themselves of the illusions which are common to every man's thoughts and which no one can entirely avoid. There is then no question here, strictly speaking, of matter for sacramental absolution, but of 'temptations and impurities which cling to thoughts of this kind'. It would seem that we are dealing here with the same thing as in the texts already quoted, which allude to confession as an opening up of conscience, in keeping with the requirements of the Rule of St Benedict (RB 4, 50; 46, 5). What follows does not correspond to what Bernard himself says in several instances,[15] but it is rather William's interpretation of Bernard's spiritual journey and a reflection of his own preoccupations.[16] Were we to believe William, we should be led to think that Bernard was astonished at such accusations because, having himself already acquired angelic purity to a high degree, he had assumed his monks were in the same state. When he discovered that they were men, he failed to understand them and was very severe. 'But', says William, because they were true religious, full of prudence and piety, they reverenced, without always understanding, their abbot's preaching. Thus when they went to confession to him, they were amazed because of the newness of what he said to them, and which seemed to give their weakness a coloration of despair. But, in keeping with some words of Job (6:10) they did not contradict the sayings of the saint, they did not excuse themselves. On the contrary they accused their weakness in the presence of the man of God, since no living soul is justified in the sight of God himself . . . . Thus they humbled themselves when they heard his reproaches . . . . '

According to William, through a process which is very

keenly analyzed, Bernard came little by little to a more exact understanding. The Holy Spirit inspired him to reflect on the reactions of his monks.[17] William's account is not representative of the normal practice of confession. His aim is to illustrate the case of a very extraordinary man and the way in which he became a saint. But at least we have here a witness to spiritual dialogue during confession. The confessor is mistaken, but the penitents are virtuous enough to draw profit from what he says to them, and this goes to prove that in monastic confession the important factor is the accusation. Counselling is sought on other occasions.

CONCLUSIONS

It would be possible to illustrate the ideas exposed in this paper with examples: as models of counsellors Bernard proposes his brother Gerard (SC 26, 7, 9), and the monk Humbert (Humb 4 and 5). As for Bernard himself, he did much counselling by correspondence, and his manner of so doing would require a special study. But the way Bernard went about counselling only goes to show what an exceptional man he was: people did not consult ordinary abbots in the same way. When he was consulted, he replied with a firmness and a self-assurance that has been considered excessive by certain people. But generally, he did so with modesty, and even humor, and this characteristic is probably the greatest proof that he really was himself one of those spiritual men whose inner growth he analyses in his treatise *On Grace and Free Choice.* Because he was humble, he did not take himself seriously, and he knew when and how to smile at himself.[18] Nor did he think he was indispensable, and he did all he could to avoid letting others become excessively dependent on him: he helped them to become and to stay autonomous because a free man frees others.[19]

If we consider the immensity of Bernard's writings, the development which he gave to certain speculative and practical problems, we cannot help but notice how relatively little he speaks about spiritual counselling. His thought about this and about what it means to be spiritual is very clear, even subtle. But he does no more than allude to being a counsellor. These allusions are found more in his sermons *De diversis* and in the *Sentences.* These texts are not, on the whole, very dense from a doctrinal point of view, but they are revealing of the day to day existence of a monastic community. When talking about counsel, Bernard uses the precise and consistent vocabulary which is characteristic of him when he writes as a theologian. But when writing about the people who do counselling, we notice a certain vagueness and variation in the words he uses. One gets the impression that he is dependent on the vocabulary handed down by monastic tradition; to it he does not attach the same importance as he does to the words of Holy Scripture, and in particular to the writings of St Paul. The important thing for Bernard, as for Paul, is first of all to be spiritual. The fact of counselling others is a consequence of only secondary importance, and it is usually the superior who does so, and only occasionally other monks.

Two main conclusions result from all that has gone before:

1. In the *doctrinal* field Bernard makes very clear distinctions between what it is, and what it is not, to be spiritual and to give counsel. Entirely rooted in grace and the presence of God, the works of Christ and of the Holy Spirit in a soul, within the living context of the universal Church and the local ecclesial gathering which is every monastery, the immedaite environment of monks, this quality of christian existence is in no way a thing acquired by natural techniques. These are not to be excluded; they can even be forms of *ascesis* and discipline—but they remain secondary to indwelling grace, which always has first place. This in no way implies that *ascesis* is of no importance: it is a strict necessity, but only as a means to supernatural growth and not to a purely psychological maturity. Bernard has no illusions as to the degree of purification to which we can attain in this life: inner growth goes hand in hand with weaknesses which must be accepted with humility and clearsightedness because they are bound up with our condition as humans. The fact of being

spiritual, and as such a counsellor, does not then authorize
the total dependence of one Christian upon another. The
counsellor must always humbly respect the workings of grace
in the person with whom he is dealing—and respect his freedom too. Thus the counsellor has no absolute power over
others except as this is required by the normal relationship
of authority and obedience between a superior and a subject.
In his treatise *On Precept* and elsewhere, Bernard has admirably
defined the limits of authority and shown that if these are
respected the generosity of obedient souls is unlimited.[20]

2. In the *practical* sphere, we see that Bernard's teaching on
counselling is extremely moderate and balanced. It is merely
a matter of living with spirituals and being helped by them
occasionally, without this practice being in any way institutionalized or obligatory: mutual help is a life experience.
There are many spirituals: all Christians and monks are virtually such. This charism is not a rare thing and requires no
special competence or specific role. Those spirituals whom
Bernard describes—Gerard, Humbert—were so without being
at all aware of the fact, and certainly in no way did they take
advantage of it. What made them counsellors was not an official nomination by some authority, or the awareness of having
any particular function, but simply the fact that people came
to them because they inspired trust.

Such are the facts, such is the teaching of Bernard on counselling. These could be judged in the light of what has been
taught and practised in other periods of history, for example,
before his own times in primitive monasticism, or, after him,
from the sixteenth or the nineteenth century onwards, or
again in the light of the custom of certain eastern orthodox
monks, certain gurus of the present day. Is St Bernard's concept of counselling a regression with regard to ancient practices? Does it meet the requirements of our own day? It
should be possible to make an objective appraisal. But to do
so, we must bear in mind the importance accorded in medieval
monasticism, within the cistercian life and elsewhere, to community living. No need was felt for extraordinary charismatics,

because it was known that the Spirit is poured abroad. Within a monastery, as in the primitive Church which is its model and even, as it were, the utopia, of a community of believers living in communion the ideal of prayer and love, brothers communicate to one another as a normal and ordinary thing whatever they may have received from others for others.

NOTES

1. The abbreviations used for the works of St Bernard (SBOp) are:
    Abb: *Sermo ad abbates*
    Adv: *Sermo in adventu Domini*
    Ann: *Sermo in annunciatione dominica*
    Asc: *Sermo in ascensione domini*
    Asspt: *Sermo in assumptione B.V.M.*
    Circ: *Sermo in circumcisione Domini*
    Conv: *Sermo de conversione ad clericos*
    Csi: *De consideratione*
    Div: *Sermones de diversis*
    Ep: *Epistola*
    Gra: *De gratia et libero arbitrio*
    Hum: *De gradibus humilitatis et superbiae*
    Humb: *Sermo in obitu Domni Humberti*
    Mor: *Ep 42, de moribus et officio episcoporum*
    Palm: *Sermo in ramis palmarum*
    Par: *Parabolae*
    Pasc: *Sermo in die Paschae*
    Pre: *De precepto et dispensatione*
    SC: *Sermo super Cantica Canticorum*
    Sent: *Sententiae*
    V Mal: *Vita sancti Malachiae*
    V Nat: *Sermo in vigilia nativitatis Domini*
2. The verb *diiudicare*, which is more frequent in biblical and
    patristic traditions than in classical literature, seems to mean not
    only 'to discern', 'to distinguish', but also 'to decide' (*statuere*), as
    is shown by the examples quoted in *Thesaurus Linguae Latinae*
    (Leipzig, 1909-1934), V/1, cols. 1156-57.
3. This formula is inspired by Job 33:14 according to a version 'Deus
    non iudicabit bis in idipsum' which is different from the text of
    the Vulgate: 'Semel loquitur Deus et secundo idipsum non repetit'.
4. St Bernard borrows this *exemplum* from one of St Jerome's

85

letters, 125, 13; CSEL, 56, 132, and not from a version of the *Vitae patrum.* The fact that he is dependent on a Latin source seems to confirm that eastern monastic texts had less influence on Bernard and the other twelfth-century cistercian writers than is sometimes asserted. This is the thrust of the works I have named under the title: 'Etudes récentes sur Guillaume de Saint–Thierry,' *Bulletin de philosophie médiévale,* 19 (1977) 49-55.

5. On this growth of the inner man, other texts are gathered under the title 'Une mystique pratique dans les Sermons de S. Bernard à ses moines,' *Studia Missionalia,* 26 (1977) 73-86.

6. Texts in which these two terms are associated are quoted by O. Prinz, *Mittellateinisches Wörterbuch* (Munich, 1967) 7, col. 1292.

7. SC 12, 5: 'Confortat alloquiis, consiliis informat'.

8. 'La paternité de S. Benoit', in *Recueil d'études sur S. Bernard* (Rome, 1969) III, 279-84.

9. See the chapter 'St. Bernard's Idea of the Role of the Young' in *Contemplative Life,* trans. Elizabeth Funder, OSB, CS 19 (Kalamazoo, 1978) pp. 23-32. See also 'The Formative Community According to St. Bernard,' forthcoming in *Tjurunga.*

10. This is confirmed by the manuscripts where the copyists have written, as being equivalent, *maior, prior,* or *senex;* SBOp 3:260.

11. *Nouveau visage de Bernard de Clairvaux: Approches psycho-historiques* (Paris, 1976) pp. 109-114.

12. See R. Arbesmann, 'Christ, the "medicus humilis" in St. Augustine', in *Augustinus Magister* (Paris, 1954) II, 623-24.

13. Sources are indicated by R. Spilker, 'Die Busspraxis in der Regel des hl. Benedikt', *Studien und Mitteilungen zur Geschichte des Benediktiner Ordens,* 56 (1938) 296-304.

14. 'Confession et louange de Dieu', *La vie spirituelle,* 128 (1968) 253-65. English translation in *Worship,* 42 (1968) 159-76. 'Confession et louange de Dieu selon S. Bernard de Clairvaux', *La vie spirituelle,* 120 (1969) 588-605; in *Contemplative Life,* pp. 108-119.

15. 'St. Bernard and Christian Experience', *Worship,* 41 (1967) 222-33; *Aspects of Monasticism,* trans. Mary Ryan; CS 7 (Kalamazoo, 1978).

16. *Nouveau visage,* pp. 27-30.

17. *Vita Prima S. Bernardi,* I, 28-29; PL 185:243-44.

18. *Nouveau visage,* pp. 94-107.

19. *Ibid.,* pp. 87-94.
20. 'S. Bernard dans l'histoire de l'obéissance', in *Recueil d'études sur S. Bernard,* III, 287-98.

THE SPIRITUAL FATHER IN THE WRITINGS
OF WILLIAM OF ST THIERRY

Thomas X. Davis, OCSO
Abbey of New Clairvaux

TRADITIONS AND CULTURES among the various peoples of the earth give evidence of the phenomenon of the sage or master, the philosopher, the shaman, the guru, the 'holy' man: a person gifted in some extraordinary manner, a 'spiritual' person who has attained the 'full' realization. Usually, such a person attracts others to himself as disciples, transforming them by his own personal influence and experience, initiating them into a 'higher' life by some form of spiritual communication-transmission at this 'higher' level. In the christian tradition, however, the only true holy person is Jesus Christ; all others are his representatives,[1] made to his image and likeness.

Jesus Christ gathered his disciples around himself not so much as a spiritual master but as the Way, the Truth, and the Life.[2] Totally new spiritual heights/depths were opened up by this Image of the Unseen God.[3] On the eve of his return to the Father, Jesus gave his disciples the Holy Spirit who by his inner unction would teach them all they needed to know.[4] The early Christians realized their differences from the other peoples in that with Christ and his Spirit there was no need for sages, masters, gurus, and other such persons.[5]

And yet, Christians seeking to lead a more meaningful life 'had recourse to brothers who were more experienced, more prudent, and had a reputation for sanctity, in order to be initiated and directed by them'[6] into this life in Christ with its mystery of participation in the divine Fatherhood of God.

In christian monastic circles, a person who had realized to a
greater degree in his own life that manner of living and
charism proper for attaining purity of heart[7] was called
an abba.

> The word *abba* assumed its meaning during the flowering
> of Egyptian monasticism in the fourth century: it denotes
> first of all and principally a spiritual man, regardless of the
> actual direction of sons. The *abba* is essentially a man of
> experience, a perfect monk who has fully realized in him-
> self the calling of monastic life, and who can serve as a
> model for others. Through contact with him and by the
> effect of his personal influence, one will become a monk.
> Ascetic perfection does not suffice to create an *abba*; one
> must also be filled with the Spirit, endowed with discern-
> ment and the gift of speaking words which are adapted to
> the spiritual needs of each individual. The number of spiri-
> tual men, of *abbates*, necessarily far surpasses that of spiri-
> tual fathers; it was only when disciples came to them that
> they became effectively spiritual fathers.[8]

A noted Tibetan master has written: 'Ultimately, our best
teacher is ourselves. When we are open, aware, and watchful,
then we can guide ourselves properly.'[9] To be open, aware,
and watchful is no small demand, for our inner spiritual path
has many illusions and obstacles: to mention just a few—our
inner dialogues with ourselves, our feelings, worries, cares,
prejudices, our personal idiosyncrasies, and even our friends,
jobs, and services in the monastery.[10] This same Tibetan
master continues:

> We need support, we need to be fulfilled, but often we can-
> not rely on friends or lovers, society, or even our own
> parents. There is no one close enough to us to really fulfill
> us. We may have our friends and relatives and be very suc-
> cessful in business, but still not be satisfied within ourselves
> —because we are lonely. We crave fulfillment of our desires,

and that craving itself creates an emotional flavor which affects whatever we do. So frustration and bitterness build up. When we stop reaching outside ourselves for fulfillment, then very gradually our desires begin to subside and we are less aggravated by our cravings.

When we are very sensitive, then transient and selfish 'loves' fail to satisfy us; we need to find someone we can truly rely on, someone we can love without fear of rejection. Then we can be free to act through our own understanding, our open hearts, our awakened energies. In this sense the teacher is a mirror of our higher self. He activates our source of inner knowledge and our sense of complete fulfillment. When we have an open heart, then the 'awakened experience' arises within us—we will know it, unmistakably.[11]

These paragraphs reflect three general and essential characteristics of the spiritual father found also in the christian monastic tradition. To be concise, these characteristics are: first, we have only one Spiritual Father—God. Christ, his Image, has initiated us into the mystery of this Divine Paternity and Fatherhood by making its full realization accessible to us through an inner anointing of his Holy Spirit. Second, other individuals can be an abba, a spiritual father, and assist us in our growth into the realization of a more meaningful monastic life and purity of heart, provided they themselves are filled with the inner anointing of the Holy Spirit given by Christ and so share in God's Fatherhood, and that they attract us as disciples and initiate and transform us by their own personal experience in a way of living built upon this mystery of Divine Fatherhood. Third, an indication that individuals are growing in this inner anointing of the Holy Spirit, that is, becoming an abba or a spiritual person, is the weakening of those fruits of transient loves in their life: frustration, bitterness, and other disordered affections and feelings. This is accomplished by an 'awakened experience' of the divine paternity, involving some form of inner stability and steadfast love, *affectus,*[12] that is both immanent and transcendent.

Admittedly, these characteristics are skeletal. As we reflect upon them in the writings and teachings of William, we shall see their fullness and richness.

THE SPIRITUAL PATERNITY OF GOD, OUR HEAVENLY FATHER[13]

According to William, the spiritual paternity of God rests on the fact that God is good. God is our Spiritual Father because of his goodness and because of what he is willing to do for us in his goodness: give us the Resurrection and the gift of our own resurrected life. Goodness—that divine incomprehensibility.

Jesus Christ, the beloved Son of the Father, is this resurrected Life. He is the spiritual person, the abba, *par excellence,* of whose fulness we have received. Our goodness, on the other hand, is a shared goodness and not identical to God's goodness. This shared goodness is precisely the ability to be a partaker of all good by a vehement, powerful free-will. Here is another mystery, but this time it is man's incomprehensibility as a likeness to God.[14] There are three ways we become like God: by the possession of life itself, by growth in goodness and virtue, and by the unity of our spirit with God's Spirit, signalled by our own inability to will anything else but the true good. The possession of life or its creation (creating grace) is not of prime importance. Growth and attraction to goodness, and convergence into the unity of the Holy Spirit (illuminating grace), is.

It is the goodness of God that attracts us to Him as our Spiritual Father. God's good will precedes our good will, as only the Father can accomplish what he promises, namely, resurrected life. Does not God first love us? Our loving response to this attraction is a vehement, powerful, well-ordered free will. This type of free will enables our 'blood' relationship to the Father to be a reality, for by it our life and its volatile emotions and affections become good, become a strong steadfast love, *affectus,* become Spirit. And from the

depths of this inner stability of *affectus* in our life, where
God, the Immutable One, is found dwelling, we gasp for life
with the words: Abba, Father!

*Contemplating God, The Commentary on the Epistle to
the Romans,* wherein is developed the power of the Spiritual
Father to attract sons, *The Nature of the Body and Soul,* and
The Golden Epistle are the primary sources for William's
doctrine on the spiritual paternity of our Heavenly Father.

THE WORD OF LIFE[15]

The Word of Life is not some pithy saying taken from our
spiritual guide or Scripture or *lectio* or the desert fathers. No!
It is the heavenly Father's all-powerful Message, who, while all
things were in silence, came from the Father's bosom as a
gentle Apostle of love. The Word of Life embraces everything
this gentle Apostle of love did and everything he said. It especially embraces the insults he received, the spitting, the buf-
feting, the cross, and the mystery of the grave and the Resurrection. All of this is nothing other than the Father speaking
to us in the Son, appealing to us by his love and stirring up
our love for him, our 'sense of life', by the gift of the Word's
Spirit, the 'Spirit of Life'.[16] Such is William's understanding
of the Word of Life, which he first presented in *Contemplating God* and which he consistently maintained throughout all
his other works.

To live this Word of Life, to make this Word of Life the
pattern of our own way of living, is for us to experience the
conferral and realization of sonship. This Word of Life comes
to us as a precious gift, a breathing of the Spirit, a kiss, a fragrance, as solitude, as our share in the Passion, as something
sweet and savory put into our mouths which, once swallowed,
eludes our grasping and leaves us gasping for more! These are
the descriptive figures that William uses to convey to our
consciousness the richness of the Word of Life, so that we may
know who we are and of what we are capable. Only this
Word of Life can make us sons of the Father; hence it is vital
for us and preparatory to any knowing of the Father.

Solitude and the Passion of Jesus are of special value for us in their practical expressions, such as life in the monastic cell, solitude of the heart, and the retreat of our conscience. In these practices the Word of Life gives the monk goodness and makes him a spiritual person, committed to the Father's good pleasure in the likeness of the Beloved, on whom rested the Father's delight. As the man of prayer himself is, so is the type of the God he forms in his mind to whom he prays! If we fail to receive into our style of living and 'our sense of life' the divine illumination and Wisdom coming from the Word, we will be unable to cry out to God in the 'Spirit of Life' from the very depths of our heart those prayerful words: Abba, Father.

THE ABBA AS A SPIRITUAL PERSON [17]

So far, this consideration of spiritual paternity has focused only on the divine dimension of our heavenly Father toward us. But there is likewise a human dimension to spiritual paternity; other persons sharing in the Fatherhood of God can be spiritual fathers, *abbates.* William, addressing himself to the human dimension, shows that this sharing in paternity is an anointing of the Holy Spirit in profound fidelity to the Father, thus making one a truly spiritual person. This anointing is what it means to be an abba in the radical sense.

Jesus is the spiritual person *par excellence.* He is the Truth and the Life, the 'holy man' whose place is in the Father's bosom, as John's Gospel indicates. And not only that, Jesus is our *place,* and we are his *place,* also. For God is the life of our soul, just as our soul is the life of the body. This mystery of indwelling is the foundation for a sharing in God's paternity and for becoming a spiritual person. In imitation of Jesus, the spiritual person is to be free from idolatry as far as is possible, that is, he must orient his life to an experience of God, without relying on an intermediary of any conceptual means—thoughts, images, visions, nor even of a carnal approach to the sacred humanity itself. In the *Sacrament of the Altar,* one is encouraged to seek and eat the spiritual flesh of Jesus, that is, to seek Jesus spiritually!

How does one begin to seek spiritually? William sees this question as a question of the quality of one's love. When we open ourselves to divine goodness, our affections and love, our reason and reasoning are purified. Through the purifying illumination that comes from divine goodness, our soul, our spirit, and our mind become poor in spirit, humble, quiet, trembling at the Lord's words, and come before his presence within us. Such was the fidelity of Jesus: poor in spirit, humble, quiet, full of profound respect for his Father's words and presence. He was able to show us how to love the Father, that is, to show us the quality of a love that is proper for loving the Father in Spirit and in Truth. In *The Commentary on the Song of Songs* William pleads to be shown a friend in whom God is, a friend who will teach others how to love God![18]

Besides the example of Jesus as the spiritual person, William sets before us Abraham and his radical faith in God. Abraham's integrity, his entire goodness, rested on the faith he had in the *promise* God made to him of what He would do for him. This promise was the call of a dead body back to life, the promise of the resurrected life. So, to be poor in spirit, humble, quiet, trembling at the Lord's words, and before his presence within us means a fidelity to letting ourselves exist according to his dispositions.

Fidelity to the Father, because of his gift of resurrected life, is the worship of the Father in spirit and in truth. Fidelity is the inner anointing of the Holy Spirit. To be anointed by the Spirit, to be acted upon by the Spirit, is an illumination of goodness so radical that this Divine Goodness dispels every possible taint of unwillingness in our hearts. As a consequence, we become a totally spiritual person like our heavenly Father, who was so good in willing to have many sons that he gave his only beloved Son over to death, even death on the cross.

To see and understand this 'substance' or goodness of the divine implies a similar illumination of our own 'substance'. Like Abraham, we measure ourselves by the type of commitment we make in faith, a radical and absolute faith to the

94

point of imitation of the Son's *kenosis*. We become a spiritual person precisely because now we *know* and *see* the Son as he sees and knows the Father, and we *know* and *see* the Father as He sees and knows the Son. Our meager, carnal thoughts of the Father die (which William considers as a kind of death of our Spiritual Father—a death of God), and we begin to worship in Spirit and in Truth.

> But because we were called as little children and not yet fit to contemplate spiritual things, divine mercy gave himself, reaching down to our very meager thoughts, with the result that whatever we did not see evidently and clearly, however much we tried to see, that same thing we had seen in a dark manner, would die when we began to see face to face. Rightly, therefore, is that which is taken away said to die, for when that which is perfect is come, that which is in part shall be done away. Therefore in a certain way and in a dark manner the Father is said to die in our regard, and he becomes our inheritance when he is possessed face to face. It is not that he dies, but our imperfect vision of him is destroyed by perfect vision.[19]

Worship in Spirit and in Truth does not make us cry out to the divinity in terms of calling him 'God', for this word 'God' bespeaks of some fear and unwillingness hidden deep within us. Rather, worship in Spirit and in Truth has us cry out in those words of total commitment and fidelity: Abba, Father.

THE ABBA AS A HUMAN SPIRITUAL TEACHER[20]

The monk is given three guardians to assist him in his approach to Wisdom, or the science of becoming a spiritual person. They are solitude, conscience, and a spiritual father or teacher. This particular spiritual father is the kind understood by the more popular concept of a spiritual father: a man who is our teacher and guide in spiritual matters. The adulterous affections which lie deep within the human heart and wander all over our life, corrupting it and giving it false orientations, make us need such a spiritual father and teacher. His role is to assist us in acquiring an inner harmony of all our faculties. Having true peace in our affective life is channelling our will into a vehement, well-ordered will. A will that is vehement and well-ordered is William's definition of love. It is not surprising, then, that he instructs us, as beginners in the spiritual life, to commit our love of God to our spiritual father and teacher. We are to give him our obedience in everything, an obedience of charity, and to have recourse to him in everything, so that eventually, as our wills become well-ordered, we may grow into spiritual powers led by the Holy Spirit. This is true wisdom, for the change will have taken place in us and not in time or place. We will experience the Spirit, the Immutability of God, as a stable inner support, *affectus,* a Spirit far beyond anything we could produce, yet a Spirit deep within our affective life.

Our affections have so powerfully gone awry that this spiritual father or teacher can cope with them only when we, his sons, become fools for the 'sake of Christ'. Folly of this type— the real meaning of the obedience of charity, poverty in the spirit, and an aspect of simplicity—consists in living in solitude and total obedience to the spiritual father or teacher.[21] It is a folly which, as we mature spiritually, gives way to genuine love, for as the softening of our inner 'substance' takes place we gradually become able to comprehend the 'substance' of the Father, the Son, and the Holy Spirit: to know the Father as he knows the Son, to know the Son as he knows the Father, and to have a unity with the Spirit wherein the Spirit himself testifies that we are the sons of God. Folly for the sake of Christ leads to Wisdom, and its taste for the things of God. Folly for the sake of Christ restores to us what William styles in *The Golden Epistle* an 'inventiveness-skill'— art of using our life intelligently.

The *Vita prima* offers another classic example of the spiritual father or teacher. St Bernard is presented as a spiritual person, the new man. As a result of being a new man in Christ, he begins powerfully and forcefully to attract disciples and to beget in them the same new life by the Word of Life. Bernard remains their teacher, giving advice for their souls and consciences, while in his own spiritual progress he becomes a fool for Christ, totally dependent upon the Father and divine providence in what regards his health and the other circumstances of his life. Unfortunately, William was unable to complete his presentation of Bernard's life.

There are fools and there are fools! There is the fool—as we see in *The Commentary on the Epistle to the Romans*—whose heart is left to itself, is blinded by itself, is not enlightened by grace. Ultimately, this fool says: There is no God![22] Then there is the fool, wisely foolish and foolishly wise, whose heart is full of inner stability, the Immutability of God, of grace and wisdom and *affectus.* This fool cries out: Abba Father!

DISCERNING GOD'S WILL

The marvelous work, *The Mirror of Faith,* opens up to us an important part of our spiritual development: the growth process wherein we begin to discern the Will of God, our Spiritual Father, who is more intimate to us than all our inmost self is to us. Not that we ever become totally independent of our human spiritual father or of human counsel, but there is to be a transfer from the one teacher to the other Teacher who is within us.

William sees a life of intense faith, hope, and charity leading us into a form of solitude necessary for this transference. For perfection in this present life is nothing else than to forget perfectly (a form of solitude) all that is behind and to advance to all that is before us by means of these three theological virtues. This form of solitude brings to our self-will purification from unessential attachments and is preparatory to a union of our will with the Will of God. If the affections of our soul conform to faith, hope, and charity, we live and walk in the Father and the Son and the Holy Spirit: we are entirely spiritual persons. Our will is penetrated through and through by the substantial Will of the Father. The Trinitarian dimension of our spiritual life—the Father, Son, and

Holy Spirit—makes us worthy to know this Will of God.

There is a passage in *The Commentary on the Epistle to the Romans* that etches out the means of being in touch with an inner discernment of the Substantial Will of the Father.

> In three ways we merit to know the will of God, [first] by being still and seeing that he is God, [second] by firmly believing that every word of God is true, for unless you believe you will not understand, and [third] by fulfilling the word and will of God according to your strength. The will of God is good when the saying is fulfilled: I desire mercy and not sacrifice, that is, when we show ourselves cheerful in the works of mercy and eager in corporal asceticism provided it is done for God. The acceptable will of God is cleanness of heart. The perfect will of God is when we are turned away from the world in our acts and affections and are turned towards God.[23]

If our human spiritual father or teacher strives to direct us towards a form of prayer or inner stillness, and an intense faith and the 'art' of actually doing—and doing well—the spiritual life, we will rapidly receive that inner illumination, that joy in the depths of our consciousness. Then, what before we could scarcely say in the Holy Spirit—that Jesus is Lord—now becomes in the same Holy Spirit a crying out all the louder: Abba, Father!

CONTEMPLATING GOD

Although there is no teaching contained in *Contemplating God* relative to an individual abba as a spiritual father initiating his disciple into 'full realization', there is a clear doctrine on spiritual paternity that engenders a new life in the human heart. *Contemplating God,* the document itself, is a handing on of the mystery of our full sharing in divine fatherhood. It shows what God, our Spiritual Father, is willing to do for us.[24]

In the opening paragraphs of this work, William sketches the renewal of the human heart as a going up into the

98

mountain-house of the Lord,[25] in search of that desert, the peaceful rest[26] which is basically an inner harmony among the affective and intellectual faculties of our personality.[27] The 'Rabboni, Master Supreme'[28] himself, will teach us, because he is 'supremely good, goodness itself'.[29] We are drawn and attracted to this Father because of his goodness, and approaching him turns out to be our transformation, as 'the beholding of your goodness is of itself my cleansing, my confidence, my holiness'.[30] And, 'may your holiness and hallowing make us holy, may your unity unite us and through, what is indeed a sort of blood relationship, may we be united to God who is love through the name of love'.[31]

This divine Father, not content simply to attract us, enters into us to look at[32] and to illumine[33] every nook, cranny, and limit of our consciousness. The Father effects this through his Son, the Word, by the breath of his mouth.[34] Because this Son has been delivered up for us even to death of the cross, he is himself all-powerful and dazzling,[35] the very handing on of love and goodness.[36] Our surrender to this 'handing on' of love and goodness is a vehement well-ordered will.[37] This aspect is very important in engendering new life. By our desire for Christ[38] and the inner anointing of the Holy Spirit[39] there is brought forth the mystery of our 'blood' relationship with God: God loving himself in the depths and freedom of *our* life.

> And you also love yourself in us by sending the Spirit of your Son into our hearts, crying Abba Father! through the sweetness of love and the vehemence of good intention that you have inspired. This is how you make us love you or rather, this is how you love yourself in us . . . through the grace breathed into us by the Spirit of your adoption, we have confidence that all that the Father has is also ours. So, through the grace of adoption we invoke you now under the same name as your only Son invokes you by right of nature . . . . We are, I say, God's offspring, we all of us, are gods and sons of the

Most High through a kind of spiritual kinship. We claim for ourselves a closer relationship with you, because through the Spirit of adoption your Son does not scorn to be known by the same name as we and because with and by him, taught by saving precept and schooled by God's ordinance, we are bold to say: Our Father who art in heaven.[40]

True, no faculty of our soul or spirit comprehends God, although God does effect a oneness and understanding[41] between himself as Father and all his sons, insofar as our affections and intellectual faculties are sanctified by the Spirit.[42] We become a spiritual person as a result. God loving himself in every nook and cranny of our soul and spirit reaches from the depths to the highest part of our spirit, where in an experience of him we encounter the Breath of God in our own gasping for life.

. . . I shall not die as quickly as all that! It may be rather that I shall not die at all, but live, and declare the works of the Lord. So I stand in the house of solitude like the lone wild ass, having my dwelling in the salty land. I draw in the breath of my love, I open my mouth in your direction, I breathe in the Spirit. And, sometimes, Lord, when I, as if with eyes closed, gasp for you like this, you do put something in my mouth, but you do not permit me to know just what it is. A savor I perceive, so sweet, so gracious, and so comforting that, if it were fulfilled in me, I should seek nothing more. But when I receive this thing, neither by bodily sight nor by spiritual sense nor by understanding of the mind do you allow me to discern what it is. When I receive it, then I want to keep it, and think about it, and assess its flavor; but forthwith it has gone. Whatever it was, no doubt, I swallowed it down in the hope of eternal life. But I pondered long on its effect on me, and in so doing I wanted to transfuse into the veins and marrow of my soul a sort of vital sap; I wanted to be rid of the taste of every other affection and savor that alone for evermore. But it very quickly passed.[43]

God is our good Supreme Master and Spiritual Father. He attracts and transforms us by the goodness revealed to us in the mystery of Christ. Our response to this goodness in Christ results in the inner anointing of the Spirit that orders all our affective and intellectual faculties and gives us a 'blood' relationship, that is, makes us too a spiritual person. Finally, full realization comes—this side of heaven—at those moments when at the highest point of our spirit we gasp for God's Breath of life.

In his other works William continues to develop the aspects and elements of this basic ensemble of what God does for us as our Spiritual Father.

THE NATURE AND DIGNITY OF LOVE

The Holy Spirit 'unites us to God through the good will that he breathes into us. And with us this vehement good will goes by the name of love, by which we love what we ought to love, namely, you. For love is nothing other than a vehement, well-ordered will'.[44] This quotation from *Contemplating God* establishes the context for the masterful presentation William gives in *The Nature and Dignity of Love* of the teacher, our human spiritual father.

Without a teacher, our adulterous affections[45] wander all over our life, corrupting it more and more by falsifying its orientation.

> Yet, happy is the person, and no other, whose God is the Lord. But in seeking happiness where it can not be found, nor along its proper path, a person wanders far from his own natural destination. Therefore, having neglected his own natural orientation, he has need of a teacher, who teaches about the happiness which a person naturally seeks through love by admonishing where and how and in what place and by what path he must seek.[46]

101

Again:

> Love, as it has been stated, is naturally rooted in the
> human soul by the Author of nature, but after the law of
> God has been ignored, it [love] must be taught by a per-
> son. It must not be taught as if love does not exist. Rather,
> the particular approach to be taught is that love can increase
> and the way to increase; that love can be integrated and the
> way to be integrated.[47]

These affections gone awry are so powerful that this teacher
of love and spiritual father can cope with them only when the
spiritual son willingly enters upon the path of a holy madness
or being a fool for the sake of Christ.

> This is why the whole discernment of the novice must be
> that he makes himself a fool for Christ, and subject him-
> self to the judgment of another especially if there is a
> senior who is known to be able to discern what God teaches
> to men. In this matter, this obedient beginner is not easily
> to be presumed capable of having freedom in judgment—
> so long as there is nothing commanded that is manifestly
> contrary to God's Will, until a long and patient experience
> will have given him an understanding in the things he has
> heard . . . for by obedience you have purified yourselves for
> a genuine love of your brothers![48]

As the teacher of love begins to fulfill this discerning role of
mediating God's teaching to the novice, he will be effective
only through the 'foolishness of it all'. But it is not quite so
simple as thinking 'another person can discern God's will for
me!' No! Rather, 'being a fool for the sake of Christ' means
producing deep down in the substance of the inner person a
softening to the grace of Christ. Thus does the novice begin
to comprehend the teacher's discernment as cultivating growth
into the full maturity of Christ;[49] that is to say, the novice
begins to experience his will undergoing transformation

through love, charity, and wisdom.[50]

It is this path of foolishness that leads from the pedagogy of a teacher into the fullness of Wisdom, our inner Teacher: Christ and his Spirit. Gradually the ability of the novice *to comprehend* does develop into a *taste,*[51] symbolizing Wisdom and Christ.

> Taste . . . symbolizes him who by the condition of the flesh has been made a little less than the angels and Moses and Elias and the other patriarchs and prophets. Thus by showing patience and humility he has made himself less and more humble in a particular way; as they destroyed their enemies by that force of the power of God, he truly taught his disciples: But if anyone strikes you on the cheek, turn to him also the other one.[52]

In other words: Christ, the Wisdom of God, was made wisdom for us.[53] And by this inner tasting, wisdom teaches us all things, yes, even the mystery of divine Fatherhood.[54]

The novice, once in touch with Christ–Wisdom as his inner Teacher, reaches the full maturity of a spiritual person. The Pasch of Christ is what he comes to identify with interiorly;[55] and the Eucharist, the Bread of Wisdom,[56] embraces his whole life to prepare him for that transitus into God himself whereby he truly becomes a son of the Most High.[57]

THE PRAYER OF DOM WILLIAM

The Prayer of Dom William invokes the Lord Jesus both as 'the Truth' and 'the Master'.[58] Clearly, this is in the mainstream of christian tradition, for Jesus is the 'holy man', the spiritual person *par excellence,* precisely because his *place* is in the bosom of the Father, in the consubstantiality of the Holy Trinity.

With a delightfully paradoxical approach, William gently encourages us to become spiritual persons by finding God in ourselves. The needed quality for our life is a worship in spirit and in truth, had by freeing our lives from 'idolatry',[59]

that is, from envisaging any conceptual form whatever for
our God or any 'sort of bodily devotion' to the 'human form'
of our Master.[60] True, we do not err by this sort of devotion,
but we do impede the spiritual prayer that aids our progress
towards that inner anointing and full 'realization' characteristic of a spiritual person. The Master himself says: 'It is expedient for you that I go away. If I do not go away, the Paraclete
will not come to you . . . '.[61]

THE SACRAMENT OF THE ALTAR

Understanding the Lord Jesus as our Spiritual Master/
Teacher, we find presented in the *Sacrament of the Altar*
another aspect of the role of the Spiritual Father. Our
Spiritual Father is the *life* of our soul. 'And in eating the
flesh of the son of man, we have life.'[62] 'Yet, there can be no
doubt that the real life of the soul rather than the life of the
body is sought after in this [the Eucharist]. As it is apparent
to all that just as the soul is the life of the body, so God is
the life of the soul, for God is love. The life of the rational
soul, consequently, is the charity of God.'[63]

William, in asking us humbly to discern in a sort of divine
manner and spiritually to eat the spiritual flesh of Jesus in the
Sacrament of his true flesh,[64] gives a sacramental dimension
to the role of the spiritual father. It is not proposed at this
point that the human person who is our spiritual father holds
the place of God in our life. Rather by this sacramental dimension not only is the focus centered on the Lord Jesus and the
mystery of the divine paternity as the life of our soul, but we
are to approach the Lord 'spiritually'. The implication is the
same as that found in *The Prayer of Dom William,* namely,
flee 'idolatry' in order to become a spiritual person full of
inner unction, for it is only this type of person who will be in
touch with the Spiritual Father dwelling at the very core, in
the very center, of his life.

THE NATURE OF THE BODY AND THE SOUL

In the section on the soul William makes a distinction

between image and identity.[65] He does not expect the soul to become identical to God by lacking nothing that is of God. Rather, the soul as an image is to reflect, represent, and typify, through some likeness, the nature of divine incomprehensibility. For the soul this image is the ability to be a partaker of all good by the possession of an inner principle of freedom from necessity—a powerful free will—so as to express by virtue this inner goodness.[66]

Any change that takes place in our life, our soul, then, is not basically the result of a change of place or time. It is the result of inner changes, especially those of the affections that channel our will. Moreover, the soul gradually perceives that it needs a more stable support *beyond yet within* itself, a type of support helpful to the re-orientation of its affections. 'For, as has been said: nothing is changed unless by the Immutable One'.[67]

These thoughts are the groundwork for William's teaching on the image and likeness of the Trinity in a person, which he develops in detail in his later works, especially in *The Mirror of Faith* and *The Enigma of Faith.* These thoughts are important for us insofar as they show what it means for a person's life *to be formed,* and they show that one's spiritual father—who must ultimately end up being the Father—must exist as one spirit with each person.

> For the will of the Father and of the Son and of the Holy Spirit conforms to itself her [the soul's] will by an unthinkable grace, by ineffable joy, by a more secret inspiration, by a most manifest operation, uniting to itself her love by a spiritual omnipotence. She is effected one in Him so that as has been said, by unspeakable groanings importuning in her, he is said rather to cry out within. And this 'I will' is the prayer of the Son to the Father. This is: I accomplish by the power of my will, who is the Holy Spirit, so that as I and you are one in substance so they may be one in us by grace. One by love and one by beatitude, one by immortality and incorruption, one in some way by that

divinity. For as many times as they have received him, he gave to them the power to be made the sons of God.[68]

Elsewhere, William will present these unspeakable groanings importuning in the soul as the cry of 'Abba, Father'.

THE COMMENTARIES ON THE SONG OF SONGS
FROM THE WRITINGS OF ST GREGORY THE GREAT
AND ST AMBROSE

The relationship between the Spiritual Father and the disciple is realized when the former confers the 'Word of Life' on the latter. This is precisely the message contained in these two works. William chose from these two Fathers of the Church passages that would present the sacred relationship as well as the specific effect of it as God's Word being poured into our spirit, our life, our soul, our consciousness. The reception of this Word of Life makes us sons of God.[69]

The heart of the Father has uttered a good word, the Son gave forth fragrance and the Spirit breathed forth and diffused it throughout all hearts: for the love of God has been poured into our hearts by the Holy Spirit.[70]

The Word of Life that will be given to us from our good Father is our inheritance.[71] This inheritance, once it thoroughly penetrates our spirit, will effect in us the remission of sins and confer the grace of sonship.[72] In order to bring out the full implication which this reception of the Word of Life has, William quotes a passage from Ambrose wherein the giving and receiving of the Word of Life is likened to a kiss.

I opened my mouth and gave forth a sigh. For a kiss is the way lovers adhere to one another and drink in the sweetness of an inner grace. The soul adheres to the Word of God through this kiss because the Spirit pours itself into the one who kisses. For even those who kiss one another are not content to offer just their lips but

106

appear to pour their own spirit into each other.[73]

This passage is reminiscent of the disciple gasping for 'Life' in an encounter with the Breath of God.

Another dimension of this Spiritual Father-disciple relationship surfaces from the texts quoted above. At the approach of the Word, the disciple's inner depths are disturbed. If the disciple opens up, the Word of Life and the Father will enter in.[74] The same idea is expressed another way: the person, kissed by the Word, enters into the bosom and hidden cleft of the Father.[75] Being kissed by the Word means being plunged into the mystery of the Passion of Jesus Christ. The entering into the bosom of the Father or having the Father enter into us—that is, praying to the Father in secret—unfolds the role of solitude in the Spiritual Father-disciple relationship.[76] That the mystery of the Passion and solitude are preparatory for knowing our Father, William will present in his own commentary on *The Song of Songs.*

> May he himself [Christ] be our head because the head of man is Christ. May he be our eye that through him we may see the Father. May he be our voice through whom we may speak to the Father. May he be our right hand through which we may offer sacrifice to God the Father.[77]

THE EXPOSITION ON THE SONG OF SONGS

For whatever God the Father does, this the Son also does in like manner . . . when he speaks to her [the soul] , he speaks himself to her; and thus it is in himself that whatever he wills her to know, he makes known to her to whom he speaks, having *wisdom* for her. And whatever he wills, he brings to pass in her or through her, being himself her strength, her justifying justice and her sanctifying sanctification. And to her who is bride *The Word of God utters himself and his Father,* in the Spirit of his mouth, to such an extent that her whole consciousness is penetrated by the fulness of illuminating grace and she can barely breathe forth the falme of her heart in these few words when she says: The voice of my beloved.[78]

This important text should be read in conjunction with the thought expressed in the Preface to *The Exposition:* 'Every man forms the Lord his God for himself, or sets Him before himself after his own manner. For as the man of prayer himself is, so the God to whom he prays appears to him.'[79] The quality of our affection and love, rather than the imagination's phantasms, brings mature spiritual knowledge of him.[80]

> Grace does this [for example, makes our likeness one of love instead of one of phantasms] for that blessed man who is poor in spirit, humble, quiet, trembling at the Lord's words, simple of soul, and accustomed to the Holy Spirit's communication.[81]

William calls for a purification of our affections and love so that our spirit, uplifted by devout love and not pretentious knowledge,[82] reaches and is touched by God's eternal immutability. And in order to have God's eternal immutability as a stabilizing influence in our heart-life, there is need for Wisdom, and Wisdom, in turn, calls for solitude and secrecy.[83] The message of William's *Exposition on the Song of Songs* concerning the tradition of the Spiritual Father is that the Word of Life coming from our Abba leads us into Wisdom, solitude, and secrecy of life in the Father's bosom. William's *Exposition* is a further development of the two previous commentaries in that he presents the Word of Life as an inward savoring of the Presence that is most profoundly within us.

The purification of our love, which replaces a love limited to phantasms, is greatly assisted by the help of another person, a fellow human being, who teaches from his own personal experience.

> If, she [the soul] says, you account me unworthy of your kiss or of your word or of the breath of your mouth, show me at least one of your friends in whom I may find the

fervor of your love, not in the faint dawn of morning or
the dusk of evening, but in the steady glow of midday light.
Show me a friend in whose heart you may lie and repose
and through whose intermediary you may feed me while
he teaches me what he has learned from you.[84]

William places these important words, which give an integral description of a spiritual father and his role, in the context
of the bride/soul, overcome by her own instability and the
corresponding absence of God in her life. The spiritual father
is to assist us to know ourselves and to find the one we are
seeking, to lead us through the periods and degrees of our purification when we are orphaned and tend to approach our God
as a Father of orphans.[85] The spiritual father leads us into
the mystery of the Word of Life, helps us to cry 'Abba,
Father', for if we sincerely gasp these words of purification,
we will *know* the mystery of God.

For this relation of the Son to the Father, whereby you
were predestined and were made the Son of God in power,
is known by those who have learned to cry in the Holy
Spirit: Abba, Father! And they understand that by this
they are made sons of God and your brothers, and the
outpouring of oil is given and apportioned to us. It is in
this that you have redeemed us, O good brother![86]

Through the purification of our affections and love, we
find ourselves in the solitude of the heart and of the spirit,
which is a sort of guileless consciousness,[87] with only one
thing to do: to savor the Presence of the Word of Life within
us. William shows that this solitude is by no means painless; it
is the absence of the Bridegroom and consequently 'undying
night, fearful solitude, tiresome waiting, no rest whatever'.[88]
How else would we become poor in spirit, humble, quiet,
trembling with reverence at the Lord's Word, ready to savor
the mystery within?[89]

THE MEDITATIONS

'Meditation Thirteen' is a good example of a delicate dialogue between a son and his Spiritual Father concerning problematic areas of their relationship. Has the Father really led the son astray in reproving him?[90] What is the effect of charity upon the labors and efforts of flesh-body?[91] In the end, the son commits his spirit to the Father and requests wisdom of him.[92]

These meditations affirm several aspects of the relationship to the Spiritual Father which we have seen so far. To select a few of them: the Voice of the Father never comes empty; it is a grace effectively touching our inner life.[93] It is charity that makes us sons of God.[94] Through the gift of the Spirit we are transformed from sons of wrath into sons of God.[95] It is the mystery of where the Master, Jesus, dwells.[96] This Master directs us with the Wisdom of the Father;[97] moreover, he teaches us to say: Our Father . . . . [98]

Two significant passages merit special emphasis. One alludes to the eventual transformation of the disciple so that he will be like his Father.

> . . . for to see what you are is to be what you are . . . . But does man ever see God as the Father sees the Son, or the Son the Father? . . . Yes, assuredly, but not in every way the same.[99]

The second is a very beautiful description of another aspect of the disciple's transformation.

> Thus with your wisdom sweetly ordering all things for them they come by a short road and lightly laden to their appointed end . . . . They do not form pictures of your love, nor do they compare it to their own by any subtle reasoning; rather, your love itself, finding in them simple material on which to work, so forms them and conforms them to itself in both affection and effect, that, besides what is

hidden within—namely, the glory and riches of a good conscience—the inner light is reflected in their outward appearance, and that not by deliberate effort but by a certain connaturality. And so much is this the case, that the charm and the simplicity of their expression and bearing provoke love of you; indeed the very sight of them sometimes moves even the barbarous and boorish souls to love you. In such people nature indeed returns to the fountain whence it sprang. Having no human teacher, they are ready to be taught by God, and when, with the help of the Spirit who has compassion on their infirmity, their spirits enter into the divine movement and their senses are controlled by a certain spiritual discipline, a certain spirituality appears even in their bodies, and their faces acquire an appearance that is more than human, having a singular and very special grace. Through devotion to good practices their flesh that is sown in corruption begins even now to rise again to glory, so that heart and flesh together rejoice in the living God, and where the soul thirsts after you the flesh also may thirst in O how many ways! For the blessed meek possess the earth of their own body; which earth, made fruitful by the faithful practice of spiritual exercises, even though it has been left to go fallow, bears fruit of itself in fastings, in watchings, in labor, being ready for every good work without contradiction of sloth.[100]

THE VITA PRIMA

William, in the *Vita prima* of St Bernard, makes some very straight forward statements about the role of the spiritual father as fulfilled by his friend. First, the spiritual father is aware that his call to be an abba comes from God and that God is working in him. God's action evokes a response from the spiritual father: he is to give life to others by attracting disciples and to renew himself, his own inner man, unto the holiness of God. These words of the *Epistle to the Philippians* (1:6) came to Bernard: 'And I am sure that he who began a good work in you will bring it to completion at the day of Christ

Jesus.' William writes:

> Bernard could take these words in no other way than if
> they had been uttered by a voice from heaven itself, and
> they filled him with great joy. As the father in spirit of his
> brothers reborn in Christ, he realized that God was working
> in him and through him, and so he began to devote all his
> efforts to spreading his scheme and finding whatever new
> recruits he could. He began to put on the new man, and to
> speak of this new way of life and other important spiritual
> questions with those with whom he had once discussed
> matters of worldly learning . . . . [101]

The precise, powerful element in this attraction on the part
of the spiritual father is charity-love-the Holy Spirit. This is
an important distinction, for other ways of attracting disciples
—popularity, personal doctrine—will not, in the long run, be
effective in the lasting renewal of the disciple's life; the charity
of the Holy Spirit poured forth from the abba will be.

> And now Bernard started to spread his idea both openly
> and privately and because the Holy Spirit gave his words
> such power, hardly any love or affection for people or
> things was strong enough to withstand its force; and so
> Mothers hid their sons when Bernard came near and wives
> clung to their husbands to prevent them from going to
> hear him.[102]

Here we see the importance of the Word of Life as the foundation of the relationship between the abba and the disciple.

> Together they set out from Tescelin's house with Bernard
> playing the part of father to those brothers of his who
> were the spiritual sons he had begotten in Christ by means
> of the Word of Life.[103]

> . . . They would try to cope with their worries [temporal]

112

among themselves as best they could, and would ask for his [Bernard's] advice on matters which concerned their souls or consciences.[104]

In outlining the basic elements of the spiritual father in the life of Bernard, with a human touch, William shows us a Bernard perhaps not too in touch with the reality of his monks' spiritual life. Yet, gradually there occurs a growing together which leads to a richer life in Christ for both master and the disciple.[105]

THE MIRROR OF FAITH

In the introductory remarks of this paper I remarked that a spiritual teacher is the 'mirror of our higher self. He activates our source of inner knowledge and our sense of complete fulfillment'.[106] In the *Mirror of Faith,* William opens up to us the way whereby we pass from a teacher who is an external mirror to us, to the real Spiritual Father, God himself, who is 'more intimate to us than all our inmost self',[107] and to our complete fulfillment. As this Will is revealed in our hearts and lives He makes us his true sons.

To become spiritual persons, we must lift up our disordered affections to the spiritual dimension of our life. Our mind and reason are purged from all evil, for faith is offered to them.

If the affections of the soul conform to faith, that man lives in the spirit and walks in the spirit, he is as if entirely spiritual. But surely those spiritual virtues are resolved into carnal affections; the whole is made flesh and it is said of that man: my spirit will not remain in this man for he is flesh.[108]

Faith is accompanied by hope and charity, 'for perfection . . . is nothing else than to forget perfectly by means of faith, hope, and charity those things that are behind and to advance to those that are before . . . ' .[109] This forgetting constitutes

113

a very rich form of solitude, whereby we move away from any type of pedagogue—persons, books, law—and move into a mature, living commitment to the Lord and into the mystery of the Father of Our Lord and Savior Jesus Christ, from whom is named all paternity. Authority predisposes to faith; faith brings with it the grace that illumines and liberates our consciousness for divine sonship.[110]

> For a person, relying upon faith, hope, and charity, and holding fast to them, does not need the Holy Scriptures unless perhaps to instruct others. Thus, many persons live in solitude, penetrated with these three virtues and without sacred books. Because of this, I think there has been fulfilled in these three virtues what has been said: prophecies will disappear and tongues will cease and knowledge will be destroyed. Yet, due to these means, such a great instruction of faith and hope and charity has arisen in these persons that they seize perfection without books insofar as there is able to be perfection in this life that can be seized through faith, hope, and charity . . . . [111]

> For formerly before faith came, we were guarded under the law, enclosed in that faith which was to be revealed and the law was our pedagogue in Christ Jesus so that from faith we were justified. But when faith comes we are not under a pedagogue but, having received the adoption of sons, we have been found sons of God, the spirit of God having been received in our hearts whereby we cry Abba, Father. Thus also in that time of grace, before the illumination of the gospels of Christ began to shine in our hearts, we have to be guarded and kept under the authority of that same gospel unto the grace to be revealed in us at the time of the mercy of God illuminating us. Therefore, in the meanwhile, may the authority be our pedagogue in Christ Jesus, so that through the humility of believing, we may merit to be illumined by grace.[112]

114

When illuminating grace will have come, we are no longer under a pedagogue for, wherever the Spirit of the Lord will be, there is liberty. For having received the Spirit of the sons of God, we ourselves are made the sons of God, both understanding and experiencing that we have God as a Father. When we have renounced all confidence in authority, we may say to that Samaritan woman what her companions said to her: we no longer believe because of your word, for we ourselves have heard![113]

Truly, no one comes to the Son unless the Father draws him. No one can enter into Wisdom and Solitude unless the Father draws him. How does this happen? By our free will, whereby we freely choose what we desire, that is, as what we desire *rightly* becomes our own free will.[114] For this process to happen, the Will of God must be one with our own free will: God must be more intimate to us than we are to our own inmost self.[115]

William has two eloquent passages on this union of wills in which he gives a particular slant often missed in the spiritual life. He means not simply some expression of external conformity or obedience to the 'Will of God' as manifested in events, persons, or 'Divine Providence'. Rather he says simply that the Will of God is deep within our own person, our own life, our own will! This is what is meant to be born not of the will of the flesh, nor of the will of man, but of the Will of God! (Jn 1:13)

For the Will of God is the hidden and highest mystery of all the sacramental mysteries which he makes known according to his good pleasure, to whom he wills, and as he wills, which, because it is divine, then in a kind of divine manner reveals to the person who is worthy—He making him worthy in the process. It is not a divine thing, it is God, for it is the Holy Spirit who is the Substantial Will of God. This is the Will of God whereby God makes all that he wills, about which it is written: All what the Lord has

115

willed he made. For the Holy Spirit makes himself known to the person to whom he gives himself. For the very Will of God makes itself known to the person in whom it is accomplished; neither is it known anywhere else than where it is . . . so no one knows His Will in which it is not accomplished, although not all know it or sense it in some persons where it is, for example, in infants and feeble-minded persons.[116]

. . . The Holy Spirit, who is the Substantial Will of the Father and the Son, influences the will of a person to Himself so that the soul, loving God and experiencing by loving, will be suddenly and entirely transformed, not indeed, into the nature of divinity, but into a kind of beyond the human form of beatitude, just short of the divine, in the joy of illuminating grace and the experience of an illumined conscience. Inasmuch as the spirit of man which scarcely before had been able to say in the Holy Spirit: Jesus is Lord, now, among the sons of adoption, may cry out: Abba, Father.[117]

The movement from an exterior spiritual father to our inner Spiritual Father, God, is a process of a discernment so extensive and comprehensive as to result in making us people of 'good will'. The absence of this good will is the sign of every possible reprobation and obdurate infidelity. The consciousness of this goodness is 'a faithful testimony from the Lord that we are the sons of God and of the grace of adoption'. [118]

THE ENIGMA OF FAITH

William's basic teaching is that the johannine doctrine, 'We know that when he appears we will be like him because we will see him as he is' (1 Jn 3:2), finds fulfillment in our soul, the inner person.[119] The more we progress in knowledge and love of God, the more we become like him.[120] But there is an important distinction to be borne in mind.

116

> . . . As in the Trinity, which is God, the Father and the Son mutually see one another and their mutual vision consists in their being one and in the fact that the one is what the other is, so those who . . . will see God as he is, and in seeing him as he is they will become like him. And there, as in the Father and the Son, that which is vision is also unity, so in God and man that which is vision will be likeness that is to come. The Holy Spirit, the unity of the Father and the Son, is himself the love and likeness of God and man.[121]

The likeness between a person and the divine Spiritual Father grows into an understanding of the Son 'inasmuch as he is the Word: not a sound striking the ears but an image presenting itself to the mind', until the disciple, illumined by this clear but inner light, yearns to behold the substance of God in that which he is.[122] This likeness is really a question of change in the disciple's manner of life so that his own substance becomes like that of his good Father.

> Consequently, when we take refuge in God, no change is made in him or his nature; however, we are changed since we who were worse are made better. So also, when he begins to be our Father he is not changed; rather, we are regenerated and made sons of God through the grace of him who gave us the power to become sons of God. And when we were made sons of God our substance truly is transformed for the better, but he begins to be our Father without any change of his substance.[123]

William's threefold way of ascent to God has been treated elsewhere in many fine works and articles. What surfaces as important in this ascent, viewed from the perspective of the disciple–master likeness, is the type of commitment the disciple makes to the divine Spiritual Father. It is a commitment so absolute that the disciple is dependent on no external person, thing, or event in his effort to learn.[124] Rather, this commitment is a sign of great love (Jn 15:8-13) and willingness to face death in one's inner depths in order to have that Likeness (Holy Spirit), to be able to come to know the Father as the Son knows him and to come to know the Son as the Father knows him.[125] This is the enigma of faith—knowing the Trinity.[126]

> When men humbly entrust themselves to the Scriptures, they become subject to them. This is the faith through which those who are blessed with a pure heart are made clean. To them is promised this vision which cannot be seen except by the pure of heart and which can be seen only if those who are to see it are purified through faith .... Therefore, the Son of God who was in the form of God, emptied himself taking on the form of a servant, so that men receiving by faith God who became man, might receive the power to become the sons of God. Toward him who is present everywhere we are moved out not spatially but through a striving for good and through good conduct. And this we could not do if Wisdom did not condescend to become adapted to our great weakness and to offer us a model for living; and in no other way than through a man, since we ourselves are men.[127]

This commitment is the love of God poured out in our hearts by the Holy Spirit who has been given us. An excellent gift it is; it makes us sons of God.[128]

Wisdom is the fruit of this change in one's manner of life, for wisdom can only be communicated from a spiritual man to a spiritual man, or by the Holy Spirit to the spirit of any spiritual person,[129] for it is an understanding of the Father. The word 'God' expresses the natural fear a person has of the Supreme Essence,[130] but the name 'Father' gives an understanding of life. When one cries 'Abba Father' to God in the Holy Spirit, the conscience of the one who cries testifies that he is a son of God.[131] This is to say, one testifies that he not only comes to some likeness and understanding of the Father through a life lived in union with the kenosis of the Son, but he also shares in likeness and understanding of the Father for the Son.

THE GOLDEN EPISTLE

Our elementary likeness to God is found in the possession of life itself. Life mirrors God, for just as it is present to every part of the body, so God is present to all his creation. This type of 'likeness to God . . . is of no real importance with God since it derives from nature, not from will or effort'.[132] It is 'evidence of a better and more sublime likeness that has been lost'.[133]

The next degree of likeness to God is found in virtue and goodness, a likeness freely willed, inspiring us to 'perseverance in good' in imitation of the Supreme Good.[134]

But that likeness which is our perfection is Unity of Spirit.[135] This unity makes us 'one with God, one spirit, not only with the unity which comes of willing the same thing but with a greater fulness of virtue . . . the inability to will anything else'.[136] This unity is the Holy Spirit, the Embrace and the Kiss of Father and Son; it is the Holy Spirit who makes us by grace what God is by nature[137] and utters in us the one word resounding in the depths of our heart 'Abba, Father'.

In order for this precious gift of likeness to God to flower into the unity of spirit, we have need of a spiritual father to whom we owe 'the obedience of charity and recourse in everything'.[138] He is to encourage us in the pursuit of good (the animal stage) and, through gradual discernment and the proper use of reason (the rational stage), entrust us to the Holy Spirit dwelling within us (the spiritual stage). Because we commit to him our charity—the obedience of charity and not the charity of being obedient—he is able to lead us into the mystery of the Charity of God, the Holy Spirit.

There are the animal who of themselves are not governed by reason nor led by affection, yet stimulated by authority or inspired by teaching or animated by good example they

119

acquiesce in the good where they find it and like blind
men led by the hand, they follow, that is, imitate others.
Then there are the rational, whom the judgment of reason
and the discernment that comes of natural learning endow
with knowledge of the good and the desire for it, but as
yet they are without love. There are also the perfect, who
are led by the spirit and are more abundantly enlightened
by the Holy Spirit; because they relish the good which
draws them on they are called wise. They are also called
spiritual because the Holy Spirit dwells in them . . . . [139]

**The spiritual father is but one of the three guardians we have
for this precious gift of likeness to God.**

In order that your solitude may not appall you and that
you may dwell the more safely in your cell three guardians
have been assigned to you: God, your conscience, and your
spiritual father. To God you owe devotion and the entire
gift of self; to your conscience the respect which will
make you ashamed to sin in its presence; to your spiritual
father the obedience of charity and recourse in everything.[140]

The guardian is to help his disciple to begin and to continue
as a 'fool for God's sake, through God's folly which is wiser
than all men's, following Christ's leadership' and thereby to
discover his own, personal, humble art of ascending to heaven.[141] This art or 'the inventiveness skill'[142] of the disciple
is the ability to live in such a way that there is an intelligent,
concrete, practical, actual 'doing' of the inward spiritual
growth through the three stages of 'the intercouse with the
Word of God'[143] wherein the disciple grows into Wisdom by
realizing that inner freedom—true piety—is having God
within him.

The man who has God with him is never less alone
than when he is alone. It is then he has undisturbed

fruition of his joy, it is then he is his own master and is free to enjoy God in himself and himself in God.[144]

COMMENTARY ON THE EPISTLE TO THE ROMANS
Abraham as Spiritual Person

If we consider the spiritual father, the abba, from the viewpoint of his own inner spiritual richness, as a person filled with the inner anointing of the Holy Spirit and thereby sharing in God's Fatherhood, and do not consider him as a 'charismatic' attracting disciples or as a spiritual master, we have an excellent insight into the nature of an abba in the person of Abraham. Abraham is a type of spiritual father for us all,[145] because he was a man whose integrity came from faith, not from observance of the Law. It was precisely this integrity that had within it a *hope* looking to the Promise, to the inheritance to be given by a God always doing what he promises.[146]

It is one thing to worship God, to commit oneself to God by doing what he commands us to do. It is quite another thing to believe and glorify God for what God himself promises to do for us.[147] A way of living in accord with either doing what is commanded or with believing what is promised a person has a profound significance for the spiritual life of that person. While we all must obey God, our basic attraction to God, our basic call to faith, must be founded on hope in God's promise to us; otherwise we can never truthfully say: 'By the grace of God I am what I am'.[148] For us to be only obedient means we can only say with the rich young man: 'All these I have observed from my youth' (Lk 18:21). Perhaps, we too will then turn away sad! In other words, to become a spiritual person one must begin by obedience, but we will never know the depths of spiritual abbahood unless our life is built upon hope in what God has promised us. It is this hope of the promise which, according to William, is written in our minds and hearts by the Finger of God, the Holy Spirit.[149]

Furthermore, what is commanded can be assimilated into

what is promised; this is the message of Christ. And this
message adds yet another dimension:

> God promised his own action, not other people's, when
> He promised sons to Abraham by the faith of the gentiles,
> and they could not be sons unless they had faith. Therefore,
> he gave the faith itself. But according to some people,
> when Scripture says: He who believes shall be saved, one
> of these acts is demanded, and the other is offered. What
> is demanded from man is in man's power; what is offered is
> in God's power. But why should not both of them be in
> God's power, both what He commands and what He offers?
> Indeed, what he commands is made the object of a request,
> when the disciples who believe in him, ask him to increase
> their faith. [*Verse 16*] Therefore everything is of faith, that
> according to grace the promise might be firm to all . . . . [150]

To be true sons of the promise, we are required to hope
against hope. Just as Abraham, in his dead flesh, was an obsta-
cle to his own hope, so, unless we allow ourselves to be 'before
God',[151] that is, to exist according to his disposition and not
glory about our own merits and ability, we are unable to be
'the faithful soul opening up the faith given us by God and
faithfully offering it to the Holy Spirit like prepared wax tablets so that he can write what he pleases'.[152] We hope to be
what he desires us to be: 'Faith in its progress is hope and in
its perfection is charity'.[153]

What is the promise of God made to us? The calling of a
dead body back to life![154] This power of the Resurrection is
the glory of God (Jn 11:40). God who calls the dead back to
life is the God of Jesus Christ, the Abba, the Father, his Father,
who raised him from the dead! The Father is the One who
raises from the dead—this is what it means for him to be
Father—and not just the one who gives life as creator.

> We should inquire carefully why the Apostle in naming
> God in whom we believe and Abraham believed, does not

122

say God the Most High, or the God who made heaven and earth, but only the God who raised up the Lord Jesus from the dead. The answer is that it is much more magnificently to God's glory that he raised the Lord Jesus Christ from the dead than that he created heaven and earth. The latter consists in making what did not exist, the former in repairing what had perished. The latter was the institution of something new, the former was the restoration of what was destroyed. The mystery of this matter had already occurred previously in Abraham's faith, for when he was ordered to immolate his son, Scripture says that he believed 'that God is able to raise up even from the dead.' Rejoicing on account of this he offered his only son, because he was not thinking of the destruction of his posterity, but of the reparation of the world and the renewal of all creation, which would take place through the resurrection of the Lord. In this way, therefore, the comparison is seen to be made correctly between Abraham's faith and the faith of those who believe in the God who raised up the Lord Jesus Christ. What Abraham believed in as future, we believe in as a past event.[155]

William suggests that the inner anointing of an abba means bestowing the power of the resurrection here and now in his life through hope, and thereby allowing him here and now to be a sharer in the Fatherhood of God, a sharer in the mystery of giving life to that which is dead, of giving life to a son who is dead.

THE POWER OF THE SPIRITUAL FATHER TO ATTRACT SONS

For William the basis of this attraction is the mystery of God's election and choice of an individual. 'God's good will precedes our good will so that he calls sinners to repentance, and these are the arms by which the enemy is assaulted.'[156] Without trying to enter into the polemic of predestination, 'a deep question leading us into the deep',[157] William says that

the divine choice of Jacob over Esau is the working of grace
and mercy precisely because, in the choice of a son, God
chooses not the sons of flesh but the sons of promise: those
who come to birth by faith and hope in the promise of God.[158]
The child of promise is one who lives in the mercy and grace
and freedom of God,[159] while the child of the flesh is one
who remains in original sin and its all-embracing and powerful
influence over the will and its concupiscences in our bodily
members (as contrasted to a 'vehement, powerful, well-ordered
'free will') and its concupiscences in our bodily members (as contrasted to the *affectus*).[160] For 'only God accomplishes what God
promises...the promise appeared more clearly in him who was
born from sterile and aged organs [Isaac] and not in the usual
course of nature, so that the divine work might be shown to be
divine and not human in the sons of God...'.[161] This again is a
prelude to the mystery of the Resurrection and the hope in our
promised resurrection to glory.

Without grace we belong to dead fish. Once attracted by
grace, we begin the spiritual journey; we are 'joined to the spirit
and are made one spirit with Him'.[162] Once we are chosen, the
Word of Scripture, the Word of the Abba, can be addressed to us
for we are not of the flesh but in the spirit.[163] Ultimately, it is the
Son's secret why one person is attracted and another is not.[164] The
attraction, because it is also a promised call, is firm; there is no
change.[165] The Word of God allows for no change, for it teaches
the mystery of the Father and the Son and the Holy Spirit.

> Whoever belong to this calling are all taught by God; nor
> can anyone of them say: I believe in such a way as to be
> called. The grace of God anticipated them all, because
> they are called in such a way as to believe. All those who
> are taught of God come to the Son, because they have
> heard and have learned from the Father, through the Son,
> who clearly said: Everyone that has heard of the Father,
> and has learned, comes to me.[166]

Taught by God, we are not to be 'conformed to this world,

but reformed in the newness of our minds. We are conformed
to the Son of God in those ways in which we are reformed so
as not to be conformed to this world'.[167] We are no longer
creatures subject to vanity and full of despair; we are now
sons, although it has not yet appeared what we shall be.[168]

Attraction to the Spiritual Father, then, is an election
coming from God's good will. It is his mercy, his goodness,
drawing us to be conformed to the Son of God, for we have
received the Word of Scripture—the Word of the Trinity
touching our hearts to love God.

> God steadily draws the heart and conscience of the sons
> of grace to remember these things, and thus He recom-
> mends his charity in our regard. Due respect being paid to
> the other mysteries of our salvation and faith, the God-man
> has this purpose in being born and in suffering and in what-
> ever else he did on earth, that he should commend his
> charity in our regard and so provoke our charity in return,
> for love responds strongest to love.[169]

We are not attracted because we first love God but because
he has first loved us and, as a consequence, we change and are
capable of overcoming all obstacles separating us from
this love.

> . . . Just as no one chooses unless he is chosen, so no one
> loves unless he is loved. Our love is an affection of the
> human mind; the love of God is an affection of grace. We
> are changed and affected when we love God, but God is
> not changed and affected when we are loved by him. Rather
> his love is the Holy Spirit, and when he deigns to give him
> to us, through him [the Holy Spirit], he pours into our
> hearts the charity by which we love him [the Father].
> Therefore, the Father loves us with the gift of his love with
> which he enriches us; we love him when we are borne with
> the whole weight of our soul towards him. This is what we
> owe to God alone.[170]

TO BE A SON OF GOD IS TO BE ACTED UPON BY THE HOLY SPIRIT

A common notion of a spiritual father is of someone to whom we go for some kind of 'direction' in order to get help and to do the right thing and so 'grow' in the spiritual life. But William, by always stressing that first and foremost God is our Spiritual Father, retains the perspective proper to a spiritual son: that God, our Father, attracts us by his goodness and mercy and that this attraction does not so much orient us as change and transform us. His goodness calls forth a goodness deep within us, and response is the beginning of a whole new way of living.

As many as are acted upon by the Spirit of God, they are the sons of God. To be acted upon is something more than to be directed. He who is directed, does something, and he is directed in order that he may do something rightly. But he who is acted upon is scarcely understood to do anything himself. And yet the grace of the Savior gives so much to our wills that the apostle does not hesitate to say: As many as are acted upon by the Spirit of God, they are the sons of God. The sons of God are acted upon so that they do what should be done, and when they have done it, they give thanks to him by whom they were acted upon, because they acted as they should, namely, with delight and love of justice . . . . The sons of God are, therefore, those who are acted upon by the Spirit, not the letter; they are those whom the Spirit excites, enlightens, and helps, not those to whom the law commands, threatens, and gives promises.[171]

We can more clearly understand what it is to receive the spirit of adoption of sons, the spirit of liberty as opposed to the spirit of bondage, if we keep in mind that we are 'being acted upon by the Holy Spirit'.[172] To be directed by another is really to retain a spirit of servitude and offer 'tablets of stone', hearts hardened in some degree by fear. Regardless of

126

how slight the degree, fear imposes a yoke of slavery befitting a carnal and not the spiritual person, who has the freedom of sons and the liberty of faith.[173]

The greatest commandment of God—love—cannot be accomplished in a spirit of bondage or written on 'tablets of stone',[174] although such an illusion may persist. What is this love that the Father has for us?

> A father usually rejoices at an only son as alone possessing the entire inheritance and having no one with whom to divide the property, but not so God the Father. He had only one Son, but was unwilling to have [only] one, and so He sent Him into the world so that He should have adopted brothers. The Only-begotten came and took on himself the sins with which we were involved, lest the grace of adoption should be impeded by them.[175]

The Holy Spirit, acting upon us, inspires in us a love of our Spiritual Father. In the Spirit we cry out to the same degree that we love; we invoke the Father with a son's affection because the Spirit is the Love, and our cry is 'Abba Father'.[176] William says of these words, 'Abba Father':

> Of these two words, one is taken from the Law and the other from the uncircumcised. Those who cry out, seek something, and what do they seek except that for which they hunger, namely, justice? The only Son of God gave his slaves the power to become the sons of God, and he admonished them to ask, seek, and knock so that they might receive, find, and have the door opened to them. In him we cry out, that is, when he pours forth in our hearts charity, without which anyone who cries out, does so in vain.[177]

This cry is the gasping for the breath of life which William has treated in his other works. One result of being acted upon by the Holy Spirit is a sort of 'death of our Spiritual Father'.

The Father himself is our inheritance, and we can not obtain his inheritance at his death, for the Father does not die.[178] But William observes, as we already noted above,[179] that the Father is said 'to die' insofar as there is a growth in our understanding of Him. In other words, the change and transformation central to a new way of living means that we experience an ever-deepening penetration into the goodness and mercy of God and a calling forth of our own God-given, inherent goodness. Our meager thoughts of the Spiritual Father die and give birth to richer life in goodness and mercy.

THE WORD OF THE SPIRITUAL FATHER

> It is important that one believe God in such a way that one believes in God. He believes in God who believes him when he speaks or promises; or he believes God who entrusts himself to him. Therefore, the prophet says about one people: their spirit was not faithful to God. To believe in God is to go to God by believing and loving and to become a member of his body or to offer one's self in obedience to his good pleasure, whatever it is, as Abraham did.[180]

In order to profit from the word of the Spiritual Father, we must make a commitment to his good pleasure. For 'he is rightly called the son of God and not of the flesh as he was born by the visit and by the word of God' (Gn 21:1-2).[181] Isaac, to whom this quotation refers, is a figure of a spiritual son insofar as his birth is due solely to the Word of the Lord. The point is that the word brings us to life as spiritual persons. This word is powerful, not because it gives us life as existence, but because it gives us life as goodness, which constitutes the power to be the sons of God.[182] Moreover, 'no soul as long as it can reason at all, is so perverse that God does not speak to it in its conscience'.[183] To be a spiritual person, then, is to live and grow in personal goodness.

The word is sanctifying, for 'every man is a liar but not

those men to whom the word of God is addressed, for Scripture pronounced them to be gods and not men, and Our Lord in the Gospel confirms this'.[184] As long as goodness is present in us, and especially if this goodness is increasing under the power of the Word of God, we are becoming holy persons, filled with the Holy Spirit who gives testimony that we are the sons of God.[185] The aim of the spiritual person is to receive this Holy Spirit in a commitment to the Father's good pleasure through a mediation of the Word.

CONCLUSION

The few references William of St Thierry makes to the human spiritual father are significant ones. They portray the spiritual father as a deeply spiritual person and spiritual teacher. Not the magnetic personality of the spiritual father but the Holy Spirit, the Substantial Will of the Father, united to the will of the spiritual father is the source of the relationship between the teacher and the disciple. This relationship rests on the *conferral* of the Word of Life, not upon the *attraction* of a magnetic personality. Were it otherwise, there would open up the possibility of some foolish act of trust, commitment, or fidelity—a counterfeit of true folly for the sake of Christ, which is the real meaning of the obedience of charity leading to Wisdom and to a taste for the things of God.

What is very important is the context of the human spiritual father: the Divine Fatherhood itself. It is not surprising that William has a lot to say about the heavenly Spiritual Father and the bestowal of the Spirit of sonship. By leading the disciple into the Word of Life by means of an inner stillness, an intense faith, and the 'art' of living well the spiritual life, the human spiritual father orients his disciple to a sharing in Christ's own experience of God as Abba. Just as Christ in his solitude, Passion, and Resurrection experienced his Father's goodness, so also, our experience of the Father, if it is an authentic love casting out the fear of any unwillingness, must also partake of the solitude and Passion of Christ. William gives the human spiritual father as one of the three guardians assisting us through our solitude and pasch into the experience of the Father's goodness.

In William's vision, we begin with the experience of a human spiritual father and rise to an experience of God, our Heavenly Father. This experience of God is Christian because it is 'an affective knowledge [*affectus*] rooted in faith in Christ, a sharing in Christ's own experience of God'.[186] This experience of God is mystical because the experience of the Father's goodness is a supernatural knowledge and love of God, incommunicable and inexpressible, save for the Spirit gasping deep within our life the Word: Abba Father! William sees the role of the spiritual father as vital to monastic, contemplative life for it leads us into contemplative prayer of a Trinitarian dimension.

APPENDIX: *AFFECTUS*

In this paper I have retained the Latin word *affectus* and give here a description or explanation of this word. *Affectus* is so technical in William's teaching that it is difficult, if not impossible, for an English translation to capture its meaning and nuances.

In his thesis[187] Patrick Ryan gives the concept of *affectus* set forth by the German scholar W. Zwingmann. This concept generally applies throughout all the works of William.

> The term is used nearly two-hundred-and-fifty times and covers several different meanings, but it may be said to indicate the deepest aspect of our tending towards God. On the one hand, ***affectus*** relates to the soul's ascent towards God (man is active); on the other, it also serves to designate the condescending grace of God, who stoops to the soul in search of Him (so that man, in a sense, is passive). It should be noted that in the second case the ***affectus*** is bound up with the work of the Holy Spirit. One may say that in the ***affectus*** God works in us and we cooperate in this divine action.[188]

William uses other words also related to *affectus,* such as *afficere, affici, affectio.* These words are also modified as *affici Deo, affici a Deo.* But it will be adequate for this study of the spiritual father simply to recall what Ryan gives for the concept of *affectus,*[189] namely, that in *The Nature and Dignity of Love* William makes a clear distinction between *affectus* and *affectio* (Ryan translates them as attachment and feelings, respectively),[190] whereas in his other works, William does not make such clear distinction. In fact, William tends to equate them on occasions.

The *affectus* is that area of the soul embracing all the affective aspects (for example, passions, affections, will, love). God works in this area by his creating grace and by his illuminating grace. Creating grace makes this area of the soul good and orients it to God. Illuminating grace affects this same area so profoundly that, ultimately, the soul is united with God in the 'Unity of the Spirit'. In this 'Unity of the Spirit' love itself is stabilized and becomes an understanding, but understanding meant in the sense of a savoring of God in an experience by which we come to know the Father and Son through the Holy Spirit.

NOTES

1. Bangalore Congress, mimeographed notes for the third day.
2. Jn 14:6.
3. Col 1:15.
4. 1 Jn 2:20, 27.
5. Mt 23:8ff.
6. Pierre Salmon, *The Abbot in Monastic Tradition* (CS 14; trans. Claire Lavoie; Washington, D.C., 1972) p. 3.
7. I. Hausherr, *La direction spirituelle en Orient autrefois, Orientalia Christiana Analecta* 144 (1955) 55-57.
8. Salmon, p. 4.
9. Tarthang Tulku, *Gesture of Balance* (Berkeley, 1977) p. 163.
10. *Ibid.,* p. 164.
11. *Ibid.,* p. 169.
12. See the Appendix for an explanation of *affectus.*
13. *Contemplating God, The Commentary on the Epistle to the Romans* (wherein is developed the power of the Spiritual Father to attract sons), *The Nature of the Body and Soul,* and *The Golden Epistle* are the primary sources for William's doctrine on the Spiritual Paternity of our Heavenly Father.
14. PL 180:714 B.
15. *Contemplating God,* the three *Commentaries on the Song of Songs, The Golden Epistle,* and *The Commentary on the Epistle to the Romans* (wherein is developed the Word of the Spiritual Father) are the basic sources for William's teaching on the Word of Life.
16. These phrases "sense of life" and "Spirit of Life" are special to William's teaching. See William of St. Thierry, *Exposition on the Song of Songs* (CF 6; trans. Columba Hart; Spencer, Massachusetts, 1970) p. 4, n. 3.
17. *The Prayer of Dom William, The Sacrament of the Altar, The Commentary on the Song of Songs, The Meditations, The Enigma of Faith,* and *The Commentary on the Epistle to the Romans* (wherein is developed the themes of Abraham and of being acted

133

upon by the Holy Spirit) are the basic sources for William's teaching on the Abba as a deeply spiritual person.

18. This friend can be anyone who is full of God's presence, including Jesus—the Emmanuel.

19. PL 180:632 CD. I am indebted to John Baptist Hasbrouck for the use of his translation (in manuscript) of *The Commentary on the Epistle to the Romans* from which this and all other quotations from this work have been taken.

20. *Contemplating God, The Nature and Dignity of Love, The Nature of the Body and Soul, The Golden Epistle, The Vita prima,* and *The Commentary on the Epistle to the Romans* are the basic sources for the Abba as a human spiritual father or teacher.

21. This obedience of charity is at the core of monastic life. See Louis Bouyer, *The Cistercian Heritage* (Westminster, Maryland, 1958) pp. 106-107.

22. PL 180:559 B.

23. PL 180:670 D.

24. *On Contemplating God* [Contemp] , 2; translated by Sister Penelope in *The Works of William of St. Thierry,* I (CF 3; Spencer, Massachusetts, 1971) p. 37.

25. Contemp 1; p. 36.

26. Contemp 12; p. 61.

27. Contemp 2; p. 37.

28. Contemp 1; p. 36

29. *Ibid.*

30. Contemp 2; p. 37.

31. Contemp 12; p. 59.

32. Contemp 3; p. 40.

33. Contemp 3; p. 39.

34. Contemp 10; p. 52.

35. Contemp 3; p. 38.

36. Contemp 10; p. 52.

37. Contemp 11; p. 54.

38. Contemp 3; p. 38.

39. Contemp 11; p. 55

40. *Ibid.*

41. Contemp 11; pp. 57-58.

42. Contemp 11; p. 58.

43. Contemp 12; pp. 61-62.

44. Contemp 1; p. 54.

45. PL 184:579 C. I have translated this quotation and all others from *The Nature and Dignity of Love.*
46. PL 184:380 D.
47. PL 184:381 A.
48. PL 184:384 CD.
49. PL 184:386 D.
50. PL 184:382 A.
51. PL 184:399 AD.
52. PL 184:398 B.
53. PL 184:399 B.
54. PL 184:399 CD.
55. PL 184:400 CD.
56. PL 184:403 B.
57. PL 184:407 AB.
58. *The Prayer of Dom William* [Orat] (trans. Sister Penelope; CF 3; Spencer, Massachusetts, 1971) p. 73.
59. Orat; p. 71.
60. Orat; pp. 73-74.
61. Orat; p. 74.
62. PL 180:353 C. I have translated this quotation and all the others from *The Sacrament of the Altar.*
63. PL 180:351 C.
64. PL 180:358 B.
65. PL 180:741 A.
66. PL 180:717 C.
67. PL 180:720 C. This same idea of God's immutability as the source of our change is expressed in the hymn for None: 'Yourself unmoved all motion's source.' This stable immutable support in our life is the *affectus.* See the Appendix.
68. PL 180:722 CD.
69. PL 180:472 A. I have translated this quotation and all the others from *The Commentaries on the Song of Songs.*
70. PL 15:1953 D.
71. PL 15:2009 D.
72. PL 15:1951 B.
73. PL 15:1950 B.
74. PL 15:2024 B.
75. PL 15:1952 C.
76. PL 15:1955 B.
77. PL 15:2052 C.

78. *Exposition on the Song of Songs* [Cant] , 141; translated by Columba Hart (CF 6; Spencer, Massachusetts, 1970) p. 113.
79. Cant, Preface, 13; p. 11.
80. Cant, Preface, 20 and 21; pp. 15-16.
81. Cant, Preface, 21; p. 16.
82. Cant 28; p. 22.
83. Cant 28; p. 23.
84. Cant 58; p. 47 and n. 20.
85. Cant 33; p. 27.
86. Cant 40; p. 32.
87. Cant 160; p. 131.
88. Cant 188; p. 153.
89. Cant, Preface, 21; p. 16.
90. *Meditations* [Med] , 13:1,2; translated by Sister Penelope, *The Works of William of St Thierry,* I (CF 3; Spencer, Massachusetts, 1971) pp. 186-87.
91. Med 13:3, 4; pp. 187-188.
92. Med 13:7; p. 189.
93. Med 4:13; p. 117.
94. Med 3:9; p. 106.
95. Med 6:7; p. 128.
96. *Ibid.*
97. Med 5:1; p. 118.
98. Med 6:7; p. 128.
99. Med 3:6; p. 105.
100. Med 12:15; pp. 175-76.
101. William of St. Thierry *et al., St. Bernard of Clairvaux*; trans. Geoffrey Webb and Adrian Walker (Westminster, Maryland, 1960) p. 30, quoting PL 185:234 C. This work is hereafter cited as Vita Bern.
102. Vita Bern, p. 32; PL 185; 235 C.
103. Vita Bern, p. 34; PL 185:236 C.
104. Vita Bern, p. 47; PL 185:243 A.
105. Vita Bern, PL 185:243 B-244 C.
106. See p. 90 above.
107. *Speculum fidei* [Spec fid] ; PL 180:382 C.
108. Spec fid; PL 180:380 C.
109. Spec fid; PL 180:367 B.
110. Spec fid; PL 180:371 B.
111. Spec fid; PL 180:367 A.

112. Spec fid; PL 180:373 A.
113. Spec fid; PL 180:373 B.
114. Spec fid; PL 180:370 D.
115. Spec fid; PL 180:382 C.
116. Spec fid; PL 180:382 A.
117. Spec fid; PL 180:391 D.
118. Spec fid; PL 180:371 A.
119. *The Enigma of Faith* [Aenig] , 4; translated by John D. Anderson in CF 9 (Washington, D.C., 1974) p. 38.
120. Aenig 5; p. 39.
121. Aenig 5; p. 40.
122. Aenig 2; p. 37.
123. Aenig 54; p. 86.
124. Aenig 60; p. 91.
125. Aenig 4; p. 38.
126. Aenig 59; p. 90.
127. Aenig 11; pp. 44-45.
128. Aenig 89; p. 116.
129. Aenig 38; p. 70.
130. Aenig 72; p. 102.
131. Aenig 73; p. 103.
132. *The Golden Epistle* [Ep frat] , 260; translated by Theodore Berkeley (CF 12; Spencer, Massachusetts, 1971) p. 95.
133. Ep frat 260; p. 95.
134. Ep frat 261; p. 95.
135. Ep frat 257; p. 94.
136. Ep frat 262; p. 95.
137. Ep frat 263; p. 96.
138. Ep frat 101; p. 46.
139. Ep frat 43; p. 26.
140. Ep frat 101; p. 45.
141. Ep frat 8; p. 10.
142. Ep frat 55; p. 31 and n. 31.
143. Ep frat 35; p. 22.
144. Ep frat 30; p. 20.
145. *Commentary on the Epistle to the Romans* [Exp Rm] ; PL 180: 587 B. John Baptist Hasbrouck's translation; see n. 16 above.
146. Exp Rm; PL 180:586 D.
147. Exp Rm; PL 180:587 A.
148. Exp Rm; PL 180:587 C.

137

149. Exp Rm; PL 180:587 D.
150. Exp Rm; PL 180:587 AB.
151. Exp Rm; PL 180:587 C.
152. Exp Rm; PL 180:587 D.
153. Exp Rm; PL 180:588 B.
154. Exp Rm; PL 180:588 D.
155. Exp Rm; PL 180:598 A.
156. Exp Rm; PL 180:640 C.
157. Exp Rm; PL 180:650 B.
158. Exp Rm; PL 180:646 CD.
159. Exp Rm; PL 180:611 A.
160. Exp Rm; PL 180:620 D.
161. Exp Rm; PL 180:647 A.
162. Exp Rm; PL 180:562 D.
163. *Ibid.*
164. *Ibid.*
165. Exp Rm; PL 180:665 A.
166. *Ibid.*
167. Exp Rm; PL 180:640 C.
168. Exp Rm; PL 180:634 B.
169. Exp Rm; PL 180:593 A.
170. Exp Rm; PL 180:643 C.
171. Exp Rm; PL 180:631 AB.
172. Exp Rm; PL 180:631 B.
173. Exp Rm; PL 180:580 D.
174. Exp Rm; PL 180:631 C.
175. Exp Rm; PL 180:631 D.
176. Exp Rm; PL 180:632 B.
177. Exp Rm; PL 180:631 D.
178. Exp Rm; PL 180:632 C.
179. See pp. 94-5 above.
180. Exp Rm; PL 180:582 C.
181. Exp Rm; PL 180:646 A.
182. Exp Rm; PL 180:658 A.
183. Exp Rm; PL 180:568 D.
184. Exp Rm; PL 180:575 B.
185. Exp Rm; PL 180:651 B.
186. Patrick Ryan, *The Experience of God in the* De contemplando Deo *of William of St. Thierry* (Ann Arbor, Michigan, 1977). Parentheses mine. The thoughts from this section of Ryan's

book have influenced the writing of this paragraph.
187. *Ibid.*
188. *Ibid.,* p. 54
189. *Ibid.,* p. 56.
190. *Ibid.,* p. 55.

Abba, *The Spiritual Guide*

THE SPIRITUAL FATHER AS SEEN BY A SPIRITUAL FATHER, BLESSED GUERRIC OF IGNY

M. Basil Pennington, OCSO
Saint Joseph's Abbey

WE HAVE IN GUERRIC of Igny a privileged witness to the spirit and teaching of the early Cistercians. He was a favored disciple of Saint Bernard and spent over twelve years with him at Clairvaux. For ten years he was the Father Immediate of Bernard's most intimate friend, William of Saint Thierry. Guerric was, moreover, a theologian of significant stature. Judging as best we can from the dates we know of him—he entered Clairvaux, c. 1125; became abbot of Igny, 1138; and died, 1157—he evidently became the Master of the School of Tournai at a relatively young age, perhaps even in his twenties or at most thirties. By that time Tournai's international attraction as the seat of Odo of Cambrai, a disciple of Anselm of Bec, had waned. Yet Odo was probably still living as bishop of Cambrai when Guerric succeeded to his magisterial chair.

Guerric's witness comes down to us in a particularly living and pure form. Besides one very enticing sermon on the Song of Songs—which gives us a faint hope that it might be part of a whole commentary which shall some day come to light—there are fifty-three feast-day sermons. Both the testimony of the *Exordium magnum*[1] —for whatever it is worth—and the state of the manuscripts[2] argue a collection that has not suffered much from editing and therefore is close to what Guerric would actually have shared with his spiritual sons in the chapter house of Igny.

140

THE SPIRITUAL FATHER-MOTHER

In one of the early sermons of this precious corpus, Guerric gives us a very important key to a significant dimension of his concept of the role of the spiritual father. It comes in the third sermon for the feast of Christmas. Considerations of the feast led easily to the thought of maternity and a gospel text invited the development:

> Whoever does his will, he is mother and brother and sister. Lord Solomon, you call me mother. I profess myself to be a handmaid. I am Christ's handmaid; be it done to me according to your word. And indeed I will show myself a mother by love and anxious care to the best of my ability; but I will always be mindful of my condition.[3] Brethren, the name of mother is not restricted to prelates, although they are charged in a special way with maternal solicitude and devotion . . . . [4]

We perceive that Guerric's very rich doctrine of spiritual maternity, finding its archetype in Mary, the Mother of God, and not neglecting the Church or the universal call of the faithful,[5] is an integral part of his understanding of the service of spiritual paternity. In this he clearly shows himself to be a disciple of St Bernard, 'our Master, that exegete of the Holy Spirit', who did not hesitate to liken himself to a mother in the service of his spiritual sons.[6]

GUERRIC'S OWN CALL

The first text that I wish to consider in this study of Guerric's understanding of the role of the spiritual father is the Rogation Day sermon in which he speaks candidly of his own election as abbot of Igny:

> I am no physician and in my house there is no bread. That is why I said from the start: 'Do not make me your leader'. It is not right for me to rule who cannot be of service. And how can he be of service who is not a physician and in

141

whose house there is no bread? He has neither the art to heal souls nor the learning to feed them. I told you this but you would not listen. You made me your superior. There was only one course open to me. If I could not escape the burden, I had to look for the remedy. I listened to the advice of the wise man: 'Have they made you ruler? Be among them as one of them'. But I cannot even do this. Lack of wisdom forbids my being put over others, lack of health prevents my being one among them. I have not the depth of soul for ministering the word, nor the strength of body for giving a good example. I am not fit to be a ruler over you nor am I fit enough to be among you as one of you. What is left to me then but to choose the last and safest place and be the servant of you all? And this I can do by thinking humbly, or rather truly, about myself. There is nothing to prevent me, in fact truth itself strongly urges me to be subject in spirit to you all, even though I am compelled by my offices to rule over you.

[2] It is you yourself, Lord God, who warn me to be subject yet command me to rule. So, confident you will grant my plea, I beg you to make me humble and helpful in the ministry you have confided to me: humble in realizing the truth about myself, helpful by speaking the truth about you. Breathe the one truth into my heart, let the other be ever on my lips. You have told us: 'Open your mouth, and I will fill it'. Put into my mouth the appropriate word that pleases the ear, so that this entire family of yours may be filled with blessings . . . .

We know that to merit the ability to teach, it is not enough to live a blameless life whereby we become your friends; we must show continuous zeal and perseverance in prayer, enough to make us seem shameless. I myself can rely on neither. All I can do is put before you the merits of those I must feed. They deserve what I do not.[7]

How Guerric came to be elected abbot of Igny has often been discussed.[8] He was a monk of Clairvaux at the time, and it has been conjectured even from earliest times that he was chosen by the Igny community at the behest of St Bernard, the Father Immediate who would have presided at the election. There may have been some influence exerted by the persuasive Bernard, but Guerric here insists on the freedom the community had in choosing him. Among the authors considering this question I rarely find any reference to a very significant document. The Acts of Milon indicate that Guerric of Clairvaux was with the bishop of Tournai in Ypres in May of 1138.[9] As Igny was virtually half way between Clairvaux and Ypres, and given the traveling habits of monks, there is basis for a strong argument that Guerric was at Igny in 1138 and, as his sermon seems to indicate, precisely at the time of abbatial election. The community had an opportunity to get to know this favored son of St Bernard, so full of learning, spiritual wisdom, and charm. But the question is somewhat apart from our present consideration. What interests us here is the qualities that Guerric would have in a man about to undertake the office of superior and spiritual father.

His requirements are very much those set forth by the Master whose *Rule* he professed. He must be a physician who knows how to heal, a wise man who can teach, but above all a humble man who sees his ministry as service and who knows he has received all that he has to give. He is to be in their midst as a living example. Knowing himself, he thinks humbly of himself; his spirit is such that he sees himself as subject to those to whom he ministers, by God's choice, by ruling. The depth of soul needed to minister the Word he has received from his Friend, the true Master. Even though he has striven to live a blameless life of continuous zeal and perseverance in prayer, he knows that what he has received has been given him, more because of the merits of his sons than by his own. It is a familial scene filled with warmth. He is to seek to serve, to rule in a helpful way, and even to try to please the ears of his monks. The 'job description' that Guerric offers in these few lines is quite complete, though other passages in his writings will add color and warmth to it.

143

A SERVICE OF FULLNESS

The only place where Guerric speaks explicitly of spiritual paternity is significantly the passage which expresses concisely the heart of his whole teaching. If the Sermon on the Mount is the summary of gospel spirituality, the Beatitudes at the head of this sermon stand as an epigrammatic summation of all that it has to say. The Cistercian Fathers have found in the Beatitudes the paradigm of the cistercian way to holiness.[10] From them Guerric offers a contextual teaching on the spiritual father. Let us listen to this significant passage:

The first virtue in this ascent, proper to beginners, is renunciation of the world, which makes us poor in spirit. The second is meekness, which enables us to submit ourselves in obedience and to accustom ourselves to such submission. Next comes mourning to make us weep for our sins and to beg God for virtue. It is here we first taste justice, and so learn to hunger and thirst more keenly after justice in ourselves as well as in others, and we begin to be roused to zeal against sinful men. Then, lest the zeal should grow immoderate and lead to vice, mercy follows to temper it. When a man has learned to become merciful and just by diligent practice of these virtues he will then perhaps be fit to enter upon the way of contemplation and to give himself to the task of obtaining that purity of heart which will enable him to see God. Tested and proved in this way in both the active and contemplative life, he who bears the name and office of a son of God through his having become a father and servant of other men will then and only then be worthy to be a peacemaker between them and God. Then he will fulfill the office of mediator and advocate, and be worthy to make peace among the brethren themselves and even among the brethren and those who are outside the community. For thus it is written in praise of our holy Fathers: 'They were men bringing peace in their houses'. If a man is faithful and constant in this office, he will often attain virtue and merit which belongs to the martyr, for he suffers persecution for justice' sake, and this even on occasion

at the hands of those for whom he is fighting, so that he
can say, 'The sons of my mother have fought against me',
and, 'with them that hated peace I was peaceful; when I
spoke to them they fought against me without cause'.
How much glory, and how rich a reward will finally crown
such perfection in heaven . . . . [11]

Spiritual paternity is seen as a stage in the normal development of the spiritual life. One must begin with renunciation.
Guerric is addressing himself here to monks, and therefore he
is placing this in the context of that renunciation of the world
that is involved in the conversion to monastic life. But he
would insist that it be in fact a true interior renunciation of
that world to which Christ's disciples do not belong,[12] of the
world of possessiveness and material aggrandizement which
fetter the spirit. I do not think Guerric's teaching should be
interpreted as limiting spiritual paternity to the monk, although his teaching is given within a monastic context. Therefore, while he speaks of obedience as at the heart of monastic
life, essentially he would be pointing to obedience in a school
of submission to the will of the Father in imitation of Christ,
an obedience one could live out in other vocations in relation
to one's spiritual father. What Guerric is saying explicitly is
that one must first be a son before one can be a father.

Poverty of spirit, submission, compunction, a quest for
virtue—the basic exercises of the active life, as this term was
then understood and is used by Guerric in this passage—leads
to a zeal for justice, in the fullest sense of that word: God
and man, each receiving his full due. But it is a question of
virtue, which stands ever in the middle, and so must be
moderated. The crusader is not apt to be a father figure.
Mercy, compassion is essential, yet it comes as a modifier of
justice. A false mercy that does not make due demands or call
forth living in all justice lacks the virility of true spiritual
paternity. The 'diligent practice' of mercy and justice brings
one to that fullness of virtue which opens out into contemplation. For Guerric it is the latter that is the means to purity of

heart—the end of the monastic life according to St John Cassian—and the clear perception of God in prayer and in all and through all.

Having come to a certain fullness of christian being and life through virtue and contemplation, one has the capacity now to engender life in others. In this fathering he shows himself like the Father of all and thus reveals himself to be truly His son.

Guerric goes on to indicate something of the nature of this paternity. Immediately he links it with service: 'father and servant'; and the service can be summed up in one word, 'peacemaker'. First of all, peacemaker with God. The spiritual father is son, closely united and formed to the likeness of the Son, and he, like the Son, is to make peace between the Father and his sons. His first role is that of prayer; he is 'mediator and advocate'. Recently when I discussed the nature of spiritual paternity with one of the great spiritual fathers on Mount Athos, he asserted strongly that the first duty of the spiritual father was to stand before the Lord in the night interceding for his sons and daughters and to visit them mystically with Christ. The father is then to lead his sons to peace among themselves and with those outside the monastery—Guerric is here speaking most specifically in the context of the abbot–father—but it is impossible for sons to be at peace with each other and their fellowmen if they are not first at peace with God. Indeed, that tranquility of order which is true peace presupposes growth in all the virtues.

Guerric is ever realistic and speaks from years of experience. He knows that fathering a group of men at different levels of growth has its pain and sorrow. The father will suffer in his fathering so acutely that he endures a veritable martyrdom. In his quest to establish justice he will suffer from those he is serving in this quest. But like his Father St Benedict, he holds out to the spiritual father the encouragement of hope, the promise of the reward.

In this brief passage then we find the way to spiritual paternity, its essential expression, and its ultimate reward.

ACCORDING TO THE TEACHING AND
EXAMPLE OF BENEDICT

We might at this point look at Guerric's sermons for the Feast of St Benedict. The role Abbot Benedict fulfilled in regard to all monks, each particular abbot is to fulfill in regard to his own sons. Guerric speaks relatively little of St Benedict in the course of these four sermons; yet they are filled with very solid benedictine teaching. Great emphasis is laid on stability, persevereance in 'the school of christian philosophy', in the exercises of wisdom: divine office, private prayer, *lectio divina,* silence, and fear of the Lord.[13] There is practical teaching on such matters as meditation, distraction,[14] and dryness.[15] In addition, there is some very beautiful instruction on fraternal love and community life.[16] Guerric might well have been speaking of himself when he says of the monk: 'Blessed indeed is the tree whose leaves are for healing and whose fruit is for life, that is, whose words bring grace to the listener and whose actions bring life to himself performing them'.[17]

Of this rich teaching I want to highlight one element which I think too significant to pass over without special mention. It is one aspect of what Guerric has to say on fraternal love. If he is in fact talking about relations between the brothers, nonetheless it pertains *a fortiori* to the relation of the spiritual father to his sons. Guerric places his teaching in the fundamental context of the two great commandments enriched by the fullness of Christ's teaching.

> To be deserving of God's friendship: this is the supreme virtue, the best gift of grace, the choicest fruit of life because it is the surest pledge of happiness . . . . And if after and because of this, the sum total and cause of all grace, you should merit that further grace, so that, beloved of God, you become beloved of men as well, what a consolation that would be amid the miseries of this life, what peace, what joy, what delight.[18]

147

To be loved by the brothers is something to be merited, and not only is it to be merited but, with proper motivation, it is something one must strive for. 'That striving . . . is neglected at their peril . . . . For it is the power and nature of true love that even when it does not feel affection it nevertheless contrives to make itself loved in return.'[19] Some have a great facility for doing this: 'For the commending of his holy love some have their own special gift from God, who makes their faces bright with oil, floods them with a gentle and pleasing graciousness, makes their every word and action agreeable in the sight of all.'[20] Others are not so blessed. 'But the obligation is the same for everyone.'[21] The monk, right from the start, is to be concerned about winning this love and seeking to learn how to make use of it. Guerric expresses a 'sincere hope' that each of his monks will attain it. He concludes the consideration with this weighty paragraph:

> Taking thought for what is good not only in God's sight but also in men's, you must neglect neither a clear conscience through love of a good name nor the esteem of men through too much trust in a clear conscience. How can you possibly flatter yourself about this clear conscience unless you are without complaint among your brethren? Unless you show you are a brother among brothers in all your dealings with them? Do you think it is enough not to scandalize them? The fact is that you do scandalize if you do not edify, that is, if you do not glorify God everywhere according to your own proper role in the community, with your own conscience and your brethren bearing witness to your goodness.[22]

As I said, it seems to me this teaching can and should be applied in an eminent way to that monk who is called upon to fill the role of spiritual father among his brethren.

In these sermons Guerric also speaks of God's spiritual paternity, undoubtedly an example for the abbot: God 'brings forth when he generates good will; he plants when he brings

148

to life; he waters when he floods the mind with grace; he tills when he imposes discipline on conduct.'[23] One of the spiritual father's most fundamental tasks, and sometimes the most difficult, is to engender good will; only then can he hope to call his sons to new life. He may by his prayer obtain showers of grace for his sons, but without that good will he will never be able to impose any sort of life-giving discipline.

In the few paragraphs where he speaks directly of St Benedict, Guerric presents him as a leader and teacher who guides his monks with charity and discretion along the simple life-giving way of the Gospel. Benedict lived as he taught, a man of faith who knew both fear and hope, a man of meekness and gentleness who yet could burn with dire zeal,[24] a model for any abbot.

GUERRIC'S OWN EXAMPLE

Guerric's sermons give many glimpses of his own exercise of spiritual paternity. Many passages make it clear that he was the recipient of the confidence of his monks, that they opened their hearts to him and revealed the inner secret working of nature and grace.[25] He insists upon the importance of their doing this and receiving guidance: 'If you are wise you will not be your own teacher and guide in the way along which you have never walked, but you will incline your ear to masters and acquiesce in their reproofs and advice . . . ' . [26] He is well aware of their constant 'falling and rising'[27] and adapts his teaching to their frailty: 'I speak in human terms because of the infirmity of your flesh, or rather because of the narrowness of your mind'.[28] He encourages and promises.[29] He traces out in many varied ways the stages of spiritual growth.[30] He watches over his sons 'with the jealousy of God', and warns them against possible evils, ready to lament their failures with an abundance of tears.[31]

Guerric knew the tension between the active and contemplative lives,[32] the call to service of the brethren and the desire to sit quietly at the feet of the Lord. But he does not record this as a clause of personal stress in the way some of the Cistercian Fathers have.[33] Perhaps this is because he is less idealistic, more comfortable in dealing with everyday reality as it unfolds, perhaps because he is more humble, ready to identify and take hope with the brothers to whom he said:

> Therefore, my brothers, if you long for the high spring, your desire is certainly to be praised. But if you have not yet attained to that, to send out your roots meanwhile to the waters that are below is a wholesome medicine. Whoever then is not successful in capturing the joys of the contemplative life, let him consider the holiness of the active life. And so let him enlarge the roots of his good desires, make his conduct more agreeable and control every circumstance of his life . . . whose words bring grace to the listener and whose actions bring life to him performing them.[34]
> . . . If anyone feels a desire for that best part which is praised in Mary, he may know that this is the reward of the man who cannot be reproached for failing to do Martha's part; it is not right that reward should be sought before merit.[35]

Yet Guerric did not hold that one way is essentially superior to the other. The Christian's goal is union with Christ Jesus, to know him and experience his love and presence; and this is granted to the busy as well as to the contemplative: ' . . . Jesus deigns to meet and manifest himself not only to those who devote themselves to contemplation but also to those who quietly and devoutly walk the ways of action.[36] . . . . Others may fly by contemplation; you at least do so by love.'[37]

It is however true, as we have seen in the text from the All Saints' Day sermon, that Guerric sees the service of the spiritual father as a fruit of contemplation, an overflowing from its fullness. In this he is in accord with the teaching he received at Clairvaux in Bernard's first sermons on the Song of Songs.[38] And in this service he found a model in Mary, the Mother of the Word Incarnate.

> She showed herself to be a Martha in her care for the
> Child's rearing in such a way that nonetheless she fulfilled
> the part of Mary in her application to knowledge of
> the Word.[39]

For Guerric Mary is the new Eve, the type of the Church,
the truest of spiritual mothers. And it is in the consideration
of his teaching on the spiritual mother that we will find those
feminine complements which bring Guerric's understanding
of the role of spiritual paternity to its fullness.

MOTHERING THE CHRIST

In the opening paragraph of this paper we quoted a significant passage from Guerric's third Christmas sermon. The
abbot is to 'show himself a mother by love and anxious care',
to have 'maternal solicitude and devotion'.[40] As he goes on
to apply the same text to his disciples, he charges them:
'Keep watch then, holy mother, keep watch in your care for
the new born child until Christ is formed in you . . . '.[41] If
this is true of the monk, *a fortiori* is the abbot to keep a
watchful care of the formation of Christ in his sons.

In his first sermon for the feast of the Assumption Guerric
speaks most fully of Mary's spiritual maternity:

> Then the blessed Mother of Christ, knowing that she is the
> mother of all Christians by reason of this mystery [being
> the New Eve, Type of the Church, Mother of Life], shows
> herself a mother by her care and loving attention. For her
> heart is not hardened against these children as if they were
> not her own; her womb . . . remains ever fruitful, never
> ceasing to bring forth the fruits of her motherly compassion
> . . . pregnant with inexhaustible tenderness.
> He was born of you once and for all, yet he remains in you
> always, making you ever fruitful. Within the locked garden
> of your chastity he makes the sealed well-spring of charity

151

always abundant.

... If the Servant of Christ by his care and heartfelt tenderness bears his little children again and again until Christ be
formed in them, how much more is this true of the very
Mother of Christ? Paul begot his children by preaching the
word of truth through which they were born again, but
Mary in a manner far more holy and like to God ... so that
first and foremost in all their needs and dangers they run
to call upon her .... [42]

Here we see in Mary, the model, many of the qualities to
be cultivated in the spiritual father: care, loving attention,
softheartedness, fidelity, compassion, inexhaustible heartfelt
tenderness, abundant charity, evangelical teaching, a fruitfulness that comes from Christ's abiding presence. He is to be
such a person that his sons instinctively turn to him in their
needs.

Anyone familiar with Guerric will not be surprised to find
St Paul coming to his mind here; indeed, it is almost to be expected. Guerric's love and admiration for Paul was all but
boundless. [43] But by evoking the Apostle here he not only
introduces another quality of the spiritual father, but also
shows the scriptural basis for attributing maternal qualities
to the pastoral office. As Guerric goes on in the sermon to
extol Mary's virtues, her chastity, humility, faithfulness,
charity, prudence, and poverty, he clearly implies Christ
must find these same in the one he will make a fruitful spiritual father.

Guerric speaks again of Mary's spiritual motherhood in the
second sermon for her birthday, indicating the source and
goal of her sons' maturity and the mother's role of desire and
loyal care:

For she desires to form her Only-begotten in all her sons
by adoption. Although they have been brought to birth
by the word of truth, nevertheless she brings them forth
every day by desire and loyal care until they reach the

stature of the perfect man, the maturity of her Son . . . . [44]

The Church, too, is a spiritual mother, and in Guerric's consideration of this reality, we find yet another, closer, type of the spiritual father, for it is actually through spiritual fathers and mothers that the Church fulfills her maternal duty. In his third sermon for the Annunciation Guerric touches on some of the more painful duties that every spiritual father must sooner or later face:

> The Church is pregnant, brethren, not as Mary was, with Jesus alone, but as Rebecca was with Jacob and Esau,[45] that is, not only with those who are good and well-behaved but also with those who are ill-tempered and undisciplined. However, these too, for the sake of Jesus, or perhaps because they possess the principle by which they are grounded in him, the womb of the Church receives and enfolds. But when the two infants struggled and fought in Rebecca's womb she, who previously had prayed to conceive, was grieved that her womb ached with pain, trouble and sorrow. She was almost sorry that she had conceived. 'If it was to be thus with me,' she said, 'why should I have conceived?' If it should happen, brethren, that the bowels of our mother should complain thus of any one of us, I am afraid that it would have been better if that man had not been conceived, except that even for such we are not allowed to despair. He who even from stones raises up sons to Abraham will not allow it. If there be any such, may he soften the stony heart in them so that their mother's womb will not ache, and may he comfort their mother's womb so that she will not grow weary carrying them, however ill-behaved they may be, until Christ is formed in them . . . .[46]

In spite of the rich biblical imagery, the passage is all too transparent to allow us to miss the open-hearted sharing of the spiritual father. Even the Golden Age knew the 'ill-tempered and undisciplined', and the abbot who had eagerly

153

welcomed them to the cloister as an answer to his prayer for
fruitfulness is now tempted to wish they had never been
admitted. Yet love of Christ and faith in Him demands another response, hope and not despair. The unruly have in
them the principle of Christ's life and it will in time come
to full life in them. In the meantime the spiritual father needs
strengthening lest weariness lead him to fail to carry out his
pastoral duties.

CONCLUSION

It would be impossible to summarize in an adequate way
this very rich teaching which, in fact, has already been
presented in very summary fashion. It can only be digested in
the patristic fashion of circling about it and bit by bit entering
into each of its facets till it becomes a living synthesis within
the receiver. It is more than obvious, especially from the way
in which Guerric, following St Paul and the Gospels themselves, has integrated the feminine and masculine, that this
teaching is equally a teaching on spiritual maternity—the
office of spiritual generation and education depends in no
wise on sex but on fullness of life. Also, as we have already
mentioned, although Guerric, as an abbot, couching his
teaching in the literary genre of sermons to his monks, expressed his teaching in a monastic frame, it is equally applicable to those who find themselves called to this ministry of
spiritual paternity in other contexts, institutional or not.
While an ecclesial office, such as that of an abbot, superior, or
pastor, might call for one who has this kind of spiritual fullness, the bearers of such life-giving spirit cannot be limited
to office holders. Guerric makes clear in his central teaching
on the Beatitudes that growing to such fullness and entering
upon the service of spiritual paternity has its place in the
normal development of the christian life. Indeed, the problem
that often confronts institutional monasticism is how to make
it possible for the monk or nun who is not called to the abbatial office to exercise such paternity when they arrive at
spiritual maturity. Certainly all should strive after such

fullness, and when it is attained its energies should not be dissipated but employed as fully as possible for the growth of the whole Christ. These considerations could lead to another paper, so let us leave them for now and seek rather simply to absorb as completely as we can the full richness of the teaching of Guerric of Igny on the spiritual father.

NOTES

1. *Exordium Magnum Cisterciense sive narratio de initia Cister-ciensis Ordinis* (ed. Bruno Griesser; Rome: Editiones Cistercienses, 1961) Dist. III, c. 9, p. 166.
2. Guerric d'Igny, *Sermons* (edd. J. Morson and H. Costello; SCh 166, 202; Paris: Cerf, 2 vols., 1970, 1973) I, 22, 69-77.
3. 3 Christmas 4-5. Where no author is indicated the citation refers to the Sermons of Guerric. The English translations used in this paper are taken from Guerric of Igny, *Liturgical Sermons* (trans. Monks of Mount Saint Bernard Abbey; CF 8, 32; Spencer, Massachusetts: Cistercian Publications. 1970-1971).
4. *Ibid.*
5. 3 Peter and Paul 1.
6. For example, Epistles 201:1, 233:3, 258, etc.
7. Rogation 1-2.
8. For example, CF 8:XVII; D. de Wilde, *De Beautu Guerrico abbate Igniacensi eiusque doctrina de formatione Christi in nobis* (Westmalle: Typei Abbatiae, 1935) pp. 16-17.
9. R. Milcamps, 'Le Bienheureix Guerric. Sa vie—son oeuvre' in *Coll.* 19 (1957) 209, n. 1.
10. See M. Basil Pennington, 'A Cistercian Way to Holiness,' CSt 6 (1971) 269-81.
11. All Saints 2.
12. Jn 15:19.
13. 1 St Benedict.
14. *Ibid.,* n. 6.
15. 2 St Benedict 5f.
16. 3 St Benedict 3ff.
17. 2 St Benedict 5.
18. 3 St Benedict 2f.
19. *Ibid.,* 5.
20. *Ibid.*
21. *Ibid.*

22. *Ibid.*
23. 2 St Benedict 7.
24. 4 St Benedict. There are two places in his sermons where Guerric speaks with unaccustomed zeal that approaches harshness—and even apologizes for it; these are the places where he denounces detraction: 1 Pentecost, 5; 3 John Baptist 5.
25. For example, 3 Annunciation 5: 'You have shared your experience with me and told me . . . ' ; 1 Epiphany 4; 2 Purification 7; 5 Purification 5; 1 St. Benedict 5; 1 Annunciation 5; 3 Easter 4; 3 Peter and Paul, 1, 2, 6.
26. 4 Advent 4.
27. *Ibid.,* n. 5.
28. 3 Advent 4.
29. For example, 4 Advent 1, 3; 5 Advent 1; etc.
30. For example, 1 Epiphany 5-7; 2 Epiphany 5; 3 Epiphany 4; 5 Purification 6; 3 Easter 5; 4 John Baptist 3; 1 Nativity B.V.M. 4; 2 Nativity B.V.M. 4; All Saints 1.
31. 3 St Benedict 6.
32. 1 Advent 3; 2 Peter and Paul 3; 4 Assumption 3.
33. For example, Bernard of Clairvaux, *Sermons on the Song of Songs* 12:9, 30:7, 52:5f, 53:1ff.; William of Saint Thierry, *On Contemplating God* 1, 12; *Meditations* 11:8f; *The Nature and Dignity of Love* 8; *Exposition on the Song of Songs* 52.
34. 2 St Benedict 6.
35. 4 Assumption 4.
36. 3 Easter 4.
37. Ascension 5.
38. Bernard of Clairvaux, *Sermons on the Song of Songs* 12. See my article 'Three Stages of Spiritual Growth according to St. Bernard,' *Studia Monastica* 11 (1969) 315-26.
39. 4 Assumption 3.
40. 3 Christmas 5.
41. *Ibid.*
42. 1 Assumption 2-4.
43. See, for example, 2 Easter 3; 2 Pentecost 1; 2 John Baptist 1; 1 Peter and Paul; 1 Assumption 3; 2 Nativity B.V.M. 1; On Psalmody 4.
44. 2 Nativity B.V.M. 3.
45. See Gen 25:24ff.
46. 3 Annunciation 7.

THE ABBOT AS SPIRITUAL FATHER IN THE WRITINGS AND PASTORAL PRACTICE OF RANCÉ

Chrysogonus Waddell, OCSO
Abbey of Gethsemani

T IS BEST TO BE CLEAR about it from the start: the title of this contribution to our symposium on the 'Spiritual Father' contains something of an equivocation. 'Spiritual father' the reformer of la Trappe certainly was, and his life and writings have much to tell us about the abbot as spiritual father. But 'father' is by no means a term which spontaneously comes to his lips or flows from his pen when the Abbot of la Trappe discourses on the duties of the abbot. He does, of course, speak from time to time of the superior as 'father'—but generally only in passing, without pausing to dwell on the implication of the term. When he writes of his own relationship with his monks, he almost invariably styles them as his 'brothers' and hardly ever himself as their 'father'. 'Mes frères', he writes; or even, in his earliest years at la Trappe, 'mes confrères', 'Mes fils'? Never.

It would go beyond the evidence at hand to speak of any really conscious disaffection on the part of Rancé with the idea of spiritual fatherhood. But the fact of the matter is that the occasional texts in which the Reformer does touch on the abbot as father only serve to emphasize the fact that such texts are, indeed, occasional and atypical.

How would the psycho-historian interpret Rancé's tendency to eschew the vocabulary of paternity? He would doubtless begin by looking straightaway to Rancé's boyhood relations with his father. If he hopes to find anything morbid

158

or troubled in this relationship between father and son, he will be out of luck. He will be equally out of luck if he tries to ferret out evidence that father fell short of son's idealized image of father: Sieur Denis Bouthillier de Rancé's career had mostly 'ups', and the occasional dramatic 'downs' were of such a nature as to enhance the father-as-hero image. True, there was a bastard son, but he was born probably after 1647, years after the death of Madame de Rancé (1638), when the future Abbot of la Trappe was already in his early twenties, and moving in circles of a smart society not particularly remarkable for scrupulosity in such matters. A bastard half-brother? *Honi soit qui mal y pense.*

But let us not make the mistake of thinking that the associations conjured up by the term 'father' were the same for Rancé as for us nowadays. A Saint Thérèse of Lisieux was able to arrive at a virtually connatural understanding of what it means to call God 'Father' on the basis of her warm and deeply affectionate relationship with her beloved Papa. It is doubtful, however, that young Armand-Jean ever called his father 'Papa'. His early letters always refer to him as *Monsieur mon père,* or *Monsieur de Rancé, mon père,* or even simply *Monsieur de Rancé,* in keeping with the formal etiquette of the period. In brief, the structure of the family-system into which the child was born on 9 January 1626, did much to color Rancé's idea of 'father'.

The Bouthilliers formed not only a clan, but something of a business corporation. Sprung originally from lawyer stock, the several branches had been quick to rise into the ranks of the lower aristocracy and into the higher echelons of power. The Bouthillier children were not just children; they were business assets. And young Armand-Jean—who was named for his sponsor at baptism, Armand-Jean Cardinal de Richelieu himself—was a case in point. An older brother, Denis–Francois, had been destined for an ecclesiastical career similar to that of his two uncle-bishops, Sébastien and Victor. Denis-Francois fell gravely ill in 1635. This was serious, really serious; for the death of the youngster would mean the loss of some ten to twelve thousand *livres* raked in annually from the ecclesiastical preferments of the moribund boy. In such circumstances, it became clear that the next oldest boy, Armand-Jean, had a vocation. Groomed as the logical replacement for his mortally ill older brother, the nine-year old received the tonsure at the hands of the archbishop of Paris. Denis–Francois died on Wednesday, 6 September 1637. Because he had been a boy-canon of the Cathedral Chapter of Notre-Dame, it was the Cathedral Chapter that buried him two days later, on Friday, 18 September. The very next day, 19 September, Monsieur de Rancé and selected members of the family escorted the eleven-year old Armand-Jean to the sacristy of the cathedral, where the prebend of the deceased Denis-Francois was officially transferred to his younger brother. By the time the young canon had reached the hoary old age of twelve, he had become commendatory abbot or prior of five different religious communities. As for his education, Monsieur de Rancé saw to it that it was the best possible. Formal schooling under the direction of three tutors began when the boy was only five, and both Latin and Greek were included in the curriculum. From time to time the father took his heir apparent to court, where the Queen Mother, Marie de Médicis, liked to cuddle and coo over the precocious youngster; but at home there was probably precious little cuddling and cooing to be had from the head of the Bouthilliers de Rancé. Warmth and affection there certainly was. But when young Armand-Jean referred to *Monsieur mon père,* he was referring to a figure of immense authority, whose principal role was the pursuit of family prestige and *gloire,* and whose paternal prerogatives were exercised by manipulating the lives and destinies of his children in the interests of family power. Less remote were the family tutors upon whom the boy depended more directly for affection, understanding, and initiation into the heady world of learning. Much as the young Armand-Jean loved and admired and respected *Monsieur son père,* then, the father-image conjured up by the elder Rancé was probably not so easily transferable to the future abbot's ideal superior and spiritual director. Thus far for the psycho-historian.

Given Rancé's passion for the Holy Rule as one of the essential points of reference for his programme of monastic life, it would seem surprising that he paid so little heed to St Benedict's terminology of abbot-as-father. In point of fact, however, though various grammatical forms of the word *pater* are to be found in the Holy Rule, surprisingly few of these refer to the abbot. The abbot is to show 'the loving affection of a father' (c. 2, 24: *pium patris ostendat affectum*); the monk is to 'look to the father of the monastery for all necessities' (c. 33, 5: *omnia vero necessaria a patre monasterii sperare*), and to perform no supererogatory work during Lent without the permission of 'the spiritual father' (c. 49, 9: *sine permissione patris spiritualis*).

There are two objections which could and should be made at this point. The minuscule listing of abbot-father texts omits the key-text from Chapter 2, 'What Kind of Man the Abbot Ought to Be':

> For he [the abbot] is believed to hold the place of Christ in the monastery, being called by a name of His, which is taken from the words of the Apostle: 'You have received a Spirit of adoption as sons, by virtue of which we cry, "Abba-Father!" ' (RB 2, 2-3)

Disconcerting as it may be to the contemporary Scripture exegete, St Benedict is here clearly saying that 'Abba-Father' is a title of Christ. And since the superior 'is believed to hold the place of Christ in the monastery', it follows that the superior, too, is necessarily an 'abba-father'. Further, Dom Adalbert de Vogüé in a detailed study, argues convincingly that the idea of Christ as father was familiar to an earlier generation of monks.[1] Agreed. But one of the clear emergents of Dom Adalbert's illuminating article is the fact that the once familiar Christ-as-father image is an idea that has been abandoned for long, long centuries. If Rancé failed to grasp the implications of the text in question, so did practically everyone else in the centuries between St Benedict and Dom Adalbert.

A second objection would be this: though it is true St Benedict rarely calls his superior *pater,* the term he most uses, *abbas,* means—as everyone knows—'father'. Therefore, in consulting a concordance of the Holy Rule for abbot-father texts, one should include not only forms of the word *pater,* but also *abbas* and its derivations. The point is well taken. If we put ourselves back into the seventeenth century, we shall realize that the word 'abbot' (*abbé, abbas*) was a term that had become virtually 'used up'. The vast majority of ecclesiastics in the non-monastic world were styled *abbé,* and were addressed accordingly: *Monsieur l'Abbé.* Rancé himself had been signing his name 'Abbé Bouthillier de Rancé' while still in his preteens, and his first extant autographed letter—written in Greek, no less, and dated 10 January 1641—is signed *Armandos abbas.* [2] *Abbé-abbas,* then, had lost much of its original impact so far as the vocabulary of spiritual paternity was concerned.

Nevertheless, in spite of his virtual eschewal of the vocabulary of spiritual fatherhood, Rancé himself was a spiritual father, and a very great one; and he rightly deserves a place in any discussion of the spiritual father in the cistercian tradition.

THE SPIRITUAL FATHER: GENERAL BACKGROUND

A.   The Spiritual FATHER

Four summary statements:

1. Any consideration of spiritual fatherhood should begin with the embarrassing fact that Jesus is quite formal on the matter: 'Call no man your father on earth, for you have one Father, who is in heaven' (Mt 23:9). What Jesus is here telling us is not so much that we really cannot call our fathers 'father', but rather that God is Father in so absolute a sense that even one's human father can claim the title of fatherhood only in a relative, derived sense.

2. Still, St Paul *did* call himself 'father'. Writing to the Corinthian community, he tells them: 'Though you have

countless guides in Christ, you do not have many fathers. For I became your *father* in Christ Jesus through the gospel' (1 Cor 4:15). Paul is 'father', then, since he has raised up new life in Christ: by the seed of the gospel he has begotten children in Christ Jesus. Communication of the word *is* new life in Christ.

3. At an early date bishops were styled 'Father', but usually with the qualification—whether explicit or implicit— 'my Father *after God*'. The bishop (and his delegate) was one who, through his preaching of the word and administration of the sacraments, communicated new life in Christ. As in the case of St Paul, fatherhood here meant raising children unto God in Christ.

4. By further extension and evolution, in the desert the name *abba* (father) was given to certain monks who had received so great a fullness of the monastic grace that through their word (word of doctrine, or even un-verbalized word of mere example) they formed disciples, communicated the Spirit, and thereby raised up new life in Christ.

In summary, the spiritual father is one who, through his charism of the word, can impart to others a certain fullness of life in Christ.

B.   The SPIRITUAL Father or Father in the SPIRIT

Biblical images of the Spirit: fire, living water, rushing wind, 'something' like a dove—all these images express a nature that is diaphanous, transparent, in full movement, intangible. At the same time, wherever the Spirit of God is at work, his activity is ordered to an effect in the order of the concrete, visible, tangible. The Spirit broods over the primæval waters, chaos is reduced to order and made fruitful (creation); the Holy Spirit overshadows the Virgin Mary, and the Word becomes flesh (incarnation); the same Holy Spirit overshadows the apostles at prayer, and the infant Church comes to the full term of its birth (Pentecost); the Holy Spirit is called down upon the elements of bread and wine, and they become the Body and Blood of Christ (sacraments); the Holy Spirit comes

163

upon the assembly of worshipping believers, and they become more truly members of Christ and of the Mystical Body of the Head (Church).

In brief, the action of the Spirit is directed towards a christological reality which assumes some concrete, tangible, visible form. Spirit achieves and perfects incarnation.

To exercise the charism of spiritual paternity, then, means to act in function of the order of the Incarnation. Far from resulting in the vaporization of the visible and material, the action of the Spirit has just the opposite effect: institutions are perfected and transformed from within; through the medium of what is concrete and visible, Christ is present with greater freedom of action; and those individuals who come more directly under the influence of an authentic spiritual father are drawn more deeply into the Mystery of Christ, so as to become themselves visible and incontrovertible witnesses to the reality of the life, death, and glorification of the Lord Jesus.

Where the Spirit is, there is poetry, art, and song. Further, the functionality and inner excellence of early cistercian architecture, of the organs of administration of the White Monks, of their monastic ritual, of their legislative deliberations, of their agricultural exploitations, are in their own way signs of the presence and action of the Spirit. This is why the most vital and authentic spiritual movements almost inevitably result in the reform and revitalization of institutional structures. This was certainly true of the cistercian reform which began in 1098; and it is just as certainly true of the remarkable reform which began at the monastery of la Trappe in 1662.

THE FATHER ABBOT *MALGRÉ LUI*

The story of Rancé's decision to embrace monastic life at la Trappe is a long one marked by a few really dramatic incidents and consisting chiefly of the gradual elimination of viable alternatives.

The main stages of Rancé's spiritual itinerary can be

discerned in two unpublished letters written to Nicolas Pavillon, bishop of one of the poorest of the dioceses of France—Alet, lost in the mountains of the Pyrenees. Pavillon was something of an episcopal St Vincent de Paul and Mother Teresa of Calcutta rolled into one. The month which Rancé spent with him in August of 1660 proved decisive—even though what Pavillon envisaged for Rancé (an episcopal career in the service of the flock of Christ) worked out rather differently than he expected.

On 28 September 1661, Rancé, who had been living in retirement at his family château near Tours for the past several years, sent the Bishop a progress-report of his efforts to dispose of all but one of the benefices he held *in commendam,* and to sell his estate and patrimony for the benefit of the poor. Where all this is to lead him, he did not yet clearly see.

> I hope . . . that after I have got all my affairs in order, God will grant me the grace of bringing me to you for yet a second visit, to receive instructions from you to serve me for guidance and consolation all the rest of my life.[3]

We move ahead almost two years, to 30 May 1663. This is the day Rancé set off for the abbey of Perseigne, there to begin his novitiate as a cistercian monk of the Strict Observance. This unpublished letter is one of the noblest pages in the whole spiritual literature of the seventeenth century, and I am sorry that I can quote only a few lines, adding explanatory notes. Rancé begins by telling Pavillon that he has carried out the main things counselled by the Bishop. He goes on to say:

> I considered myself duty-bound to introduce the Reform of St Bernard [Strict Observance] into the abbey I had retained [*in commendam*], with a view to removing from it the disorder which had been entrenched there for a long, long time.[4]

A masterpiece of understatement. The earliest mention of la Trappe I have so far found in Rancé's correspondence is in an unedited letter addressed to the Chancellor, Pierre Séguier, in 1649.[5] Our twenty-three year old commendatory abbot calls the attention of the Chancellor to the clandestine return of one of the monks of la Trape (sic!) who had been perforce lying low these past several years, after shooting down one of the local peasants in cold blood. This incident serves well to set the tone of the abbey, for this malefactor was by no means the only miscreant in the community at la Trappe.

As for the buildings, the account by Dom Dominique Georges is instructive. As Vicar General of the Strict Observance, Dom Dominique had visited la Trappe, and in 1686 he presented a detailed report of his visitation to the Fathers of the General Chapter held at Cîteaux.[6] He contrasts the flourishing state of the buildings with what Rancé found when he first arrived at la Trappe. Monastic enclosure had long been a dead letter, and seculars of both sexes had free and easy access to the cloister—or at least to what was left of the cloister. What had once been parlors now served as stables, and to get to the second floor (not to be counselled, since the floors had rotted through) one had to use a ladder. Monks and seculars used the refectory in a creative way; it served admirably for bowling when the summer heat and inclement weather rendered the game incommodious outside. As for meals, the monks fended for themselves. And since the dormitory was uninhabitable, each had his own personal provisions for lodging. The archives were in a state of chaos, and, since many important documents had perished, the legal title to monastery lands and property was in danger of being lost. The church, too, was in shambles, and the bell-tower on the verge of collapse. And everywhere, muck and filth and filth and more filth. As for the community, it officially numbered six monks and a laybrother—or was it only five monks? Hard to say, since the prior had had to take French leave to escape a sentence of hanging.

And who had been responsible for all this? Rancé, the

commendatory abbot who for years had collected the revenues through his agent, but who had failed to provide for the welfare of the community for which he was responsible before God. His duty was now clear. Rancé announced to his motley crew of pseudo-monks his intention of entrusting the abbey to the Strict Observance. The response was less than enthusiastic. Rumors soon began circulating around the countryside. After all, it was not as though the unreasonable Rancé would be the first abbot ever to be assassinated by his community.

Perhaps the best picture of community morale at this juncture is given by Monsieur de Saint-Louis, a distinguished cavalry officer who had just returned on furlough to his estate some ten or twelve miles distant from the disreputable abbey. Writing years later in his Memoirs, Monsieur de Saint-Louis tells us:

> I had hardly arrived when I learned, through a friend who had come to see me, of the danger to which the Abbot la Trappe was exposed. He had just to say the word 'Reform' for the six or seven wretched monks who were staying there at his abbey to rise up in revolt. They were thinking of nothing short of running him through with a dagger, or of doing away with him by poison. They were so blinded that they did not even try to keep their detestable plot a secret, and they had absolutely no regard for possible consequences. These criminals—two of whom had been under court sentence for their crimes—were known throughout the province as persons capable of anything, and it was impossible not to feel sorry for Monsieur l'Abbé de la Trappe. Still, no one did anything about it, for fear of what these mad men might do in retaliation.
>
> I no sooner learned of the dangerous situation in which this illustrious abbot was, than I felt interiorly urged to go there and offer him my services . . . . He was surprised at such an offer coming from a gentleman who was a perfect

167

stranger; but he received my compliments and the offer of
my services with every possible expression of gratitude,
and he answered my proposal with such wisdom and com-
posure that I was really quite edified. He told me, among
other things, that the affairs of God have to be handled
differently from those of the world, and that, in enjoining
these bad monks to do good, he had to try to make them
love the good. During the course of our entire conversation I remarked in him an uncommon nobility of spirit and
courtesy, and I was especially struck by that tranquility of
soul which seemed to make him despise the danger that
threatened. And I simply could not understand the consideration he had for people so little worthy of it.

It is true that I was then short-sighted in my understanding,
and that I failed to reflect on the fact that, when it pleases
God for us to undertake something for his glory, charity
and only charity should be our motive. And this was the
way in which the Abbot of la Trappe wished to lead back
those rebel spirits.[7]

The charitable but firm attitude of this puzzling commendatory abbot eventually won over the recalcitrant monks—at
least to the point where they were willing to sign an agreement entrusting the unlikely abbey to the Strict Observance.
The contract was signed on 17 August 1662. As for the individual monks, all coercion was avoided. Those wishing to transfer to another abbey of the Common Observance were not
only free to do so, but would receive an annual provision of
four-hundred *livres.* Three of the monks opted to remain at
la Trappe, but of these only one actually joined the Reform.
The other two remained at the abbey for a while, before
eventually moving elsewhere on the monastery property,
where their needs were amply provided for by the Abbot.[8]
Meanwhile our commendatory abbot had asked and received
the assistance of the superior of the near-by Abbey of Perseigne (one of the houses designated as a novitiate-house of

the Strict Observance). A colony of six monks arrived in time for conventual life, so long interrupted, to begin once more on the Feast of Saint Bernard, 20 August 1662.

Rather much is left unstated then in Rancé's restrained, 'I considered myself duty-bound to introduce the Reform of St Bernard into the abbey which I had retained, with a view to removing from it the disorder which had been entrenched there for a long, long time'.

Important pastoral note! There can be no significant reform or renewal of community unless there is present as an essential condition a group of sincerely committed like-minded and fully aware individuals. 'My son,' says Ramandu to Prince Caspian, in C. S. Lewis' *The Voyage of the Dawn Treader,* 'it would be no use, even though you wished it, to sail for the World's End with men unwilling or men deceived. That is not how great unenchantments are achieved. They must know where they go and why.'[9] Even at this early date, when Rancé was still only commendatory abbot of la Trappe, he understood that a community of monks, if they are to live at real depth, must know where they are going, and why. Those monks who had been 'monks unwilling or monks deceived' had been charitably provided for. There was now a nucleus of a community capable eventually of sailing for the World's End, capable of entering with full awareness and deep joy into the paschal journey, into the Great Voyage that leads from this world to the Father.

In our own contemporary situation, there is, of course, an understandable bias in favor of 'pluralism'; and often the implicit assumption is that any real community should not only respect, but love and encourage those differences which mark off one member from another. But when these 'differences' concern matters of fundamental orientation and basic options, the result can become problematic. There are, after all, many different kinds of community, and not all communities are formed for the same purpose. One of the chief functions of any authentic spiritual father within a monastic community is to discern spirits with a view to realizing the potential of the unique individual in such a way that fidelity to his particular vocation makes for the strength and harmony of the community, while at the same time the community brings out what is best and most characteristic in each individual member.

At any rate, it might well be objected that if Rancé had really understood what community life is about, he would have managed to keep together under one roof not only the recruits from Perseigne, but the monks for whom provisions were made either in other monasteries of their own choice, or on the property of la Trappe. Personally, my own feeling is that Rancé showed great respect for the individuals by pro- viding them with the environment most suited to their con- crete situation. There is a limit as to how many 'men unwill- ing or men deceived' can be contained within even the most fervent community, without turning that community into a sociological hell.

As for the community of la Trappe under its illustrious reformer, it was considerably less monolithic the closer one looked. The Vicar General of the Strict Observance, Dom Hervé du Tertre, abbot of Notre-Dame de Prières, who made the regular visitation at la Trappe in 1676 and 1678, was struck at the diversity of personalities. In his first visitation card[10] he notes that the forty-six members of the community all come from different provinces, and that, of these, some had been 'students from various colleges, others cavalry men, others soldiers, others clerics, still others priests of the diocesan clergy or of religious congregations; there were doctors of theology, religious of various Orders, such as Canons Regular, Hermits of Saint Augustine, Benedictines—even from the Maurist Congregation—Celestines, Franciscans, religious from the Congregation of Val des Choux, and even Cistercians from both Observances, the Common and the Strict, as well as monks from divers conditions and professions, and of every different age-group.'

Nevertheless, and despite this great diversity, difference,

170

and disparity, we found them so closely united by the bond of charity, so much at one in everything, so devoted, one and all, to their duties, and so universally zealous for regular observance, and enjoying together so profound a peace, that during the three entire days spent in carrying out the regular scrutinies, we received no complaint: neither the superiors against the inferiors, nor the inferiors against the superiors, nor the inferiors against each other. Not only did we not perceive or note any discontent, murmuring, division, dissension, alienation, partiality, aversion, or mutual dislike, there was not even the slightest appearance or even the mere shadow of any of these things . . . . [11]

Uniform the observance was, and yet the spiritual itinerary of the individual monks passed through geographically diverse regions. Monsieur de Saint-Louis, whom we have already met, was particularly struck by Rancé's genius for discerning the particular graces of individual vocations.

I remember seeing one day three persons of outstanding virtue. 'Look,' [the holy Abbot] said to me, 'there are three gentlemen, each going to God by a quite different route.' This he knew, because they came to him for spiritual direction. But seeing that I was surprised at what he had said, he added: 'That should not surprise you, Monsieur. Eternal Wisdom leads men by an infinitely diverse number of ways, none of which resembles the others. You would have a hard time finding four [monks] in this community who are being sanctified in the same way: for the science of a director consists particularly in examining with a great deal of application the temperament, the inclinations, and the degree of grace of each individual, so as to conform to it as much as possible. Without this, [the spiritual director's] ministry will be useless for the souls who are in his hands.'[12]

Nor should we be too quick to assume that, so often as an

individual failed to find peace at la Trappe, Rancé's attitude
was anything less than respectful of the individual's particular
grace. There is, for instance, a very moving letter dated
27 August 1673, and written to one of his own monks who
had made profession only to find, with the passing of time,
that the life at la Trappe was simply too tough for him. Without the slightest indication of recrimination, Rancé shares
the fellow's pain and heart-break. He writes:

> I have asked R. P. Abbé N. to provide you with a place
> where you can render to God in peace and in repose what
> you have promised him . . . . I feel more pain over our se-
> paration than I can express, and I have never experienced
> anything so hard and difficult to bear. But one must acquiesce
> to the way God leads us . . . . I beg you to believe that, wher-
> ever God's Providence places you, you will be as present to
> me as you have always been, and that your salvation will
> be just as dear as always, and that nothing can break the
> bonds of charity by which God has wanted us to be united.
> I shall be praying for you incessantly as for the rest of our
> brethren, and you will always be among their number in
> my heart. I conjure you, too, to keep in your own heart
> the place that I ought to have there, and not to think that
> you are dispensed from praying the Lord for me simply
> because you are no longer under my direction . . . . [13]

But to return to the crucial period of first beginnings, when
Rancé was as yet only commendatory abbot of la Trappe,
I feel that already he showed the prudence characteristic of a
spiritual father in the cistercian tradition: great understanding,
respect, and love for the individual in his concrete spiritual
situation—but always within the context of the community.
If the Mystical Body is for the individual member, the individual member is also for the sake of the Mystical Body; and if
the community is for the individual monk, the individual monk
is likewise for the sake of the community.

Back to Rancé's letter of 30 May 1662, to Bishop Pavillon:

> I lived there [at la Trappe] to try to consolidate the good
> which was not as yet too solidly established; and I thought
> that if I lived with the religious of the Reform, and like
> them practised abstinence from meat, this might serve a
> good purpose by way of providing an example of some
> sort to the non-Reform religious; and that, even though
> they might not accept the same way of life, they might
> at least begin conducting themselves in a more orderly,
> more religious manner. After having lived in this way for
> several months, the thought came to me of embracing
> the regular life. This experience did not last any length of
> time; but it was not long before I felt it again, stronger
> than before. It stayed with me for more than two months,
> though I said nothing about it to anyone . . . . [14]

Pastoral note! Rancé's vocation as spiritual father begins
crystallizing within the matrix of this still fragile, nascent community. There is to be a mutual interaction which will only
intensify as abbot and community together grow: the spiritual father, thanks to the community; the community, thanks
largely to the spiritual father. There is a curious parallel to
this phenomenon to be noted in the non-christian Far East,
though in a (for us) exaggerated form. Lama Anagarika
Govinda writes:

> Religious leaders depend as much on the faith of their
> adherents as their adherents depend on the initial inspira-
> tion which they receive from their leaders. Once this
> mutual process has started, it grows like an avalanche . . . .
> It is for this reason that we should not expect religious
> leaders taken out of their surroundings and their spiritual
> and traditional background—like many of the high Lamas
> who fled from Tibet and are compelled to live in com-
> pletely uncongenial surroundings, in a kind of spiritual
> vacuum—to display the same super-individual forces which

173

centered upon them before they were deprived of their natural conditions of life and of the contact of those who had faith in them.[15]

My point here is that, even at this early date, when Rancé is still an 'outsider', the 'mutual process' described by Lama Govinda had begun, and it was the community through which Rancé received both his monastic vocation and his personal charism as spiritual father. Too seldom we think of the spiritual father as the one who gives, the spiritual son as the one who receives. But the dynamic in this relationship is often considerably more complex, more rich: for the father receives through his giving, and the son gives birth to the father.
To continue with Rancé's letter:

> This plan [*dessein*] seemed at first fraught with difficulties and with things contrary to my temperament and to all my natural inclinations; but all this simply vanished, and I experienced an ardent longing to go ahead with the idea.[16]

Our father-in-the-birthing refers to 'this plan'. We assume he means the idea of becoming regular abbot of la Trappe. But the antecedent is rather different: ' . . . the thought came to me of embracing the regular life'. With his wonted penchant for simplifying otherwise complicated issues, Rancé here omits mention of the fact that his personal preference had been to join the community as a simple monk. His decision to become regular abbot crystallized only after a later consultation at Paris, in April 1663, with Msgr de Choiseul-Praslin, bishop of Comminges. This prelate had been instrumental at an earlier date in Rancé's conversion from a life of mild dissipation and ecclesiastical dry-rot. The point the bishop now made was this: with Rancé just a simple monk, the next commendatory abbot might be as bad as Rancé himself before conversion.[17]
The letter continues. His spiritual director in Paris prudently advised a period of waiting before committing himself. Three months passed. Another trip to Paris: Rancé's attitude

is the same, but he can not yet speak his unqualified 'Yes'.
Six more weeks at la Trappe. In April the moment of grace
came. The 'Yes' was spoken. He went to Paris a third time,
and received his director's *Fiat* (and also the advice of
Msgr de Choiseul-Praslin). 'I know that the life I am under-
taking is beyond my strength,' Rancé tells Pavillon, 'but I
also know that nothing is beyond the scope of God's power,
and that he can bring to perfection in me the work that his
mercy has begun.'[18]

King Louis XIV allowed la Trappe to become a regular
abbey (for the duration of Rancé's abbacy only), and the
abbot-elect went to Perseigne to begin his novitiate. Dom
Armand-Jean Bouthillier de Rancé was about to become
a father.

PREPARATION FOR A FATHER'S ROLE

Frère Armand-Jean entered upon his novitiate at Perseigne
with total abandon. Predictably enough, by the end of October his health had collapsed. At the end of two months of
recuperation at la Trappe he was back at Perseigne against all
odds and expectations. His health was always to remain pre-
carious. The rest of the novitiate was far from being smooth-
sailing. The nearby abbey of Champagne had become the
scene of civil-war between the Strict Observance members of
the community and the Mitigated. The novice was dispatched
thither to effect a *rapprochement* between the warring parties.
Rancé arrived in the nick of time. The Common Observance
brethren had invoked the help of the local gentry to effect a
coup, and things might have worked out otherwise had the
leader of the party of seculars not turned out to be a personal
friend of our novice. Order returned at last. The mission took
two weeks from Rancé's novitiate, but it was a valuable
lesson—a real education in the pastoral implications of the
War between Observances. Soon after this initial success, the
Superior of Perseigne wished to send the novice off on a similar mission. Rancé refused to cooperate further in the travesty
which his novitiate formation was about to become. Reluc-

tantly, the Vicar-General of the Reform, Abbot Jean Jouaud, agreed that the novice had a point.

Meanwhile, Rancé had been plunging himself into cistercian sources. There can be no doubt that the most important work he studied at this time (if not even earlier at la Trappe) was a book which was to serve him admirably as a practical point of reference for his monastic programme at la Trappe. *Du premier esprit de l'Ordre de Cisteaux* is a book which should be familiar to anyone interested in the world of seventeenth-century Cîteaux.[19] The author was Julien Paris, abbot of Foucarmont (1645-1671), and an outstanding champion of the Abstinent party. Though one distinguished cistercian historian has described the book as 'an oversized pamphlet, an apology for the Strict Observance,'[20] this description does scant justice to the work which corresponds perfectly with its full-length title: *On the Early Spirit of the Cistercian Order: With a Discussion of a Number of Things Necessary for the Understanding and Re-establishment of the Government and Way of Life of the Founders of This Order.*

The plan of the book provides for four main parts. Part One deals with the early Order, and discovers the spirit of the first Cistercians by a survey and analysis of the Order's early history, key-legislation, and early practices. Chapter IV is devoted to the pivotal principle that is the heart of the book: the true cistercian spirit is bound up with the integral observance of the Holy Rule. The following chapters show how the concrete cistercian usages harmonized with the prescriptions of St Benedict. Part Two studies the administrative machinery of the Order. For our present purpose, the really important section includes several chapters devoted to the role of Superiors. There is included, in fact, a kind of 'Mirror of Abbots' composed of cistercian texts and a few pages by St John Climacus. More of this in a moment. Part Three traces the decline of the Order as reflected in the Order's history and in the attempts of General Chapter, king, and pope to check the disintegration of the mortally sick organism. One of the three chief causes of decline is spelled out in detail as the fault of Superiors ignorant of the nature of their pastoral ministry to their communities. (Rancé, take note!) Part Four recapitulates much of the earlier material, and asks the question: does the Order have to be renewed in its early spirit? Obviously! How? By re-establishing the integral observance of the Holy Rule. And how is this to be done? By a return to the institutions and practices of early Cîteaux.

Dom Julien spells out the main features of his back-to-early-Cîteaux programme, and our abbot-elect finds himself provided with a practical programme for monks. His own reforming work at la Trappe will depart only in matters of detail from the blue-print traced by the Abbot of Foucarmont. Perhaps it should be remarked in passing that, with Cîteaux in the heydey of St Bernard as the norm of authenticity, not only the Common Observance, but the Strict Observance as well fell short of the ideal. Years later, confined to the infirmary, and looking back to the beginning of the la Trappe reform, the *ancien abbé* wrote:

> When I entered the Cistercian Order, my idea was to adopt usages quite the contrary to those I saw established there, and, since the Order seemed to me to have been quite holy in its beginning, I resolved to conform myself as much as I could to the rules which the Founders had prescribed by their example.[21]

The major portion of Dom Julien Paris' 'Dictionary for Abbots'[22] consists of a florilegium of texts about the abbot drawn from the Holy Rule and from the writings of St Bernard. From the Holy Rule our author culls ten points directly concerning the abbot's responsibility towards himself, but these are followed by ten points dealing with the abbot and his religious. Chapter and verse from the Holy Rule are quoted in Latin in the marginal annotations. The abbot, then, ought:

1. To act in such wise that his religious not only work out their salvation, but do so with real advantage to themselves.

2. To remember that he is responsible not only for the faults of his religious, but for their failure to advance in virtue.

3. To take care that their imperfections do not become more serious because of his neglect.

4. To love them in such a way as also to hate their vices.

5. When dealing with their faults, to remember that he himself is weak.

6. To make corrections, but without going to extremes.

7. To be persuaded that the souls under his guidance are weak and that they have to be solicited as such.

8. Nevertheless, to reprimand and chastise severely those who are negligent, turbulent, rebel, and froward, and to exhort with gentleness those who are obedient, docile, and tractable, so that they persevere in the good and daily make new progress in virtue.

9. To warn and reprimand those whose characters are more docile and reasonable once or twice by word only, so often as they do something wrong, before going on to harsher correction, and to punish the proud and arrogant at the very beginning of their faults by disciplines and other similar mortifications such as will hinder a relapse.

10. To accommodate himself to the nature and capacity of each individual so as to win them for God and lead them to heaven by means of the duties of their profession.

The Bernardine florilegium is composed of a parallel series of nine maxims, each of which is accompanied by a series of texts by the Mellifluous Doctor:

1. The first and most important of all the rules . . . for those who undertake the guidance of others, is to wait till God calls one to do so, and not to take the initiative on one's own.

2. One should not take on this burden if one is not filled with grace and virtue, and particularly a great and perfect charity.

3. The abbot has to know how to obey before he can know how to command, but, even so, the ability to live a virtuous life under the conduct of another is no sign that one is ready

to act as a guide for others.

4. Three requirements on the abbot's part: (a) good example, (b) exhortation, (c) prayer.

5. The abbot must be more concerned for the salvation of the brother than for his own personal inclinations.

6. The superior ought not to be surprised or discouraged when he encounters really hard cases; he should tell himself that is precisely for them that he is abbot.

7. Gentleness is always to be preferred to rigor and severity.

8. When gentleness proves unavailing, get tough.

9. The superior must always be deeply concerned for the salvation of those in his charge, because he is answerable for them to God.

Next follows a series of examples showing how St Bernard himself put these maxims into practice. A fourth section reflects the popularity of St John Climacus at this time—and here the saint is presented not so much as a model of asceticism, but as an outstanding director of souls. The material consists of a twenty-point programme for superiors, taken from St John's letter 'to Pastor'. A fifth section deals in a fair amount of detail with the problem of avoiding an extreme of rigor as well as an extreme of weakness. I rather suspect that this section is Dom Julien's personal contribution to our Directory for Abbots. Eleven examples of too much rigor are given, and seven of too much indulgence, and then ten suggestions for striking a happy medium. Finally, a sixth section deals with particular points of practice excerpted from the early Cistercian Usages.

This is really quite a collection of texts, and the above schematic outline fails to suggest the richness of much of the material.

At the end of his year-long novitiate, Rancé's cistercian formation had been neither prolonged nor systematic, but the wonder is that he profited from this year of grace as much as he clearly did. The papal bulls authorizing him as regular abbot of la Trappe arrived at Perseigne on 19 June 1664. A week later, on 26 June, he pronounced his solemn vows.

On 19 July he was blessed as abbot by the exiled Irish prelate, Patrick Plunket. And on 20 July he came home to la Trappe.

THE SPIRITUAL FATHER IN ACTION

The new abbot did not remain with his brethren very long. At a meeting of the Strict Observance abbots held in Paris at the beginning of September, Rancé was appointed, despite his vehement protests, one of the two delegates to be sent to Rome as representatives of the Abstinents in the settlement of the War between Observances. He was to be absent from his community for two long years. Rancé found the whole Roman experience sheer hell, but this period of forced exile from la Trappe ultimately proved helpful for Rancé's monastic thinking. As representative of his Observance, he gained a deeper familiarity with the Order's past and present history, and, in his spirited defense of what he considered to be the cistercian spirit and ideals, he perforce assimilated at greater depth much of the material heretofore known only in a more casual way from his reading of Julien Paris. The Roman experience also helped to clarify for him an important point: if the salvation of la Trappe were to depend on the successful outcome of the battle of Observances, and on a general reform of the Order as a whole (in France), chances of salvation would be slim indeed. He was totally committed, of course, to the Abstinent cause, but he was also a realist. A decade later, in a letter dated October of 1675, he would comment sadly that, 'It is true that it was sixty years ago that the Reform began, but it is also true that they [the Abstinents] were more concerned with taking over monasteries than with forming religious'.[23] As for Rancé, he was concerned with forming religious, and, though he was generous enough in giving reform-minded Superiors advice when asked, and though he even occasionally sent monks of la Trappe to other communities in the interest of reform, his own efforts centered almost exclusively on his own beloved community. 'My very dear confrères,' he had written his brethren from

Paris, as he headed romewards in 1664, ' . . . be wholly convinced that I shall be carrying you with me in the depths of
my heart, and that at every moment and wherever I am, you,
for whom God has given me so strong an attachment, will be
very much present to me . . . . Pray to God for me, and think
on this: that from now on my salvation and your salvation
are inseparable according to the order of Divine Providence . . . ' . [24]

Pastoral note. In these days of temporary abbots, I suppose
that there are not many abbots who can realisitically consider
their personal destinies all that closely bound up with the
community. We are in a historically different context from
that of seventeenth-century la Trappe. But surely we can
regret the fact that something is so often missing in the dynamics of spiritual direction in many of our communities, something which was very present at la Trappe: the conviction
that, in matters of spiritual direction, both director and
directed were inseparable in their personal involvement as
regards the spiritual question or problem under discussion.
When a monk went to Abbot Rancé with a problem, the
Father Abbot experienced that problem, not just as that
monk's problem, but as *his* problem, too. And this was bound
to affect the quality of their relationship and the dynamics
of direction.

So, my point here is that Rancé, as spiritual father, experienced a deeply personal commitment to, and involvement
with his brethren; but that he also had, in his programme of
formation, an objective point of reference furnished by
tradition. It is that second point which I wish to examine a
bit more closely.

AN OBJECTIVE NORM OF REFERENCE

The Reformer of la Trappe was a man virtually without
ideas of his own. Brilliant he was—to a certain extent. He
knew how to put a lexicon to excellent use; he was a splendid
stylist in whichever language he cared to speak or write (and
he was as fluent in Latin and Greek as he was in French); and

if, when he received his doctorate in theology at the Sorbonne, he stood at the head of his class, this honor was surely not out of deference to his family connections, but the honest recognition of the excellence of his scholarly achievement. However, he lacked the real scholar's ability to move from that which has been acquired to new conclusions and corollaries. His method of argumentation consisted almost exclusively in drawing up lists of *auctoritates* in support of whatever point he was belaboring at the moment. His broad reading in Church history and his very real familiarity with the writings of rather many of the Fathers and other ecclesiastical writers greatly facilitated his task of assembling long lists of prooftexts.

This tendency to look outside himself to 'authority' as concretized in Tradition (the Scriptures, the Fathers, the *magisterium,* the early Cistercians, even the writings of recent canonized saints) was accompanied by a genuine self-diffidence. I like enormously the letter he once wrote to a superior who had asked him to share what he had learned in prayer about the formation of novices. Rancé replies that, since God does not explain things to sinners the same way he does to his saints,

> it is quite impossible for me to satisfy your request. I have too much sincerity to foist my imaginings off on you as though they were real, and I am not so virtuous that God deigns to hold converse with me and to declare his intentions to me by means of prayer . . . . [25]

Does this mean Rancé has nothing to say about the formation of novices? Hardly. God might not have held a private tête-à-tête with Rancé concerning novitiate formation, but God's will in such matters can be learned from sources more prosaic, but just as authentic as the way of private revelation.

I think Rancé's point is a good one. The spiritual father who operates too exclusively by the mystic glow of his interior illuminations places both himself and his *dirigé* at the mercy of his possibly malfunctioning ganglion cells. Whatever Rancé's horror of quietism might have been, he was not in the least anti-mystical, and he respected in himself and in others spiritual illuminations that were really spiritual illuminations. But he was honest about it all when he had no personal lights, and his constant point of reference was to tradition and to authority rather than to his interior lights.

Another pastoral note. It is only speciously comforting when Rancé assures the spiritual father that he can learn how to form novices by ways more prosaic than mystical locutions. For this presupposes, on the director's part, a knowledge of which prosaic sources he should draw upon, and it also presupposes that he does the actual drawing. In other words, Rancé insists on a spiritual father having a basic technical and practical competence. Perhaps his most systematic discussion of this point is to be found in his *Treatise on the Sanctity and on the Duties of the Monastic State,* in which he discusses, in Chapter 9, the charity and duties of Superiors. The question is asked: is it necessary that a superior be very learned in order to be sufficiently qualified to instruct his brethren with advantage? Rancé begins by stating a general principle which St Bernard would have whole-heartedly endorsed:

> Science should be regulated and measured according to the state and conditions of the persons who are to be instructed; and therefore it can be asserted, without danger of erring, that a man who knows everything relating to his profession, who understands its principles, its nature, and its rules, that such a man, I say, possesses all the knowledge proper for him, and that God requires in him; and that, consequently, he is sufficiently qualified to fulfill the duties and obligations which his state imposes on him.[26]

Rancé now applies the principle to the concrete case of a 'doctor or an ecclesiastical pastor' whose knowledge should extend far enough to include practically everything knowable:

'He ought to know, perfectly well, all the dogmas and
mysteries of faith, the Holy Scriptures, tradition, ecclesiastical history, the decisions and rules of the Church
[Canon Law], a profound knowledge of the writings of the
holy Fathers . . . ' . Quite a curriculum. As for the mere
superior of religious, he is a man 'destined to direct only a
few persons, whose life ought to be spent in retreat, in
silence, in the mortification of the senses, and who, having
his mission only for the purpose of teaching piety, and not
for expounding doctrine, has no need for such profound
learning . . . ' . He concludes that the one thing the superior
has to know is 'Jesus Christ, and him crucified'.[27] There
follows a very beautiful passage on this 'great book of Christ
crucified'. The reader will feel no need of reading farther to
be convinced that this is an appalling instance of that anti-
intellectual stance which is synonomous with the name of
Rancé. But let him read on. How do we come to a knowledge
of Jesus Christ, and him crucified? By a constant study of
Holy Scripture. A new question: do you then allow superiors
no other studies but that of the Holy Scripture?

> Superiors being established only for the purpose of guiding
> those whom our Lord had committed to their direction, in
> the practice of everything most elevated, pure, and holy in
> religion, it cannot be doubted but that they are obliged to
> have a perfect knowledge of it; and, as the whole system
> of religion consists in the truths of faith, and in the holy
> maxims laid down and delivered to us by Jesus Christ for
> the direction of our lives, it is equally certain that the duty
> of a superior is to read, to hear, to meditate on the sacred
> writings, since they are the sources from which these
> maxims and divine truths flow.

More follows:

> To this sacred occupation, he must join the study of the
> works of the holy Fathers which treat of the conduct and

rule by which we should square all the actions of life, and, moreover, as he ought to understand his state in a perfect manner and in its fullest extent, he must read with care and attention whatever the saints have written concerning his obligations, and the history delivered down to us by ecclesiastical writers, of the lives, actions, rules, and doctrine of the ancient holy monks.[28]

This, writes Rancé, is 'the precise circle of the sciences necessary for a superior'. Anti-intellectual? Hardly! The superior's intellect is in the service of his ministry every bit as much as the intellect of the theologian, and it is every bit as active; only the scope of its focus and concern is different. Rancé asks of the spiritual father not only a perfect knowledge of Scripture (and how many superiors have this knowledge nowadays?), but the equivalent of a comprehensive grounding in ascetical and mystical theology and in everything touching on monastic history and spirituality.

If you wish to argue that the superior's scope of knowledge is too restricted, you have every right to do so, and I will not argue. But here the point is that, according to Rancé, the spiritual father is duty-bound to have a solid grounding in *all* the above-designated areas of knowledge. Actually, Rancé himself raises the question: does this 'narrow sphere' of knowledge really suffice for a superior to assist his brethren in their spiritual advancement? He answers by commenting on the example of a skilled lawyer whose competency to teach law should not be challenged just because he is not also an astronomer. In a later paragraph our author admits that a superior might possibly have to study in areas outside the scope of his profession, but that happens by 'a particular order and disposition of Divine Providence'. For me, one of the most telling arguments he proposes in support of his contention that the superior should avoid wasting time on things less directly connected with his mission, is this: the superior should be persuaded that he belongs no more to himself, but that his time, his person, and his life belong to his brethren; in a word, if he loves them as he ought, and as much as he is obliged, his days will appear too short to fulfill the full extent of his duties, and to satisfy the efforts of his love; and, hence, so far from engaging himself in any affairs that have no connection with his state, he will not, without scruple, deprive his brethren of one single moment of his time, since he will be persuaded that they should be all employed in their service.[29]

SENSITIVITY FOR THE CONCRETE SITUATION AND THE INDIVIDUAL

An objective norm and point of reference will not be all that helpful unless the spiritual father has an insightful understanding of the person he is directing, and of the concrete circumstances in which that person is. Rancé's own keen sense of the concrete and of the uniqueness of each individual is a fact that must be borne in mind as often as we read his writings—especially his letters. His counsels are never contradictory, though his recommendations about the same matter sometimes differ; but this depends on the individual addressed and the attendant circumstances.

It is, for instance, quite typical of Rancé's sensitivity for the individual that, when the retired cavalry office, Monsieur de Saint Louis, retired to the property of la Trappe to live as something of a recluse, Rancé's provisions for his rugged way of life included a staff of three servants and a stable of two horses. Or again, take Monsieur de Saint Louis' favorite valet, Hans. 'He had a failing quite common among Germans,' our recluse writes with true gallic *hauteur.* 'He loved his wine.'

But he was so weak-headed that it took only a few drops to get him so addle-brained that he was absolutely incapable of anything whatsoever. I had put up with it while I was in the service, but I did not think the sanctity of the place where I had retired [la Trappe], or the type of

186

life I had embraced, allowed me to keep a domestic whose bad example could give scandal. Besides, when I used to see him in that 'condition', I often had a hard time keeping from becoming angry. I made up my mind to send him away, and spoke about it to Monsieur de la Trappe. He listened to my reasons with his usual calm, and then spoke. 'But what are you going to do, Monsieur? Are you going to be remedying the evil? Not at all. You will be giving this poor fellow the occasion to offend God all the more often. Since the time he has been with you, it is only three or four times a month that he falls into this "excess." But just as soon as he leaves you, there will not be a day when he will not be drunk.'[30]

Hans stayed on. He never drank another drop and he died a good christian death a few years later.

Perhaps one of the most remarkable documents attesting to Rancé's fine feel for the concrete situation is the *Règlements* he drew up, at the request of the local bishop, for a community of nuns Rancé himself had founded in the nearby town of Mortagne. The tiny congregation—the Daughters of Christian Doctrine—was to ensure the education of the girls of poorer family in the region. For a time when the main purpose of many such congregations was being rendered difficult by Constitutions or Usages geared more to cloistered religious than to teaching Sisters, the *Règlements* drawn up by our fiery ascetic are astonishing. Morning and evening prayer in common, but no Divine Office; modest garb, but no religious habit: 'since they are obliged to be in the world, they dress in modern fashion so as not to look ridiculous'; a promise, but no vows; Sunday Mass and Vespers in the parish church . . . . [31]

But even within the closed world of la Trappe, where the life-style and monastic commitment were the same for all (or almost all), each individual monk was understood by Rancé in terms of his own uniqueness. The abbot was there to see that God's will was done and that the monk was sanctified; this is a theme to which Rancé constantly recurs under one or another aspects. This demands total openness on the part of the monk, if his spiritual father is to provide him with exactly the right direction required by that particular monk in that particular situation.

> . . . The superior should know perfectly the persons who are under his charge, without which the authority he has received for no other purpose than to preserve good order would produce nothing but trouble and confusion; as, without the aforesaid knowledge, he would act without light; he would consequently act without prudence; he would be directed by nothing but humour and fancy; his conduct would be like to that of a blind man who does everything by conjecture, or like that of a physician who undertakes to cure the sick of whose maladies and constitution he remains entirely uninformed.

> It being therefore evident that the superior, in order to be properly qualified to direct his brethren, should have a perfect knowledge of them; this being admitted, it naturally follows that they ought to have an entire confidence in their superior; for without such a disposition on their part, it is impossible he should know them, since it is equally certain that, unless he acquires this knowledge either by some extraordinary means or by revelation, he can form only some uncertain notions of them, founded on mere conjectures. Hence the brethren must certainly give him a full description of the state of their interior, manifest the motions of their hearts, and unfold clearly its most latent recesses— which can never be the case unless they have an entire confidence in him.[32]

Though Rancé provided a number of confessors for his community, no one ever went to them. All preferred to have 'Father Abbot' as both director and confessor. Here Rancé was on somewhat delicate terrain. According to early cistercian practice, the monk not only could choose the abbot as proper and ordinary confessor, but had to approach him as confessor at least once a year (and as often as he fell under censure or a reserved sin).[33] The Order's discipline on this point was changed by Pope Clement VIII in 1593, in the interests of greater liberty of conscience on the part of the religious.[34] At la Trappe, then, there could have been no question of the monk *having* to go to confession to the abbot, but, according to the papal Constitution of Clement VIII, any religious who freely wished to do so could—and with Rancé as abbot, everyone freely wished to do so.

The practical point arises, then. Can a monk look elsewhere than to his abbot for spiritual direction? Rancé makes a distinction. If it means a breakdown of communication between abbot and monk, obviously not. But

> there may be found other directors in monasteries, who have been commissioned to supply the inability of the principal superior, which inability proceeds either from non-residence, or from the superior's incapacity, infirmities, or disorderly life. Such a mode of direction is just, is founded on lawful principles, and there is no danger in believing that the inferiors shall derive from it necessary assistance and comfort.[35]

But our Reformer also admits of other less exceptional instances of direction undertaken by persons other than the superior:

> There are others who have the care of souls in monasteries which are governed by abbots, who are entitled priors, deans, ancients, or presidents, as we find in the ancient monastic rules; but it is to be noticed that it was neither the indocility of the brethren, nor any other illegal cause, that gave birth to such an arrangement: the superior established them to the end that, dividing his pastoral charge with them, they might assist him in his functions, when, on

189

certain occasions, he found it impossible . . . to attend to the wants of his brethren.

The person thus chosen is always a man of much piety, who not only acts by virtue of the commission he has received from his abbot, but is influenced in his ministry by the same motives; who is always careful to give the abbot an exact account of the brethren's dispositions, even to their least thoughts. Thus confidence is not injured, but remains entire; unity is preserved; this subordination does not enervate in any manner the first and principal authority; and the superior, being informed of everything, is by that means personally enabled to prescribe proper remedies for every disorder, to calm every uneasiness, to dissipate every dangerous thought which might disturb the brethren. In a word, he rules all, and the whole community regularly moves under his direction. But here you easily remark, my brethren, that I speak not of sacramental confession, the secret of which is inviolable, as you all well know.[36]

As is clear, then, the sharing of the abbot's pastoral responsibility in no wise compromises the principle of unity of direction. And, clearly, what Rancé here envisages is quite different from the standard practice of many communities, where individual directors exercise their pastoral ministry independently of other directors, and often enough in total independence of the abbot.

I realize full well that I should have given this entire subsection the title 'Abbot as (Almost) Sole Director'. If I have not done so, it is because this emphasis on the abbot's ministerial function vis-à-vis each individual is meant as a service to each and every monk, whose richer life depends on his father abbot's comprehensive understanding of his concrete spiritual state. As Rancé saw it, the abbot was for the monk, not the monk for the abbot.

But in the next to last citation given above, Rancé refers to a superior's incapacity or disorderly life. Which brings us to an essential point in Rancé's teaching.

THE LIMITATIONS OF THE ABBOT
AS SPIRITUAL FATHER

The benedictine maxim that the abbot represents Christ in the community was understood quite differently by Rancé than by many a latter-day Trappist. Because the abbot takes the place of Christ in the community, it has sometimes been assumed that any fool thought that passes through the abbot's mind is an expression of the mind of Christ. Little wonder that we are currently witnessing the rise of the temporary abbot and the trend to democratize community structures.

Rancé and Bernard (and surely Benedict) were at one: the abbot has the place of Christ in the community as often as he has the mind of Christ and as often as his actions and decisions are in conformity with the mind of Christ. As often as he acts contrary to the Gospel or to the Holy Rule, he is not Christ; as often as he acts from fear or selfish motivation or political considerations, he is not Christ; as often as he renders it difficult for his monks to live his commitment to the full, he is not Christ. 'Superiors', Rancé writes,

> when their commands are according to the divine law,
> enjoined for your perfection, formed by the spirit of your
> rules, and within the sphere of your profession, should find
> in you submission without bounds; so, in like manner,
> when they require anything contrary to the law of God,
> when they withdraw you from the ways of perfection
> instead of assisting you to advance, and when they aim at
> the enervation and destruction of the rules for the pre-
> servation of which they have received their authority—in all
> these cases, I say, you are not bound to obey them, and you
> should remember that he who said 'he that hears you hears
> me, he who despises you despises me', declares in another
> place 'that it is better to obey God than man', and that
> 'when the blind leads the blind, both fall into the pit'.[37]

Or again:

The religious should attend [the abbot's] doctrine in all things, place themselves in his hands, and give themselves up to his direction without reserve. But if, on the contrary, his incapacity, his negligence, his indifference for his state, and the impropriety of his conduct are such as to produce sufficient motives to diffide in his direction, it is then necessary to walk more cautiously and to consider the superior's manner of life with more exactitude. Saint Bernard teaches us that in such a case we ought to possess prudence and liberty: prudence in order to discern whether there is anything in his orders contrary to the law of God, and liberty to the end that we may be able to resist the order if any such opposition should be evidently found in it.[38]

And he concludes with this summary statement:

You must take notice that when [the abbot] speaks in the name of Jesus Christ, that is, when he proposes nothing but truth and the will of God, that then he must be obeyed as Jesus Christ himself, and, moreover, you should evince by all your words and actions that you respect his person and character, though at the same time you find it necessary to adopt different sentiments from those he inculcates.[39]

Total openness and dependence—but without derogation to prudence and liberty.

THE FATHER ABBOT AS REPRESENTATIVE OF CHRIST AND WITNESS TO TRADITION

The key texts for an understanding of Rancé's concept of the abbot as representative of Christ are to be found, as we might expect, in his splendid commentary on Chapter Two of the Holy Rule, 'On the Qualities of the Abbot', in his *Commentary on the Rule of Saint Benedict.*

Consistent with total commitment to his brethren, our Abbot begins his remarks by stating that the loftiness of the

brethren's vocation to perfection can be gauged by the qualities demanded on the part of the abbot.

Firstly, the abbot must carry out the meaning of the name
'superior'—*nomen maioris.* 'Do not think,' writes Rancé, 'that
this name *maior* is a name of domination or of lordship. On
the contrary, it signifies in this context only a simple ministry . . . . ' This ministry, he explains, is simply the expression
of what Jesus means when he says, 'Let he that is the greater
among you, become the lesser; and he that is the leader, as he
that serves' (Lk 22:26).

> And if a superior wants to put into practice what this ex-
> pression signifies . . . he must enter into all the needs of his
> brethren, be they spiritual or physical; he must render them
> all the offices of charity in his power; he must be so atten-
> tive and so alert to all that concerns them, that not a single
> one of their needs escapes him.[40]

And when our Commentator gets to the words, 'He is considered as the one who holds the place of Jesus Christ', he
entirely neglects what this means as regards the monk's stance
vis-à-vis the abbot, and deals solely with the abbot's stance
vis-à-vis the brethren. The abbot does for his monks what
Jesus did for his disciples, so that he too can say, 'Those whom
you gave me have I kept, and none of them is lost' (Jn 17:12).
All his efforts are to be devoted to the sanctification of the
brethren, and he is to be occupied day and night with their
salvation to the fullest extent possible. The spiritual father
must have for his brethren the same charity that Jesus had for
his disciples. How did Jesus form his disciples? Chiefly in four
ways: by (a) his word, (b) his example, (c) his watchfulness,
and (d) his prayer; and Rancé treats of these four functions in
brief. But the general principle is that the abbot must 'do in
the monastery what Jesus Christ himself would do if he were
there'.

> He should follow Jesus Christ step by step as much as he

possibly can in all the functions touching on his state as superior; and as Jesus Christ—as he himself attests—told his disciples all that the Father had taught him (*Omnia quae-cumque audivi a Patre meo, nota feci vobis*), so also [the superior] ought, after his example, to teach his brethren everything that concerns their profession, all the maxims they should follow in their conduct; he should point out to them the ways that are safe, the principles that are certain, for fear that they let themselves fall into error, and that they take the wrong path. He should enlighten them, stir them up, support them, reprimand them, console them, and make himself, as the Apostle says, 'All things to all,' so that there is not one but who is saved and preserved for Jesus Christ: *Omnibus omnia factus sum, ut omnes facerem salvos.*[41]

In this last sentence there are three words which might easily be overlooked, but which are essential for Rancé's understanding of the father abbot's ministry. These words are: *for Jesus Christ.* The pastoral ministry is ultimately a christological reality not only because it is rooted in Christ's self-giving and sacrificial love, but because it is carried out for love of him, and directed towards him in its paschal finality.

Hundreds of instances could be cited in which the Reformer of la Trappe put this teaching into practice! Let one example stand for all. The Reform is at a critical juncture, and Rancé is called to Paris to take part in the deliberations of the superiors of the Strict Observance. He writes to his higher superior to excuse himself from attending:

One of the brethren here has been at the gates of death for the last two months. True, God has given him all the dispositions I could want him to have in this situation; but the moment of death is assuredly the moment of greatest temptation, and I have to tell you that for me to leave him in that extremity would mean to subject myself to a well-nigh insupportable violence. God has entrusted him to me,

194

he has placed him in my hands, and it seems to me that God wants me to place him back into his own hands. And unless I receive his last breath and close his eyes, I do not believe that I will be able to render God the account he is going to ask of me. Yes, I realize that I owe everything to our Observance, and that there is nothing more important for me than the affair being treated of at present. But I am only one part [of the Observance] , and the least important part at that, and God has charged me, as head of this house, with its direction; and the obligation that I have to watch over the souls whom he has deigned to commit to my care seems to me more binding than all other obligations.[42]

But just as the abbot was, for Rancé, Christ among the brethren, so also was he the living embodiment of monastic tradition. There are very few letters of counsel he wrote to reform-minded superiors in which he did not stress the fact that the superior is obliged to manifest in his own person the living tradition in which his brethren are to be formed. He himself, of course, was the first to put this maxim into practice.

It was a question of monastic formation by contagion, and, if his own place relative to the community was so special, it was not because he was apart from his brethren, or above them in any way, but because he personally recapitulated in his own person their tradition, their ideal, their community experience. And however grim their penitential life, howsoever austere their regime may appear to us outsiders, Rancé made it a thing of joy for them, thanks to his own enthusing example. Writing to the Duchess of Liancourt in 1670, the historian Félibien des Avaux shares his impression of the visit he made to la Trappe in September of that year. 'His [Rancé's] words,' he writes, 'are accompanied by such a joy-filled air, that it is easy to see how deeply convinced he is of the things he talks about.'[43] And he makes the following perceptive comment: 'These are no timid, spineless slaves led by a valiant captain. These are free men, men who are generous, and who march after their head whom they obey with the utmost love . . . . '[44]

We are back in the desert, in a sense, where learning how to be a monk consisted simply in living with an *abba,* doing what he did, and picking up something of the spirit/Spirit which suffused his words and his silence, his action and his repose.

THREE ADDITIONAL NOTES ON RANCÉ
THE SPIRITUAL FATHER
   If this article were not already too long, the following three points would deserve extended development.

The Christological Dimension of Monastic Life
According to Rancé
   No matter how energetically and sincerely Rancé insisted on the Rule and early cistercian institutions, and, no matter how fiercely he defended particular points of la Trappe observance (humiliations, spiritual reading rather than studies, rigorous silence), all these were of a secondary nature in his order of priorities. What comes first is Jesus Christ, and, for Rancé and his brethren, monastic life means nothing except insofar as it means the following of Christ. It is a question of integral Christianity: Jesus the starting-point of monastic observance, Jesus the substance of monastic observance, Jesus the goal of monastic observance. (No need to point out that this christological dimension ensures the Trinitarian fullness of the monk's life with Father, Son, and Holy Spirit.)
   Apart from this christocentricity, Rancé's teaching on penance and humiliations and practically everything else is as intelligible to us as would be (to most of us) Swahili or Geez. Perhaps the key text is the following.

   As the penitence of a monk owes its birth, strength, and merit to the penitence of Jesus Christ, so ought it to be a continual *retracing*, a faithful *imitation* of *his* penitence.[45]

Rancé insists: 'To know what the penitence of solitaries ought to be, we must consider what the penitence of Jesus Christ was.'[46] The idea of Jesus as a penitent is a bit foreign

196

to most of us, but Rancé understands by the penitence of our Lord all that he did and endured for love of us and for our salvation. The penitential exercises of la Trappe, then, were envisaged as so many ways of participating in what we would call the Mystery of Christ.

Pastoral note one: the spiritual father should be bent on ensuring the specifically *christian* content of his spiritual son's monastic experience.

Rancé and the Material Environment of la Trappe

One of the Reformer's major achievements was the excellence of the material environment which he provided for his brethren. When he became regular abbot in 1664, major reconstruction work had already begun. Virtually a new monastery had to be built. It is difficult nowadays to appreciate the impact the monastery made on visitors in its material aspects: order, harmony, simplicity, functionality, austere beauty, perfect cleanliness (the French expression *salé comme un trappiste* gained currency at a much later date). It is instructive to read the descriptions of the place in the various published and unpublished accounts of 'My Visit to la Trappe'—though the best illustrated and best documented one is surely the *Description du plan en relief de l'Abbaye de la Trappe* (Paris, 1708), which the solitary of Sénart, Frère Pacôme, drew up at the request of Louis XIV. Rancé was a good father; he provided for his brethren an environment which reflected, sustained, and fostered their pursuit of the life of the spirit.

Pastoral note two: the spiritual father's concern should extend to the material environment he provides for his brethren.

The Rancéan Programme: For Ascetics or for Contemplatives?

This sub-title is, I suggest, a bit stupid, but it does correspond to the terms of an objection frequently voiced by people who know little about la Trappe and still less about Rancé.

Abba, *The Spiritual Guide*

Rancé was no contemplative, we are told, and his monastic programme was a regime of heroic mortification without a truly contemplative dimension.

When is a person an ascetic and when is he a contemplative? Most of the really ascetically-minded monks and nuns I know are people whose lives are marked palpably by an authentic contemplative dimension. Perhaps this contemplative dimension has a deep connection with the ascetic dimension, and quite possibly it is because of the contemplative orientation that their asceticism is such an authentic, positive element in the way they live the Mystery of Christ.

Indeed, I personally think that one of the strongest points in the Rancéan programme at la Trappe was its perfect continuity with a monastic contemplative tradition which went haywire only when people started tossing around the word 'contemplative', stopped thinking about being just monks, and began worrying about being 'contemplatives'. Let me explain.

The desert fathers, Cassian, Saint Benedict, Saint Bernard—and Rancé: You come to the monastery, where you: (a) overcome vice, and (b) acquire virtue. This is done under the aegis of the Holy Spirit, whose action becomes stronger and less inhibited as one grows in virtue. Imperfect motivation (fear, hope of reward) becomes purified, till perfect love has cast out all fear, and the monk's life is now one of spiritual freedom in which he tastes and experiences the divine realities known hitherto only in an imperfect, non-experiential way. The elimination of vice and the acquisition of virtue made up the 'active' life in traditional monastic terminology; whereas what happened when the Holy Spirit took over in a more totalizing way was the 'contemplative' life (or 'speculative' or 'theoretical' life).

It is perfectly clear that at la Trappe under Rancé plenty of this tasting of divine realities was going on. Granted, much of the documentation on which such a judgement is based has to be demythologized, and the various literary genres taken into account. Even so, there is no accounting for that which

198

remains unless we postulate the existence of a goodly number of monks who were operating on the strength of a pretty full outpouring of the gifts of the Holy Spirit. The mutual love and respect, the contagious enthusiasm, this astonishing fidelity to 'obligations of the monastic state', the uninterrupted prayer of so many individuals—all indicate that the ascetic life had flowered for many into a certain fullness of the life of the spirit. Obviously, there were many individuals who were still on the way. After all, Monte Cassino and Clairvaux were not just for what Saint Benedict would call the 'perfect' monk, but for monks on the way to becoming 'perfect'. Just like at la Trappe.

Pastoral note three: if the spiritual father makes a distinction between 'ascetic' and 'contemplative', it should ultimately be with a view to uniting the two in the deepest possible organic relationship.

CONCLUSION

There is really no conclusion called for. What has preceded is only a non-systematic listing of a few ideas which come to mind when I pass in review the life and teaching of Rancé, spiritual father of his brethren at la Trappe.

La Trappe, of course, is not popular nowadays, and really has not been for a long time. This is perfectly understandable, since the 'la Trappe' many of us have known is only a distorted caricature. Rancé's la Trappe and the Trappist phenomenon of the nineteenth century are light-years apart (though truly, I would not want to be the least bit disrespectful of the extraordinary nineteenth-century Trappist phenomenon, which has its own admirable features). In the present climate of renewal, there are some of us who are impatient of the past, and who want to move 'forward' without too much looking backwards. Others of us would prefer to apply to our own monastic institution what St Bernard suggests when he speaks of the Church as being *ante et retro oculata*—with eyes that look backwards (so that we know where we come from, where our roots are), and eyes that look forward (to the eschatological fulfillment of our individual and collective destiny), so that we can live in full awareness in the present moment. For me, the question for those of us who hold to the need of this gazing backwards is whether the sweep of our vision into the past should include the seventeenth-century la Trappe? I rather doubt that many 'Yes-es' will be heard in response. Perhaps this is for the best—even though I per- sonally feel that, in our cistercian history, seventeenth-century la Trappe shines as a blaze of glory in affirmation of the inexhaustible fecundity of the cistercian heritage. There was, however, a holistic quality about Rancé's return to tradition, with an organic unity and functional relation between indivi- dual elements and the whole cistercian life as he conceived it. Our own reference to the past is perforce more atomistic: we have to choose this or that element, discard particular points of usage as no longer viable, adapt other points of usage or institutions to the point where one can understandably won- der whether any continuity remains between starting-point and point of present arrival. (Can the temporary abbot, for instance, function as spiritual father nowadays the way the abbot ideally functioned as father at Monte Cassino, Clair- vaux, and la Trappe?)

Whatever problems and tensions there might be in the area of monastic renewal within the cistercian family, it is clear enough that we have at present everything, absolutely every- thing, needed to live monastic life to the full, with joy and dedicated enthusiasm. And even though it might be ill-advised for us to take much heed of the la Trappe of Rancé's vision, I personally feel quite satisfied that much of what is noblest and deepest about our life has reached us thanks to the fidelity and faith of Rancé and his community. And since I am ending on this personal note, I might as well admit that, in occasional discouragement, I sometimes think that the real strength, the real beauty, the real quiet splendor of our life is less a pledge of a springtime of cistercian monasticism yet to come, than the remnant of a past season of autumnal splendor. Perhaps you know the poem by Robert Frost, 'A Boundless Moment', in

which a fellow trudging through a New England forest at
winter's end in March suddenly catches sight, in all the winter
barrenness, of a patch of color, a 'Paradise-in-bloom'. Is it
March anticipating May? No, he realizes as he moves on—only
'A young beech clinging to its last year's leaves'. And that
terrifies.

NOTES

1. English translation, 'The Fatherhood of Christ', in *Monastic Studies* 5 (1968) 45-57, from the original French, 'La paternité du Christ dans la règle du Maître', in *La vie spirituelle* 501 (1964) 55-67.
2. Unedited letter; original in Collection Tournouër; bibliographical note in H. Tournouër, *Bibliographie et Iconographie de la Maison-Dieu de la Trappe au Diocèse de Sées* (*Documents sur la Province du Perche,* 4e Série, No 2; Mortagne, 1905) p. 198, n. 793.
3. Unedited letter, Utrecht, Rijksarchief, Fonds Port-Royal (no No), a first of a series of three letters to the bishop of Alet.
4. Second letter in the series described in the preceding note.
5. Unedited letter; Paris, Bibliothèque nationale, MS francais 17391: Correspondence du Pierre Séguier, Tome 25, f. 216r.
6. Frequently printed. This excerpt translated from M. de Maupeou, *La Vie du tres-reverend Pere Dom Armand Jean le Bouthillier de Rancé* . . . (Paris, 1703), T. II, pp. 251-74—Procés verbal de l'état spirituel et temporel de l'Abbaïe de la Trappe, dressé par le R. P. Dom Dominique Georges, Abbé du Val-Richer, Superieur et Vicaire general de l'étroite Observance, dans la visite qu'il fit de ce Monastere le 16 Novembre 1685 et presenté au Chapitre general tenu a Citeaux en 1686. (Accent marks—or rather lack of them—as in the text, so also in later notes.)
7. Unedited *Mémoires* of Le Honreux de Saint-Louis, Paris, Archives du Ministère des Affaires Etrangères, MS France 1442, pp. 13-18.
8. See the not yet printed mimeographed paper by P. Lucien Aubry, 'Personne et Communauté: Rancé et la Trappe,' p. 2 (226).
9. C. S. Lewis, *The Voyage of the Dawn Treader* (New York, 1952) 172.
10. Frequently printed. Material here taken from Dom Pierre le Nain, *La Vie de Dom Armand-Jean le Bouthillier de Rancé* (Paris, 1719) II; 719-23.
11. *Ibid.,* pp. 719-20.

12. M. de Saint-Louis, *Mémoires,* pp. 167-68.
13. *Lettres de Pieté ecrites à differentes personnes* (Paris, 1701), Tome I, Letter 71, pp. 330-32.
14. Letter indicated above, note 4.
15. Lama Anagarika Govinda, *The Way of the White Clouds* (London, 1966) 93.
16. Letter indicated above, note 4.
17. Aubry, *Personne,* p. 3 (227).
18. Letter indicated above, note 4.
19. First printed at Paris in 1653, with two subsequent augmented editions in 1664 and 1670. References here to edition of 1670.
20. Louis Lekai, *The Rise of the Cistercian Strict Observance in Seventeenth Century France* (Washington D.C., 1968) p. 184.
21. Le Nain, *Vie,* Livre VII, Chap. XV, p. 674.
22. Paris, *Du premier,* pp. 302-341.
23. Unedited letter in Troyes, Bibliothèque municipale, MS 2183, f. 43r. Though dated from October, a note on f. 43v indicates November.
24. Le Nain, *Vie,* Tome I (ed. of 1719), p. 64.
25. *Lettres,* Letter 47, p. 206.
26. Rancé, *Treatise on the Sanctity and on the Duties of the Monastic State* (Dublin, 1830) I, 138, corresponding to Ch. 9, Question 2, of the original French text (numerous editions—two in 1683, another without date, and still other editions in 1684, 1701, 1846). Citations from *Treatise* are taken (with occasional simplification of punctuation) from the rare, flavorsome, but not always accurate translation of 1830, made by the future abbot-founder of Mount Melleray Abbey.
27. *Ibid.,* p. 139.
28. *Ibid.,* Question 3, pp. 139-40.
29. *Ibid.,* Question 5, pp. 142-43.
30. M. de Saint-Louis, *Mémoires,* pp. 126-27.
31. So far as I know, only one copy exists of the *Reglements pour les Filles de la Doctrine Chretienne de la Ville de Mortagne* (Paris, 1698), in Paris, Bibliothèque Mazarine, printed catalogue N⁰ 43285 (with the *ex libris* of the bishop of Séez, Msgr Turgot).
32. *Treatise,* Chap. 8, Question 1, p. 109.
33. See Paris, *Du premier,* pp. 290-91.
34. Text printed in full, Paris, *Du premier,* pp. 292-94.
35. *Treatise,* Chap. 8, Question 4, pp. 118-19.

36. *Ibid.,* pp. 117-18.
37. *Treatise,* Chap. 8, Question 5, p. 120.
38. *Treatise,* Chap. 8, Question 2, p. 113.
39. *Ibid.*
40. *La Régle de Saint Benoist nouvellement traduite et expliquée selon son veritable esprit . . .* (Paris, 1689) I, 124. Other editions of 1688, 1703, and 1704.
41. *Ibid.,* pp. 126-27.
42. *Lettres,* T. 2 (Paris, 1702), Letter 4, pp. 14-15.
43. Many different editions. Here taken from the first edition, *Description de l'Abbaye de la Trappe* (Paris, 1671) pp. 108-109.
44. *Ibid.,* p. 81.
45. *Treatise,* Chap. 12, p. 214 (introduction to Question 1).
46. *Ibid.*

CONTEMPORARY CISTERCIAN PRACTICE

THE SPIRITUAL FATHER TODAY

Edward McCorkell, OCSO
Holy Cross Abbey

T HE FATHERHOOD OF GOD is ultimately the source of any spiritual fatherhood among men and women of any time, culture, or religion. This great reality of God's Fatherhood is found in all the great religions of the world. Since I come from a Judaeo-Christian background, I would like to mention briefly, at the beginning of this paper, something that, no doubt, will be treated at some length in other papers. I refer to the Old and New Testaments of the Bible.

In the great song of Moses in Chapter 22 of the book of Deuteronomy, the inspired author asks the people of Israel: 'Is not this [Yahweh] your Father, who gave you being?'— clearly indicating God's Fatherhood. Shortly after his question, the sacred writer counsels the reader to 'ask of your father, let him teach you'. We see indicated here already the spiritual mission of the father of a family. He is a teacher, he transmits to his sons and daughters the 'word of God', and in doing so he becomes a spiritual father. More striking still is a figure like Abraham, whom we call 'our father in faith' in our eucharistic liturgy. In a divine encounter, Abraham heard the word of God coming to him: 'Look up to heaven and count the stars if you can. Such will be your descendants.' And, continues the author of Genesis, Abraham put his faith in Yahweh.

St Paul takes up this text of Genesis in his letter to the Romans, chapter four, and points out that the faith of Abraham, not his circumcision, made him the father of

207

all believers. He is quite explicit: 'In this way Abraham became the ancestor of all uncircumcised believers.' Long before Christ came, the idea of a spiritual father, transmitting life, has emerged. That life is passed on by means of a spiritual reality we call faith.

With Jesus, of course, the fatherhood of God is revealed perfectly in his own person. As he said to Philip: 'He who sees me, sees the Father'. He clearly came to give us a share in his sonship. 'I go to prepare a place for you, so that where I am, you also may be', that is, at home in my Father's house as an adopted son.

Is there, in our christian tradition and theology, a real sharing in the fatherhood of God, as well as the sonship of Christ? I ask this question before taking a look at the 'spiritual father today', because I believe any insights or experience that we might have today need to be tested in the light of the authentic roots from which we derive any genuine spiritual life we can claim to possess.

What we are dealing with in an assembly such as this is, I believe, not only the concept of 'spiritual father', but a real, concrete transmission of spiritual life, as real as the penetration of the seed into the ovum in the physical 'fathering' process. Men and women today are hungering for a genuine experience of spiritual life. How often, in their search, they are frustrated and disappointed because they come upon counterfeit presentations or manifestations of 'spiritual life' that dissipate like a cloud in the bright sun. To return to our question: is there, in our christian tradition and theology, a real sharing in the fatherhood of God? Jesus seems to give us a clear answer to that question in his words, recorded by Matthew in Chapter 23 of his Gospel: 'You must call no one on earth your father, since you have only one Father, and he is in heaven'.

How then does St Paul speak of himself as in labor, giving birth to his disciples spiritually and, in sending Onesimus, the slave, back to his master, Philemon, write: 'I am appealing to you for a child of mine, whose father I became while wearing these chains . . . a part of my own self.' We do not have a contradiction here, but simply a clear indication that it is the unique fatherhood of God that gives meaning to any share in his fatherhood on the part of a 'spiritual father'.

In our monastic tradition we have a whole line of spiritual fathers: the fathers of the desert, the fathers of the Church, our father St Benedict, our cistercian fathers, Robert, Alberic, Stephen, Bernard, and the others. Blessed Guerric, abbot of Igny, himself a spiritual son of St Bernard, liked to use the text of St Paul about being in labor till Christ was formed in his monks.

What about today? We hear the lament that there are few, if any, real spiritual fathers today. Actually the word used more commonly in our own time is 'master' or 'director'. Father Flavian Burns, who was a spiritual son of Father Louis (Thomas Merton) and then became a spiritual father himself as abbot of Gethsemani, gave us a retreat at our monastery and mentioned this complaint. His comment was that the problem is not so much a lack of spiritual masters or directors as a lack of discipleship. Too many aspire to be spiritual father, guru, staretz, he remarked. Clearly one does not become a spiritual father as one does a doctor of theology by going through some course. It is a gift, a charism, given by God, usually the fruit of years of faithful living of a deep, interior life. Being a teacher of mystical theology or spirituality, a priest or confessor, a superior, even an 'abbot' of a well-organized western monastery does not thereby guarantee that one is a spiritual father.

St Benedict was endowed with the genius and the charism needed to blend and wed what was best in the double stream of monastic life that came down to him: the anthonian or eremitical and the pachomian or cenobitical. However, there has been an unfortunate development in western monasticism. It is parallel to the 'straitjacket' theory ably delineated by Gerald and Patricia Mische in their timely book, *Toward a Human World Order.* Just as in the world of 1978 the value of

209

basic human development tends to be subordinated more and more to the imperatives of national security, we monks— at least Cistercians—can get caught in the 'straitjacket' of economic administration and self-sufficiency. We relate this to the value of 'poverty', but I believe we have come a long way from what our cistercian fathers meant by being 'poor with the poor Christ'.

I mention this because one of the reasons I was asked to give this paper is that I am an abbot. I was superior of a small monastery in Chile for about four years before coming to Berryville, where I have been abbot eleven years now. I quickly found myself caught up in the administrative machinery that plagues most of our institutions today. Much of the monastic rhythm was affected by the demands of the economy. As has often been said, 'the tail tends to wag the dog'. Being self-sufficient, in the cistercian tradition, tends to become the cog around which the rhythm of the life revolves. Evidently, in the more balanced twelfth century, this demand was not inimical (less so at least) to the proper balance needed for seeking the 'one thing necessary'.

St Paul asked the Corinthians in the beginning of his first letter to them: 'Where are the philosophers now? Where are the scribes? Where are any of our thinkers today?' We might ask ourselves: 'Where are the spiritual fathers today?'

There is a special problem that has emerged in our time— though it is not entirely new. Part of Alvin Toffler's *Future Shock* that has become 'present shock' is the widespread break-up of family life. The experience of fatherhood and sonship is commonly very unhappy, even traumatic. Recently I was shocked to read of a father murdering his six children ranging in ages from three to twelve. In another case—closer to home since we knew the man involved—a father was murdered by his son, who attacked him with a hatchet while he was sleeping in bed. Many youths have painful experiences in their relationship with their fathers, so that it is psychologically difficult, if not impossible, for them to relate even to God as Father.

210

Thus a topic like the one given to me—'the spiritual father today'—will readily turn off a lot of our young people. On the other hand, our youth are very perceptive and sensitive. If they discover someone who is really and genuinely spiritual, they will submit to him or her as a disciple and even as a son or daughter.

It is the widespread practice in our Roman Catholic Church to call priests 'Father'. Unfortunately, because of their preoccupation with administration and social demands, they often repel youth by their aggressive approach. Being celibate, they often come across as frustrated and seeking a kind of substitute fatherhood. Some mention must be made of this malaise in our time.

Shortly before he died, when he was on his way to the Bangkok Conference, Father Louis (Thomas Merton) gave a conference on prayer in Calcutta, India. In the course of it he said: 'You will not believe me when I tell you some of the things that are being said, of people going to a priest in confession, complaining of their inability to pray. The priest says, "Why pray? I don't pray. Why should you? Prayer is irrelevant. Prayer is medieval. It is immaturity . . . . Your action is your prayer and if your action is twenty-four hours a day, your prayer is twenty-four hours a day".' This is the life of prayer which is relevant to the world. It is exceedingly dangerous. In America some Catholic theologians have elected to go along with the popular theology: God is dead. The keynote is 'horizontal'. God is no longer transcendent. He is nowhere else but purely and simply in my neighbor.

This is one of the reasons why so many youth flocked and still flock to a place like India, seeking a real 'guru'. When they find one, they readily submit to a discipline that is even harsher and more demanding than our old trappist regime. I know of one such American who made a retreat with us recently. I had first met him some years ago when he was a beginner and immature. Now he has developed a life of prayer and genuine self-denial, considering himself to be son of a spiritual father in the hindu tradition. He had gone the

211

way of many youth in the 60s—sex, drugs, and the like—and in his dilemma he went to a psychiatrist. Yet, it was only when he submitted himself to a spiritual father that he began to emerge into sanity.

As a Roman Catholic priest and a cistercian abbot I recognize and pay tribute to the real presence of real spiritual fathers in traditions other than my own, christian and non-christian. We have heard about this in other papers at this Symposium.

Two of our young monks at Berryville pointed out to me, in sharing their views of my topic, that it is unfortunate that no paper was assigned with the topic of the 'spiritual child'.[1] Perhaps we should have invited someone to give a paper from that view and enter into dialogue.

It was also pointed out to me that ultimately both spiritual father and 'child' have to recognize that they are in the presence of a profound impenetrable mystery. It calls for genuine humility and reverence on the part of both. Such an attitude of humility will help both recognize the need for the healing power of love both on the psychological level and the deepest spiritual level, where the Holy Spirit penetrates with his divine therapy.

I believe we have in the person of the Holy Spirit a common ground on which we can enter into dialogue with our non-christian brothers on this subject of spiritual fatherhood. A spiritual father is one in whom the Holy Spirit 'breathes' his life of prayer, giving him the capacity to communicate life. What he does, how he lives must flow from who he is—a man of charity and compassion. It is in this way that he transmits spiritual life more than by his words.

I believe that the wisdom of the desert is still operative today. To share just one brief word from the apothegmata, or sayings of the desert fathers: Abba Poemen was once asked by a brother: 'What shall I do, Father, that I may learn to fear the Lord?' Poemen replied: 'Go and become a disciple of a man possessed by the fear of the Lord and from his fearing the Lord you, yourself, will learn to fear the Lord.'

I would like to conclude this paper with a few reflections from Father Louis' (Thomas Merton's) little book on spiritual direction: The whole purpose of spiritual direction is to penetrate beneath the surface of a man's life, to get behind the facade of conventional gestures and attitudes which he presents to the world, and to bring out his inner spiritual freedom, his inmost truth, which is what we call the likeness of Christ in his soul. This is entirely a supernatural thing, for the work of rescuing the inner man from automatism belongs first of all to the Holy Spirit. The spiritual director cannot do such a work himself. His function is to verify and to encourage what is truly spiritual in the soul. He must teach others to 'discern' between good and evil tendencies, to distinguish the inspirations of the spirit of evil from those of the Holy Spirit.

I believe we need to recapture something of the character of the spiritual father of the earliest day of christian monasticism, who 'did much more than instruct and advise. The neophyte lived in the same cell with him, day and night, and did what he saw his father doing. He made known to the father "all the thoughts that came into his heart" and was told, on the spot, how to react. In this way he learned the whole spiritual life in a concrete and experimental way. He literally absorbed and reproduced in his own life the life and spirit of his "father in Christ".'

The seventeenth-century benedictine mystic, Dom Augustine Baker, who, as Merton points out, fought a determined battle for the interior liberty of contemplative souls in an age ridden by autocratic directors, has the following to say on the subject and with this I will end my paper: The director is not to teach his own way, nor any determinate way of prayer, but to instruct his disciples how they may themselves find out the way proper for them . . . . In a word, he is only God's usher, and must lead souls in God's way, and not his own.

---

1. An initial oversight remedied in the paper 'Spiritual Sonship: A Report on Experience', and in the following paper as well —ed.

THE SPIRITUAL MOTHER TODAY

Jean-Marie Howe, OCSO
Abbaye N.-D. de l'Assomption d'Acadie

M Y CONTRIBUTION to this Symposium can only be one of reflection on my own experience in this domain. I hope that this experience, limited as it may be, will touch upon and join at its essential level the experiences that others may have had.

Perhaps it would be best to take you on my journey, which really began about twenty years ago. The beginning was not conscious. I did not set out on a journey. It just happened, and in retrospect I know about when it started. It began the moment that my eyes were able to see a spiritual reality in the face of a person. I learned to 'see', my 'eyes' opened, so to speak. That is what gave the initial impetus to my journey, a journey which has shown that the end is in the beginning and the beginning in the end.

My spiritual journey began when I met a spiritual mother.

The experior manifestation of the spiritual in the person of a real spiritual mother or spiritual father—perceptible and visible in a certain way, although undefinable and often unrecognizable—has been important for me ever since this first experience of it. Once begun, my journey went on continuously, relentlessly; for once the initial discovery was made, the pursuit of the reality became almost irresistible. In fact, irresistibility is the one word that best describes this whole journey.

For several years it was the face that determined the journey, because it was something in the face that touched, that awakened a consciousness in me. It was this that made

214

further quest an inner necessity. I learned that the first face 'seen' was a key, for it has enabled me to recognize the same thing when it exists in other faces. As time went on, it happened that other such persons appeared on my route. This gave me a special experience of persons, of spirituality, which has had its repercussions on my efforts to communicate spiritual life to others.

I cannot really say what happened to my consciousness, but I know that it opened and was increasingly receptive. The face became the *lieu* of spiritual life for me, for it was there that I acquired a 'sense' that has developed and remained with me ever since. By it a whole spiritual world opened, a spiritual vision took form. My own life became more and more an immersion in this world, which is essentially an immersion in the Mystery of Christ.

As this part of the journey was going on, something else was happening. Spiritual formation and guidance became my task and has been my concern ever since. The personal journey that was taking place simultaneously was the impetus to all I was to do in this area. It was this journey that helped me to sense what was in the writings of Père Placide Deseille, and which made me pursue intensely the reality which I had in a way already grasped.

It was almost with passion that I went into the study of Père Placide's books and tapes of a retreat he preached explaining the *Principles of Monastic Life.* Through him, this journey led me to the desert spirituality, the monastic spirituality of the East and West, and, without realizing it at the time, the doctrine of the Cistercian Fathers. What took hold of me was the dynamic relationship of the image and likeness. It was a development of the whole spiritual life based on the image: the return to the heart, the whole life of the heart, the journey into the heart which is also a journey into consciousness, an ever-deepening heart, an ever-deepening consciousness. In the *Asian Journal* Thomas Merton said that 'what is really essential to the monastic quest . . . is to be sought in the transformation of consciousness in its ultimate ground'.[1]

Although there were intellectual aspects to this journey, it was a journey into the heart. This is essential for the communication of spiritual life, for if one wishes to attain the heart of another, it is from one's own heart that life must flow.

What is to follow, then, are simply my efforts to communicate this spiritual life to others.

The spiritual mother is what she is. She is on her own journey, responding to a call from 'beyond'. At the same time she is present to this world. If she has 'antennas' sensitive to truth, along with a desire and capacity for fullness of being, she will be open to many things of value today. If she has a certain insight into human nature and personalities, she will be able to meet people as they are, where they are, and journey with them into the realities of the spiritual world, taking into consideration the particular needs and affinities of each person. It is understood that what underlies all work with individuals is a certain sense of God and some understanding of the divine pedagogy.

I have found that some people require very little material for their journey, but they must keep going into it, going down into it—finding depth in that way. Others need a great deal; they find it necessary to look at things from many different angles in order to find depth. Their way is richer in a sense. Yet, the end of both is the same—depth, and depth is the 'key'. There are still others with whom I have had experience who are almost unaware of the nature of spiritual life and of their actual relationship to it, but who are no less driven by a desire for the Absolute. The spiritual milieu works on them, molds them, and they become what they are without being too conscious of any of it. Very often they are people who have a certain limpidity, clairvoyance, and straightforwardness. There may be an absence of piety and intellectuality, but there is at the same time something very real there. There are two qualities I have found to be of vital importance in any spiritual quest: a desire for the Absolute and a basic capacity for human truth.

216

How is the spiritual mother to communicate life to those who seek it, and what exactly is the nature of communication at this level? For me, it is a question of the opening of consciousness, the awakening of the heart, of the *sens intime* of spiritual realities. This awakening is tantamount to guiding a person into the experience of a whole new world, a world which demands a different vision (a vision perceived through the eyes of the heart), and to helping the person to see the realities of that world.

This spiritual world continues to grow through many different channels. Once this 'sense' of the spiritual is awakened, the eyes are sensitized to related realities wherever they may be. So, it seems to me that the *raison d'être* of the spiritual mother is to succeed in opening this 'sense' of the spiritual in those with whom she works. It is through this 'sense' that they enter into a spiritual world that is immense.

The method that I use for awakening this consciousness is somewhat analagous to the experience of immersing oneself in water, as opposed to that of swimming on the surface. By 'immersion' I mean the sinking into, the letting go of self and just 'being', allowing the water to penetrate all the pores. By 'swimming' I mean action—doing something, going toward a predetermined goal, choosing the means, observing one's progress, paying attention to what is happening as a result of all this action. The application to spiritual life seems obvious.

Since 'immersion' is my way, it is upon this that I shall concentrate. It is a question of immersion in the Mystery of Christ. On the physical level, it is an immersion of the person in the concrete realities of the monastic milieu, that is, the Rule, the community, the vows, asceticism, solitude, silence (or, for someone not in monastic life, immersion in a suitable environment). On the intellectual level, it is immersion in Scripture and in monastic doctrine, ranging from the Desert Fathers to the Cistercian Fathers to contemporary theologians and authors who echo the essence of monastic thought. Spiritual immersion is the life of the heart, discovered and enriched through prayer, *lectio divina,* and the liturgical and sacramental life. Finally, there is a deeper level of immersion, that which is the goal of all three previous levels. It is no less than actual participation in the Mystery of Christ: immersion in Christ himself, transformation, divinization of the entire being.

Monastic life has its roots in being. When I think of being, I think of substance, of the heart. Our substance, our heart, must be truly penetrated by the Mystery of Christ. For such penetration to be possible, immersion is essential, and immersion in the Mystery of Christ presupposes *kenosis,* which is an emptying and, at the same time, an openness. It demands *ascesis,* rectification of the heart, interiorization, with ever-increasing receptivity. In the measure in which our substance is changed, our prayer is changed because our prayer is the expression of what we are, of what is deepest in us. My way of prayer has been the Jesus Prayer ever since my real journey began. It accompanied me; as the years went on, I discovered that my journey was taking place in it. The method of prayer varies with the individual, but it must lead to the heart where prayer is alive. The heart must be liberated in order to have real prayer.

One cannot speak of substance, of being, without touching on the vows. The contents of the vows, I believe, have finality. Poverty, chastity, and obedience are essential for any real experience of God. They make our substance capable of being penetrated by him. Stability gives continuity and conversion of manners gives depth to that relationship with God.

Continuity seems to me to be one of the secrets of spiritual life. Continuity in immersion. In that way an awakening of the heart, an opening of consciousness may progressively and almost unconsciously take place. The 'sense' which is awakened is very fragile. It demands continuity in order to exist, otherwise it will be eclipsed because it lacks milieu. One entry in Julien Green's journal[2] can be interpreted in this light. He speaks of two ways: the narrow and the wide. The narrow way is like a ledge jutting out on a mountain. One must stay close to the rock, which is God, if one does not wish to fall into the abyss below. Paradoxically, however, if

one does step off the narrow way, one does not fall into the
the abyss. The way simply becomes wide, the abyss disappears.
It is as though there never were an abyss, a mountain, a
narrow way.

In order to have immersion that is real, there must be simplicity. Père Charles Dumont made an accurate distinction
between sincerity and simplicity when he said: 'sincerity is
to say the truth, it is to say what one thinks or how one sees
things, while simplicity is to submit to the reality'.[3] 'To submit to the reality' has always been something I have tried to
arrive at with myself and others. Reality, facts—to learn to
see reality, to see that a tree is a tree, to deal with facts.
The bare facts of spiritual life are tremendous, much greater
than what can be said about them.

It seems to me that a certain 'atmosphere' pervades this
method of immersion. Something of that atmosphere can be
found in the following two texts: Nathaniel Hawthorne's
short story *The Great Stone Face* and Hermann Hesse's novel
Siddhartha. Even though clothed in a secular and even
fictional guise, both illustrate this experience of transformation of being through immersion. In the first it is a question of
transformation by looking and in the second transformation
by listening.

> Ernest had no teacher, save only that the Great Stone Face
> became one to him . . . . He attracted little notice from the
> other inhabitants of the valley; for they saw nothing
> remarkable in his way of life, save that, when the labor of
> the day was over, he still loved to go apart and gaze and
> meditate upon the Great Stone Face . . . . They knew not
> that thence would come a better wisdom than could be
> learned from books, and a better life than could be moulded
> by the defaced example of other human lives . . . . The pure
> and high simplicity of his thought, which, as one of its
> manifestations, took shape in the good deeds that dropped
> silently from his hand, flowed also forth in speech. He
> uttered truths that wrought upon and moulded the lives of
> those who heard him . . . . Ernest began to speak, giving to

219

the people of what was in his heart and mind. His words
had power, because they accorded with his thoughts; and
his thoughts had reality and depth, because they harmonized
with the life which he had always lived. It was not mere
breath that this preacher uttered; they were the words of
life, because a life of good deeds and holy love was melted
into them. 'Behold! Behold! Ernest is himself the likeness
of the Great Stone Face!'[4]

I will remain by this river, thought Siddhartha . . . . May
my present path, my new life, start from there.
In his heart he heard the newly awakened voice speak and
it said to him: 'Love this river, stay by it, learn from it.'
Yes, he wanted to learn from it, he wanted to listen to it.
It seemed to him that whoever understood this river and
its secrets, would understand more, many secrets,
all secrets.[5]

In both of these experiences the essential qualities are the
same: being, simplicity, continuity of experience and time,
plenitude, and beauty. Transposed into a vision of monastic
life, they have been very helpful for awakening in a person a
certain 'sense' of things. It should be remarked, however,
that even transposed, they only go up to a certain point.
There is a step beyond which is not found here and which is
too important not to mention: the possibility of being taken
over by God, of becoming a holocaust—the experience to
which our quest may lead and toward which we direct
our steps.

When it is a question of being, of substance, of 'real', it is
a question of time, much time usually. In the *Citadelle*,[6]
Saint-Exupéry noted the difference between someone who
was carried up to a thousand mountain tops and who was
thus able to observe a thousand landscapes (without really
knowing one) and someone who climbed up one mountain
by himself, experiencing all the steps of the journey. The
latter takes time, but in experiencing one mountain the

person is capable of understanding all the landscapes
to come.

Though not always looked upon in that way, the spiritual
life, and, *a fortiori,* monastic life, is a quest, an adventure.
The Quest of the Holy Grail and *The Lord of the Rings* by
Tolkien are vivid texts illustrating this point. However, I see
the quest as a quest by 'immersion' and not by 'swimming'.
One's attitude is that of attention, constant attention, waiting (not pouncing on a particular object or running after a
particular object), remaining suspended above the whole, so
to speak, waiting and allowing the true object to come to
you in its reality. Of course, this does not take anything away
from the idea of quest as an adventure, an adventure which
involves the whole being, giving vitality to one's whole life.
The quest is an answer to a call: 'the drawing of this Love and
the voice of this Calling'.[7] Without a call there would be no
real quest. The call becomes a wound, a wound for the absolute, for the Truth, for God, and it is by this wound that what
is most real in us awakens and sets out on the quest. Prayer
itself is a progressive ever-deepening wound opening into
Christ's wound; sanctity is a divine wound.

Perhaps one of the most characteristic traits of my approach
to communicating spiritual life to others is the use of symbols
and images. I have found that they can be real catalysts of
life. They provide a whole world of echoes to which the heart
can respond. There is something delicate and light about symbols and images; they leave space to breathe in and make the
beauty of doctrine felt. It would be pointless to give many
examples of the symbols and images that I use, because my
spiritual world is full of them. But, I will say a few words
about three of them. 'River of water' and 'river of wine or
fire' is an image of a deep underground river in us, the deepest
level of spiritual life. The river of water is plenitude: it is at
this level that one arrives at willing what God wills; and the
river of wine or fire is divinization: it is at this level (if one
can call it a level) that one cannot not will what God wills.
There are two images that I like for describing the progress of

the spiritual life. One is the face. The progress from image to likeness can almost be 'seen' if one 'knows' the face. The other I found in Kahlil Gibran's *Procession:* the reed and the song. A person becomes more and more a reed as he is hollowed out by the spiritual life. The life that grows in him is a song that becomes more and more divine.

The *raison d'être* of the methods used for communicating spiritual life is to facilitate as far as humanly possible a rebirth. Olivier Clément writes of monasteries as 'places for rebirth'. There is also a more personal aspect to this communication. One could say that the journey made by the spiritual mother gives her the capacity to enter into the journey of another as from the interior, and there to lead the person into the spiritual world, perhaps to a rebirth. If the spiritual mother has at some time in her life gone through a trial of some magnitude, she is able to descend into the depths with someone undergoing one of similar intensity and day by day make the difficult passage with the person. It may well be that through this spiritual mother the person may cross a threshold into a different level or zone of spiritual life. Rebirth, the passage to another order, requires a death similar to physical death, against which we may struggle even though the death is desired for what is beyond.

It's evident that when a spiritual mother agrees to travel with another person, she agrees to be changed by the other. And often it happens that together they arrive at something that neither can claim as all her own nor can she distinguish her own share from the other's. Throughout my whole journey I have experienced the truth of this kind of relationship.

One really assimilates very little in a lifetime, so we must not think that we have to have many things. We must live out our spiritual journey just as it is. The important thing, always, is that our experience in the spiritual life be authentic. Every step must be a step in the reality, and we must try to profit to the utmost from each step. Progressively we enter into the spiritual world, and God becomes more and more a reality for us. One may live in this reality as simply as one lives in the common reality of daily life without special attitudes and comportments. It is just that this other world has become *real,* and one can dwell simply in this spiritual world. The real in the spiritual life is greater than anything we can invent and cannot in fact be invented at all. All real transformation is the work of the divine and not the human. Simone Weil wrote an unforgettable page illustrating this point. She says that 'there are false imitations of the love of God, but not of the transformation that it operates in the soul, for one has no idea of that transformation other than passing through it oneself'. She also says: 'Although there is no fire present in a cooked dish, one knows nonetheless that it has passed through fire'. And on the other hand: 'Even if one might have believed that he saw the flame, if the potatoes are raw, it is certain that they did not pass through the fire'.[8]

Comparatively recently, on my personal journey, a turn in the road appeared that brought to light yet another resource for communicating spiritual life. What marked this turn in the road was a rediscovery of the psalter and of a method for entering into it. It all happened quite by accident.

One day I began reading the psalms aloud to myself, softly and slowly, listening to the words more than saying them. In order to get the impression of movement of journey, I began to tap on the table slowly and regularly; at the same time I listened. Gradually I found myself, as it were, walking into the psalm. There was no meditation or reflection, just movement into . . . . The psalm began to reveal something through the words and yet beyond them. I experienced a psalm; in that experience there came to me the 'sense' that had opened for me by way of the face many years before and that had progressively made its way to a deeper level of consciousness.

Since then, this has been my way of praying the psalms, and a whole experience in that area has come into being. A new vision took form which was the same as the other and yet different. Perhaps it is the same one seen from another level. At any rate, the psalter revealed itself as a special means for the communication of spiritual life to others.

It was recently brought to my attention that my experience
with the psalms is somewhat reminiscent of a description of
peak experience and Haiku poetry by Brother David Steindl-
Rast.[9] For example, with respect to Haiku poetry, Brother
David writes:

> Haiku is, paradoxically, a poem about silence. Its very
> core is silence . . . . All that matters is the silence. The
> Haiku is a scaffold of words; what is being constructed is a
> poem of silence; and when it is ready, the poet gives a
> little kick, as it were, to the scaffold. It tumbles and the
> silence alone stands.[10]

There seems to be some similarity between what is being said
here and my way of experiencing the psalms. The psalm does
become a kind of scaffold of words (Spirit-filled words) and
as our substance penetrates the exterior of the words, we can,
as it were, give a little 'tap' and the words disappear, leaving
us immersed in the Mystery.

Once a psalm is experienced, a pull, an irresistible attraction, makes itself felt, which causes one to leave everything,
so to speak, and walk into the psalms. The way through the
psalter is the way of a poor man. To use an image: a dusty
road, and dusty boots (which might some day stand still at the
still point of the turning world)[11] walking on and on into the
psalms and out of self. Immersion. *Kenosis.* Substance.

There is a real force in the psalms, as Dom André Louf
points out in his book *Seigneur, Apprends-nous à Prier.*[12] It
seems to me to be a force of yearning, a force of drawing into
the Mystery of Christ. The psalter appears to me to be an
opening, a door to the Parousia, the plenitude of the Mystery
of Christ. Christ is Alpha and Omega, beginning and end,
beginning and end of the desire which inhabits us. Between
the beginning and the end there is a whole spiritual journey
possible. Walking into the psalms is walking toward the heart.
Coming through the psalms is coming into the heart. Walking
into the psalms is walking into the heart of Christ, into the
heart of humanity, into our own heart. It is immense. Walking
and listening. Listening to what? Listening to the voice of

Christ and in it the voices of all humanity through the ages. St Augustine hears in the pslams the voice of Christ praying to his Father and also the voices of the members of Christ, his Mystical Body, praying through him to the Father. It is in this tradition that I find myself. Siddhartha, listening to the thousand voices of the river (the different voices of humanity) which ultimately he heard as one voice, is an image which, transposed, gives much insight into this understanding of the psalms.

Walking deeper and deeper into the psalms, immersed in them, one should listen attentively for the unchanging bass, the 'I am', the Absolute, the Eternal, which flows under the ever-changing melodies, the various thematic subjects of the psalms. To hear the 'I am': this is to find the plenitude, the white light containing all the colors, the full Mystery burning in a moment. It is at this 'still point of the turning world' that our hearts are in union with Christ's heart, beating at the heart of the world.

I have discovered that simply praying the psalms with another by the method described above can help the person to grasp something of this whole spiritual world or open it to him. Should the result be an opening of a 'sense', then the person would be ready to set off on his own journey. And that journey is important.

The world today is a suffering world. The cries of humanity reach us on all sides. Those cries demand a response. Christ saves and heals the world. As we journey toward the Father, in the Son, by the Spirit, the life which has taken root in us can grow even to the point of making us a holocasut through whom He blows, through whom He burns, so that the words we speak are words of fire, the words we pray are prayers of fire.

> A brother went to the cell of the abbot Arsenius in Scete, and looked through the window, and saw the old man as it were one flame; now, the brother was worthy to look upon such things. And after he had knocked, the old man came out, and saw the brother as one amazed, and said to him,

'Hast thou been knocking here for long? Hast thou seen aught?' And he answered, 'No'. And he talked with him, and sent him away.[13]

The spiritual mother or father who can help in some way that life to be born is in a serious endeavor. That life can save and heal the world, although this is most often hidden from the eyes of the world. The quest and its fulfilment is often unseen, unknown. This is echoed in Tolkien's tale. When Frodo returns to the Shire from the quest that saved it, 'few people knew or wanted to know about his deeds and adventures';[14] and if they had known, they would not have understood. Frodo was left with a wound that would never heal and which forced him to continue his journey, beyond . . . .

Those in whom that life is born are wounded and cannot stop their journey.

All I have been able to offer you is my experience. It did not take long to put down on paper, but I can make mine the words of Corot. In speaking about a painting that he had done rapidly, he said: 'How much time did it take me? five minutes and my whole life.'

NOTES

1. Thomas Merton, *The Asian Journal* (New York, 1973) 316.
2. Julien Green, *Le Bel Aujourd'hui* (Paris, 1958) 243-4.
3. Charles Dumont, 'L'esprit de Cîteaux dans la mentalité actuelle' (conférence), Conférence régionale, *Cîteaux* (June, 1976).
4. Nathaniel Hawthrone, *Complete Novels and Selected Tales* (New York, 1937) 1170-83.
5. Hermann Hesse, *Siddhartha* (New York, 1951) 82-83.
6. Antoine de Saint-Exupéry, *Citadelle* (Paris, 1948) 145.
7. T. S. Eliot, *Four Quartets* (Little Gidding).
8. Simone Weil, *La Connaissance Surnaturelle* (Paris, 1950) 96.
9. David Steindl-Rast, *At the Still Point: Reflections on Haiku Poetry and Monastic Life.*
10. *Ibid.*
11. *Ibid.*
12. English translation *Teach Us to Pray* (London: Darton, Longman, Todd; New York: Paulist). Ch. 5: 'The psalm as response to the Word.'
13. *The Desert Fathers* (trans. Helen Waddell; Ann Arbor, 1960) 125.
14. J.R.R. Tolkien, *The Lord of the Rings* (Toronto, 1973) 305.

SPIRITUAL SONSHIP: A REPORT ON EXPERIENCE

William Wilson, OCSO
New Melleray Abbey

THIS SYMPOSIUM IS REMARKABLE for the number and quality of papers and studies on Spiritual Fatherhood and Motherhood. My contribution here is a homely sidelight, but I hope you will find it stimulating and informative to hear a rank and file monk report on his personal experience of, and reflections on, being a disciple, a spiritual son in a cistercian monastery.

A young person can be, and I certainly was, a bundle of confused good and bad impulses. Entering the monastery, not yet twenty years old, I was a tangled skein of good intentions, hopelessly unrealistic ideals, lethal misconceptions, and a great deal of unrecognized ego ambitions. I had already made enough mistakes in life to know that it doesn't always work out well when you simply follow your strongest impulse—even when that impulse seems very religious. A young person often has a vague sense that he doesn't have purity of heart, lacks discretion, and cannot be sure of distinguishing God's will among the many voices clamoring in his heart. How aptly I thought the proverb quoted in the Rule of St Benedict applied to me: 'There is a way which seems right to a man, but its end is the way to death.' (Prov 14:12; RSV text used here and throughout)

And so I sought someone who could help me discern the will of God. As a novice in the monastery it was the novice master and also my confessor. Remotely, it was the abbot. But the abbot was a more distant figure and his spiritual fatherhood more general. Without any doubt, it was the spiritual fatherhood of these men which saved me from the constant peril of being led astray by my own ambitions during the novitiate.

Looking back, I can see some of the important aspects of being a disciple, a spiritual son. A son must have faith, a theological faith, in his spiritual father. He must believe that the spiritual father is God's Providence guiding him along new and unknown paths of interior life. A disciple must begin by *trusting* in the better judgment of his master. Moreover, he must trust that this father really loves him and has only his best interests at heart in all the guidance he gives. He must be convinced that the spiritual father is loyal to the welfare of the disciple, and not biased in favor of his own personal interests or those of the group to which he belongs. Having such a faith and hope in his 'Abba', the disciple owes him a very special love of gratitude. It is the responsibility of the spiritual father or mother to fulfill these expectations of the disciple as well as he or she can. There is a specific love which the spiritual guide owes to the follower. The self-love of the neophyte is not a reliable source of true benevolence even toward himself. Left to his many desires, often conflicting and sometimes totally destructive, the confused self of the young disciple would often follow wrong and hurtful impulses. So he chooses to follow the directives of the more achieved self of the spiritual father. The latter, therefore, should try to love the spiritual son better than the son is able, at present, to love himself. The father's self has been more integrated by grace. He shares his 'self' with the son, allowing him to live by his fatherly wisdom, until the son himself acquires a certain degree of discretion. In other words, the spiritual father ought to love his son and guide him as his own true self. Besides this love, the father must believe and trust, just as his spiritual son does, that God will use him, in spite of his personal sin and ignorance, to guide the disciple in the right path. The fullest exercise of concrete acts of faith, trust, and love are equally important on both sides of the relationship if it is to achieve its optimum effect. Notice the concreteness of the theological virtues in this case. Here we do not believe, hope in, and love the mysteries of our faith in any general way. Rather, the disciple dares to believe that the Holy Spirit will act, guide, and sanctify him through his concrete and practical inter-action with this particular man.

A word of caution. Suppose the spiritual father consciously or even unconsciously foists on to the disciple his own religious idiosyncrasies? In fact, this will happen almost inevitably. In the beginning, the disciple will have no means of discernment. He will imbibe a certain number of merely subjective intel-lectual and spiritual viewpoints while he is drinking in the great spiritual tradition of the Church from the fountain of his spiritual father. If the spiritual father is blatantly incom-petent, even a beginning disciple will recognize the error of his outlandish doctrine. Usually the strictly subjective ele-ments of the spiritual father's teaching are so minor and harm-less that the young disciple will neither recognize them nor incur any serious loss by accepting this influence. Later on, when he is practised in knowledge and discretion, the disciple will be free to drop certain optional views and practices which may have been right for the spiritual father but prove to be useless baggage for the disciple.

If we are spiritual fathers or spiritual mothers, we must not impose our views, our devotions, our ways of thinking upon our disciples. We want our disciples to become like Christ, not like us—to be formed in the image and likeness of God, not our own. But it is really very difficult to let someone we know and love, someone under our guidance, grow into a mentality and spirituality different from our own. Can we be detached enough to allow them to be different? Are we secure enough in our own spirituality not to be threatened when a disciple grows in a pattern uniquely his own? Can we go even further and encourage our spiritual children to become them-selves in any way God fashions them, regardless of how dif-ferent they are from us? We are true spiritual fathers and mothers only to the extent that we can do this. Insofar as we try to guide and limit our disciples in ways that are merely our own personal options, we are fakers and charlatans. Eli, the priest of Shilo, was cursed for not correcting his sons according to the flesh. But in dealing with young Samuel, his son according to the spirit, Eli is a model for spiritual fathers. The old priest did not try to form the boy in his own ways. He taught Samuel to obey God: ' . . . If He calls you, you shall say, "Speak Lord, for your servant hears"?' (1 Sam 3:9).

Let me return to my own experience of discipleship. I remember what went on between me and my spiritual father during those early years. For the most part, he had to keep on, repeatedly checking my unconsciously self-centered ego ambitions. There is a strong tendency, in the aggressive but immature, to try to become great or outstanding or holy in religious life by exaggerated efforts. The fervent disciple lacking discretion wants to fast extremely, study extremely, work extremely, pray extremely, be humble extremely. I bless my early spiritual fathers who patiently and constantly forbade me to carry out my 'good intentions'. They taught me the error of my ways. Eventually, but very slowly, over the years I began to be able to see the difference between a a spiritual ego-ambition and a true leading of the Holy Spirit. The growth process continues, and I still need a spiritual father to help me make such discernments in particular instances. Now that I am older, perhaps the more difficult task of my spiritual father is stirring me up to a little more generosity in fasting, prayer, and work.

From these recollections I learn that one of the first and greatest duties of a spiritual son is to desire and to try to learn discretion from the master. Correlatively, one of the principle duties of a spiritual father is to teach the disciple discretion. The spiritual father or mother ought to explain discretion frequently and give a living example of it in their lives.

Adrian Van Kaam, in *Religion and Personality,* wrote that a true sense of self-worth and authentic self-love, far from being present at the outset, are the last things a person attains after

much experience of the spiritual life. I agree entirely. I see
now how tremendously I was helped during the first years of
monastic life by the love and affirmation I received from my
spiritual fathers. I can say in all truth: I was able to survive
those years only because I knew I was loved, affirmed, believed
in, by my spiritual fathers. I was quite unsure of myself,
whether I was any good or not, whether I was 'real' or not. At
times the self-doubt would have been completely paralysing.
But in the midst of that terrible experience of un-selfhood, I
kept on repeating over and over: 'Father so and so loves me.
He really loves me and he believes in me'. At such difficult
times I virtually lived on the strength of his faith in, and love
for, me. It held me afloat when I would have sunk if I had been
left to my own self estimation.

Here present are many abbots and abbesses, and others who
serve as spiritual fathers or mothers. The human reason why
you are chosen to be spiritual leaders is that you are magnified
in the eyes of your sons and daughters. It is God's Will that
you appear to them to be extraordinary. To your spiritual
children you seem wiser, holier, more spirit-led than others.
That is why they chose you to be their spiritual father or
mother. For them personally, you are one of the finest
christians they have ever known. That being so, can you imagine the astonishingly great significance your valuation of your
spiritual child has in his or her heart? If the person who knows
me best in this world is also one of the very best people I
know, and he loves me and thinks highly of me, then nothing
else under heaven could more powerfully convince me of my
own lovableness and worth. This is one of the essential and
most precious dimensions of the relationship between spiritual
father and son: that the son sees his own goodness and value
reflected in the love and esteem of his spiritual father. And
vice versa. As the disciple deeply realizes that he is thoroughly
known and loved by his father, he will advance in authentic
self-love; and his ability to believe in and accept love from
others and from God will increase.

During those first years I had a little confusion about

232

loyalties, for I was spiritual son of both the novice master and my confessor. By the end of the novitiate I realized that a monk should have only one spiritual father in the strict sense. Of course there are many other spiritual relationships which are helpful and even necessary for spiritual growth. We need confessors, advisors, teachers, preachers, senior monks, peers, and friends. But there really can be only one spiritual father. No disciple can serve two masters. He will have to give primacy to the will of one or of the other. In my experience, the spiritual father had come to be that one sacramental person chosen by the monk, in whose preferential will the disciple freely believes the hidden will of God is revealed for him. This description will become clearer as we procede.

There may be good reasons for having a spiritual father other than one's abbot. In this case, the spiritual father will have to be careful to situate his ministry within the larger context of the disciple's ultimate filial loyalty to his abbot. I believe that, according to the Rule of St Benedict, the abbot is ordinarily the spiritual father of his monks. But just as he delegates much of the material administration of the monastery to a procurator, he likewise has power to delegate a share of his spiritual paternity to certain of his monks. For example, the novice master is appointed by the abbot to be the immediate spiritual father of the newcomers, while the abbot remains the ultimate spiritual father of the whole community. Because of the large number of monks, or the press of other duties, or the personal needs of particular monks, the abbot does not serve as immediate personal spiritual father to each monk.

During my first three years of simple vows, the former close relationship with the novice master gave place to a much looser bond with the junior master. This situation intensified the spiritual son relationship I had with my confessor. By the end of these three years, I realized I had no close relationship with my abbot. At that point it was difficult for him to admit me to final profession. He simply didn't know me well enough. So I asked him to be my spiritual father in the strict sense.

From then onward the priest who heard my confession was
also counselor and friend. But he was no longer my unique
spiritual father. I continue the practice of asking my abbot to
be my spiritual father. I don't think it is always best for every
monk to have the abbot as his immediate personal spiritual
father, but it has been a great blessing for me.

During this most recent decade of spiritual sonship I have
learned a new meaning and practice of obedience to my spiritual father. I'd like to tell you about this. My earlier ideas of
obedience represented it as 'doing what my spiritual father
commanded, or at least permitted'. To obey his commands
and never to act without his permission. Such were the norms
of my former idea. In the light of personal discoveries in
recent years I can no longer subscribe to such an inadequate
conception of religious obedience.

Let me share a very personal meditation on the gospel
scene of Our Lord's agony in the garden. I present it merely
as a monk's scriptural meditation which led me to a new
understanding of obedience. The synoptic gospels show us
Jesus accepting the will of God in the garden of Gethsemane.
I have come to believe that the Father offered Jesus alternatives in the garden. The Scriptures do not tell us much about
what other courses of action Jesus was free to take instead of
handing himself over to his enemies there in the garden.
Would it not have been acceptable to the Father had his
innocent Son slipped away from the hostile crowd in Gethsemane the way he did when the people of Nazareth were
ready to throw him over the brink of the hill? We don't
know. But I think there is good reason to believe that the
Father would have been pleased if Jesus had chosen to subdue
his enemies physically in the garden. We read that at the
simple request of Jesus, the Father would have immediately
sent more than twelve legions of angels to rescue him from
his enemies (see Mt 26:53). So I have chosen to believe that
Jesus had other alternatives acceptable to the Father. I do not
believe that the Father's love for the Son was in any way
conditional or dependent upon Jesus' choice to die on the

cross. In my view, then, Our Lord was not laboring under any
threat of loss of his Father's love should he choose not to
drink the cup of his passion. Not even human lovers, if their
love is real, demand absolute obedience as the price or the
condition of their love. So I cannot imagine the heavenly
Father making an absolute demand of his Son's obedience
unto death on the cross. The way I understand it, the Father
offered the Son several possible choices, but revealed his
preference that Jesus freely die on the cross for the salvation
of the world. I believe God the Father revealed a preference
to his Son, and not a demand. There is a world of difference
between a preference and a demand. It is one thing to reveal
your preference to someone you love and whom you leave
perfectly free. It is an altogether different thing to demand
that someone do what you want done as a prerequisite to
your loving him. I see the act of obedience of Jesus as loving
conformity with the preference of his Father, not as an act
of submission to an inexorable fate imposed by a stern Master.
It is to me as if the Father had said to Jesus: 'My Beloved
Son, you may do this or do that, and I will be pleased with
you because I love you. But if you are willing, I would have
you drink the cup of Passion and Death.' If my belief is right,
then the agony of Jesus in the garden was not a matter of
trying to bend his will into conformity with a divine command.
It was, rather, the agony of a man perfectly free to avoid
death, struggling to accept death because it was the mere
preference, not the absolute demand, of his Beloved Father.
Love obeys the preference of the beloved. The loving son,
Jesus, obeyed to death the preference of his Beloved Father.

The result of this meditation is a new concept of christian
obedience. Specifically, christian obedience includes and goes
beyond submission to commands and prohibitions. Christian
obedience conforms to the preference of the Beloved. Practising this kind of obedience to my spiritual father has become
one of the essential vital functions of my spiritual sonship.
I call this kind of obedience 'preferential' because it goes
beyond commands and seeks to obey preferences.

Does this preferential obedience foster immature dependency? To lean on a spiritual father—or anyone else—to make one's decisions for one, to avoid moral responsibility, to refuse to be author of one's own actions—all of this represents the worst of moral immaturity. But let me show you that it has nothing in common with preferential obedience.

Life is a sequence of moral situations, each one of them more or less complex. Many of them are exceedingly complicated. Every life situation has its own moral implication: it calls upon you to act in a certain way. We can classify all life situations objectively as being either clear and certain in their moral implication or unclear and uncertain. Here are a few examples of a clear moral situation: a man finds himself in circumstances in which adultery would be possible and easy. A woman sees a blind man feeling the ground in search of an object he has dropped, which she sees. In such cases the person knows spontaneously and immediately what ought to be done. It is gross immaturity for a disciple to ask his spiritual father to help him decide what to do whenever the situation is objectively clear. As spiritual fathers and mothers you should not tolerate such infantilism among your disciples. Hopefully, we disciples will know better than to approach you when we should listen to the call of the moral situation and obey it.

But there are many other moral situations which do not give clear indication of what ought to be done. A disciple does well to take counsel with the spiritual father to gain from him any information he may have pertaining to the obscure moral situation. But this is not yet 'preferential' obedience.

Sometimes both the spiritual father and the son experience the ambiguity of an objectively uncertain moral situation. Then, and then only, is the time to practise preferential obedience. An example: a certain monk had been in the monastery quite a number of years when his family raised the question of a home visit. The case had merit because he had not seen any of his relatives except for one visit from his mother. Moreover, permission for such visits was already being granted. But a monk who embraces 'preferential' obedience is not content to do things merely because he can get permission for them. After long consideration neither he nor his abbot could determine with certainty whether it would be the best way of loving to remain in the monastery or to make the home visit. Although willing to give the monk permission to visit his family, still the abbot had a lingering preference for the monk not to go. The monk obeyed this preference of the abbot, judging that this obedience was the best act of love he was capable of in the situation and believing that the abbot's preference revealed the preference of God for him at that time.

I have been asked if this preferential obedience leads to increasing dependence on the spiritual father. Actually, the reverse is true. This form of obedience leads to increasing dependence on the Holy Spirit, while recourse to the spiritual father decreases. The obedience due to the legitimate commands of our superiors admits of no diminution. So there is no spiritual growth that would free us from the obligation of obedience to them. But the exercise of preferential obedience disposes a person to be led immediately by the Holy Spirit, because every act of this obedience is itself a response to an invitation of the Spirit. This form of obedience, required by no law, expresses consent to an occasion of grace offered by God's Spirit: his preference for our greatest good. But more than this, preferential obedience disposes its adherent to docility to the Spirit because of the humility, faith, and love that it embodies. It takes humility to walk by the judgment of another, especially when neither reason nor law obliges one to do so. In obeying the preference of your spiritual father, you are impelled neither by his reasons nor by church law. And it takes faith, a kind of covenant faith in which we trust that God will respond to our graced initiative. We believe that God will accept our obedience to the preference of a human spiritual father as a symbol embodying our desire to obey our heavenly Father's preference. Moreover, we trust and believe that God will lead us by means of the 'sacrament' of the spiritual father's preference. Preferential obedience, as humility and faith in act, arises from our desire to love and to grow in love. It is therefore love coming-to-be. This exercise of love, humility, and faith disposes a person for increasing sensitivity to the impulse of the Holy Spirit. Progressively, without reflection and almost unawares, the monk simply knows what to do (how to love best) in the uncertainties of each moral situation. Less and less frequently does he find himself confused and unsure of how he ought to act. He never makes a decision no longer to consult or follow the preference of his spiritual father so that he can henceforth be free to follow the Spirit. That would be a mistake. It is just that he is unselfconsciously being led by the Holy Spirit more and more so that his experience of moral situations as 'uncertain' progressively decreases. So there will be an unintentional diminution of occasions for practising preferential obedience in proportion to the growing connatural inclination of love received from the Holy Spirit. Preferential obedience is, therefore, an ascetical and mystical means by which the practitioner comes more and more under the immediate guidance of the divine Spirit within him. Far from alienating the disciple from the spiritual father, this spiritual development is the deepest preference of the authentic spiritual father.

Sometimes secular psychologists think this obedience is equivalent to a sickly cult of inferiority. How wrong they are! They do not realize that the spiritual father in no way dominates the disciple. Actually, it is the believing will-act of the disciple that creates and maintains the status of the father. The spiritual father has no authority, no power of any kind over the disciple, except what the disciple himself, by his free choice, confers upon him. It is the spiritual father who depends on the disciple. No Christian can ever set himself up as a master and teacher capable of guiding others. We Christians well know that we have only one Father, one Teacher, one Guide: the Divine Spirit. In christian tradition, those who serve as spiritual

guides realize that no power or competence of their own
enables them to be instruments of the Holy Spirit toward a
disciple. It is only the willing faith of the disciple, in which
the master humbly joins him, that allows the Spirit of God to
lead a Christian to holiness by means of the ministry of a
spiritual father or mother.

In this last part of my talk I'd like to tell you what spiritual
sonship means to me now—now that I am in my middle years.
My relationship with my spiritual father is the principal
governing relationship of my whole life. I love some other
people more intensely than I love my spiritual father. Yet the
love between a disciple and his master is unique and in some
way supreme. For it is within the context of the love relationship between me and my spiritual father that I pass judgment upon and put order into all my other loves.

Quantitatively, the work my spiritual father now does for
me most is to be a silent affirmation of my life—a life I live in
the open before him. I do not mean that my spiritual father has
any right or any desire to pry into the natural secrets of the
intimacies of my life of prayer and friendship. Nor do I think
it is in any way desirable to burden him with all the details of
my interior prayer and relationship with others. He respects
the privacy of my life and trusts me in my private domain.
Yet, he is welcome to see any part of my life. There is no
domain that I would hold back from his concerned interest.
His general knowledge and approval of my life of prayer and
human relationships encourages me and gives me confidence
and strength. He knows my sins and weaknesses because I tell
them to him. Yet he continues to believe in me! Because he
trusts me, I can dare to trust myself.

At times I still lose the thread of the meaning of my experience, especially interior experience. Prayer can seem to
vanish, and God with it. At such times my spiritual father
lets me see with his faith vision. He offers me his believing
interpretation of my life. And it is good. At other times, no
less frequent, he listens to my report both of the chaos of my
interior experience and the sense I see in it by faith. His

acceptance of my chaos and my self-understanding is very strengthening.

I have become convinced that the development of christian interior experience, under the action of the Holy Spirit, leads to an ever deepening awareness of one's own moral weakness, sin, confusion, and spiritual poverty. It is faith alone which enables the progressing contemplative to endure the increasing darkness, emptiness, and impoverishment. However, this invincible faith is itself nourished by the believing presence of the spiritual father. The spiritual father cannot spare his disciple the horrors of these dark nights. Nor can he share them. Every man is a solitary in his mystical experience, whether of heavenly light or of divine darkness. As it is written: 'The heart knows its own bitterness, and no stranger shares its joy' (Prov 14:10). Nevertheless, the very presence of the spiritual father in the life of the disciple is most reassuring during periods of intense, passive purification. For no matter what ordeals of doubt and confusion the spiritual son goes through, no matter how weak and overthrown he may feel, there stands his spiritual father, strong, firm, unshaken in his faith that God is doing his work in the soul of the disciple. This too is a precious service you spiritual fathers and mothers can render to your children.

Finally, in my spiritual father I have an ever present model of a life given over to God in prayer and given to men in service. It is an inspiration to have inter-personal contact with such a spiritual father. And whenever my own discernment is uncertain, I still look to his preference to find the Perfect Will of God.

THE EASTERN AND WESTERN TRADITIONS

COMPARATIVE STUDIES

241

THE GURU: THE SPIRITUAL FATHER IN THE HINDU TRADITION

Francis Acharya
Kurisumala Ashram

AS AN ALTERNATIVE to 'spiritual father' I have chosen 'guru', its equivalent in the hindu tradition. Spiritual fatherhood is a key concept in biblical revelation. It is not absent in the hindu tradition, even in its very strict sense, and as such it is related to the word 'guru' which occurs in vedic literature for any person of importance such as father, mother, teacher. 'To the Master who has taught them the highest *brahman,* that beyond which there is nothing, the disciples say: "You are indeed our father, for you ferry us across to the further shore, beyond the reach of ignorance".'[1] And the Code of Manu explains: 'The man who teaches the Veda, be it little or much, is called guru because of the benefits conferred by such instruction. The *brahman* who is the giver of birth for the sake of the Veda and teacher of prescribed duties becomes by law the father even of an aged man, though he himself may be young.'[2] The Institute of Vishnu has this to say on our subject: 'He who fills the ears with holy truths, who frees from all pains and confers immortality, let the student consider as his father and mother.'[3]

Yet, on the whole, spiritual fatherhood does not attain in hindu spirituality any place comparable with that which it enjoys in Christianity. It is at the very center of Christ's life and mission, and we can truly speak of an identity experience. It sums up the religious experience of the Word of God made flesh. It is the repeated experience of the Son of Man, an

243

experience by which he came to realize himself, to realize his
true self as Son of the Father, one with Him in the Holy
Spirit, as it is recorded in the Gospel: at his baptism in the
river Jordan, at his transfiguration on the mountain, and
repeatedly in his prayer life, as when he was filled with joy by
the Holy Spirit and he sang the blessedness of his unique
sonship, or when he prayed at the Last Supper that the Father
might set his seal on this sonship by giving it the glory which
he, the Son, had had with the Father before the world was
made.

Yet, in spite of the unique theological quality of Christ's
experience of the divine fatherhood, the spiritual father of
the christian tradition—and more so perhaps in its western
wing—has often shrunk to being a very particular type of
person, one who belongs exclusively to the ecclesiastical
world and, more strictly still, to such ecclesiastical institutions as seminaries, religious congregations, and monasteries.
His function often merges with that of the confessor, be he
an 'ordinary' or an 'extraordinary', though in some circumstances he cannot be the confessor of his spiritual sons. In its
most widespread acceptance the spiritual father must also be
distinct from the religious superior—even from the abbot of a
monastic community. Such a clear-cut understanding with
its subtle distinctions could hardly fit the hindu tradition!

In this connection it may be useful to make a general
observation concerning Hinduism. By whatever way we
approach it we are struck by its complexity. The hindu tradition is indeed a vastly complex phenomenon. The word
'tradition' itself has connotations very different from its
strictly defined and authoritatively preserved christian
counterpart. To the western cartesian mind it appears as a
motley collection of ideas, philosophies, and sectarian beliefs.
Yet Indian masters see the same reality in a different perspective; as Sri Aurobindo put it: 'That vast, rich, thousand-
sided, infinitely pliable, yet very firmly structured system we
call Hinduism'. This essay on the guru may help us to see
how he can be an intermediary, a helper to solve the problems

of doctrine, and a mediator in reconciling the apparently
conflicting schools of spirituality (or paths to salvation) and
the *sadhanas* (or spiritual disciplines).

First, the complexity is certainly there, but, under the
diversity of geographical, social, religious, and cultural traditions, behind the pluralism of peoples, languages, and customs, there is an unmistakable unity resting on many values.
We will mention only one here, but it is exemplary for other
fields. Nature plays an important part in this unifying
process—unceasingly at work in Indian culture in spite of the
widely different climatic conditions. The land more than the
sea has shaped the lives of the people of India. Its great rivers
have been invested with sacredness, while their flow into the
sea continues to this day to evoke the merging of the individual soul with the universal soul.[4] India's mountains have
always been considered areas of holiness calling man to the
peaks of asceticism. Its forests have traditionally been the
place of *gurukulas* or *ashrams,* where men and women retire
for a life of meditation after they have performed their duties
as householders.

Unity in diversity remains one of the dominant features of
India as a whole and more particularly of her approach to the
ultimate realities. It is asserted in a vedic aphorism—which is
universally accepted and unceasingly quoted:

Ekam Sat, Viprash bahudah vadanti

[Reality is one, sages speak of it in many ways].

In spite of this diversity and complexity—and some would say
syncretism—it remains true to say that spirituality as a value
of life is a conspicuous feature of the genius of India and
probably its most outstanding contribution to the life of the
world community. India's pride, increasingly acknowledged
by the West, though not always for its most authentic expressions, is her God-awareness. Inherited of old from her
rishis and sages, it has been carried along through the ages in
the life of her people despite the vicissitudes of her history,
and it is still very much alive today. Gurus are the most
influential agents of this God-awareness, while the Vedas, the

record of their experiences and their spiritual attainment, are
its most revered embodiment. The Vedas are a vast complex of
spiritual and metaphysical intuitions and deep psychological
insights, but also of religious and philosophical agnosticism
as well as magic and even superstition. The Vedas rest on a
few fundamental experiences. The supreme Reality is beyond
the reach of human apprehension. It is one-without-a-second,
beginningless, endless. It is supreme fulness of existence,
consciousness and bliss, *sat-cit-ananda.* It is at once the ground
of all fleeting existence and the Self of man's own self. It is
the most fulfilling experience of man, yet also a mystery of
which the least inadequate human expression is: 'Not this,
not this'.[5]

How exactly this mystery is related to man and his quest
for fulfilment has been a matter for fierce controversy down
the ages, some schools even rejecting the Upanishadic teachings.
But the basic intuition of the transitory nature of all phenomenal existence remains to this day a conspicuous feature of
the hindu way of life, accompanied by its natural corollary
of a profound respect for anyone, man or woman, who has
the courage to translate it into action by embracing a life of
total renunciation and finding joy and peace in the constant
awareness of the Presence on which all things rest. It shows
no sign of being outmoded, but witnesses even in our own
days a renewed vitality.

Another universally shared view in India about the spiritual
quest is that of the *margas,* the paths that lead to spiritual
attainment: *jnana marga*—the way of knowledge or wisdom,
bhakti marga—the way of loving devotion or commitment,
and *karma marga*—the way of action or service. The western
view of these paths has been hardened somehow. They have
been cast into two patterns often experienced as conflicting:
the active life and the contemplative life, and often the
distinction seems to rest exclusively on rules of external
behavior, of activity and rest or non-involvement. The Indian
margas, while preserving their distinctive features, are generally
considered and experienced as complementary. Though one

may predominate, it is felt that all three are components of the psychological and spiritual make-up of humankind. In another respect they represent successive phases of human life. The western ecclesiastical classification of actives and contemplatives is not found in India. The prevailing view is rather that what matters is 'realization'. This may require leaving the world, at least for a time, sometimes for a lifetime. One can withdraw from the mainstream of life as in our own days has Ramana Maharshi who, after years of extreme asceticism, remains totally non-involved except for making himself available in utmost simplicity both to his family, who have built an ashram with him at the center, and to any enquirer who comes to seek advice or to experience the truth of his presence. Or one can turn again to the world and become involved in various activities: in spreading the message of Divine Life as Ramdas from his ashram on the west coast in South India, or as Swami Sivananda in the Himalayas. One can consecrate one's life to higher education, like Rabindranath Tagore at Shantiniketan near Calcutta, or to the more ambitious enterprise of creating a new man, a new humanity, like Sri Aurobindo at Pondicherry. One can also enter the field of social uplift, like Vinoba Bhave, or even politics, like Mahatma Gandhi. These are all spheres of activity for true gurus, where they can reveal their ability to awaken us to a higher consciousness, their charism for helping to realize the all-pervading Presence. In all these fields in this century they have had a deep influence, not only on the revival of Hinduism but also on the renaissance of art, literature, and ultimately on the re-birth of India through *swaraj*—self-rule. Is it not from them also that the world movement towards putting an end to colonialism as well as other forms of domination of one person over another, one nation over another, has gathered much of its strength? And is it not even now leading us all to that universal brotherhood for which we are longing, the new man, recognized by all as son of God, *harijan,* according to Mahatma Gandhi, or *amritasya putra,* son of immortality, in the words of the Vedas?

While the guru can be considered as the backbone of Hinduism, the spiritual quest in Hinduism has been described as hunting for the guru. It has also been said that the guru is the symbol of Indian culture, of the entire religion, of the spiritual heritage of India. In Christianity pre-eminence goes to God, who takes the initiative in speaking to man and in planning out and launching and working out his economy of salvation. And ultimately this is entrusted to the Church. In the *Sanatana Dharma,* the Eternal Order or Law, which Hinduism claims to be, salvation is realized, perceived, and apprehended by *rishis, munis,* acharyas, or gurus. Guruship is a freely formed institution emerging from experience and preserved in the Sacred Scriptures and spiritual writings, as the prophetic life or the priesthood is preserved in our Scriptures and in the lives and sayings and rules of the monastic fathers. But their influence seems to have penetrated more deeply and more permanently into the personal and social life of the people. To treat exhaustively of the guru we would have to turn not only to sacred writings but also to such fields as history, the arts, psychology, sociology, and even politics.

To sum up, it remains true to say that the guru is the nearest Indian equivalent to the spiritual father in the christian tradition, yet it is far less confined to the professionally religious sphere of life which is its milieu in the West. Like God, whom he makes present, the guru is an all-pervading reality, permeating even the profane spheres of life. This was brought home to us recently. A mechanic of our neighborhood in Kerala, a Hindu and father of several children, had been working for some months at coupling a second-hand Kirloskar oil engine with a generator for operating our milk cooler. As he failed repeatedly to find his way, one day in great perplexity (he had burned the coil for the second time) he exclaimed: 'I must go and see my guru'. By this he meant the man who had taught him the trade. But he expected from him not simply a technical advice but also a 'grace', a 'blessing', without which he feared he would not be able to bring his work to completion.

It would not be fair, however, to absolutize the ideal of the Indian guru. Indians themselves have their own reservations about them. Answering the question, 'Who is the True Guru?,' the *Bhavan Journal* of Bombay, the fortnightly journal of Bharatia Vidya Bhavan, the most influential cultural association of India, recently quoted Sri Samartha Ramadas, a Maharashtrian saint, as saying: Talking of gurus, they are legion. Men with mantras, mystic powers, men with minds festering with desires, sorcerers and tricksters with nimble tongues. No good ever comes of them. They are surely not dispensers of liberation. One upsets our minds, the money grabber; one derides others, the curious-minded; one has no devotion, the hot-headed; one is intent on pleasures and one creates troubles; these are not men to confer emancipation. One whose non-attachment is superficial, whose mind is bristling with desires, one who without practice holds forth on Vedanta, these too are no good. The one who matches his words to deeds and behaviour is the right guru. One given to true devotion, realized, discriminating, dispassionate, learned and subtle, such a guru alone can give you the highest place.[6]

Moreover, if we understand the guru in his essential function of spiritual guide or preceptor, it would not be right to describe him as an exclusively Indian institution. On the contrary, all the great religions have made a place for spiritual teachers and know accordingly the master-disciple relationship. Swami Vivekananda has brought out its central place in religion. It is a significant fact that where this relation still exists between the teacher and the taught, there also gigantic spiritual souls grow, but in those who have thrown it off, religion is made into a mere diversion. In nations and churches where this relation between teacher and taught is not maintained, spirituality is almost an unknown value.[7]

THE GURU, EDUCATOR OF ANCIENT INDIA
The root of the word 'guru' is the same as that of the latin
gravis, heavy, a word which easily takes on spiritual connotations, as the english 'grave', or, in the Bible, the aramaic
kabod, heavy, which came to designate the glory or the
radiance of God. In the Indian tradition, when used for a
person, 'guru' designates a man of weight, a venerable or
respectable person, as father, mother, or even simply a relative older than one's self. The word comes close in modern
usage to designating a spiritual person or a preceptor, one
who teaches the law and religion and from whom the student
receives the initiatory mantra with the sacred thread, the
ceremony by which he becomes a *brahmachari,* to lead the
chaste life of a student of sacred knowledge. Thus the guru
as a distinct person of Indian society appears first in the
world of education. He is a teacher, a preceptor. Another
word which designates the same function and occurs even
earlier than 'guru' is *acharya:* 'He who knows the rules of
right behavior', the spiritual guide or teacher whose privilege
it is to invest the student with the sacred thread and to instruct him in the Vedas, in the law of sacrifice and religious
mysteries.[8] The two words have been used indiscriminately,
though *acharya* is often reserved for a learned person. But to
this day *acharyas* are considered as gurus. Yet the gurus are
often more charismatic figures, and they have generally stolen
the show, and more so beyond the borders of India. In the
Upanishads the guru is described as an elder who is to be
approached with reverence by the *brahmana,* the *brahmin*
student. He is the teacher from whom *brahma*-knowledge is
to be sought and for this he is expected to be versed in the
scriptures and established in *brahman:*

> Having scrutinized the worlds won by works,
> let a ***brahmana*** arrive at non-attachment.
> That which is not made is not won by works.
> For the sake of this knowledge, let him approach
> with sacrificial fuel in hand,
> a teacher who is learned in the Scriptures and established

in *brahman.*

§

Unto him who has approached in due form,
whose mind is tranquil and who has attained peace,
let the teacher who knows teach in its very truth
that knowledge about *brahman*
by which one knows the Imperishable One, the true.[9]

Buddha himself describes the guru as 'The *brahmana* whose
self has been cleansed of sins, who is free from conceit, whose
nature is not stained by passions, who is self-controlled, who
has studied the Vedanta and lived a chaste life, he indeed is the
man who can expound the doctrine of *brahman*'.[10]

Education in vedic India, as all over the ancient world, was
not for the masses. It was generally conducted away from the
cities, in sylvan retreats with the simplicity of life which this
required, in an atmosphere of recollection and serenity con-
ducive to mental concentration. Apart from the environment,
the real creative force in education came from the teacher,
the guru. The earliest gurus belonged to the *brahmin* caste
whose exclusive privilege it was to be the teachers of the Vedas,
of its rituals and its chants. But when, with the Aranyakas
and the Upanishads, the interest turned from the seen to the
unseen, from the sacrifices believed to support the cosmic
order (while enhancing the devotees' earthly life) to the
realization of the non-earthly *atman* within him, the guru
assumed new qualities and so did his relationship with his
students. The guru-shishya relationship is at the heart of
Hindusim, both in the early tradition which is seen as a
continuous revelation based on sacred texts, *sruti,* handed on
by the *rishis,* the sages who have 'heard' the Veda, and in the
post-vedic era of *bhakti* which opened the path to realization
to millions. In the Upanishads, tradition can be learned only
by hearing, and the guru is he who knows how to utter it,
how to recite it with its correct rhythm, vibrations, and
intonations. Education is based on the student's individual

251

treatment by his teacher, with whom he has to live in order to imbibe the inward method of the teacher, the secrets of his efficiency, the spirit of his life and work. The method he is to use is *upasana,* meditation, by which the student approaches his subject—the word he has heard or read—mentally, for concentrated and deep reflection. The *brahmachari* lived with his guru, not simply as a boarder for a set number of semesters, but as a member of his family. His routine duties provided a number of experiences. He was to go daily to collect wood from the forest and bring it home for tending the sacred fire. We see the students approaching their teacher with fuel in hand as a token that they are ready to serve him and tend his household fire, and this also is food for meditation: 'The *brahmachari* puts on fuel to enkindle the mind with fire, with holy luster'.

The *brahmachari's* next duty was to tend the teacher's house and cattle. Tending the house was training for him in self-help, in the dignity of labor, by manual service for his teacher and the student brotherhood. Tending cattle was education through a craft as part of the highest liberal education. The students received a valuable training in the love of the cow as the animal most serviceable to man, and in the industry of rearing cattle and dairy-farming, with all the other advantages it gave of outdoor life and robust physical exercise. Another of his duties was to go out on a daily round of begging. It was not selfish begging for his own benefit, but for the ashram to which he belonged. Its educative value is explained in the Satapatha Brahmana, which points out that it is meant to bear fruit in creating in the student a spirit of renunciation and humility.[11]

In these schools the *brahmachari*s came for their period of studentship proper, leading to the second *ashrama* or stage of life, that of the householder. But some would prefer to continue and dedicate their whole life to the pursuit of learning and religion in the spirit of this passage in Brihad Aranyaka Upanishad: 'Wishing only for that world [*brahman*], mendicants leave their homes. Knowing this the people of old did not wish for offspring . . . and they, having risen above the desire for sons, wealth, and new worlds, wandered about as mendicants.'[12]

The influence of the *gurukuls* was not confined to the small group of students who lived with the master; it extended to society. We hear of kings who come from distant regions to sit at the feet of the master in search of enlightenment. Sometimes the guru-disciple relationship arises between husband and wife—Yahnavalkya and Maitreyi—or between father and son—Uddālaka Aruni and Svetaketu. Sometimes it is transferred to the sphere of the gods, as in Katha Upanishad where it is Yama, the god of death himself, who leads Naciketas from the desire of earthly life to that of a life of good works and finally to enlightenment about the great transition, the crossing over to the further shore, by which man conquers re-death. We also find in the sacred writing philosophical debates in the form of competitions as they still take place today. These were a favorite practice among monks and wandering mendicants, a means by which they spread their own beliefs and views.

THE BESTOWER OF INITIATION

The conferring of *brahmacharya diksha* or of *sannyasa* is one of the fundamental duties of the guru. Because no one can become a guru without having a disciple, it is true to say that one becomes a guru by giving *diksha* to the first disciple. But, at the same time, by this the guru recognizes the spiritual worth of the seeker, his fitness to embark on the path that leads to liberation. This is the formal duty of the gury, one by which he finds himself rooted in the heart of institutional religion: its *samskaras* or sacraments—sixteen in number—which mould the life of a Hindu from conception in the womb of his mother to the burning of his corpse after death on the burial ground.

The guru's proper *samskaras* are *upanayama*—the conferring of the sacred thread—and *sannyasa,* the great renunciation of which the contents are remarkably described as unsullied

253

brahmacharya (chastity), true *vairagya* (non-attachment), perfect *jnana* (wisdom), and the desire for selfless service (*niskama seva*). As a whole hindu *samskaras* have remained close to nature, they make greater use of its symbolism (the physical realities of nature, of matter) than our christian sacraments. The whole cosmos and its four elements (earth, water, air, fire) are made to contribute to the initiation of man in to the most significant stages and states of life. *Upanayama* is the sacramental imparting of a new birth from which the candidate emerges as a *dvija,* a twice-born. It is also the guru's formal admission of the student which makes him into a *brahmachari,* a student of sacred knowledge, one who treads the path leading straight to *moksha,* salvation. *Sannyasa diksha* comes as the seal of *brahmacharya diksha.* It elevates the *brahmachari* to a higher sphere of spiritual attainment described as liberation from bondage, including social obligations—even the most conventional ones. Through increasing God-awareness the *sannayasin* becomes an embodiment of truth: 'One who craves not and hates not, one who is above all opposites and therefore is established in freedom'. 'By the grace of the Spirit, he sees the Spirit in all things and therein finds fulfilment . . . liberty . . . deliverance from the oppression of pain.'[13]

Both these initiations consist of very elaborate rituals lasting several days: fast and *pranayama,* recitation of *jabamala* (rosary), mantras, fire sacrifice, readings, and sacramental actions. But, on the whole, the kernel of their structure is very close to, if not identical with, the consecration of the monk in use in the eastern churches. They consist essentially of prayers, readings of the sacred scriptures, and sacramental actions. The following are common to the two traditions: tonsure, stripping, bathing, and clothing. Proper to Hinduism is the giving of the mantra, whispered in the ear of the seeker. This can be a name of God, but it is not necessarily a prayer. The sound (*sabdam*), with its vibrations, is often the determining element which will be the vehicle of the guru's grace or *shakti,* imparting spiritual energy to the disciple.

254

But again in this matter of guru and the initiation he gives
we find ourselves confronted with that 'infinitely pliable
though very firmly structured system called Hinduism'.
Hardly any of the prominent gurus of our time perform these
samskaras. They are left to professional *sannyasins.* At Sivananda Ashram, Rishikesh, the guru known as the President of
the Divine Life Society, reserves to himself only the giving of
the mantra and some prayers and chants. Further still, a considerable number of gurus have ceased giving *diksha* altogether. Sri Aurobindo and Ramana Maharshi, who saw
thousands of disciples who came to them from India and
overseas, never gave *diksha* nor did they receive any disciple
in the traditional sense. They held that God is the only guru
and that no human being can be a substitute for him. Though
they did not deny the possibility of a spiritually experienced
person helping another along the same path, they insisted
that the real source of help is transcendent. Some famous
hindu holy men, like Sri Ramakrishna, refused to think of
themselves as gurus in spite of their many disciples, and this
for the same reason: they saw God as the only guru. This was
also the case of Gandhiji, the Mahatma, who occasionally
referred to his own disciple Vinobaji as his guru. For the
Sikhs the sacred scripture is the only guru: *Guru Granth.*
For others, guru is anyone or anything you choose to induct
yourself into spiritual life or mystic experience. Anything
through which one approaches illumination is guru.

The same flexibility is manifested in the diversity of manners of conferring *diksha.* It is not that the *samskaras* are
depreciated or abandoned, but that they are transcended. In
the ancient monastic orders which took their origin in the
eighth century from Sankaracharya and the great acharyas
who created the Vedantic schools, *brahmacharya diksha* and
sannyasa diksha are still indispensable for all their members.
This remains the rule in most of the modern ashrams which
owe their origin to a particular guru. Yet in the world of contemporary gurus where their mission is understood as consisting
almost exclusively in the awakening of divine consciousness

in the aspirants—even when they themselves have received a full-fledged *sannyasa diksha*—several other ways also recognized by tradition will be used, depending on the guru's own view and on the capacity or the life situation of the disciple.

A common way of imparting *diksha* is by whispering the mantra in the disciple's ear. This mantra becomes then the center of the seeker's devotion, and it is usually kept secret. He repeats it over and over again and concentrates upon it at the time of formal initiation. This is not magic. Its nature is that it has been given by the guru to whom he has surrendered and that it is his own. *Diksha* is also given by contact or touch and by a glance which establishes a spiritual communion and by a word which awakens a sense of the Divine in the disciple. In the *shaktipath diksha* the guru's charismatic power enters into the disciple, sometimes unexpectedly even at a first meeting, sometimes after a long time, sometimes also simply by thought when the disciple is physically distant from him. What is essential and common to all such initiations is that something of the consciousness of the self-realized man enters into the eager consciousness of the disciple. This can be sudden, even dramatic. A story is told of Swami Vivekananda. One day as he was sitting in *samadhi,* a man attracted by his recollection paid homage to him by touching his feet. Vivekananda came to his normal consciousness and, realizing what had happened, exclaimed: 'My dear friend! What have you done? Your whole life will now be changed'. And indeed it turned out to be so. The man gave up his profession, entrusted his wife and child to his relatives, and became a *sannyasin.* When he touched the feet of the swami in deep meditation, there came to him a spiritual power which transformed his life. It is difficult not to think here of our Lord performing a healing miracle when his garment was touched by the sick woman whose faith literally stole away his healing power.

256

TEACHER OF MEDITATION

The guru's function is not confined to giving *dikshas,* even if they are charismatic. He is essentially an educator, a teacher, and he remains today very much so. Education in ancient India included of course the three Rs, but its aim was sacred knowledge as it had been crystalized in the Vedas. The Rig Veda, the most ancient, consists mainly of hymns to be chanted at the daily or seasonal ceremonies, sacrifices, and ritual observances. These hymns are the work of men trying to come to terms with the creation by personifying in the form of gods the powers at work in it. All along there is an underlying search for understanding these as diverse manifestations of one supreme God, of Divinity itself. This search becomes more insistent in the Brahnanas and Aranyakas where questions arise about the nature of the gods themselves. It reaches its climax in the Upanishads, which means 'approaches', but they are in reality the consummation of Vedic teaching—centered on the very nature of existence. They establish the ancient equivalence felt between the human and the divine world on a new foundation, the assumed identity between the individual soul, *atman,* and the universal soul, *brahman.*

This ultimately provided the real purpose of education, attainment of the highest knowledge, saving knowledge, leading to *mukti,* salvation. But the first task of the teacher was to train the student in *upsaana,* a meditation in which importance is given to various objects of meditation. The whole process of meditation was framed into four steps: *sravana, manana, nididhyasana,* and *darshana,* already found in the famous colloquy between the sage Yajnavalkya and his wife, Maitreyi, on the *atman,* the Self:

> Mark well, it is not for the love of the All
>   that the All is dearly loved,
> rather it is for the love of the Self
>   that the All is dearly loved.
> Mark well, it is the Self that should be seen,

> that should be heard,
> the Self that should be thought on
>   and deeply pondered over, Maitreyi.
> Mark well, by seeing—*darsana*—the Self,
>   by hearing it—*sravana*—
> by meditating on it—*manana*—
>   by pondering deeply on it—*nididhyasana*—
> is this whole universe known.[14]

It is interesting to observe here how the four steps towards the attainment of supreme knowledge of the Upanishads are close to, if not identical with, the four rungs of western monastic *lectio divina: lectio, meditatio, oratio, contemplatio.* It seems that the two traditions have discovered or created from their origins the same path towards realization or communion with God. That a similar itinerary of the mind has been devised quite independently and even several centuries earlier by the *rishis* of India suggests that we have here a fundamental experience of humankind in its quest for God.

Sravana means hearing. It is the hearing by listening to the instruction of the teacher or by reading. In its highest form it consists in receiving through the ear of the heart the knowledge that vanquishes sorrow. The knowledge thus received through the ear was aptly called *sruti,* 'what has been heard', which is the term still used for revealed knowledge corresponding to our Bible. *Manana* corresponds to *meditatio.* It is the work of the *manas,* the mind, its natural activity: a searching for understanding in the process of assimilation through deliberation and reflection. It is the most active stage of meditation. It is known as *svadhyaya* when it turns to be more of a study. *Nididhyasana* is the highest stage of meditation proper, it leads straight to realization, the realization of the truth. It has been defined by Patanjali as 'the steady stream of consciousness of the one Reality'—we could say initial contemplation. The fourth stage we have indicated here, *darsana,* is not usually included in the lists, but it is the universally acknowledged goal of the three other steps. It is known by diverse names: realisation, illumination. We have chosen *darsana,* the vision, as the sacrament of the contemplative realization of God. As the Bhagavad Gita puts it: 'When he sees me in all and he sees all in me' (VI, 30).

Upasana meditation is thus a mental approach which looks at things not for the sake of analysis but in the light of their relation to the ultimate reality, the light of unity. We could point to a similar experience in the christian tradition: 'A monk is one who feels himself one with all men, who sees himself in every man' (Evagrius). It is in this sense that meditation brings about an inner transformation, a becoming. The personality is elevated by an inner growth and expansion. Realization through purification and refinement culminates in identification, in oneness. The light of contemplation expands the consciousness in God, as Gregory the Greate wrote of St Benedict. Such contemplative knowledge and communion is also experienced in the Jesus Prayer as an inner light shining in the heart, which becomes thus the place of God, the place of the vision of God, as he makes himself present to his devotee. This establishes him in his full self-realization, as the image of God. The Indian tradition speaks of the 'experience of pure light by concentration on the lotus of the heart,' in the encounter of the Self.

The main task of the guru consists therefore in developing and strengthening the mind of the *brahmachari* student for the acquisition of the highest knowledge. This is the fruit of the training in meditation. It includes, of course, yoga, defined by Patanjali as *citta vritti nirodha,* the arresting of the fluctuations of the mind. Yoga has its own three stages of meditation following *pratiyahara,* the withdrawal of the senses from their objects for the stilling of the mind when the inner gaze, usually restless, is made to rest still between the eyebrows. Our three stages are: *dharana, dhyana,* and *samadhi.* They are, in fact, three degrees of concentration. In the first, the mind is still struggling to concentrate on its object. In the second, the distracting images are shut out and the mind is fixed on its object, but there is effort, strain, and there remains a conscious self direction. In the third, *samadhi,* concentration is effortless and the object alone shines in a new light while the subject appears, as it were, to have merged with the object.

GUIDE TO REALIZATION

Again here we should not take *samadhi* too easily for granted, nor should we think of all ashrams and *gurukuls* as turning out realized men every year as our colleges turn out graduates. The Upanishads themselves tell us of the short-comings of both disciples and gurus. Svetaketu, on his return home as a fully initiated *brahma-charyi* who had studied the holy Vedas for twelve years, is found by his father 'proud of his learning and having a great opinion of himself'. He is then told: 'Have you asked for that knowledge whereby is heard what is not heard . . . whereby is known what is not known?' And when the father explains this the young man replies: 'Certainly my honored masters knew not this themselves. If they had known, why would they not have told me?' And then follows the exchange of questions and answers on the essence of the fruit of the banyan tree and the salt in the water, leading to the great realization of Svetaketu. It is exemplary of the Upanishads' teaching on the indwelling Spirit:

'Bring me a fruit from this banyan tree.'
'Here it is, father.'
'Break it.'
'It is broken, Sir.'
'What do you see in it?'
'Very small seeds, Sir.'
'Break one of them, my son.'
'It is broken, Sir.'
'What do you see in it?'
'Nothing at all, Sir.'
Then his father spoke to him: 'My son, from the very essence in the seed which you cannot see comes in truth this vast banyan tree. Believe me, my son, an invisible and

260

subtle essence is the Spirit of the whole universe. That is Reality. That is Atman. YOU ARE THAT.'

'Explain more to me, father,' said Svetaketu.

'So be it, my son. Place this salt in water and come to me tomorrow morning.'

Svetaketu did as he was commanded, and in the morning his father said to him: 'Bring me the salt you put into the water last night.'

Svetaketu looked into the water, but could not find it, for it had dissolved.

His father then said: 'Taste the water from this side. How is it?'

'It is salty.'

'Taste it from the middle. How is it?'

'It is salty.'

'Taste it from that side. How is it?'

'It is salty.'

'Look for the salt again and come again to me.'

The son did so, saying: 'I cannot see the salt. I only see water.'

His father then said: 'In the same way, O my son, you cannot see the Spirit, atman. But in truth he is here.

An invisible and subtle essence is the Spirit of the whole universe. That is Reality. That is Truth. THOU ART THAT? *TATVAM ASI.*'[15]

The gurus warn their disciples against seeking mere learning, mere book knowledge, 'for that is mere weariness of the tongue.'[15a] 'Not by the study of the Vedas is the *atman* attained, nor by intelligence, nor by much book learning.'[16] And the disciples, some at least, are aware of it. One confesses to a sage: 'I am learned in the Scriptures, *mantravid,* but I have no knowledge of the *atman, atmavid.* I have heard from persons like you that he who knows the *atman* vanquishes sorrow. I am in sorrow. Lead me then, I pray, beyond the reach of sorrow.'[17]

In the case of Svetaketu, it was his own father, his father by the first birth, who became his guru, as he led his son to that experience which each one of us has to have and no one can have for us. By this the guru reveals himself not only as a teacher of meditation but also as a guide to realization.

The dialectical method in favor with the *rishis* for this purpose consisted in giving an enigmatic definition of *brahman,* one that would prompt questions from the listener. The puzzle of the definition proposed lay often in the restricted, sometimes minute, field of reflection it offered the student: the little seed, the glass of salted water. But this narrowing down resulted in the concentration of his thought. As new objects appear when they are caught in a beam of light, new questions surged in his mind, questions which led him through deeper insights and interiorization to a unifying knowledge of the world and of all things. And from the Self that indwells all things dawned the mysterious unity: 'The Self that indwells all things is within you,' the inner realization of the oneness of *brahman* and *atman,* of the ultimate reality of the universe and of his own self. 'This, my *atman* within the heart, is that *brahman.'*

Atman is above, Atman is below
Atman is North and South, East and West.
Atman is the whole universe.
He who sees, knows, and understands this,
who finds in Atman the Spirit,
his love and his pleasure and his union and his joy
becomes a Master of himself. His freedom then is infinite.[18]

Contrary to what was often held in the past, western thinkers now generally agree that no school of thought understood this identity in terms of pantheism. And in that sense no school broke away from the authentic upanishadic experience by which the mind transcends the data offered for observation to penetrate into the deeper layers of inner awareness. Yet for this, two ways were followed. One is 'apophatic'; it consists in denying all the limitations or restrictions which would go against the identity of the subjects and the Absolute. It is not the individual *atman* which is identical with *brahman,* observes Suzanne Siauve, but the subject freed from all his conditionings, the idiosyncrasies that make him appear as individual, including his impression of being different from the object of his own knowledge which is precisely the ground of his being. The other path preserves the distinction between *atman* and *brahman* and understands the identity in terms of a relationship. *TATVAM ASI* ('Thou art that') does not mean identity between two ultimate realities. It means that God is the soul of my soul, the spirit of my spirit, the support of my being in an eternal dependence on his love.[19]

It is this last interpretation that puts more emphasis on the teaching and the role of the guru. His task is to reveal to the disciple the unity of the Vedas, to make him aware of their convergence towards perfect harmony, which is also perfect knowledge of God. His aim in opening the mind of the disciple to the knowledge of the greatness of God is to awaken in him *bhakti,* devotion, a devotion which is illumined through and through by knowledge. The true guru thus leads his disciples according to their capacity, regulating the hours of study and meditation, of work and service for their growth *jointly* in knowledge and love. But in the *bhakti marga* this is above all the fruit of divine grace; the guru is only the instrument of this work. From him is expected primarily the right interpretation of the Vedas. Madhva, one of the most eminent representatives of this school, gives great freedom to his disciples in the choice of their guru. If they do not find any experienced, competent, true guru, they should rather seek their own way to realization with the occasional help of devout and experienced persons. In case they discover that their guru is really not competent, they should seek a more competent guru, and for this, he adds, there is no need to ask the former's permission.

THE MEDIATOR OF DIVINE LOVE

The *bhakti* movements conceive the relationship of the devotee to God in terms of grace and love, a relationship eminently personal. But the *bhaktas* speak also of *guru bhakti,* love and devotion for the guru, and they seek the grace of the guru. By this they do not equate the guru with God, for they unambiguously hold God's transcendence. They introduce, so to say, within the devotee's relationship with God new qualities which turn out to be channels of divine grace and love. The guru becomes God's instrument for the disciple, his representative in the strict sense of making him present to the devotee. This sacred character is bestowed on the guru through a *diksha,* a sacramental initiation which like the other *samskaras* both symbolizes and confers on him the capacity of being a true mediator.

In *Saiva Siddhanta,* which stands closer to Christianity than any other hindu religious system and represents the high level of India's deeply religious experience, God is love. In this school, rituals as well as beliefs make the guru a channel of divine love. The *diksha,* initiation ceremony, expresses clearly the transfer of power coming from God. When the guru lays his hand on the head of the disciple to bestow on him the sacred initiation, this hand is no more his own hand; it is God's hand. The preparatory rituals have made his hand into a vehicle for the divine descent through a consecration comparable to that of the *murtis,* those images of stone or metal to whom daily worship is offered. The spiritual relationship of the guru with the disciple originates from a divine initiative. The disciple should not think it is he who discovers his own guru through his own searching. It is Siva, God himself, who comes to him through the guru who is made to meet him. The unseen Lord, appearing in visible form as guru, lends his aid with motherly love to his devotees. Sometimes God appears directly in a vision to the devotee who has been seeking without finding. It is God who seeks the devotee, indeed he literally longs for him, as much as the cow, when her udder is swollen with milk, looks for her calf and calls it. 'When I knew not his form, even then he fixed his love on me, planted himself within my thought and flesh and thus made me his' (Manikkavacakar). The guru is grace incarnate. The world does not realize that Siva's appearance in the human form of a guru is like a decoy for the purpose of snaring man to his side. The

Sastras themselves require the divine guru for their elucidation; therefore he ought to be sought after by every aspirant who desires to be delivered. To secure this liberation God's unseen presence in the soul as its light does not suffice. His grace manifested through the guru is necessary.

In the *Vaishnavatie* school of Ramanuja that spread to North India, where it gained the allegiance of Kabir and is still very much alive today in the Kabir *panths* or ashrams, the devotion is more centered on the person of the guru known as divine teacher. He is believed to be more than a mere channel of the Divine. The shortcut to God is *prapatti*, surrender, abandonment of the devotee to God, which is experienced as a gift of himself accepted by God, who takes charge of him who makes so unconditional a surrender. *Bhakti* should not be of the monkey type, which clings to God and guru by the devotee's own exertion, like the baby monkey holding his mother round her waist while she jumps from branch to branch, but of the cat type, that is, by giving oneself completely to God, like a kitten held in its mother's mouth. As a man in time of famine offers himself to be the slave of the master who will care for feeding him, the devotee makes himself the servant of God who will henceforth feed him.

Overwhelmed by God's grace, the devotee who surrenders to the guru experiences liberation from maintaining himself by force. Instead of the constant exercise of asceticism and of good works as well as concentration, and in the awareness of his total powerlessness, he joyfully lays down his burdens at the feet of the guru. And God who is love feels bound, by such a surrender, to lead his devotee to salvation. In the ritual which consecrates the disciple's surrender—*samasrayana*—a challenging substitute for our monastic vows—the guru holds the part of the witness. He introduces the disciple to God, prays for him, in his name, even asking pardon for his former sins, and finally he gives him a new name, ending not with *ananda*, bliss, as is the case with many of our swamis, but with *dasa*, servant, slave. This expresses his new condition, his

265

new state, following the consecration. More interesting still for us Christians, this *diksha* does not simply bind the disciple to God. It creates a bond with the whole community of those who have gone through the same consecration and particularly between the guru and the disciple. This bond is experienced as a spiritual solidarity; the *prapatti*—the disciple's surrender— rests on the guru's own surrender to God. His surrender to God is the disciple's security. He carries the burden of all his disciples and, with himself, entrusts them to God. The guru is described as *Vedanta Decika,* the fearful lion king of the mountains, moving freely, unchallenged by any other power and carrying with him in his mane all the little parasites that rest in it. Some of us would prefer another word to convey the guru-shishya relationship!

The guru's function as mediator takes on here a new dimension, unique in Indian thought and dominated by the belief in reincarnation. According to the law of *karma,* man is the maker of his own destiny. His life is the outcome of this rigorous law: it is the sum total, or rather the balance sheet, of the profit and loss of his own actions, good and evil. Strictly speaking, no one can do anything for anyone else. This view tends to leave no place for any fellowship or sharing or ultimately for any deep relation bearing on one's destiny, as our neighbor is for us only the instrument, or rather the witness, of a destiny which we have to undergo.

The guru-disciple relationship in Ramanuj's Vaishnavism does away with the law of *karma* by acknowledging the guru's role as mediator, a function for which he is consecrated. On account of this, he literally takes charge of the disciple, even to the point of suffering for his sins; he has also special power to make intercession for him. As a counterpart to this and as a result of the new relationship that has been created, the disciple is expected to pray for his guru. Eventually, he even has the duty of pointing out his failure to remain on the right path. This relationship consecrated by the *diksha* is no longer subject to external circumstances; it is rooted in the absolute. Madhva's vision of all beings in the realm of salvation is one of

266

interrelationships of gurus and disciples, in an increasing process of receiving the Divine Light from each other.

DEVIATIONS?

While this understanding of the guru prevailing in the *bhakti* movements—the most influential in Hinduism—shows the deepest insights into the relationship of the guru with the disciple and of both with God, it is on account of the implications of this view that the guru tradition of India is exposed to real deviations. The common man seeks mediations and the assurance of quick advances on the path to salvation. His guru will then easily clothe himself or be endowed by the disciple with divine powers. He is made the channel through which the divine flows and reaches men, sometimes in an unexpected and sudden manner. He is not only one who has an experience of God and can therefore show the way to others. He has the power to communicate this experience, so to speak, materially.

Such beliefs are rooted in the ancient writings of Hinduism, and especially in the more popular type: the Epics, *Mahabharata,* and *Ramayana* and the myths of the *Puranas* which are often simply bewildering to the uninitiated. This tradition magnifies the powers—*siddhis*—of the ascetic who has acquired by his *tapas* such tremendous energy and power that it can frighten even the *devas,* the gods! They then send temptations to the *rishi.* Only a very slight slip may suffice to make him lose in a single instant the fruits of many years of *tapas:* a slackening of his mental concentration, a movement of irritation; the *rishi* curses his tempter and all at once loses his powers. But the curse works out, because his word is effective. This is an attribute of the true guru. He is *satyavac*—his word works out what is said. To this is related the power of the mantra, the short formula which often because of its sound alone actualizes or enlivens the relationship between guru and disciple.

THE GURU IN THE ANCIENT AND CONTEMPORARY TRADITIONS

Let us now summarize our enquiry concerning the guru in the hindu tradition. And first in the words of this tradition itself.

> The guru is the dispeller of darkness and the revealer of light. He is the destroyer of the sins of the disciples. He makes the disciple like himself. He is a man of vision, one who destroys ignorance and who gives knowledge. He imparts grace, bestowing joy and peace on the disciple. In a more simple manner, he must be a man of good conduct, without sin, firm in mind. He must be imbued with a *sat* character that is real and truthful, because he has experienced truth. He is God-oriented and an indefectible friend of the disciple.[20]

At its highest, the guru institution offers experiences and aids which the West has never enjoyed in the same manner and which are now lost to a great extent. It has, if not always answered the needs, at least inspired devotees for the last 3000 years. It has drawn to itself men of great practical and intellectual distinction from within India and even from outside. It has survived conquerors and profound cultural changes. It continues to offer its rewards—though these are sometimes elusive—to those who come to it wholeheartedly accepting its discipline. 'Most of those I met who had done so,' writes Peter Brent in *Godmen of India,* a popular yet very factual and balanced book, 'seemed to me to be men and women who had benefitted as a result. They were quiet, certain, happy, dedicated; their lives were rich, their inner world expanding. They did not merely tell me so, they seemed to be people of whom it was true.'[21]

Finally we wish to mention that the image of the guru as it appears to a keen enquirer in India today is quite in conformity with the picture we have drawn from the ancient tradition of India. It will suffice to quote the same book:

> The guru is first the focus of the disciple's attention and emotion. In normal life these are dispersed, elicited by

many events and people. The guru cures this condition of dispersal, draws the disciple's energies together in a way which may be a preliminary to redirecting that energy inwards. Second, the guru, human being demonstrably similar to the disciple, sets the experience within human scale. The myth of his divinity may add intensity to the disciple's devotion. The fact of his humanity allows the disciple to operate without being crushed by a constant sense of eternity, omniscience, omnipotence, without feeling that he is contending with the Absolute without allies. Third, it is clear that the guru can help the disciple directly, either by explaining difficulties, helping to solve the problems met with, while practising the techniques and giving general encouragements, or by scolding or setting the disciple baffling problems, even by violence. Fourth, he is the respository of whatever doctrine, religious or scientific, is currently in use to explain the disciple's experiences. They may be very important because insanity, or at best disorientation, might be the outcome for the disciple. Fifth, he is the example, the proof that the way leads somewhere worthwhile. The guru's own sanity, detachment, serenity, strength, integration and loving-kindness show that the hard journey the disciple has to make will prove worthwhile in the end. Possibly, sixth, he may be a source of developed mental power which, when transferred to the disciple, can transform the latter's life.[22]

A very personal witnessing in this respect and much closer to us comes from Abhishiktanandaji—Dom Henry Le Saux, O.S.B.—in his autobiography, published in 1974. The facts go back to the years 1950–1955 when he was an exclaustrated monk and the founder of an Indian benedictine ashram in Trichinopoly diocese, South India. He had experienced the *darsana* of Ramana Maharshi at Thiruvannamalai: 'When looking deep into his eyes—eyes so full of peace and love— I sensed something of the call to the within which seemed to well up from the very depth of his consciousness, merged as it was in the primordial mystery.' But he goes on to confess that he was still too fresh from Europe and not sufficiently attuned to the mysterious language of silence to make this a real turning point in his life.

A few years later he came into contact with Swami Gnananda—a sage from the East, as he calls him—who was then living in a poor unknown village of Tamil Nadu as its guru. He first narrates how the old man was venerated as an epiphany of the invisible Presence by the people who had asked him to settle down in their place. Here is the account of his first visit:

> At this point the devotees began to arrive. Men, women, children, prostrated themselves respectfully, even affectionately. One could easily see that for them this was no empty conventional gesture or rite enjoined by good manners. Quite obviously the bodily prostration revealed the far deeper prostration happening ceaselessly in the secret place of the heart. One saw faith, love and complete confidence in this man who had become for them nothing less than the *epiphany of the invisible Presence,* the outward manifestation to their human eyes of the grace and love of the Lord who dwells undivided both in the highest heavens and in the deepest depth of the heart.

And now his own meeting with his guru: Vanya—the benedictine monk—had approached this man almost as a tourist and, lo and behold, the swami took possession of his very being. The monk realized that the allegiance he had never freely yielded to anyone in his life was now given automatically to Gnanananda. He had often heard of the irrational devotion disciples showed to their gurus and their total self-abandonment to the guru. All these things had seemed utterly senseless to him, a European with a classical education. Yet now at this very moment it had happened to him, a true living experience tearing him out of himself. This little man with his short legs and bushy beard, scantily clad in a *dhoti,* who had so suddenly burst in upon his life, could now ask of him anything in the world, even to set off like

Sadashiva, a dumb and naked wanderer for ever, and he, Vanya, would not even think of asking him for any sort of explanation. He was not afraid of speaking of the 'mystery of the guru', for it is a meeting with the divine, 'the experience of meeting with men in whose hearts the invisible has revealed himself and through whom the light shines in perfect purity.' Reflecting later on this inner initiation, he writes:

> The guru and the disciple form a couple, a pair of which the two elements attract one another and adhere to one another. As with the two poles they exist only in relationship to one another . . . . A pair on the road to unity . . . . A non-dual reciprocity in the final realization. The guru is one who has himself attained the Real and who knows from personal experience the way that leads there; he is capable of initiating the disciple and of making well up from within the heart of his disciple, the immediate ineffable experience which is his own—the utterly transparent knowledge, so limpid and pure, that quite simply 'he is'.

Is it not in fact true that the mystery of the guru is the mystery of the depth of the heart? Is not the experience of being face to face with the guru that of being face to face with oneself in the most secret corner, with all pretence gone?

The meeting with the guru is the essential meeting, the decisive turning-point in a person's life. But it is a meeting that can only take place when one has gone beyond the level of sense and intellect. It happens in the beyond, in the fine point of the soul, as the mystics say.

The most significant outcome of this encounter is that the guru introduces the disciple to his real self:

> What the guru says springs from the very heart of the disciple. It is not that another person is speaking to him. It is not a question of receiving from outside oneself new thoughts which are transmitted through the senses. When the vibrations of the master's voice reach the disciple's ears and the master's eyes look deep into his, then from the very depths of his being, from the newly discovered cave of his heart thoughts well up which reveal himself. What does it

271

matter what words the guru uses? Their whole power lies
in the hearer's inner response to them. Seeing or listening
to the guru the disciple comes face to face with his true
Self in the depth of his being, an experience every man
longs for, even if unconsciously.[23]

WESTERN GURUS?

In what manner can such functions be exercised in the
West? It is not easy to say. Yet let us first observe that there
is a need for it. The wide gap created by the positive sciences
between a world dominated by technology and, on the other
hand, the wisdom of old with its interests centered on
interiority (in India the *atman,* the inner self) must be bridged.
There are signs that this has already begun. The current
interest taken by the present generation, saturated with the
benefits of technology, in the things of the spirit and in the
interior journey—aroused partly by the impact of the spiritual
disciplines of the East—will not easily be reversed. In all
probability it has come to stay. Now if, as we believe, this
stems from, this points to, something essentially true and
real about man's nature and his destiny, then western man
must ultimately realize this truth in his own terms. He cannot
simply borrow and clothe himself with exotic patterns.
Hybridization of this kind invariably ends in the deterioration
of both the cultural values that are made to mate. Whatever
he borrows from another culture has to be grafted onto his
own language and thought-patterns, that it may suck juice
and sap from the depths of his subconscious. Except, of course,
in the case of a first awakening, he will require for this a master of his own, not one imported from a culture in which
masters have a place precisely because their roots lie in that
culture. In all respects the guru-shishya relationship as it is
known today is heavily determined by the facts of hindu
society. If anything similar is to develop in the West it must
be equally part of western culture. Let us not repeat, though
in a reversed manner, the mistake of the western churches
who went out to the four corners of the world to plant the

Gospel and instead planted their own life style and all its trappings. In spite of four hundred years of intense missionary activity and efforts of gigantic magnitude, the outcome remains minute, at least considering the scale of the task before them. Though they have made incredible investments of talent as well as of finance, of love of neighbor with utter self-sacrifice, the kind of which makes saints like Francis Xavier, the returns are very limited and certainly completely out of line with the first expansion across the Roman Empire of a Christianity which took place with the power of the Spirit and made inculturation its rule.

It would require another symposium to picture the image of the master which is required for this new birth, but is it not presumptuous to say that it may differ much from that of the missionary guru who comes presently from the East to the West. Yet if new explanations have to be found for his powers and if devotion to him is to be couched in new terms, if the very qualities we look for in him are altered, in essence he will still be the guru, the guide and mentor of the inward path, the bringer of light.

NOTES

1. *Prasna Upanishad* VI, 8.
2. *Code of Manu* II, 149-50.
3. Ed. Max Mueller, vol. 7, no. 47.
4. *Mundaka Upanishad* III, 2, 8.
5. *Brihad Aranyaka Upanishad* IV, 4, 22.
6. *Bhavan Journal* XXIII (1977) 340.
7. *Complete Works* IV, 28.
8. *Code of Manu* II, 140 and 171.
9. *Mundaka Upanishad* I, 2, 12-13.
10. S. Radhakrishnan, *The Principal Upanishads,* p. 679.
11. XI, 3, 3-5.
12. IV, 4, 22.
13. *Bhagavad Gita* V, 2-3 and VI, 20-23.
14. *Brihad Aranyaka Upanishad* II, 4, 5.
15. *Chandogya Upanishad* VI, 12-14.
15a. *Brihad Aranyaka Upanishad* IV, 1b-2.
16. *Katha Upanishad* 1, 2, 23.
17. *Chandogya Upanishad* VII, 1.
18. *Ibid.,* VII, 25, 2.
19. 'Le Guru dans la Tradition Hindoue', *Axes* VI/1 (1974) 13.
20. B. Bhatt, 'Authority in the Guru-Sishya Relationship',
Jeevadhara VI (1976) 362. The relationship of this image of the guru
with the spiritual father in the Catholic Church today, but also the
differences, appears significantly in the following portrait made a few
years ago by the late Father Daniélou: 'What is expected from a spiritual father is first knowledge of spiritual things, discernment of the
spirits, that is the art of discerning what comes from the Holy Spirit
and what comes from the devil. Knowledge of the human heart. The
spiritual father must be prudent, capable both of stimulating on the
path of perfection and of warning against excessive zeal. He must be
humble; he must respect the diversity of God's ways and of the spiritual
vocations and not impose his own views.' Liminaire, *Axes,* VI/4 (1974) 7-8.

21. Peter Brent, *Godmen of India* (Penguin Books, 1974) p. 292.
22. *Ibid.,* p. 339.
23. Abhishiktananda, *Guru and Disciple* (London, 1974)
pp. 26-30.

THE SPIRITUAL FATHER:
TOWARD INTEGRATING WESTERN AND
EASTERN SPIRITUALITY

Yves Raguin, SJ
Ricci Institute, Taiwan

THE SPIRITUAL FATHER is the person who communicates the faith and guides the faithful on their way to God. He is at the same time the father and the master. This tradition, in Christianity, goes back to Christ and his disciples. Although Christ told his apostles not to call anyone 'father', because there is only one father, the Father in heaven (Mt 23:9), the tradition of calling the spiritual master 'Father' started early in the Church. Then, in the monastic tradition, the 'spiritual father' was at the same time the head of the monastic family and the spiritual guide of the monks. But ultimately the appellation 'Father' takes its full meaning from the unique paternity of the heavenly Father, as Paul says in the Epistle to the Ephesians (3:14-15).

In the same way, we have only one Master, Christ (Mt 23: 10), and if we call someone 'master' it is only in reference to Christ who is the only Master, because he alone knows the secrets of the Father. Being 'the way, the truth, and the life' (Jn 14:6), Christ is the absolute Master, knowing God and man. But the Spirit is also called the master of spiritual life, because he is the Spirit of the Father and the Son. He knows all the intimate secrets of God and dwells in us to make these secrets known to us.

Although, in christian spirituality, there is a great insistence on the role of the Holy Spirit as the only master of spiritual life, still it is a fact that those who claim to have the Spirit as their only master and who put aside all other guides may easily fall into grave spiritual aberrations. And the fact that God came to speak to us in human language justifies fully the role in the spiritual life of those we call spiritual fathers or masters.

We should compare what we may call the western tradition regarding the role of the spiritual father with so-called eastern spirituality. This latter tradition is very vast, too vast to be reduced to something homogenous. But it is still possible to highlight some of the main aspects of the Indian and Chinese traditions relating to the question of the spiritual father or master.

In Christianity, the spiritual father or director is usually nothing more than a wise and experienced guide who directs his spiritual sons and daughters on their way to God along the path of Christ. He simply helps them to be faithful to Christ and docile to the action of the Holy Spirit. But the Indian 'guru' or the buddhist 'master' have to be themselves real 'seers'; they must have a real experience of the spiritual or divine world. Nobody can be a master unless he has gone the whole way of experience. This means that much more is normally required of the eastern gurus and masters than of the western spiritual fathers, as if the West were content with having Christ as the perfect 'seer', without asking the spiritual fathers and masters to be 'seers' themselves.

But it is only by letting Christ take 'shape' in him that the spiritual father can be a real master. He thus becomes like the visible instrumental guru, the one in whom the true guru begins to take on a form for the disciple as he awakens. This 'true guru' is the inner guru who manifests himself at the moment of ultimate spiritual experience.[1] This short quotation opens a possible perspective of integration of the western and eastern spirituality.

THE MASTER AND THE EXPERIENCE

The disciples of Jesus called him 'Rabbi', which means 'master'. At the beginning they understood the term in the line of the Jewish tradition. Jesus was seen as the master who explained the Law. But soon Jesus claimed to be more. He was not an ordinary master of the Law. This appears clearly in his conversation with Nicodemus. 'Amen, amen, I say to you, we speak of what we know, and we bear witness to what we have seen' (Jn 3:11). And John says in another passage: 'No one has at any time seen God. The only-begotten Son, who is in the bosom of the Father, he has revealed him' (Jn 1:18). Christ is not simply an ordinary rabbi, he is the great seer, and the person who sees him sees the Father. That is why he is the Master, the only master. Peter had the decisive word when he said: 'Lord, to whom shall we go? You have the words of everlasting life' (Jn 6:68).

All this shows the depth of the experience of Christ. For him to teach his disciples to pray is to tell them how to relate to his Father who is also their Father. He taught them to pray in teaching them to say 'Our Father who art in Heaven ...'. But this prayer would not have the depth it has, had not Christ shared the experience of his own oneness with his Father. This experience of the relation to his Father at the depth of his being is in the line of Zen. For Christ, seeing one's nature (the *kenshô*[2]) is to realize the identity of his divine nature with the Father's nature. In this respect we may see him as the greatest of all Zen masters. No one in human history had such a deep experience of God in seeing his own 'original nature'.

We may say that Christ in his humanity lived 'in faith' his union with God, but at the depth of his self there was an experience of who he was, the Son of the Father, sharing with him the one divine nature. This is what makes Christ a perfect master. Never has a man had such an experience of God. Buddha himself never claimed to be more than a human being. He had seen the way of liberation from *samsâra* to *nirvâna.* He had seen the way and wanted to show it to others.

278

With these limitations, he has been one of the greatest masters and spiritual fathers in human history. The ideal of the master in Buddhism always goes back to Buddha as a model.

When Christians say they have only one master, Christ, Buddhists say, they have only one master, the Buddha. But there is a great difference in language between the two. Christ speaks of God his Father. Buddha has discovered how things are. His experience is not of a God but of Reality, whatever it may be. This Reality for him is not the transient world or the fleeting ego, but what is beyond or at the depth of them. This he has seen and experienced and he wants to help others to this experience.

> The Zen Master is first and foremost one who has experienced, seen and tasted the essential world in which he himself is constantly deepening his own 'at homeness'. He does not speak of himself as one who 'has arrived', but as the one who must continually go on from here. But at the same time he speaks with authority and has great self-confidence in the fact that what he has experienced is the real world and no one can prove him wrong. His own experience has filled him with such a deep peace that it is manifest in his personality. It enables him to move with freedom and ease and it gives him a tremendous power in being able to guide others, with great humility.[3]

The Master is the one who knows from experience and has tasted what most people never have tasted. In this respect Christ is a Master because he has had an experience of God no one ever has had or ever shall have. This point of experience is very important. Christians tend to insist on faith, and it is true that the essential is faith, because not everybody is called to the experience about which we are speaking. But the fact that the buddhist way is based on experience and not on faith reminds us of the necessity of experience if one is to be a real Master. To be a Master is a gift from beyond, and nobody can assume this title without being given that experience. There are, as there always have been, many self-appointed 'masters' who simply sell methods without being able really to show the way, because they have not travelled far.

Those who seek God out of their own deepest nature have always looked for guides. Once upon a time, these men were called spiritual fathers or directors. Today, they are known as counsellors, gurus, zen or yoga masters. Whatever we like to name them, they deal with the same basic reality. There exist men who have found the way to God. There is no end to their journeyings. When they set out the first time, they were alone; it was hard going up mountains and across deserts. When they reached the end, they started going back and forth to the plains, helping others who wanted to climb God's mountain too. Solitaries they remain, but they never travel alone because their disciples go with them.[4]

This is what Christ did during his whole life, first alone, then with the disciples he called 'my friends' and 'my little children'. All the time he went back and forth from his human condition to his Father, becoming for his disciples the perfect image of the Father, and father himself. Master as he was, he showed in perfection the humility all real masters on earth are seeking.

A proud master is nonsense, for his experience, if it *is* of the beyond, is a gift he has received, not an achievement of which he can be proud. This is the whole meaning of Christ's washing the feet of his disciples and saying, 'You call me Master and Lord, and you say well, for so I am. If, therefore, I the Lord and Master have washed your feet, so you also should wash one another's feet' (Jn 13:13-14). This is the sign of the great Master who knows that he comes from the Father to reveal his secrets. In fact, the Master is at the feet of his listeners humbly asking them to listen to his wonderful invitation to ascend the mountain of the Lord.

When God tells his people: 'Listen, Israel', it is more a humble prayer than an order. When Christ tells the Samaritan woman, 'If you knew the gift of God, and who it is who says to you, "Give me to drink", you perhaps would have asked of him, and he would have given you living water' (Jn 6:10), he

is in fact humbly begging her to listen to the wonderful message
he has for her. This is again the humility of the Master.

In the Indian tradition the real guru is a man who prefers
to be hidden. Happy the one who can discover him. This is why
the search for the guru is so important. 'Not many hear of him;
and of those not many reach him. Wonderful is he who can
teach about him; and wise is he who can be taught. Wonderful
is he who knows him when taught.'[5] The man who is a guru
leads his disciple along the paths he knows until the disciple
has met the indwelling inner guru. Once the inner guru has
been found, the outer guru, the man, disappears. Did Christ
not mean something similar when he told his disciples he
had to leave them? 'And now I am going to the one who sent
me . . . . But I speak the truth to you. It is expedient for you
that I depart, for if I do not go, the Advocate will not come
to you . . . . Many things yet I have to say to you, but you
cannot bear them now. But when he, the Spirit of truth, has
come, he will teach you all the truth . . . ' (Jn 16:5; 7; 12-13).
This is why the Holy Spirit is the inner Master who makes us
understand what Christ has told us. He reveals the secrets
of God.

This reminds us of the Indian tradition of the two gurus,
the instrumental guru and the definitive guru who appears at
the time of the inner enlightenment. The definitive guru 'is
advaita, non-dual. He alone is the guru who can make one
take the high dive; he appears and reveals himself only at the
moment of the divine! The other guru is the guru *murti,* the guru
in visible form, the one who can only show the way.'[6] In
Christianity we have the ordinary guru who is a man, the
spiritual master or father, then Christ and his Spirit who is
properly the inner guru, the ultimate grand guru, the one who
with Christ knows all the secrets of God.

THE SPIRITUAL FATHER, GIVER AND MASTER OF LIFE

Early in the christian tradition the two functions of father
and master became closely connected and embodied in the
apostles. The apostles called to life by conferring baptism

and transmitting the message.

In Paul the two aspects are really one. But for him 'father-hood' is also 'motherhood', as is clear from the images he uses. He writes to the Galatians: 'My dear children, with whom I am in labor again until Christ is formed in you!' (Ga 4:19). He knows very well that this spiritual paternity comes from the only Father of all. The same way, Paul knows that he is not himself the ultimate master. The real master is Christ, who teaches the faithful through the interior master, the Holy Spirit who comes 'into our hearts, crying "Abba! Father!" ' (Ga 4:6). It is with these perspectives that Paul sees his own mission as spiritual father and master of his flock. The Father in heaven represents the masculine aspect; the Church on earth represents the feminine aspect; and the Spirit itself can be seen here, as often in the Bible, as a 'feminine' power. All these aspects of the mystery of divine life are very important to grasping the depth of spiritual paternity, or rather parenthood, in the christian tradition.

Because he saw himself as the father of his Christians, Paul was conscious of being their master and model, because he had the experience of Christ. This consciousness was very deep in him, and he fought to be recognized as one who has 'seen' Christ. He wrote to the Ephesians: ' . . . I suppose you have heard of the dispensation of the grace of God that was given to me in your regard; how by revelation was made known to me the mystery, as I have written above in belief; and so by reading my words you can perceive how well versed I am in the mystery of Christ . . . ' (Eph 3:2-4).

Paul was very conscious of having been the father of many in their regeneration through faith in Christ. He told the Corinthians how the apostles are 'cooperators with God' in evangelisation, and he added as a conclusion to his teaching:
I write these things not to put you to shame, but to admonish you as my dearest children. For although you have ten thousand tutors in Christ, yet you have not many fathers. For in Christ Jesus, through the gospel, did I beget you. Therefore, I beg you, be imitators of me, as I am of Christ. For this very

reason I have sent to you Timothy, who is my dearest son and faithful in the Lord. He will remind you of my ways, which are in Christ Jesus, even as I teach everywhere in every church (1 Co 4:14-17).

The model of the spiritual father remains God the Father, but God revealed and heard in Christ through the guidance and light of the Spirit. Only once in the Gospel does Christ relate to his disciples and other people as 'father'. 'My children, with what difficulty will they who trust in riches enter the kingdom of God' (Mk 10:24). After the last supper he calls his disciples 'friends' or 'my children'. 'Little children,' he says, 'yet a little while am I with you' (Jn 13:33). Later he tells them: 'I will not leave you orphans . . . ' (Jn 14:18). And immediately afterward he identifies himself with his Father in relation to his disciples: 'But he who loves me will be loved by my Father, and I will love him and will manifest myself to him' (Jn 14:21). Christ is the perfect image of the Father, and 'to see him is to see the Father' (Jn 14:9).

This identification of Christ with the Father will have a great influence on christian spirituality. The spiritual master is not simply the one who reveals the truth and shows the way, he is father and mother. We have seen this in the letters of Paul and we can give more examples from John's letters. John was filled with love for his 'children'. 'My dear children,' he wrote, 'let us not love in word, neither with the tongue, but in deed and in truth' (1 Jn 3:18).

It seems that this mystic view of paternity is specific to Christianity because of the revelation made by Christ of his Father. Behind all this we may see the intimate connection between two fundamental attributes of God, who is 'love' and 'light'.

Among the Fathers of the Desert, the notion of spiritual paternity was very important. These men who left the world were seeking at the same time the guidance of a master they could regard as their father. It was said of the disciples of St Pachomius that 'after God, Pachomius was their father'. God is the only real father, but after God these great hermits

283

shone with all the radiance of spiritual paternity.[7]

Before the existence of organized monastic communities of contemplatives, the seekers of enlightenment in both East and West were looking for a master, one who could lead them to contemplation. We know from the tradition how disappointed the five first disciples of Sakyamuni were when he put aside the ascetic practices he had been performing for years. They thought he was renouncing his quest. But he did it because he knew there was no hope of enlightenment in these practices.

Reading the liturgical texts from the time between Ascension and Pentecost, we see how the early Church saw the ascension of Jesus to heaven. He was the one who had opened the way for them. Having entered the kingdom of Heaven, he would take his faithful with him. He had not simply opened the gates of heaven to our contemplation, he entered himself into the Holy of Holies, the bosom of the Father. This explains the sense of exultation of those who had found a master who could lead them into the mysteries of God. This has been the joy of all those who have met someone who has entered the mystery and is able to lead others into this same mystery. This is a 'joy which is rare indeed,' as a roshi said, 'to meet a congenial soul, a congenial living being who underwent similar experiences concerning ultimate matters. With the exception of the experience itself there is hardly a joy that equals this . . . ' . This explains the hardships endured by disciples who wanted to put themselves under the guidance of a spiritual father or master, in the West as well as in the East. Nothing could deter them from seeking guidance from men whom they considered as the ones who had seen the way.

This explains the flight of thousands of people to mountains and deserts in the search for immortal life, enlightenment, or the vision of God, in the East as in the West. Here we should say something about the development of monasticism in China as well as in the western world, but this is not the place.

In the West as in the East, the foundation of communities of 'contemplatives' saw as a result the spiritual father, the original master, becoming the father of a household. In principle, at least in the Occident, the father of the community was modeled on the *paterfamilias* of roman society. But, according to monastic tradition, the father, the abbot or *abbas,* had a double function: to be the father of the monks *and* their spiritual guide. He had to be a man of deep spiritual experience in order to be able to guide his monks individually as well as in community. But as time went on, those chosen to be abbots were selected more for their aptitudes for governance than for their spiritual experience. This is why, inside the communities, there were besides the father abbot spiritual men who were the monks' personal counsellors, yet still the discipline and the spirit of the monastery were in the hands of the abbot.[8]

With time, contemplative life became a specific type of life distinguished from an active one, but this did not mean that the monks living in these communities were 'contemplatives'. Most of these groups were started naturally, because there was there a holy man, a master whose experience attracted disciples. After the death of such a master, it often happened that no other master was there to take his place, and while great efforts were made to keep his spirit alive, it was impossible to institutionalize the master's spirit. We know from history how difficult it is to maintain the spirit of a great founder. If there is not constant renewal through the mystical experience of many individuals, the best monasteries become 'dead' institutions. This phenomenon is to be observed in the East as in the West. It is well known that great spiritual movements are built on the experience of one man or a few men. A monastery, be it christian or zen, dies spiritually if there is no master alive in the monastery. A 'dead' monastery comes back to life with the coming of a spiritual father and master.

After having been pushed to action and involvement in all sorts of works and movements, Christians are again being called to inner attention by the masters of modern times—

inner attention to themselves, to others, and to the whole
of creation.

THE SEARCH FOR THE FATHER/MASTER
AND THE
MASTER–DISCIPLE RELATIONSHIP

Those who feel attracted to a deeper spiritual experience
seek irresistibly for a guide to be their father and master. The
search is sometimes very painful, because masters are rare,
and it seems to be only by chance that we meet the one who
is meant for us. There is no universal master. A mountain
guide knows 'his' mountain, and all the ways to the peaks and
valleys. That is why it is dangerous to run after a master just
because many people flock around him. He may be 'the one',
he may not be. Most of the time, meeting the master seems to
be pure 'accident'. In fact, there is already something between
the master and disciple before they meet. And when they
meet there is in the heart of the disciple something like a voice
saying, 'This is the one!'

There are many examples of the search for a master in
Hinduism and Buddhism, probably more than in Christianity,
because the human guru is more important in the East than in
the West. But there are in Christianity many examples of this
search or of sudden encounter between the disciple and the
one who will be his master. This is God-given. In Buddhism
they say that there is an affinity which draws the disciple and
the master near to one another. The problem is to find the
master or the guru who can lead. First the disciple must find
a master that suits him or her. This is very important—that the
master and the disciple be on the same 'wave length' so to
speak. In Zen it is not advised to change masters. When you
find the one you feel you can relate to, it is best to stay with
him at least until you have come to 'kenshô'. Going from
master to master can only hinder one's practice and confuse
the disciple. After 'kenshô' however people often go to other
masters to test their own enlightenment through questions
and answers.[9]

There is much that could be said about the role of the guru in Indian spirituality, and we may draw some examples from this later. Now we will speak mostly about the role of the master in zen training. In the course of the training the disciple, Only the roshi, with his long years of experience and acutely discerning eyes, can gauge the exact degree of his [the disciple's] comprehension and give him the necessary direction and encouragement at this critical point. An accomplished roshi will not scruple to employ every device and stratagem, not excluding jabs with his ubiquitous baton (*kotsu*) when he believes it will jar and rouse the student's mind from dormant awareness to the sudden realization of its true nature . . . . The strategy of placing the student in a desperate situation where he is relentlessly driven from the rear and vigorously repulsed in front often builds up pressures within him that lead to that inner explosion without which true satori seldom occurs. However, such extreme measures are by no means universal in Zen.[10]

This means that the student or disciple puts himself totally into the hands of his roshi, because the roshi is the one who knows how far his disciple has gone on the way to *kenshô*. He knows also the way he will react under the kind of pressure described above. This way of acting in Zen is very similar to many examples we find in the lives of the Fathers of the Desert. Orders were given by the spiritual father to his disciple, not primarily to test his obedience, but to provoke in the heart of the disciple a total conversion and total change of mentality, as the one required by Christ of his followers. Only under such pressure could the disciples experience the truth of the words of Christ which apparently contradicts human reason. Such pressure was put on the apostles when Jesus in Capernaum (Jn 6:22-71) explained that they should eat his flesh and drink his blood. The result was the *kenshô* of Peter, the realization that he belonged to Christ totally and that for him there was no other way. We may see in the same light the great trials of Christ, the temptation in the desert, the agony in the garden, and his derelicton on the cross. We may see in these great trials three of the main steps to the realization in his humanity of who he was, the Son of God. No roshi ever has submitted his son-disciple to such a trial, and no son-disciple ever had such a *satori.* In the history of Christ it is the Father himself who puts his Son to trial. As it has been written in the *Letter to the Hebrews:* 'He, Son though he was, learned obedience from the things that he suffered' (Heb 5:8). This obedience is the total dependence of Jesus on his Father.

This brings us to a very important point in the question of the relation of the father-master with his son-disciple. In the hindu tradition the authority of the guru is total. This may be puzzling for a Christian, because, as Sr Vandana says:

the guru is not a mere man to his disciples. I have seen the same deference and devotion poured out at the Guru's feet and the same generous offering made there as at a holy shrine, as holy as Badrinath. The Guru by his Kripa enables a man to get direct knowledge of the Self, purifies him from sin, removes all darkness; in fact the Guru is Brahman. 'I will be with you wherever you need me, do not fear,' the Guru assures the disciple. In return, he exacts a strict obedience, prompt, willing and 'blind' without criticism or complaint . . . . But however exacting the discipline, there is a bond of love . . . . In any case as Chidananda Swami explained: 'The power is God's, not mine.' Aurobindo had also said: 'The power is not my personal property. It is a higher Force acting in the world; only one Force.'[11]

A Christian would probably give such an obedience and veneration to Christ alone, never to a man. But we should not forget that the guru should be a selfless man, a man through whom God is acting directly, not with any demonstration of personal power, not making ostensible use of what we may call his 'spiritual powers'. But, this being said, there is no difficulty in seeing in a spiritual father and master the image of Christ, and in respecting and loving him for what he is. Christ very often so reveals himself through a man that we can really see Christ living here in this man for us.

The roshi in the zen tradition is different from the guru

of the hindu tradition. Since there is not in Zen any background of divinity whatsoever, it is impossible to see a roshi venerated the way some gurus are. There is no element of the 'divine' in the relation between the roshi and his disciple. The roshi appears more 'human' than the guru because the zen experience is a human experience. It opens to the Absolute, but without the religious connotation we find in Hinduism.

The zen master does not pretend to have special powers. He is just a man who has had the ultimate experience of *kenshô*. He has realized himself at such a depth that he is totally one with himself, free from any kind of hindrances and ties, and totally open to others. This freedom is absolute freedom and not at all communication of spiritual powers. He cannot give his experience to another or make the disciple come to an experience. He can only help the disciple remove whatever obstacles are in the way of coming to a true enlightenment experience. Often he speaks of the four wheels of a car: if they are all on the track there is no problem, it rolls along right to its goal; but with most of us one or two of our wheels are off the track. This is why *dokusan* [private encounter with the Roshi] is so important. It is very important for the disciple to be as open as he or she can in the *dokusan* room . . . . Then it is very important to follow the instructions of the Roshi as faithfully and as purely as one can. Gradually one is able to trust the Roshi more and more.[12]

The whole effort and attention of the roshi are intended to help the disciple on his way to the *kenshô*. Communication between the master and the disciple occurs not so much in words as in speechless communion. It is the long experience of the roshi which enables him to follow his disciple in a way which allows little verbal communication. 'The most crucial point,' says Sister Kathleen Reiley, is when a disciple comes to an initial enlightenment experience; that is when the master must discern whether it truly is a real Zen experience or only a passing psychological state. If the '*kenshô*' is approved then *dokusan* takes on a new flavor. When the

289

disciple has finished his training, the relation between the roshi and his disciple becomes deeper and deeper. The disciple begins—deepening and deepening the practice of 'just-sitting'—and living in the awareness of the empty-infinite of just eating and sleeping, laughing and crying . . . . There is no way to describe the joy and depth of unity that exists in realizing that the disciple and Master are ONE in this mystery of empty-infinite.[13]

These examples taken from Hinduism and Zen Buddhism, as well as from Christianity, show very clearly the importance of the human guide in the way to ultimate spiritual experience. Although we claim that the Holy Spirit is the only Master, we know on the other hand that the so-called 'spiritual' movements have led astray many people who claim that they obey the Spirit alone. In no sane spiritual tradition has there been a dispensation from human spiritual guidance. This is the general law of human spiritual experience.

One of the most striking signs of our times is this search for gurus and roshi. I am afraid that our spiritual fathers, directors, or masters are very pale figures in comparison with some of these non-christian gurus and roshis. On the other hand, we should not think that all those who claim to be gurus and roshis are real ones. They may be simply selling methods of prayer or 'kenshô in four days'.

But we should look more attentively to the qualities required from real gurus and roshis. We know that, first of all, they should have experience of spiritual things and of the Ultimate. They should have undergone a long training, and dare to lead people only when they are sure of the quality of their own experience. If we do this, I am sure that we will turn more attentively to Christ, the greatest human guru of all times, and to the Holy Spirit, the incomparable inner master. Both of them are together in one, the perfect manifestation of God the Father, the ultimate mystery of God.

If we do all this, we may be able to say with Christ, almost with the same fullness, what he said of himself to his Father: Righteous Father, the world has not known you, but I have known you, and these have known that you have sent me. And I have made known to them your name, and I will make it known, in order that the love with which you have loved me may be in them (Jn 17:24-26).

NOTES

1. From *Guru and Disciple,* by Abhishiktananda (Henri Le Saux, OSB), trans. Heather Sandeman (London, 1974) pp. 28-29. I have quoted freely, paraphrasing the text.
2. The term *kenshô* is the Japanese reading of the Chinese *chien-hsing,* which means 'to see one's nature', one's 'true nature'.
3. Sr Kathleen Reiley, MM, A note to 'The Role of the Master in Zen and his relation to the disciple, from the point of view of a young disciple' (1978).
4. Y. Raguin, SJ, 'The Spiritual Master, Christ's Style,' *Sursum Corda* (Australia) 13, 7 (February 1975) 291.
5. *Katha Upanishad,* II, 7-9
6. Abhishiktananda, *Guru and Disciple,* p. 108.
7. *Dictionnaire de Spiritualité,* 'Direction spirituelle', col. 1044.
8. See Rembert C. Weakland, OSB, 'The Abbot as Spiritual Father', *Christian Monks and Asian Religions: Proceedings of the Second Asian Monastic Congress, Bangalore, October 14–22, 1973. Cistercian Studies,* 9 (1974) 231.
9. Kathleen Reiley, MM. Note 3 above.
10. Philip Kapleau, *The Three Pillars of Zen* (Beacon Press) 87.
11. Sr Vandana, RSCJ, 'The Guru as Present Reality', a paper presented at a Seminar on 'Guruship' held at the Christian Institute of Sikh Studies, Batala, Punjab, December 6–8, 1974.
12. Sr Kathleen Reiley, MM, note 3 above.
13. *Ibid.*

PATH TO WISDOM: EAST AND WEST

Joseph Chu-Công, OCSO
Saint Joseph's Abbey

L ET ME BEGIN by recounting a story: a university student was visiting Gasan, a distinguished master of Tenryuji Temple of Kyoto (1853–1900), and he asked him: 'Have you read the christian Bible?' 'No, read it to me,' said Gasan. The student opened the Bible and read from Saint Matthew: 'And why are you anxious about clothing? Consider the lilies of the field, how they grow: they neither toil nor spin; yet I tell you, even Solomon in all his glory was not arrayed like one of these . . . . Therefore, do not be anxious about tomorrow, for tomorrow will be anxious for itself. Let the day's own trouble be sufficient for the day.' Gasan said: 'Whoever uttered those words I consider an enlightened person.' The student continued reading: 'Ask, and it will be given you; seek, and you will find; knock, and it will be opened to you.' Gasan remarked: 'That is excellent! Whoever said that is not far from Buddhahood.'

The topic graciously assigned to me for this Symposium was 'The Spiritual Father: A Comparative Study'. I have decided to treat the subject under the aspect of Wisdom, in a way which I hope is wide enough in scope to cover all the nuances of the topic, but concrete enough to stimulate your interest.

In its broad sense, wisdom is taken to mean the intelligent and intuitive application of learning, the ability to discern the intangible inner qualities and essential relationships of things; it is insight and evaluation combined. In a more academic sense, wisdom is taken to mean the teaching of the ancient wise men relating to the art of living, especially those teachings that concern the philosophical and theological problems of the universe: man, God and/or the Absolute. In this sense I would describe wisdom as the apprehension of a truth through the realization of our original and essential oneness with it. There is also a religious meaning to the concept of wisdom: the apprehension of the All-Embracing-Reality, or God, or the Absolute— again, not so much by way of learning as by a realization of our original oneness with this Reality. This All-Embracing-Reality is realized and expressed in different ways by different people. It is God, it is Buddha or Perfect Being, it is the Absolute. In any terms, man is part of that All-Embracing-Reality, and wisdom is said to be reached when man realizes his oneness with it.

In this essay, I shall attempt to present a comparative study of St Bernard of Clairvaux (1090–1153) with Mumon Ekai (1181– 1260), a zen master. After a brief biographical note on the two masters, I shall treat the subject in four stages:

(1)   the vision of wisdom itself;
(2)   this vision as realized by Bernard and Mumon;
(3)   the ways and means each used to transmit this wisdom to their disciples;
(4)   their practical instructions on the path to wisdom in daily life.

This is a comparison and not syncretism, in which everything is the same. Bernard represents Christianity, which is a religion in the full sense of that word, whereas Mumon represents Zen Buddhism. Zen is not a religion in the western sense: it has no creed, no dogma. Zen can be taken as a religion only if by religion we mean direct contact with the 'Origin', or the 'Root' of all things. 'Zen concerns itself,' says Joshu Sasaki Roshi, 'with the roots of all things, which corresponds to the seat of God.'[1]

It might even be helpful to note at this point that the word Zen can mean two things: 1) a Zen school of Buddhism; and, 2) Zen taken as life, truth, enlightenment. In the second sense, Zen is not limited to Buddhism, but is, as zen masters claim, a basis or horizon for considering all religions, all philosophies, all cultures.[2] Here I take Zen in this broad sense as life, or truth itself, apart from its narrow sectarian interpretation as a Zen school of Buddhism.

The term 'spiritual father' is not taken here in the purely christian sense of a desert father, or one who by long experience in the desert learned the life and then exercised a genuine 'paternity', helping his disciples to cultivate by means of asceticism those seeds of the spiritual life which, though planted in them at baptism, often remain undeveloped. The term here is taken in the broader sense of any spiritual master who, by virtue of his learning and experience, is equipped to help others make progress in the spiritual life.[3] Ideally speaking, the spiritual master will help others to reach the height of sapiential knowledge, or wisdom. A spiritual master of any period of time or of any culture employs an intuitive understanding of others to help them find their spiritual path which will lead them to the high contemplation—their only goal—which is wisdom.

BIOGRAPHICAL NOTES

Bernard of Clairvaux (1090-1154)[4]

St Bernard was born in 1090 at the castle of Fontaines-lès-Dijon. From his youth he demonstrated an amazing combination of temperament and grace. He was a poet, a lover of nature, an artist, a musician, a thinker, a biblical exegete, a mystical theologian, a writer, and a master.[5] Bernard was esteemed on all sides. He was called forth and agreed to launch into the public affairs of the Church. Despite his important role in ecclesiastical business and politics, Bernard's first and most cherished responsibility was to train his monks. Whenever possible, he personally undertook the formation of his novices.

Bernard strongly insisted on the necessity of a spiritual master both for himself and for everyone else. He expressed this in a phrase of such clarity that it has become axiomatic: 'He who takes himself for master, becomes the disciple of a fool'.[6] He warned his monks to be on their guard against self-confidence. 'There are some,' he wrote, 'who fearlessly walk the road of life without a guide or master. Let them be on their guard, they fancy that they are both disciples and masters.'[7]

One of the greatest lights among the authors of the Middle Ages, Bernard has left a large body of writings, many of them sermons. Best known, perhaps, are his letters. Less well known but equally valuable are his works in the form of formal treatises, such as *De consideratione* which Bernard dedicated to his disciple, Pope Eugene III. In this treatise Bernard proposed to Pope Eugene a programme inspired by the monastic tradition according to which he himself was living. He laid stress on the interior life and on the essential value of contemplation over action. The most important of all Bernard's collection of discourses is the group of eighty-six sermons on the *Song of Songs,* which form his greatest and most significant single work. Nowhere else does his spiritual insight and experience manifest itself with such depth, vitality, and spontaneity as in these discourses, which are the fruit of his mature years. The commentary on the *Song of Songs* is a magnificent treatise on the union of the Incarnate Word with the Church, and the mystical union of the Word with the soul. It manifests Bernard's penetrating insight into the mystery of Christ and the mystery of the Church.

Bernard's role as spiritual master in the path to wisdom has been clearly shown in Dante's famous poem, *The Divine Comedy.* Dante was given as guides three persons: Virgil, Beatrice, and St Bernard. Virgil guided Dante, as it were, through the 'Purgative Way', Beatrice through the 'Illuminative Way', and St Bernard through the 'Unitive Way'. Beatrice's 'illuminative way' is, however, more or less 'intellectual' and not 'sapiential'. It was up to St Bernard to guide Dante through the path of wisdom by love. It is love that leads us to contemplation or wisdom. St Thomas Aquinas wrote: 'The greater a man's love, the more perfectly will he see God, and the more blessed will he be.'[8] Reflecting on St Thomas' statement, Étienne Gilson wrote:

> In the mind of anyone who understands this, the role of
> St. Bernard in the Divine Comedy assumes an intelligible
> aspect and at the same time that of Beatrice appears in its

true light. The outcome of the sacred poem is nothing else than the union of the soul with God, the image of the beatific vision. If Beatrice were the light of glory, the Divine Comedy would conclude with a look from her eyes, and a smile from her lips. But Beatrice retires and appoints in her place this man whom love has transfigured into the image of Christ—Bernard of Clairvaux.[9]

Dante himself wrote:

O Beatrice! Beloved guide, sweet friend!
She said: 'That which now overmasters thee
Is might which nothing can evade or fend;

Herein the wisdom and the power see
That opens between Heaven and Earth the road
Long yearned for and awaited ardently.'[10]

And I, who now drawing ever nigher
Towards the end of yearning, as was due
Quenched in my soul the burning of desire.

Bernard conveyed to me what I should do
By sign and smile, already on my own
I had looked upwards, as he wished me to,

For now sight, clear and yet clearer grown,
Pierced through me the ray of that exulted light,
Wherein, as in itself, the Truth is known.

Hence my vision mounted to a height
Where speech is vanquished and must lag behind
And memory surrendered in such plight.[11]

Mumon Ekai (1181–1260)

Mumon Ekai was born in 1183, toward the end of the Sung Dynasty. He studied Zen under Getsurin, the seventh successor of master Yogi Hoe (d. 1049) at Manjuji Temple. Getsurin, famous for his severity, gave Mumon the koan, or a paradoxical problem known as *No,* to study. After six years of hard work Mumon still had not solved his problem. He swore he would not sleep until he understood the koan. One day, when the noon-drum was being struck, he suddenly came to a realization. The next day he went to Master Getsurin for *sanzen,* for an inter-view. His realization was approved by Getsurin. More on this later.

By the time Mumon was thirty-six, he was recognized as a monk with a promising future, and had visited a great number of prominent Zen masters. At the age of sixty-four, in 1248, he founded Ninnoji Temple. After his retirement in later years, he was still sought after by learner-monks. The Emperor Riso invited him to the Palace and had him preach. The records tell that he always wore poor garments and showed no pride, and he spoke succinctly and pointedly to everyone. He died in 1260.

Mumon's literary work was the *Mumonkan,* or *The Gateless Gate,* which he wrote when he was forty-six. The *Mumonkan* is a collection of forty-eight koans, or sayings of the ancient zen masters, of some seventeen centuries between Shakyamuni Bud-dha and his disciples and Shogen and Waken, contemporaries of Mumon. The book, published in 1229, consists of only nineteen printed pages. But hundreds of pages have been used by later generations in commenting on it.

The *Mumonkan* is now a relatively well-known text in the West. At least five complete translations into English are known to us.[12] Fr Heinrich Dumoulin has translated it into German too, with commentary and verses as well as explana-tions and annotations. He has used the *Mumonkan* as a basis for a brief but comprehensive study of the history of Zen Buddhism during the T'ang and the Sung dynasties (618–907, and 980–1052, respectively). In the preface to his work, *The Development of Chinese Zen After the Sixth Patriarch in the Light of the Mumonkan,* Dumoulin writes:

The *Mumonkan* is, after the *Hekiganroku*, the most important koan collection of Chinese Zen. This work, the product of the last great flourishings of Zen Buddhism in China in the thirteenth century, is of great significance in relation to the entire history of Chinese Zen. In the center of most of the koan stories, stand the Zen Masters of the T'ang Period, those original and dynamic figures who lend a unique authority to Zen in contemporary China. Master Mumon himself represented the second flowering that once again displayed the worth of the transmitted heritage.[13]

Mumon Ekai dedicated the *Mumonkan* to the Emperor Li-tsung in celebration of the fourth anniversary of his coronation (1229). The Memorial to the Throne states:

We have arrived at January 5th, the second year of Jotei, 1229, a congratulatory day for Your Majesty. Your humble servant, monk Ekai, on December the 5th last year published a commentary on Forty-eight cases [koans] of the spiritual activities of the Buddha and the Patriarchs. I pray for the eternal health and prosperity of Your Majesty. I respectfully desire that Your Majesty's wisdom may become even more clarified day by day, and your life be as eternal as that of the universe itself. May all the Eight Directions sing the praises of your virtue, and the Four Seas take delight in your effective unmoving activity.

Mumon gave the reason for the title of his book, *The Gateless Gate,* when he wrote: 'In all the teaching of the Buddha the most essential thing is enlightenment. While there are so many gates leading to it, the most central one is a gateless gate. His verse was:

The Great Way is gateless;
There are a thousand alleys.
If you pass the barrier
You walk alone through the universe.

THE VISION OF WISDOM

St Bernard thought the word *sapientia,* 'wisdom', was derived from *sapor,* 'flavor'. Wisdom is a kind of seasoning and a pleasant flavor which makes things savory and good

299

tasting. Speaking of the virtues of obedience and patience as
wholesome but dry and insipid food, Bernard wrote:

> For both these foods a condiment is needful, so needful that
> without it both will be found not only insipid to the taste
> but even destructive to life . . . . Nowhere can be found so
> good a condiment as wisdom. It is, indeed, the tree of life by
> which Moses sweetened even the [bitter] waters of Mara . . . .
> It is the oil for want of which the door was shut against the
> foolish virgins; it is the salt by which the command of God
> must season every sacrifice. This is the reason why we call
> people unsalted, when we wish to signify that they are want-
> ing in wisdom.[14]

A wise person is one who relishes or experiences things as they
are: *Est enim sapiens, cui quaeque res sapiunt prout sunt.*[15]
Taken in this sense, wisdom can be applied to almost any kind
of knowledge. 'Wisdom is that by which we value and esteem
things in accordance with the worth and merit of each, so that
what possesses the highest value attracts our affection most
strongly.'[16]

There are several kinds of wisdom: wholesome wisdom,
wisdom of the flesh, and wisdom of the world.

> Wisdom of the flesh is death, and the wisdom of the world is
> an enemy of God. The only wholesome wisdom is that which
> comes from God, and which is chaste and peaceful. The
> wisdom of the flesh is impure instead of chaste, and the wis-
> dom of the world is rather contentious than peaceful. The
> wisdom which is from God is chaste in that it seeks not the
> things that are its own . . . but the will of God. And it is
> peaceful inasmuch as it does not abound in its own senses,
> but rather acquiesces in the judgment and counsel of others.[17]

True wisdom is the fulfillment and ultimate purpose of a life
spent in pursuit of good. Wisdom is the love of good. 'Wisdom
is a relish for what is good. But we have lost this spiritual relish
almost from the very first appearance of our race.[18]

This faculty of experiencing the good is a high power which
guides the senses and illumines the intellect and renews the
heart. When wisdom gains admission to the soul, it reveals to it

the foolishness of following the senses. It purifies the intellect and leads and renews the palate of the heart. With its spiritual taste thus restored it begins to have a relish for the good, and a relish for Wisdom, greater than which there is no other good.[19]

The wisdom which is the greatest good is God himself, and a person is not only wise but also blessed when this Wisdom is experienced. Bernard wrote: 'One who tastes wisdom as wisdom exists in itself is not only wise but also blessed. Because this is to see God as God is in himself.[20] To taste God as he is in himself constitutes supreme wisdom, because it puts one in the blessed state.

But, 'What is God?' Bernard asked. And he answered: 'God is pure Being.' Clearly no better answer occurs than, 'One Who is . . . . Indeed, this is fitting, nothing is more appropriate for the eternity which God is. If you should say of God anything, good or great, blessed or wise, or any such thing, it is summed up in this phrase which says, "He is". For his being is what all things are.'[21] God's 'isness' is our 'isness', a zen master would say. Again Bernard asked: What is God? Length, I say. What is that? Eternity. He is also width. And what is that? Charity. And in what boundaries is this charity confined in God who hates none of the things he has made. His bosom encloses even his enemies.[22] Again, what is God? The height and depth. Consider his power as height and his wisdom as depth. His height is known to be unattainable, and his depth to be equally inscrutable.[23] Bernard borrowed the words of the Book of Wisdom to express his notion of this all-embracing God: O powerful Wisdom, reaching everywhere mightily! O wise power, disposing all things sweetly. One reality, multiple effects and various operations. And that one reality is length because of eternity, width because of charity, height because of majesty, depth because of wisdom.[24] And with Paul he exclaimed: O, the depth of the riches of the knowledge and wisdom of God, how inscrutable his judgments and how unsearchable his ways![25]

Bernard was not satisfied, however, with the notion of God as *being* only. If he had used a zen expression he would also have said, I think, that God is non-being as well. Bernard wrote:

If you should add a hundred such attributes, you would not go beyond his essence. If you should say these things you would add nothing; if you should not say them, you would take nothing away. If you have already perceived how singular, how supreme his being is, do you not judge by comparison whatever God is not, is non-being rather than being?[26]

This is tantamount to saying that God transcends both all-being and non-being. When we transcend the duality of all-being and non-being we attain true wisdom. The experience of God as all-being and non-being is made possible to us through the mystery of Christ and the Church.

Who is Christ? Christ is the power of God and the wisdom of God. Christ is the wisdom which comes from the Father's bosom. Speaking of Wisdom which built itself a house (Pr 9:1), Bernard wrote: 'This Wisdom is Christ, the power of God and the Wisdom of God, God himself. Coming to us from the bosom of the Father, he built to himself a house, his Mother, the Virgin Mary.'[27]

The experience through wisdom (*Prajna*) of non-duality, including all that Master Mumon and countless other masters before him realized and handed on about this experience, Jesus also knows, and that in a pre-eminent manner, through knowing himself. It is all included in Jesus' word: 'My Father and I are one'; 'I am in the Father and the Father is in me'; and 'I come from God; I proceed from God; I am going to God.'[28]

Christ, the eternal Wisdom, became the Wisdom-in-time for the Church through the Holy Spirit, who is the Spirit of Wisdom, the Bond of Love. Through the Holy Spirit Christ reveals to the Church not knowledge only but sapiential knowledge or loving wisdom.

Christ reveals himself, and the Father as well, to whom it pleases him. And it is certain that he makes this revelation through a 'Kiss', that is, through the Holy Spirit, a fact to which St. Paul makes reference in Corinthians (1 Co 2:10). It is by giving the Spirit, that he shows us himself. For the Spirit himself is the act of receiving revelation. He reveals in the gift, and his gift is in the revealing. Furthermore, this revelation through the Holy Spirit not only conveys the light of knowledge but also lights the fire of love, as St Paul again testifies (Rm 5:5).[29]

The Holy Spirit is the 'Kiss' which unites Christ and the Church just as it unites the Father and the Son. Bernard asked:

> Do you wish to see the newly-born bride receiving this un-precedented kiss. Then look at Jesus in the presence of the apostles. He breathes on them and says: 'Receive the Holy Spirit'. That favor given to the newly-born Church was indeed a kiss. What?, you say. That corporeal breathing? O no, but rather the invisible Spirit, who is so bestowed in that breath of the Lord that he is understood to proceed from him equally from the Father (Jn 15:26), truly the kiss that is common both to him who kisses and to him who is kissed.[30]

The Holy Spirit is, then, according to Bernard, God's very inwardness to himself—the kiss of the one who kisses, as well as the one who is kissed.

In zen vocabulary, we can very well call the Holy Spirit the mystery of the non-duality of the Father and the Son, and the inexpressible communion of all in God. In the Holy Spirit the love which is the very life of God himself comes to completion, for in him the cycle of Being concludes with the return of all to the Father. Bernard wrote:

> If any of us is so filled with desire that he wants to depart and to be with Christ, he will find himself locked in the arms of Wisdom [the Holy Spirit] ; he will experience how sweet divine love is as it flows into his heart . . . . The soul freely traverses the meadows of contemplation, and in the Spirit, follows the One she loves without restraint wherever he goes.[31]

Zen distinguishes between vertical and horizontal wisdom. Vertical wisdom is that penetrating insight which leads to knowing things as they are. It goes upward, as it were, to the higher understanding, or rather a realization of truth. Horizontal wisdom leads to knowledge *about* things. It is common in human learning and thinking for us to reach a certain level of knowledge and then go on expanding that level. It is said that in zen practice and life the aim is not to elaborate, but to penetrate.[32]

303

Vertical wisdom is called also 'Transcendental Wisdom'.
Transcendental in the sense of transcending or going beyond the
mere knowledge of things. It is knowledge, or *awareness as such,*
beyond the duality of subject and object which is the realm of
philosophy. Transcendental wisdom is knowing; knowing, that is
to say, subject, predicate, and object are all the same.

Mumon Ekai understands wisdom in this vertical or transcendental sense. For him, to be wise is to know things in their
'suchness'. It is to know things as they are in themselves. Mumon's notion of such wisdom is illustrated in the following
incident: during the first century of Japanese Zen there occurred
the remarkable journey of the monk named Hotto Kakushin
(1207–1298) who went from Japan to China. After a long
search for a zen master, he met the famous zen master of the
time, Mumon Ekai. From the very beginning the relationship
between master and disciple was exceptionally intimate. Master
Mumon (No Gate) asked the newcomer during their first
encounter:

'There is no gate here whereby you can enter. Therefore
how did you come in?'
'I came in', Kakushin replied, 'by the No-gate (Mumon).'
The master now asked, 'What is your name?'
'My name is Kakushin (Enlightened Mind).'

On the spot Master Mumon composed the following verse:
Mind is Buddha
Buddha is Mind
Mind and Buddha in their *Suchness*
Are in past and future alike.[33]

For Master Mumon, as for all zen masters, 'Suchness' is what
a thing is, the nature of a thing, for example, the nature of man.
To each the 'Suchness' of a thing is to attain supreme knowledge or ultimate wisdom. Ernest Wood asserts that 'if the term
God, divested of all anthropomorphism, or taken in his "Suchness," is used for the original power, or self-being, then the Zen
view has always been that one can know God by overcoming the
impurity which one's mind imposes on one's "seeing".'[34]

Zen masters assert that 'Suchness' is 'Voidness', and 'Void-

ness' is 'Suchness', because the 'Suchness' of anything is devoid
of any other thing. This is true when one tries to think about
God. In thinking about God we must pass beyond all limitations.
The 'limits' by which we distinguish one being from another are
the boundaries of that being's existence and the means of discovering or locating the individual in a framework of time and
space or in the relationship of one thought to another; but these
'limits' or boundaries which serve to reveal the 'Suchness' of a
being are not the 'Suchness' itself.

To reach the 'Suchness' itself of any being, we must pass
beyond and leave behind those very boundaries or 'limits'
which once served to bring the individual to our attention and
which enabled us to distinguish this individual from ourselves
and from all other aspects. To move from this knowledge of
discovery, from this horizontal knowledge which grasps boundaries and distinguishes one limit from another, towards the
knowledge which touches the 'Suchness' of the object known,
as it were through the 'Kiss of Wisdom' or through enlightenment, requires a new faculty, a new mind, a mind that has the
directness of the heart and the unifying function of the 'Kiss'.
It is to go into the 'Suchness' of a being where there is no gate,
because the gate itself is a limit that swings between oneself and
the object known. This is a motion which is said to be 'pure'
because it leaves behind those very limits which both reveal
and obscure the existence of the object itself.

Wisdom is able to abandon the limiting boundaries which
might have served to describe its own functions and move
into the 'Void' where the object is just 'Such' apart from any
limits that might serve to distinguish it from other objects or
even from the one knowing. Thus the 'Void' in which wisdom
knows and into which wisdom moves is a 'Void' only in the
sense that is void of limitations, but in the greater sense the
'Void' is being itself. Abhishiktananda (Henry Le Saux, OSB)
writes:

> When man thinks seriously about God, striving to grasp him,
> take his measure and mentally to realize his presence, his
> intelligence is soon baffled and his thinking lets him down.

305

The time comes when the thought itself vanishes in that over-whelming brightness . . . . There is nothing on which he can lay hold, to which he can cling. On the contrary, everything slips away—his body, his thought, his very awareness of him-self and of his own personality. His being draws within and called simply to *be* appears to him as being swallowed up in the 'void' . . . . The realization of the mystery of being leads to nothing less than this. It is fullness and emptiness at the same time. The Vedantic *pursam* and the Buddhist *sunya* (that is, empty, or void).[35]

Mumon's realization of ultimate wisdom has been described by him as the experience of 'Voidness'. The verse he wrote at his death was:

The Void is unborn
The Void does not perish
If you know the Void
You and the Void are not different.

Voidness or emptiness may suggest a deprivation of all mental operations, as occurs in a trance. It is not so. Abbot Soyen Shaku wrote: 'Voidness describes the "deep things of God" which are absolute and not relative. For when we say, "God is", it may be taken as meaning that "He is" as we individuals are.'[36]

The assertion of the 'Void' goes beyond the negation of sub-stantial reality and the doctrine of the inconsistency of all things. All phenomena as such, including the five aggregates (form, sensation, mental functions, rational knowledge, and consciousness) are declared 'Void'. This 'Void' free of all particularities and of all concreteness, is beheld by the enlightened eye of wisdom (*Prajna*), the organ of intuitive knowledge, which brings about all-knowing. The *Prajna-paramita Sutras* declare that

After the eye of wisdom has comprehended the 'Void', has unmasked all false appearances, and has destroyed attach-ment to illusory concepts, it beholds in enlightenment *things as they are,* and also the human spirit in the simple 'Thusness', or 'Suchness' of being.[37]

For a zen practioner no effort is too great to grasp the 'Voidness' of all things. How to grasp this 'Voidness' or 'Transcendental Wisdom' is the most absorbing topic of all the *Wisdom Sutras*—the *Prajnaparamita.* When it has been successfully carried out the zen discipline comes to an end. The *Prajnaparamita Sutras* are eagerly studied and recited in zen monasteries even today.

D. T. Suzuki calls 'Voidness' the gospel of the *Wisdom Sutras,* and the fountainhead of all the Mahayana philosophies and practical disciplines. He asserts that If God is the ultimate ground of all things, he must be 'emptiness' itself. When he is at all determined in either way good or bad, straight or crooked, pure or impure, he submits himself to the principle of relativity; that is, he ceases to be God, but a god who is like ourselves mortal and suffers. To be established nowhere thus means 'to be empty.'[38]

Suzuki quotes St Bernard's comment on Isaiah 10:15: 'The ability to glorify God comes from God alone', and concludes that 'All relative existences are as such empty and unborn'.[39] Suzuki did not have access, apparently, to the *De consideratione,* in which Bernard expounded the notion of the non-duality of all-being and non-being of God, or, in the zen sense, the 'emptiness' of God.

For Mumon, wisdom is the religious sense of enlightenment. Through our faculties we first become aware of a thing as an object to us, but when, through this religious sense of enlightenment, or wisdom, we take hold of the thing, then we—the seizer—and the seized become one; the awareness of dualism ceases, and there is an understanding of the complete identity of subject and object which is known as all-knowledge or *satori* in Japanese and *wu* in Chinese.

A way toward the working out of this identity was given by Mumon in Case (or koan) XVIII of the *Mumonkan* entitled 'Tozan's Three Pounds of Flax':

A monk asked Tozan, 'What is Buddha?'
'Three pounds of flax,' he replied.[40]

Blyth has commented at great length on Case XVIII of the

307

Mumonkan. He reminds his readers of the Buddhist 'Trinity' or the 'Three Bodies' (*Trikajas*), and tries to tie this notion in with the christian mystery of the Blessed Trinity.[41] Master Mumon did not even hint at the thought of the 'Trinity'. His comment on Case XVIII was:

> Old Tozan's Zen is rather like a clam;
> When it is just opening the two halves of the shell,
> You can see the liver and the intestines.
> But though this may be so, just say, 'Where can we see
>   Tozan?'

Mumon's verse on Case XVIII was:

> 'Three pounds of flax,' artlessly,
>   spontaneously it comes out.
> The words and the meaning are intimate,
>   indivisibly intimate.
> He who explains this and that, yes and no,
>   the relative,
> Is himself only a relative person.

As a rule, the koan is not to be explained, but must be realized. All the terms used in this Case XVIII have an absolute, not a relative, sense. The words 'Tozan's Zen' indicate the moment Tozan reaches the realization of the Absolute Truth. Mumon substitutes for the 'Three Pounds of Flax' his own words, to express his inner realization of Truth, that is, 'Zen Clam'. His question was: 'How do you realize the absolute Truth when you look inside the clam?'

Enlightenment, or *satori,* at its highest point brings the realization that the substratum of existence is 'Void'. Out of this 'Void' all things ceaselessly arise and into it they endlessly return. This 'voidness' is positive and dynamic. The richness of the 'Void' is found in traces and hints wherever Creation reveals itself to the searching heart. It is detected by artists and poets, it is reached for by sages and musicians, it is pointed to in the vividness of a sunset and hinted at in the harmonies of a great symphony, or the free rhythm of Gregorian chant—but it is none of these.

THE VISION OF WISDOM AS REALIZED
BY THE TWO MASTERS

Bernard's realization of Wisdom was expressed in what he called 'The Visit of the Word'. In his seventy-fourth sermon on the Song of Songs he said:

> I have received the visit of the Word
> and indeed not once but many times;
> but although he has often come to my soul
> I have never been able to ascertain
> the exact moment of his entrance.
>
> Certainly he does not enter through the eyes
> for he has no color, nor through the ears
> since he has no sound, nor through the organ of smell.
> For his mingling is with the mind, not with the atmosphere.
> But neither can he be said to come from within me.
> I have ascended to what is highest in me
> and behold I have found the Word to be higher still.
> I have descended to explore the lowest depths of my being
> only to find that he was deeper still.
> I looked to the exterior, I perceived him beyond what is
> outermost; and if I turned my gaze inward,
> I saw him more interior than what is inmost.
>
> Then I realized the truth of what I read that,
> 'In him we live, we move, and have our being'.
> Blessed is the soul in whom he is, who lives for him
> and is moved by him![42]

I have commented on Bernard's account of this experience elsewhere.[43] Let me repeat here only the main points.

The term 'visit' means an intimate presence, an awareness, a union of the Word and the soul. For Bernard, the 'Word' means both the Eternal Word which is the Eternal Wisdom from the bosom of the Father, and the Incarnate Word which is Wisdom-in-time for all men. A constant meditation of the

309

'Word' is true wisdom, true philosophy, the source of salvation, the royal road.[44]

Bernard's consciousness of the presence of the Word in his mind and heart is, in the vocabulary of Zen, a pure awareness which Thomas Merton defines as 'the one in which one experiences reality not mediating an object, a concept or a symbol, but directly, and the one in which clinging to no experience and to no awareness, one is simply aware'.[45] There is no duality-experience of any kind. It is essential that we transcend the level of the senses and intellection in order to reach this level of pure awareness. Because 'the Word is simply with the mind', as Bernard said.

Bernard realized Wisdom, or the All-Embracing-Reality. This went beyond his own power and, transcending the zenith of his consciousness, he found the Word deeper than the inmost part of his being. He left the Word at its outermost reaches only to find that the Word is still beyond. This is certainly the experience of Wisdom. 'Wisdom is one in itself,' Bernard wrote, 'but it is manifold in its effects and operations. Wisdom is length because of its eternity; breadth because of its charity; height because of its majesty; and depth because of its understanding.[46] This experience of Wisdom as Wisdom exists in itself puts one in a blessed state. 'He who experiences wisdom as wisdom is in itself is not only wise, but blessed.'[47]

According to Mumon Ekai no verbal expression can fully describe the truth of the realization of Wisdom. He said: 'It is like a mute person who had a dream. He has had it. That's all.'[48] Mumon's own realization was reported as follows: Mumon Ekai went to see Getsurin, the seventh successor of Yogi Hoe, at Manjuri Temple. Getsurin, who was famous for his severity, gave him the koan *No* (*Wu* in Chinese, and *Mu* in Japanese) to study. After six years of hard work Mumon had still not solved his problem. He swore he would not sleep until he understood *No,* and when he fell asleep he would go out into the corridor and bash his head against a post. One day, as the noon-drum struck, he suddenly came to a realization, and composed the following verse:

310

Out of a blue sky the sun shining bright, a clap of thunder!
All the living things of the great earth open their eyes widely.
All the myriad things of nature make obeissance.
Mount Sumeru, off its base, is dancing a polka.
The next day, when he was interviewed by Getsurin, he
wanted to tell him about it, but Getsurin asked him: 'Where
did you see the god? Where did you see the devil?' Mumon
said 'Kwatz!' Getsurin said 'Kwatz!' and they 'Kwatzed' each
other *ad infinitum,* more or less. He composed a stanza:
No! No! No! No! No!
No! No! No! No! No!
No! No! No! No! No!
No! No! No! No! No![49]
Because words often fail sufficiently to convey the experience, we often see the Zen masters uttering a cry of joy, as
Mumon, uttered the word 'Kwatz!' This word means nothing;
it is simply 'Kwatz', an exclamatory utterance which does
now allow any analytical or intellectual interpretation. It was
said that when Master Baso (788), an epoch-maker in the
history of Zen, uttered 'Kwatz!' to his disciple Hyakujo, when
the latter came to the master for the second time to be instructed in Zen, his 'Kwatz!' deafened Hyakujo's ears for the
following three days.[50]
It is difficult for the uninitiated to understand the significance of Mumon's realization as it is expressed in the above
two verses. The following paragraphs which describe the
characteristics of zen experience by zen masters might be
helpful to give us some ideas.
A. *Momentariness:* The realization of truth comes upon
one abruptly and is a momentary experience. This is why
Mumon wrote: 'Out of the blue sky the sun shining bright.
A clap of thunder.' Another Zen master declared: 'O monks, lo
and behold! A most auspicious light is shining with the utmost
brilliancy all over the oceans, all the Sumerus, all the suns and
moons, all the heavens, all the lands—each of which number as
many as hundreds of thousands of kotis. O monks, do you
not see the light?'[51]

311

B. *Feeling of exultation:* This feeling of exultation follows because the realization is the breaking-up of the restriction imposed on one as an individual being. Realization does away with the tension of opposites caused by our ordinary thinking. The feeling that follows the realization is that of a complete release, a complete rest, a sense of coming home. This is why Mumon wrote: 'Mount Sumeru, off its base, is dancing a polka.'

C. *Authoritativeness:* The realization is the final knowledge; no amount of logical argument can refute it. It is as clear as an apple on the palm of one's hand. Realization is a form of inner perception which takes place in the most interior part of consciousness—hence the sense of authoritativeness, meaning, finality. Thus Mumon wrote: 'All myriad things make obeissance' [that is, they do as I wish them to do].

D. *Intuitive insight:* At the moment of realization one acquires a 'seeing' which is quite a different quality from what is ordinarily called knowledge. It is the seeing into the nature of things, or, as Bernard said: 'To experience things as they are'. The knowledge contained in the realization, or enlightenment, is concerned with something universal and at the same time with the individual aspect of existence. 'Satori is the knowledge of an individual object and also of reality which is, if I may say so, at the back of it.'[52] Thus Mumon wrote: 'All the living things of earth, all myriad things of nature make obeissance' [that is, they gaze at me].

E. *Sense of beyond:* With realization, one feels that the experience is one's own, but it is rooted elsewhere, it is beyond. The individuality which one found rigidly held and kept separate from other individual existences becomes loosened from its grip and melts away into something indescribable. Mumon could not express this state of affairs except to say 'No! No! No! No! No!'

No, or *Mu,* when given to the uninitiated, stands by itself. The Zen masters claim it as an eye-opener. The disciple is not to think about it, for no logical thinking is possible. *No* literally means 'Nothing', but ordinarily when this is given as a koan it has no reference to its literal meaning. It is *No,* pure and simple.

For the enlightened man *No* is the gate of Zen. *No* is 'Void', it is 'Emptiness'—*Synata*—the essential nature of all things, the Perfect Being-Nature, the Supreme Wisdom.

WORD AS MEANS LEADING TO WISDOM

Christianity, like the religion of Abraham and Moses in the Old Testament, is in its very essence the mystery of an encounter between human beings and God. From the beginning of Genesis and throughout the Bible we are represented as standing in the presence of God and as entering into dialogue with him. First it is Adam and Eve. After the Fall, God spoke to us only indirectly through prophetic intermediaries. But in Jesus, God once more entered into conversation with humankind directly and literally face to face. 'In many and various ways God spoke of old to our fathers by the prophets, but in these last days he has spoken to us by his Son, whom he appointed the heir of all things, through whom also he created the world.'[53] And Paul wrote: 'And we all with unveiled faces, beholding the glory of the Lord, are being changed into his likeness from one degree of glory to another; for this comes from the Lord who is the Spirit.'[54] In Jesus Christ the Father has spoken the last word to us. Jesus gives thanks to God the Father and addresses him in prayer. He also teaches us to say for ourselves, 'Our Father'. We see thus the significance of the words in Scripture.

The Old Testament was written in Hebrew. For the Jew, the word was a history to be lived. He had no interest in defining the word; he wished to live the actual life God put at his disposal. He asked for understanding. The Hebrew word is not simply the translation of a thought; it is a living and acting reality. It is not the *logos* in the classical sense of the Greek, but the Hebrew *dabar,* which is translated 'word' as well as 'event' as 'thing that happens'. *Dabar* is the 'word-event', the 'word-thing'.[55] The whole Bible is a series of God's redeeming events, the greatest of which is the coming of Jesus

Christ. Jesus Christ achieved all that the word of God is said
to have achieved in the Old Testament. Jesus is the Word
which becomes flesh and dwells among us. Jesus is the summit
and the fullness of the self-revelation of God to men through
his words (Jn 1:18).

Bernard was a man of the Bible. He saw the Bible as an experience, as a means of participating in the redemption in
Jesus Christ of the whole human race. Scripture led him to
the experience of God. Jean Leclercq observes that

> For Bernard, Sacred Scripture was not so much a subject .
> of study as one of prayer. It is necessary to 'taste', to 'feel',
> how good God is. Bernard used this vocabulary of spiritual
> sensations with pleasure. For if the charity of God is at the
> origin of revelation, it must be at its end point. All things
> tend toward love, and this supernatural sensibility leads to
> willing surrender. The word of God encourages dialogue; it
> waits for the echo, the response which will be the word
> of man.[56]

Bernard wrote: 'The soul that thirsts after God gladly rests
and lingers in his inspired word, knowing that therein, without doubt, she shall find him for whose company she yearns'.[57]
As for himself he wrote:

> I will search the treasures of spirit and life hidden in the
> profound depths of these inspired utterances. This is my
> inheritance, because I am a believer in Christ. Why should
> I not endeavour to find the wholesome and savoury food
> of the spirit beneath the unprofitable and unpalatable letter,
> as the grain amongst the chaff, the meat in the shell, or the
> marrow in the bone?[58]

William of St Thierry, Bernard's first biographer and friend,
observed that 'Bernard read Scriptures with simplicity, with
great care and very often. It was in the waters of this original
source that he drank and found replenishment far more than
from the other streams of learning that were derived from the
Scriptures. It was his great delight to pass hours reading
Scriptures.'[59] According to Bernard:

> The words of God are, indeed, pregnant with meaning as

mysteriously profound as they are full of sweetness and
grace. For by the sweetness of its sound it soothes our
affections, by its abounding wealth of meaning it nourishes
and strengthens our minds, by the depth of its mystery it
bewilders our intellect.[60]

To express his eagerness for reading Sacred Scripture, Bernard
quoted the famous saying of Gregory the Great: 'In the ocean
of this sacred reading the lamb paddles, and the elephant
swims' [*in hoc sacrae lectionis pelago agnus ambulat, et
elephas natat.*][61] For this reason he added: 'Let no one be
astonished or take it amis if in examining the Scripture
I give rein to my inquisitiveness as if I were in the wine-
cellar of the Spirit, since I know that life is found in this
way and among such things my spirit draws
strength.'[62]

Bernard reminded us that in expounding Scriptures we
must remember that the Scriptures are wont to present the
unknown and invisible things of God to us by means of figures
drawn from things we know, thus offering us, so to speak, a
rare wine in a common cup. Holy Scripture, by means of
human words, speaks wisdom hidden in a mystery, and com-
mends the Divinity to our love, investing it with human affection; and from familiar images of earthly objects as from a
chalice of vile materials the Scriptures bring forth the rare
and precious, even the mysterious and invisible things of God.[63]

Bernard warned us that 'The word of God is not a sounding
but a piercing word, not pronounceable by the tongue but
efficacious in the mind, not sensible to the ear but fascinating
to the affection'[64]—because 'it is the Son of God, the Word,
the Wisdom of the Father who raised human reason by his
might, taught it by wisdom, drew it to things interior.'[65]

For Mumon Ekai the word used as a means leading to wisdom is the 'zen word' or the koan. In the preface to his
Mumonkan he wrote:

While I was spending a summer at Lung-hsiang in Eastern
China in the first year of Shao-ting [1228] I had to look
after a number of students who wished to be instructed in

315

Zen. So I made use of the ancient masters' koans as a piece of brick which is used for knocking at the gate. The students were then disciplined each according to his ability.

Before we consider the nature of the koan and its functions, attention should be given to the question of Mumon and the use of words.

Some Zen scholars think that Zen seems to deny the inner relationship between words and reality. Dumoulin writes:

The Zen masters, in resorting to gestures, grimaces, and all possible signs, not infrequently end in the grotesque. One cannot unconditionally approve of their attitude towards language. The basic error is apparent already in the Lanka-Sutras: it regards the relationship between syllables and reality, word and meaning, and doctrine and truth as merely external, similar to the fingertip with which one points to the moon. Fingertip and moon remain infinitely separate. The words of Master Mumon are similar. 'It is as one who seeks wisdom in the words, or who attempts to beat the moon with a stick or who scratches an itch over the shoe: what real concern have they with truth?'[66]

We can sympathize with Dumoulin if Mumon's comparison of the use of words to 'beating the moon with a stick' were taken literally. What Mumon meant, however, was that if we use many words drawn from memory to expound a truth, it is useless. Zen does not lay stress on logical words or philosophy in the unfolding of religious consciousness. What Zen emphasizes is the intuitive understanding of ultimate religious truth or wisdom. D. T. Suzuki's remarks on this subject are interesting:

Zen claims to be a specific transmission outside the written Scripture and to be altogether independent of verbalism, but it is Zen masters who are most talkative and most addicted to writings of some sorts. Almost every master of note has left what is known as *Sayings* which were more or less filled with paradoxical expressions altogether off the ordinary logical line of human understanding. The masters seem to be particularly delighted to lead the readers to bewilderment with their apparently irrational and often irrelevant utterances. But the fact is these utterances issue from the master's most kind and loving heartedness as they wish to open for their students the higher way of observing things enabling the latter to rid themselves of the entangling networks of relativity.[67]

In his introductory remarks to the commentary of the Song of Songs, Bernard also said: 'We must remember that love reveals itself not by words or phrases, but by action and experience.'[68] We know, however, that Bernard took twelve thousand words to explain that love to his monks, and left the explanation unfinished! Tai-hui (1089–1163) said in a letter to Chen-ju-Tao-jen:

> There are two errors now prevailing among the followers of Zen. The one thinks that there are wonderful things hidden in words and phrases. The second goes to the other extreme, forgetting that words are the pointing finger, showing one where to locate the moon. Blindly following the instruction given in the sutras, where words are said to hinder right understanding of the truth of Zen and Buddhism, they reject all words or teaching and simply sit with eyes closed. What a pity! . . . Only when these two erroneous views are done away with is there a chance for real advancement in the mastery of Zen.[69]

As a matter of fact, in Zen there is strong belief in the power of words. It is said that beneath a single phrase there exists life and death; within a single response there lies release and there lies capture; upon a single expression rests the myriad transformation which it is impossible for any man to know. This is why the master usually works hard to help the disciple to know the many subtle meanings within a single word. There is a group of koans called in Japanese 'Gonsen koans', the study and investigation of words. By studying and meditating on these koans the students will attain insight into the mystery of words.[70]

Space does not allow me to present a survey of the koans and their use as they developed in history. Suffice it to note that the Japanese word *koan* comes from the Chinese words *kung,* 'public', and *An,* 'records'. Koan thus means, 'public records'.

The Zen masters have stated clearly what a koan is and for what purpose it is used. When asked to explain why the teaching of the buddhas and patriarchs were called 'public records', that is, koans, Chun-Feng Ming-pen (1263-1368) answered:

> The koans may be compared to the case records of the public law court. Whether or not the ruler succeeds in bringing order to his realm depends in essence upon the existence of the law. *Kung,* or 'public', is the single track followed by all sages and worthy men alike, the highest principle which serves as a road for the whole world. *An,* or 'records', are the orthodox writings which record what the sages and worthy men regard as principle . . . .
> Now, when we use the word 'koan' to refer to the teaching of the buddhas and patriarchs, we mean the same thing. The koans do not represent the private opinion of a single man, but rather the highest principle, received alike by us and by the hundreds and thousands of bodhisattvas. This principle accords with the spiritual source . . . .
> It cannot be understood by logic; it cannot be transmitted in words; it cannot be explained in writing; it cannot be measured by reason. The koans are a torch of wisdom that lights up the darkness of the feeling and discrimination, a golden scraper that cuts away the film clouding the eye, a sharp ax that severs the root of birth-and-death (or duality), a divine mirror that reflects the original face of both the sacred and the secular. Through it the intention of the patriarchs is made abundantly clear, the Buddha-mind is laid open and revealed. For the essentials of the complete transcendence, final emancipation, total penetration and the attainment of identity nothing can surpass the koan.[71]

The main features of the koan are as follows: every koan is a unique expression of the living nature of 'Perfect Being' which cannot be grasped by the bifurcating intellect. All point to the 'Original Face', or the true Self-Nature, the equivalent of which for a Christian would be the 'Image of God'.

Koans appear bewildering, even bizarre, to persons who are uninitiated in Zen. Those who grasp their spirit know that they are profoundly meaningful. The merit of koans is that they compel us to learn these truths not simply with our head but with our whole being, not allowing us to sit back and endlessly theorize about them in the abstract.

Perhaps one can say that the koan generates insight through the 'friction' of paradox rather than through the deduction of reason, or through the progression of scientific investigation. Greek thought strove to teach truth through the logical deduction of conclusions from self-evident first principles. This gave us the profound, but static and unmoving, view point of logical truth. Empirical thought, which is the basis for today's scientific technology, arrives at new truth through the progressive method of observation, question, hypotheses, and verification through exact experimentation. This has given us the world of scientific truth. But Zen thought generates insight through the direct confrontation of paradox—often expressed in a koan. This paradoxical word generates such a feeling of interior discomfort with one's present condition of understanding that one is pushed to move beyond by the inner invisible drive to truth: to move beyond familiar ways of understanding, to move beyond the limits of relative knowledge towards the absolute. It is an instinctual way of teaching, similar to that of the mother eagle who pushes the baby out of the nest into the empty world beyond.

The complete 'solution' of a koan involves the movement of the mind from a state of ignorance called delusion to the awareness of living truth. This implies the emergence into the field of a new consciousness different from the ordinary thinking way.

Paradoxical statements are the inevitable result of the zen way of looking at life. The whole emphasis of its discipline is placed on the intuitive grasping of the inner truth deeply hidden in our consciousness. And this truth thus revealed or awakened within oneself cannot be imparted to others through any dialectical formulas. It must come out of oneself, grow within oneself, and become one with one's own being. What ideas or images can do is to point to the truth. This is what Zen masters do.

WISDOM IN DAILY LIFE

A wise person is not born but made. As a rule wisdom is not to be found early in life, but only after a long practice of discipline. It is, therefore, natural that all masters, christians and those of other traditions, have placed great stress on the exercises of a moral life, charity, and prayer, or meditation. Space does not allow me to elaborate on these exercises. Here are only a few essential points.

A. *A moral life:* For Bernard, the ethical question is central to the Gospel. Expounding the word of God to his monks, he presupposed they were 'mature people', enlightened men taught in the way of the Spirit,[72] men who already knew the two great enemies of the soul, a misguided love for the world and an excessive love for the self.[73] Bernard wrote strong words to Pope Eugene III: 'Although you know every mystery, if you do not know yourself, you are like a building without a foundation.'[74] His last words to his monks, quoted from Paul (Eph 5:8), were: 'Let us walk like children of light'.[75]

Mumon's last words in his postscript were: If you have passed the gate, Mumon is useless to you. If you have not passed it, you are still deceiving yourself. It is easy to be clear about the Nirvana Mind [the Absolute] but it is not easy to be clear about the Wisdom of Differences. If you clearly understand the Wisdom of Difference, you can make your country one worth living in.[76]

Even if it were easy to attain the knowledge of timelessness, spacelessness, selflessness, otherlessness—the Absolute—to apply this knowledge to the relative world of daily living is troublesome. Nevertheless this troublesome task is the only thing which will justly reflect the creative work of Chapters One and Two of the Book of Genesis. Enlightenment, or

wisdom, does not itself make a master of Zen. It is one
thing to have a thorough knowledge of all the characteristics
of enlightenment, quite another thing to live a life which
expresses that knowledge.[77]

B. *Love and compassion:* Bernard deeply experienced the
Gospel truth that 'God is love'. When man, by his love for
God, is fully conformed to him, the experiential union, or
wisdom, is reached. He wrote:

> It is by conformity of love, brothers, that the soul is
> wedded to the Word, when, namely, loving even as she is
> loved, she exhibits herself, in her will, conformed to him
> to whom she is already conformed in her nature. Therefore,
> if she loves him perfectly she becomes his bride. What can
> be sweeter than such a conformity?[78]

The first fruit of a sapiential union of the soul with God is
an ever greater love for one's neighbor. It is impossible for a
soul blest with such a grace to keep for itself the joy it experiences. This love accommodates itself to everyone; it
embraces both friends and foes; it makes the 'feeling' of
other its own.[79]

In order to bring home to his students an example of love
and compassion, Mumon gave Case XXIII in *The Gateless
Gate:*[80]

> Hui-Neng Daikan [d. 713], the sixth patriarch of Zen,
> received from Konin Daimon, the fifth patriarch [d. 673]
> the bowl and robe. Because of the jealousy of some of the
> monks, Hui-Neng left the monastery at night, taking the
> bowl and robe with him. Some brother monks pursued him,
> intending to wrest the treasured objects from him. Among
> them was a tall, stern and rough monk, named Emyo.
> Hui-Neng knew Emyo was coming, so he sat and waited,
> placing the bowl and the robe on a nearby rock. When
> Emyo appeared, Hui-Neng said to him: 'These objects just
> symbolize the truth. If you want them, take them.' But
> when Emyo tried to lift the bowl and robe, they were as
> heavy as mountains. Trembling with shame, he said: 'I came for
> the teaching not for material treasures. Please teach me!'

Hui-Neng said: 'Do not think: "This is good!" "This is not good!" At such moments, what is your Original Face?' At these words, Emyo's entire body was bathed in perspiration; he was enlightened. In gratitude he said: 'You have given me the secret words and meanings. Is there yet a deeper part of the teaching?' Hui-Neng replied: 'What I have told you is not secret at all. When you realized your own true self, the secret belongs to you.'

Emyo said: 'I was under the fifth patriarch many years but could not realize my true Self until now. Through your teaching I find the source. A person drinks water and knows himself whether it is cold or warm. May I call you my teacher?' Hui-Neng replied: 'We studied together under the fifth patriarch. Call him your teacher, but just treasure what you have attained.[81]

Commenting on this story Mumon wrote:

The Sixth Patriarch should say that this is a state of emergency, needing grandmotherly kindness. It is like peeling a fresh lichi, removing the pip and then putting it in your mouth for you. All you have to do is just gulp it down.

C. *A Living Faith:* For a Christian, faith is the acceptance of the words spoken to us by God, and the surrender of our whole being—body and mind—to him. According to Bernard, faith is essential for attaining wisdom. He wrote:

With the power to understand invisible truth, faith does not know the poverty of the sense; it transcends the limit of our human reason, the capacity of nature, the boundaries of experience.[82]

For a Zen Buddhist, faith is a belief such as is described in the words of Shakyamuni Buddha who, after his religious awakening, said: 'How wonderful! Every sentient creature is endowed with the intrinsic wisdom and virtuous characteristics of Tathagatha [that is, Suchness] !' The determination to struggle with the barriers, or koans, set up by the masters, is in the first place generated by faith in the reality of this intrinsic wisdom, this Bodhi-Mind.

Along with this faith a spirit of inquiry is needed. Faith

and the spirit of inquiry are complementary and mutually conditioning. The power of a spirit of inquiry paves the way more surely to enlightenment chiefly because the spirit of inquiry awakens the faith which lies dormant at the basis of our being. To stimulate faith and the spirit of inquiry in students, Mumon gave Case XLVI in *The Gateless Gate*— Sekiso's Hundred-Foot Pole:

> Sekiso said, 'How can you go on further from the top of a hundred-foot pole?' Again, an ancient worthy said, 'One sitting on the top of a hundred-foot pole has entered the Way, but is not yet the real thing. He must go on further from the top of the hundred-foot pole, and reveal his true self in the ten directions.'

In his comment on the koan Mumon wrote:

> Going beyond the top of the pole and turning his body about—what is there here to dislike or to praise? But even so, tell me, how we proceed onwards from the top of a hundred-foot pole? Aha!

We are asked by Mumon to jump off the top of a hundred-foot pole! How are we going to make this jump out of death into life? Mumon said in his verse:

> If the [third] eye [intuitive faith] in the forehead is darkened
> And we mistake the star on the balance for the measurement,
> We throw away our body and soul
> And blindly lead other blind people.[83]

To make this jump requires a faith and a striving spirit. Just to be on our lofty intellectual pedestal is not enough. Not logical trickery, but a surrender of our whole being is needed to effect a penetration. It is, Mumon tells us, like climbing up to the end of a pole one hundred feet long and yet being urged to climb on and on until you have to execute a desperate leap, utterly disregarding your life. The moment this is executed you find yourself safely on the full-blown-lotus pedestal, that is, you are enlightened. Bernard was not less emphatic on the subject. 'What is the reason,' he asked his monks, why she

323

[the soul] is so little industrious in a matter which concerns her highest interest? Industry, my brothers, is a very important endowment of our nature. But if it fails to perform its functions, are not the rest of our natural gifts and faculties thrown aside, as it were, with the rust of decadence?[84] Striving and perseverance made aridity fervent.[85]

D. *Meditation:* Bernard advised Pope Eugene to 'Take time for meditation!',[86] because meditation purifies the mind, controls emotions, guides actions, corrects excess, improves behavior, confers dignity and order on life, and imparts knowledge of divine and human affairs. Meditation anticipates adversity when all is going well, and when adversity comes, it stands firm. In this, it displays both wisdom and fortitude.[87]

For Bernard meditation and contemplation are not quite synonymous, although both terms are used interchangeably. Meditation is the searching of the mind to discover truth, whereas contemplation is the true and sure intuition of the mind concerning something, or the apprehension of truth without doubt.[88]

Bernard put great emphasis on meditation on the Word of God. 'The man who thirsts for God eagerly studies and meditates on the inspired words, knowing that he is certainly to find the One for whom he thirsts.'[89] But in meditation on the Word of God one must leave the surface of the letter in order to enter the depth of its meaning, for only then can he taste the meat and the marrow. We must search for the treasures of the Spirit and life hidden in the profound depth of these inspired utterances. For it is the Spirit who quickens, that is, who gives understanding.[90]

In order to explore the profound depth of sacred truth we must develop what Bernard called a 'sense of taste'—*interiorum sensuum gustu.* 'Sacred Scripture,' he wrote, 'not content to flatter our eyes with the beauty of its literary cloth, wants to satiate us with the succulence of its profound meaning. It was written for us, not only to delight us with its external form, but also to feed the internal sense of taste as with the marrow of the wheat.'[91]

324

As concrete steps toward deep meditation, Bernard advised, (1) be still, and (2) go inward. Stillness is essential in meditation: in fact, it is the essence of meditation. 'Be still and know that I am God.'[92] We should not be content to meditate on God in creation only; he must enter into our own inmost depth.

By a special privilege, the soul wants to welcome him down from heaven into her inmost heart, into her deepest love; she wants to have the one she desires present to her not in bodily form but by inward infusion, not by appearing externally but by laying hold of her within.[93]

This going inward is nothing distant, nothing esoteric, nothing complicated. It is the depth and lucidity of the Gospel because 'The Kingdom of God is within you'. 'It does not behove you, O man, to cross the seas, to penetrate the clouds, or to climb the Alps [in search of God]. No great journey is necessary for you. Seek no further than your own consciousness [soul]: there will you find your God!'[94]

Scripture invites us, saying: 'Open your mouth and I shall fill it' (Ps 81:11). Our nature, created by God, is capable of the infinite, and can be filled only with the infinite. When we reflect on the word of God, it helps us to be mindful that we are capable of the Infinite God, that God desires to fill us with his infinity. Think of yourself as the infinite 'sky' that is pure and limpid. Think of your consciousness as a vast universe. This universe is Christ and is being filled by Christ at every moment (Eph 1:23). We are the plentitude, the fullness, the completion of Christ as Paul expressed it (Eph 1:23; 5:26). We can make a koan out of any word of God. For example, we can ask ourself: How do I realize Christ in the words: 'The Church is the fullness of him who fills the universe'? Every word in this short sentence is dynamic. Notice that it is in the 'present' tense. It is also infinite, because it is all-embracing. It carries with it the seed of expansion, and as it becomes self-activating it will go on infusing us with divine life.

We must train ourselves to go beyond the 'meager letter', as Bernard advises. Christ said: 'It is the Spirit that gives life,

325

the flesh is of no avail. The words I spoke to you are Spirit and life.'[95]

An analytical understanding is never sufficient to reach wisdom or grasp a truth, especially a religious truth, nor can external religious observance bring about a spiritual trans- formation in us. We must experience or, as Bernard said, 'We must taste'. We must realize in our inmost consciousness the meaning that is implied in a doctrine, then we will be able not only to understand it but to live it in practice.

All Zen masters after Shakyamuni Buddha knew this well, and they endeavored to produce knowledge, so to speak, out of meditation, that is, to make wisdom grow out of personal, spiritual experience.

Although Zen is sometimes described in the West as the Meditation School of Buddhism, it is not in its present form strictly buddhist, and it certainly is not a passive form of meditation, as the word Zen so often implies in the West. In both East and West there is much so-called meditation which is nothing but a fixing of the mind on a concept or on an object. It is necessary to state clearly that zen meditation is a strenuous task of consciousness, whether it takes the form of a periodic effort, or aims at being the constant background in the midst of all our other material and mental activities.

These remarks apply to both the Soto and the Rinzai Schools of Zen. These differ in that the Soto method aims at observing one's own mind in tranquility (also called serene reflection, or Mokusho Zen, which means the quiet sitting still in silent meditation[96] or the quietness of no-thought) while the Rinzai gives the student's mind a hard task usually involving a vigorous or violent treatment of a koan problem. The Rinzai method may even involve an ear-splitting shout designed to knock the thinking process 'off its perch'. In either case meditation is not a supression of thought or an ignoring of facts, but a more complete response to them. Thus it is a discovery of the limits of the mind coupled with a will simply to go on, to reach beyond. Zen is often described in the last analysis as a 'leap in the dark', or more accurately 'a leap into the dark'.[97]

Mumon was one of the strong advocates of the koan meditation, or koan exercise, in China. The method of the koan
is to stop the discursive traces of intellection. By it students
of Zen prepare their consciousness to be the proper ground
from which intuitive knowledge (*prajna*) is able to burst
forth.

In the *Mumonkan,* or *The Gateless Gate,* koan *No* heads
the collection of forty-eight koans. Mumon himself worked
hard for six years to solve that koan, under the experienced
guidance of his master Getsurin. Commenting on this koan
No, Mumon gave his disciples the instruction needed to work
it out in their turn under his guidance. These instructions can
be applied in the study of the other koans. I quote in full
Mumon's directions:

In Sanzen [the practice of Zen] you must try to pass
through the barrier [koan] of the patriarchs. In the attainment of exquisite *satori,* you must completely exhaust
your mind. If you do not pass through the barrier of the
patriarchs and do not exterminate the exercise of your
mind, you are all ghosts leaning against the grass and trees.
Now say what the barrier of the patriarchs is. This one
word *No* indeed expresses the only barrier of Zen Buddhism
in which there is no gate. Taking this into consideration,
I have come to call this book *Zen-chu Mumonkan.* Those
who have passed through it can see Joshu in person and,
more than that, can go hand in hand with the successive
patriarchs, can enjoy the closest intimacy with them, and
can see with the same eyes and hear with the same ears
as theirs. Is this not a pleasant thing? Is there not any fellow
to swallow completely this barrier?
Raising this one doubt 'What is *No*?' throughout your body
in the three hundred and sixty bones and eight thousand
pores, devote yourself to the realization of the word *No.*
Keep it day and night and don't interpret it as voidness or
there-is-not, the opposite of there-is. Just as if you had
swallowed a burning iron ball, never spit it out even if you

feel like vomiting, and it will melt away all your former
false knowledge and perceptions. If you have continued in
this condition for a long time and have become so pure and
ripe that the inside and outside naturally come to be one,
I can expect that you will surely realize *satori* yourself just
as a dumb person who, having a dream realizes what it is.
You are enlightened dashingly, you will be astonished to
feel as if heaven and earth have crashed into nothing. You
will feel as if you stand with the great sword of General Kan
in your hand. When you meet Buddha, you will have
already killed the Buddha. When you meet the patriarchs
you will have already killed the patriarchs. You can be calm
and peaceful even on the scaffold, and you can behave
yourself cheerfully during life as if you were always in
paradise even though you transmigrate, as it is traditionally
said, through the four kinds of birth in the six worlds of
living beings according to your karma.

Now, how you shall hold on to *No*? Keep holding the one
word *No*, using all your energy. If you do so without any
discontinuity *No* will be manifested just as when a candle is
lit in the dark it immediately shines bright. No discontinua-
tion! Then and there Buddhahood is manifested.[98]

The whole of this long commentary may be summarized
thus:

1. The practice of Zen includes the receiving of private instructions, hearing lectures (*teichos*), sitting in meditation. To be
   attentive in the details of daily life is also crucial.
2. Zen cannot be approached from the suppositions of logic. We
   must stop all thought forms in order to look into the source
   of thoughts. Emotionality and sophistication must be
   cut off.
3. Do not think that enlightenment must be this or that.
4. Search for truth from within.
5. Do not consider *No* as being or non-being. Once *No* is
   solved, we see and hear what the greatest men of the past
   saw and heard. We grasp the world of enlightenment. We
   realize the unification of the 'self' and the 'Self'.

6. The result is a state of peace and truth. We will be able to live with spontaneity and joy.
7. To attain this state, unremitting effort is needed, but persistence will end in the birth of yet another living witness to the Truth or Wisdom.

The practical application of these elements, especially the 'wrestling' with the koan and the interview with the Roshi (*dokusan*) can be seen as dynamic only if one has attended a *Zen Sesshin* guided by an experienced Zen Master. This practical method of Zen training is one of the decisive factors in the encounter of East and West as represented by Bernard and Mumom.

Mumon's forty-eight koans in the *Mumonkan* have the purpose of leading the student to the realization of supreme wisdom, or the true Self. The following koan might serve as a summary of Mumon's vision and his effort to help his disciples:

> There was an old woman who kept a teahouse at the foot of Mount Taisan, where there was located a Zen monastery noted all over China. The monastery temple was supposed to give wisdom to the one who worshiped there. Whenever a traveling monk asked her which was the way to Taisan, she would say: 'Go straight ahead!' When the monk followed her direction, she would remark, 'Here is another common church-goer!' Zen monks did not know what to make of her remark. Someone reported this to master Joshu, who said: 'Wait until I investigate'. Joshu started out and, coming to the teahouse, asked the old woman which was the road to Taisan. Sure enough, she told him to go straight ahead, and Joshu did just as many other monks had done. Remarked the woman, 'A fine monk, he goes just the same way as the rest'. When Joshu came back to his brotherhood, he reported, 'Today I have found her out through and through.[99]

Mumon's question to his students was: 'Tell me now, what was Joshu's insight into the old woman?' You yourselves may ask, 'What did the old master find in the woman when his behavior was in no way different from that of the rest of the monks?' I leave this to your own solution in accordance to your own situation.

For both Bernard and Mumon, a good moral life, love and compassion, a life of faith and striving, are essential conditions to realize true wisdom. Mumon tells us to go straight ahead in the form of a koan:

How do we proceed onward
From the top of a hundred-foot pole?

And Bernard tells us:[100]

If any of us is so filled with desire that he wants to depart[101] and to be with Christ,[102] with a desire that is intense, a thirst ever burning, an application that never flags, he will certainly meet the Word in the guise of a Bridegroom on whatever day he comes. At such an hour he will find himself locked in the arms of Wisdom.[103]

Path to Wisdom

Joshu Sasaki Roshi, 'Zen, the Root of All Things,' *Cross Current*, 24 (1974) 205.
2. See Zenkei Shibayama, *A Flower Does Not Talk* (Vermont, 1972) 16.
3. See Thomas Merton, 'The Spiritual Father in the Desert Tradition,' *Monastic Studies* (1968) 88.
4. For further information on St Bernard as spiritual father, read 'St Bernard—the Father of His Sons' by a Monk; 'St. Bernard, Spiritual Director in the Church,' by François Vandenbrouke; 'St. Bernard—Spiritual Director' by Edouard Wellens. These essays can be found in *Saint Bernard and the Church* (trans. Monks of St Joseph's Abbey; Spencer, Massachusetts, 1955). The original text of Edouard Wellens can be found in *Coll.* 15 (1953) 90-103.
5. Jean Leclercq, *Bernard of Clairvaux and The Cistercian Spirit,* trans. Claire Lavoie; CS 16 (Kalamazoo, 1976) pp. 16ff.
6. Letter 87, 7; *The Letters of St. Bernard,* trans. Bruno Scott James (Chicago, 1953).
7. *Sermo super Cantica Canticorum* [SC] , 77, 6.
8. Thomas Aquinas, *Summa theologiae,* I, 12, 6, resp.
9. Etienne Gilson, *Dante the Philosopher* (New York, 1949) 48.
10. Dante, *The Divine Comedy,* trans. Dorothy Sayers (Baltimore, 1966), Paradise: Canto XXIII, 34-39.
11. *Ibid.,* Canto XXXIII, 46-55.
12. Nyongen Sensaki and Paul Reps, 'The Gateless Gate,'' in *Zen Flesh Zen Bones,* ed. Paul Reps (Rutland, Vermont, and Tokyo: Tuttle, 1957). Sohaku Ogata, 'The Mu Mon Kwan,' in Zen for the West (London: Rider, 1959). R.H. Blyth, *Zen and Zen Classics,* vol. 4, *Mumonkan* (Tokyo: Hokuseido Press, 1966). Zenkei Shibayama, *Zen Comments on the Mumonkan,* trans. Sumiko Kudo (New York: Harper & Row, 1974). Katsuki Sekida, *Two Zen Classics: Mumonkan & Hekiganroku* (New York: Weatherhill, and Tokyo).

Abba, *The Spiritual Guide*

13. Heinrich Dumoulin, *The Development of Chinese Zen after the Sixth Patriarch in the Light of the Mumonkan,* trans. Ruth Fuller Sasaki (New York, 1953) p. 1.
Wu-mem-kuan, Der Pass ohne Tor, trans. Heinrich Dumoulin; *Monumenta Nipponica Monographs,* 13 (Tokyo, 1953).
14. *De diversis* [Div], *sermo* 2, 4; SBOp VI/1:82. Translation mine.
15. Div 18, 1; SBOp VI/1:157-58.
16. SC 50, 6; SBOp II:81.
17. *In nativitate domini* [Nat], *sermo* 1, 5-6; SBOp IV:248.
18. SC 85, 8; SBOp II:312. Also, Bernard of Clairvaux, *On Grace and Free Choice* [Hum], trans. Daniel O'Donovan; CS 19 (Kalamazoo, 1977) p. 75.
19. SC 85, 8; SBOp II:313.
20. Div 18, 1; SBOp VI/1:157: 'Cui vero ispa in se est, prout est, sapientia sapit, est non modo sapiens sed beatus est. Nempre haec est videre Deum sicuti est.'
21. *De consideratione* [Csi] V, 13; SBOp III:477-78; CF 37:155.
22. Csi V, 27; SBOp III:489-90; CF 37:173.
23. Csi V, 29; SBOp III:491; CF 37:176.
24. Csi V, 27-28; SBOp III:489-90; CF 37:176.
25. Csi V, 29; SBOp IIi:491; CF 37:176.
26. Csi V, 13; SBOp III:477; CF 37:155.
27. Div 52, 2: SBOp VI/1:275.
28. SC 8, 7; SBOp I:40; CF 4:51, citing Jn 10:30, 14:10.
29. SC 8, 5; SBOp I:38; CF 4:47.
30. SC 8, 2; SBOp I:37; CF 4:46.
31. SC 33, 2; SBOp I:234; CF 7:145.
32. Ernest Wood, *Zen Dictionary* (Vermont, 1972) p. 152.
33. Heinrich Dumoulin, *A History of Zen Buddhism* (New York, 1963) 149.
34. Ernest Wood, *Zen Dictionary,* p. 139.
35. Abhishiktananda, *Saccidananda* (Paris, 1970) pp. 104-106. The etymological derivation of the Sancrit word *sunyata* is from the root 'swell'. A 'swelled' head, as we know, is an 'empty' head. See Edward Conze, *Buddhist Wisdom Books* (New York, 1972) p. 80.
36. Soyen Shaku, *The Sermons of a Buddhist Abbot,* trans. D. T. Suzuki (New York, 1971) p. 143.
37. Heinrich Dumoulin, *A History of Zen Buddhism,* p. 34.
38. D. T. Suzuki, *Essays in Zen Buddhism,* Second Series, p. 342.

332

39. *Ibid.,* p. 311.
40. The Case can be paraphrased as follows: 'A monk asked Tozan when he was weighing some flax: "What is Buddha?" Tozan said: "This flax weighs three pounds".'
41. R. H. Blyth, *Zen and Zen Classics,* IV, *Mumonkan,* pp. 143-46.
42. SC 74, 5-6; SBOp II:242-43.
43. See my 'Religious Awakening: Saint Bernard and The East' in *Saint Bernard of Clairvaux,* ed. Basil Pennington; CS 28 (Kalamazoo, 1977) 209-268.
44. SC 43, 4; SBOp II:43; CF 7:223.
45. Thomas Merton, *Mystics and Zen Masters* (New York, 1967) 237.
46. Csi V, 29; SBOp III:492; CF 37:176.
47. Div 18, 1; SBOp VI/1:158.
48. *Mumonkan by Mumon* (trans. Joshu Sasaki Roshi; Los Angeles, 1970) p. 3.
49. R. H. Blyth, pp. 1-2.
50. D. T. Suzuki, *Essays in Zen Buddhism,* First Series, p. 295.
51. D. T. Suzuki, *Essays in Zen Buddhism,* Second Series, p. 39.
52. D. T. Suzuki, *Essays in Zen Buddhism,* Second Series, p. 35.
53. Heb 1:1.
54. 2 Co 3:18.
55. For an excellent treatment on the Word of God, see George Auzou, *The Word of God* (St Louis, 1960) p. 160 ff.
56. Jean Leclercq, *Bernard of Clairvaux and the Cistercian Spirit,* p. 22.
57. SC 23, 3; SBOp I:140; CF 7:28.
58. SC 73, 2; SBOp II:234.
59. *St. Bernard of Clairvaux,* trans. G. Webb and A. Walker (London-Westminster, Maryland, 1960) p. 42.
60. SC 67, 1; SBOp II:188.
61. Div 94, 2; SBOp VI/1:352. Gregory's *Moral., Epist.;* PL 75:515.
62. SC 16, 1; SBOp I:89; CF 4:114.
63. SC 74, 2; SBOp II:240.
64. SC 61, 3; SBOp I:223.
65. Hum; CF 13:49.
66. Heinrich Dumoulin, *A History of Zen Buddhism,* p. 50.
67. Zenkei Shibayama, *A Flower Does Not Talk,* p. 9.
68. SC 1, 11; SBOp I:7; CF 4:6.
69. D. T. Suzuki, *Essays in Zen Buddhism,* Second Series, p. 92.
70. See Isshu Miura, *The Zen Koan* (New York, 1965) pp. 52-56.

71. *Ibid.,* pp. 4-7.
72. SC 1, 1; SBOp I:3; CF 4:1.
73. SC 1, 2; SBOp I:4; CF 4:2.
74. Csi II, 6; SBOp III:414; CF 37:353.
75. SC 86, 4; SBOp II:320.
76. R. H. Blyth, *Mumonkan,* p. 312.
77. Thomas Merton and D. T. Suzuki carried on a lively dialogue on the 'Moral Life' for both Christian and Zen. See Thomas Merton, *Zen and the Birds of Appetite* (New York, 1968) 99-139. For a fascinating discussion on Zen and ethical issues, see Alan Watts, *Beat Zen, Square Zen, and Zen* (San Francisco, 1959).
78. SC 83, 3; SBOp II:299. After St Bernard, the fourteenth-century christian mystics also stressed the element of love as the way of sapiential union or divine wisdom. The Author of the *Cloud of Unknowing* wrote: 'Pierce that Cloud [of Unknowing] with the keen shaft of your love!' *The Cloud of Unknowing,* trans. William Johnston (New York, 1973), p. 63.
79. SC 57, 9; SBOp II:124-25.
80. The kernel of this story is the koan: 'Do not think: "This is good!" "This is not good!" At such a moment, what is your Original Face [your true Self]?' The story obviously has its moral note.
81. R. H. Blyth, *Mumonkan,* p. 170.
82. SC 28, 9; SBOp II:198; CF 7:95.
83. R. H. Blyth, p. 297 ff.
84. SC 83, 2; SBOp II:299.
85. SC 9, 7; SBOp I:46; CF 4:58.
86. Csi 1, 8; SBOp III:403; CF 37:37.
87. Csi 1, 8; SBOp III:403; CF 37:37.
88. Csi II, 5; SBOp III:414; CF 37:52.
89. SC 23, 3; SBOp II:140; CF 7:28.
90. SC 73, 3; SBOp II:235.
91. *Sermo in Dominica IV post Pentecosten* [IV pP], 2; SBOp V:202.
92. Csi I, 8, quoting Ps 46:10; SBOp III:403; CF 37:37.
93. SC 31, 6; SBOp I:223; CF 7:129.
94. *In adventu Domini* [Adv], *sermo* 1, 10-11; SBOp IV:168-69.
95. Jn 6:63.
96. For a complete treatment of the 'Practice of Zen through Observing One's Own Mind in Tranquility', see Gar C. Chang, *The Practice of*

Zen (New York, 1970) pp. 67 ff.
97. See Ernest Wood, *Zen Dictionary,* p. 81.
98. *Mumonkan by Mumon,* pp. 1-2.
99. *The Mumonkan,* Case XXXI: Joshu's Old Woman. For another famous old woman, see Case XXVIII: 'Blow out the Candle'.
100. SC 32, 2; SBOp I:227; CF 7:135.
101. Depart here means to dissolve the ego-self.
102. Christ here means the risen, the cosmic Christ, of whom Paul speaks (Eph 1:23), the Christ whose fullness we are.
103. 'Arms of Wisdom': here the duality of subject and object, of Christ and the soul is transcended.

I am grateful to Fr Robert Morhous, ocso, for reading this manuscript and offering many insightful suggestions.

THE SPIRITUAL GUIDE: MIDWIFE OF THE HIGHER SPIRITUAL SELF

Sister Donald Corcoran, OSB
Transfiguration Monastery

THE BOOK OF ECCLESIASTICUS counsels that one should seek a person of understanding, cleave to a person who is wise, then go to that person early in the morning, letting one's feet wear the steps of their door.[1] Saints beget saints, an old saying goes. Each of us could probably recall the impact on our lives of a certain pastor, religious teacher, or perhaps the religious belief and devotion of a parent or relative. Looking to history, one finds countless personalities—Bodhidharma, Charles de Foucauld, Rumi the Persian, the Baal Shem Tov, Jacob Boehme, Francis of Assisi, Gandhi, Ramakrishna, Benedict of Nursia, Aurobindo—the power of whose spiritual lives had a way of spilling over into successive generations. The compelling attractiveness of the personal holiness of someone like Mother Teresa of Calcutta stands as a contemporary example of the words John Cassian put into the mouth of the desert father Archebius: 'A saintly life is more educative than a sermon'.

Discipleship is a common human phenomenon. One learns to be a carpenter from a master-carpenter, gourmet cooking from a gourmet cook. In the practical arts—certainly no less in the education of the religious spirit—one learns from a master. A master is accomplished, enthusiastic, highly disciplined. But more importantly, the master is one who has travelled the path; he knows its struggles, pain, failures, renewed efforts. It is not surprising, therefore, that the 'master–disciple' relationship should be one of the fundamental commonalities of the great religious traditions of man. For to be a disciple of a master in the spiritual means *par excellence* in many traditions.

The guru is the backbone of Hinduism. So also the roshi in some sense *is* Zen Buddhism, the sheik *is* Sufism, the zaddik *is* Hasidism. To find the quintessential spirit of a particular religious tradition it is best to look to its great guides, for here one finds that tradition as a *lived* experience and not merely a set of doctrines and concepts. The master–disciple relationship takes one to the heart of a religion. Furthermore, the eminently personal and human quality that makes the stories of master and disciple so attractive also enables them to bear significance across cultural boundaries. There is a strikingly similar wisdom, humor, and even teaching manner in the stories of Desert Fathers, hasidic masters, or zen masters.

To study the genuine master–disciple relationship is to come in contact with one of the noblest forms of human encounter. Kierkegaard felt that the relationship of religious guide to disciple was the highest type of relationship, surpassing even friendship. Perhaps one could say that it is the highest form of friendship. Indeed, the ancient gaelic term for the spiritual guide, *anamchara,* means 'the friend of one's soul', and the buddhist words for spiritual guide *kalyana mitta* mean 'beautiful friend'. Friendship is an important model for understanding the master–disciple relationship.

Many metophors throw light on the function of the master or guru. The spiritual guide in the East is often explained by the metaphor of the boatman who takes one to the 'other shore' of spiritual deliverance. Other models are friend, personal model, wounded-healer, catalyst, transmitter, initiator, hermeneut or interpreter, 'soul-maker' (James Hillman's psychology), and finally 'midwife' of spiritual rebirth. It is the last metaphor which I believe is perhaps the most suitable image of the function of the spiritual guide, since it underscores the spiritual process which the disciple experiences and to which the guide or master is simply an assisting agent. It is the journey which is important, not the guide.

Basically, the spiritual process in the great religious traditions can be understood as a process of transformation. This transformation is a shedding, a transcendence, a death, to the empirical, phenomenal ego and the discovery, emergence, birth, of a deeper spiritual self or identity. All genuine human religious experience is a participation in the Paschal Mystery. St Paul speaks of leaving behind the 'old man' and finding the 'new man' in Christ. Sufism speaks of *fana* (extinction of the superficial self) and spiritual rebirth or reintegration (*ba'qa*). Hinduism sees the spiritual process as transcendence of the *ahamkara* (literally, the I-maker) in order to discover the deep self (*atman*). One form of Japanese Buddhism speaks of death to the small ego (*shogu*) and rebirth as the large ego (*taiga*). Jung's psychology sees the journey to psychological wholeness (the process of 'individuation') as the progressive shift in the center of gravity of the personality from ego (conscious personality) to the self (the integration of the unconscious). The psychologist Stanislov Grof has discovered a deep propensity for 'rebirth' in the structure of the human psyche. Thus spirituality is transformation, and authentic transformation is a passage to the deep self. To understand the authentic spiritual guide demands that we first understand the authentic spiritual process. To understand the authentic guide we must understand the authentic spiritual journey.

Despite evident commonalities in the diverse manifestations of the master–disciple phenomenon, it is important to recognize important differences arising from basic cultural sensibilities. Westerners tend to be affronted, for example, by the worship of the guru in India. They tend to be suspicious of complete submission, extreme signs of reverence and adulation. Yet taken in the context of the eastern, especially hindu, belief in *jivan-mukti*—the belief that a living person can be totally delivered, can totally 'realize' divinity in this life—such adulation has some internal consistency. Culturally, the East seems to esteem the blind loyalty and trust of childlike dependence, whereas the West values an ideal of self-assertive independence.

Pre-eminent among the great guides of history are the founding personalities of the great religions—Buddha, Mohammed, Christ. The master is the center of a circle of disciples. The master at the center with a surrounding ring of disciples forms a *mandala.* The master is the source of spiritual power in the group. He is the fountain, center, source of inexhaustible spiritual wisdom.[2] The perfection, completeness, of the teaching is symbolized by the circle or *mandala* of disciples. Hinduism calls these superior teachers 'gurus for the world' (*jagad gurus*). So also, one discovers, many of the religious classics of mankind are the literary testimony of great spiritual guides. The insights of great spiritual teachers have frequently come down to us mediated by the personal experience of a disciple or group of disciples. The New Testament of the christian Bible and the Gospel of Sri Ramakrishna would be two examples of this. The real significance of the spiritual classics can never be touched by a merely notional or conceptual understanding. The *Spiritual Ladder* of John Climacus, *The Instructions for Practical Living* of Wang Yang-Ming, the *Yoga Aphorisms* of Patanjali require a degree of involvement on the level of experience in order to be truly appreciated. Their true reading demands the *disposition* of a disciple, in other words.

The more I have studied great spiritual guides in many traditions the more I am impressed with their characteristic humility and their consciousness of themselves as mere *means*—their consciousness that something greater is operating through them. The religious guide simply helps to create a 'place' for the numinous experience to happen. The guide nudges, cajoles, intimates, encourages, asks socratic questions. Yet more than all this, the guide embodies the teaching. One hasidic story tells of a disciple who said it was enough to see his master tie his shoelaces. The guide is more than a teacher. The guide *is* the teaching.

Besides considering the nature of a true or authentic master, we must equally consider the nature of authentic *discipleship*. Many have said that the lack of christian spiritual guides (a debated question) is perhaps due to the lack of genuine disciples. The hindu tradition says: 'When the disciple is ready, the master appears'.

The master–disciple relationship is truly mutual. The master does not do all the giving. In Jungian terminology, the master–disciple relationship is a manifestation of a two-part archetype that should not be *split;* it should not be divided between two persons (one superior, the other inferior). For 'master–disciple' are parts of the nature of *each* person in the relationship. The element of 'master' (teacher, guide) in the spiritual guide activates the potential and growing inner master in the disciple, just as the strong and eager 'disciple' in the student activates the inner 'disciple' in the guide. There is a type of chiasmal relationship as far as the psychological dynamics of the relationship is concerned. In an authentic master–disciple relationship there is no abuse of power.[3] There is an inner authority respected in the disciple. There is also a deep humility and disposability in the master. The true healer is the wounded healer. So also the one who cares for souls teaches the most effectively when he/she is deeply a disciple.

In several traditions I have found the occasional belief that in some sense the master is 'created', or made possible by the disciple. Swami Abhishiktananda (Dom Henri Le Saux), who became a *sannyasin* in India, explained the master–disciple relationship through the vocabulary and concepts of Indian Advaitic spirituality:

> The guru is most certainly not some master or professor, or preacher, or spiritual guide, or director of souls who has learned from books or from other mean what he, in his turn, is passing on to others. The guru is one who has himself first attained the Real and who knows from personal experience the way that leads there; he is capable of *initiating* the disciple and of making well up from within the heart of the disciple, the immediate ineffable experience

which is his own—the utterly transparent knowledge, so limpid and pure, that quite simply 'he is'.

Is it not in fact true that the mystery of the guru is the mystery of the depth of the heart? Is not the experience of being face to face with the guru, that of being face to face with 'oneself' in the most secret corner, with all pretence gone?

The meeting with the guru is the essential meeting, the decisive turning point in the life of a man. But it is a meeting that can only take place when one has gone beyond the level of sense and intellect. It happens in the beyond, in the fine point of the soul as the mystics say . . . in the meeting of the guru and disciple there is no longer even fusion, for we are on the plane of the original non-duality . . . . What the guru says springs from the very heart of the disciple. It is not a question of receiving from outside new thoughts which are transmitted through the senses. When the vibrations of the master's voice reach the disciple's ear and the master's look goes deep into his soul, then from the very depths of his being, from the newly discovered cave of his heart, thoughts well-up which reveal him to himself. What does it matter what words the guru uses? Their whole power lies in the hearer's inner response to them. Seeing or listening to the guru the disciple comes face to face with his true self in the depth of his being, an experience every man longs for, even if unconsciously.[4]

This long but beautiful passage from Abhishiktananda underlines the fact that authentic discipleship may be equally as important as authentic masterhood. There is no 'master' without a disciple.

The wisdom of all spiritual traditions underscores the essential point that one is not to seek a guru but to seek God or the spiritual path. One is to pursue the path—with or without a personal guide. The guide is merely a companion for the journey. A Sufi tale offers wise advice related to this matter:

Mussa Najib was asked why he charged a fee from those who came to his sessions: and why he often did not even address his audience. He said: 'I charge for this object lesson: people believe that knowledge must be freely given, and consequently mistake everything which is free for knowledge. I do not always lecture because among Sufis, "the master finds the pupil". The pupil has to be physically present, but he may be absent in every other sense. When I discern that a pupil is "present" then I "find" him, even it is silent to him. Seek and *you* will be found.'[5]

This story is similar to the hindu aphorism: 'When the disciple is ready the master appears'. The disciple is ready when he is sincerely eager to devote himself *completely* to the path. Then the disciple is 'ready' for a guide. Yet the human, personal guide should not be considered a necessity, a *sine qua non.* The guide is simply a *means.* Many traditions emphasize that it is the divine, numinous power that is the true guide. It may act through a human person or it may not. In the christian tradition the Holy Spirit is frequently referred to as the true guide of souls. In our own tradition of monastic spiritual fatherhood, the 'elder' is spoken of as *pneumataphore,* a bearer of the Spirit. The sum of the spiritual process for the Desert Fathers was summed up in the apophthegm 'Give your blood and receive the Holy Spirit', that is, 'hand over your life and be reborn in the Spirit'. The notion of the spiritual life as 'acquisition of the Holy Spirit' is a central theme among the russian *startzi* who are in some sense modern successors of the Desert Fathers. In his study of the notion of the 'cure of souls' in the christian tradition, John McNeill concludes that the russian *startzi* are perhaps the best models of the christian guide.[6]

Guidance can come in many forms. Perhaps the human, personal guide, especially in its profoundest form of master-disciple, should be considered an extraordinary grace, at least in the West where the role of the spiritual guide has not been as common or as institutionalized as in eastern traditions.

Certainly the human guide is not indispensible. One of the great hindu spiritual leaders of modern times, Aurobindo Ghose, for example, did not have a personal, living spiritual teacher. While there is a consistent concern in the christian tradition for the care and guidance of souls, the master–disciple type of phenomenon is *not* central to Christianity. There is no sense of persons-to-person transmission as in Zen but rather transmission generation to generation through the exoteric structure and teaching of the Church. There are, however, two sub-traditions, one might say, within the christian tradition, in which a type of master–disciple relationship similar to those of the East does appear. These two sub-traditions appear among the Desert Fathers. What is frequently called 'spiritual direction' in the christian tradition is not as deep an experience as the master–disciple relationship, at least, generally speaking.

In our own day the term guru is frequently used in a wide sense. It is applied to a spiritual guide in various traditions and not just to the classic guide of India. Guru has taken on a generic sense in our culture. In the widest sense, any factor which contributes to religious growth is in some sense guru. Life itself is in some sense spiritual guide. Scripture, nature, community, monastic environment and way of life, conscience, the psyche itself (especially in the Jungian sense) can be considered guru.[7] Though the term guru or spiritual guide can be validly used in this wider sense, it is usually understood in the special sense of a *type* of teacher in many traditions. And it is usually understood to mean the relationship of a living disciple with a living master. Some traditions speak of 'spirit' guides, guides who come in dreams. In other words, I understand by 'master–disciple' in this paper the specific notion of guidance in the *interpersonal* context.

Contemporary persons are becoming increasingly aware of the 'inner guide'. Deprived of adequate exterior forms of guidance, persons increasingly look *within* to the resource of their own deep selves for guidance. This notion of developing the inner guide seems to have particular meaning in the context of Jungian psychology. Ira Progoff, whose roots are in Jungian psychology, has, for example, provided a type of secular spiritual discipline in his Intensive Journal Method. Jung himself experienced the guidance of a strong inner personality in himself whom he named 'Philemon'. Mary Watkins, in her book *Waking Dreams,* explores the imaginal as a door to the deeper self and speaks of 'image as a guide'.[8] There is a similar approach in Roberto Assagioli's psychosynthesis. A Zen story tells of a monk, Zuigan, who cultivated this sense of the inner guide:

> Zuigan called out to himself every day 'Master'. Then he answered himself, 'Yes, sir'. And after that he added, 'Become sober'. Again he answered, 'Yes sir'. And after that he continued, 'Do not be deceived by others'. 'Yes, sir, yes, sir', he answered.[9]

The christian foundation for a notion of inner guide rests on its understanding of the person as *imago Dei.* According to St Augustine, God dwells in the deepest recesses of the soul, the *memoria,* where he teaches us as 'internal Master'. Classic spiritual teachers have always provided means for attuning oneself to this 'inner guide' through prayer, *mantrum,* silence, meditation, or whatever spiritual discipline may represent their tradition. In our own day a wealth of knowledge is appearing dealing with techniques for evoking and developing the 'inner guide.' The research into altered states of consciousness by such mind-researchers as Jean Houston, biofeedback, dream diaries, psychological journals, guided affective imagery, creative imagination, are all means of touching the deep resources of the self. In addition there is the blending of classic spiritualities among themselves—as in christian Yoga or christian Zen. The increasing confluence of classic spiritualities with some frontier movements of contemporary psychology, such as transpersonal psychology, is perhaps a sign of an emerging spirituality for the 'new age', and thus one might even hypothesize about the emergence of a new style of guide.

The resurgence of the guide phenomenon in our day brings an urgency to the need to develop a sensitivity for the *authentic* master–disciple relationship. Criteria of assessment are lacking. Though it may not be possible to devise a list of criteria that would have litmus-paper accuracy for distinguishing the true guide from the spiritual charlatan, one can gain great sensitivity for authentic elements by acquainting oneself with the classic stories of the great masters in several religious traditions.

Certainly one of the most important elements of the master–disciple relationship is the element of transmission. There is a growing recognition of the importance of tradition as a *context* for spirituality by scholars such as Huston Smith and Jacob Needleman.[10] Thomas Merton, in a talk given in Calcutta shortly before his death, stated that in some sense the direct transmission of the inner heart of monastic life from master to disciple is essential to monasticism. It is important then to focus on the role of guide as transmitter. In the face to face interaction of master and disciple there is usually a strong sense of 'handing on' (*paradosis*), a direct and charismatic transmission. Thus in many traditions there stretches for generations a type of spiritual genealogy which clearly traces the links in the line of transmission. Personal authentication of the transmission becomes an important aspect of the master's function. Thus, at least in the first generations of Ch'an (Zen) Buddhism in China, the begging bowl of Hui-Neng was passed on from master to disciple as a symbol of the transmission of the authentic teaching. There is also the frequently found symbol of the passing on of the master's cloak or mantle, as in the biblical story of Elijah and Elisha. Yet, in one sense, *nothing* is transmitted. This has been frequently insisted on by Ram Dass, for example. The transmission is not so much a passing-on of ideas, concepts, or teachings, as it is the evocation of a deep and abiding experience in the disciple. What is transmitted is not so much a way of life as life itself.

Occasionally, the passing of spiritual power from master to disciple—or perhaps it would be better stated, through master to disciple—is sometimes even visible to or experienced physically by the disciple. There is, for example, the noted story of the Russian *staretz,* Seraphim of Sarov, who allowed his disciple, Motovilov, a felt experience of the Holy Spirit. Certain shivite gurus in India, such as the currently popular Swami Muktananda, belong to a tantrically influenced tradition in which the power of the guru passes visibly to the disciple or is felt physically. This transmission of power is called *shaktipat.*[11]

In many traditions the master's ability to assess authentic spiritual experience is highly intuitive. Thus, for example, a zen master frequently perceives Enlightenment in a disciple simply by his non-verbal behavior. In addition, the master's experience, his whole manner of life, acts as a type of touch-stone or tuning-fork to which the disciple 'attunes' himself. This is why the 'formation' of the disciple frequently occurs simply by living with the master. Another aspect of the guide's discernment is the necessity of prescribing various disciplines and means to fit the uniqueness and diversity of personalities. The classic masters—zen, hasidic, desert—were all experts in understanding human nature and thus were master pedagogues.

The master–disciple relationship, is from a human point of view primarily and eminently a *caring* relationship. The care of a spiritual master is one of the greatest forms of human benevolence. A young English writer who travelled throughout India investigating the mysterious attraction of the guru personalities concluded simply that the world needs great lovers, and this is something a true guru is in a deep and genuine way.[12] Martin Buber said of the hasidic masters that their teaching methods are the same as God's—complete love and acceptance but also firmness. No one is more accepting, no one is more demanding, than a genuine spiritual master. The great spiritual guides are the great lovers, it is true, but very often perversion comes close to the truth and misuses it. Certain 'gurus' or self-proclaimed spiritual masters seem, for example, to play upon people's need for affection. Followers are held in a type of emotional bondage. The emotional and affective vacuum of mass society presents a situation ripe for the spiritual charlatan. Young people frequently seek a type of surrogate parent. It is important then to understand the authentic emotional bond in the interpersonal relationship of master and disciple, and also to recognize its perversions.

Friendship is perhaps the best model of the affective element of the master–disciple bond. In my own discussions with zen practitioners about their relationship with their roshi I have found that even in the apparently austere and formal inter-action of roshi and student there is a deep affective bond. The love of a genuine master for his disciple is a love that frees, creates, and enables another. It does not bind another in emo-tional dependency. The master and disciple's affective energy is really focused on the divine, the numinous, the Absolute—the goal of the spiritual process, so there is a freeing factor at the heart of the relationship. Furthermore, since the master is a channel of God's love, there is a particular quality of depth, beauty, and tenderness manifest in the affective quality per-vading the lives of genuine masters. The human emotional bond acts as a kind of sacrament of divine love. There must be a deep joy in the master when he/she sees the spark of life grow in a new generation. 'And now I call you friends, for I have given you everything I received from *my* father.'

The love of the master for the disciple and his/her concern for the spiritual welfare of the disciple is creative. This quality in the master evokes and engenders the true personality of the disciple. A contemporary jungian psychologist, James Hillman, speaks of psychology as 'soul-making', the evocation of the deep self. Hillman believes that it is eros (caring) that evokes psyche (soul). Eros is far more than brutal and blind passion. It is caring—the type of generativity that Erikson sees in the mature personality. Hillman proposes a new view of the task of psychology. Hillman believes that the major psychoanaly-tic schools are inspired by a basic myth. So, for example, Freud's psychology is based on the Oedipus myth, Jung's psychology is based on the hero myth. Hillman sees his approach based on the classic myth of Eros and Psyche and sees psychotherapy as a process of educating eros through folly and suffering. The psychotherapeutic process is a matter of being cared for enough to learn truly to care for one's self. Thus the analyst in jungian terms is a projection of the Self. The spiritual master is a projection of the Self of the disciple. All the components of the psyche in jungian terms have a guiding aspect—shadow, the contrasexual (*anima* and *animus*), and the Self. The process of psychic development to wholeness is a journey, and the deep aspects of our self speak as guides in that journey. It is not surprising that frequently in dreams or myths the 'self' will be represented in the figure of a Wise Old Man or Wise Old Woman—the *senex* or elder. The psychotherapist and the religious guide as 'soul-maker' is a kind of psychopomp to the deeper Self. And the quality of the analyst or guide that affects this journey is the quality of care. The great spiritual masters are the great soul-makers precisely in the sense meant by Hillman.[13]

SPIRITUALITY AS INITIATION

Genuine spirituality is a type of initiation. Therefore the initiation archetype can provide valuable insights into the authentic function of the spiritual guide. Though the initiation process itself has come under considerable scrutiny by scholars, the role of the initiator in the process has been somewhat neglected.

Initiation arises from humankind's search for transformation. Everywhere humankind has felt the inadequacy of the human situation. Faced with suffering, death, and a sense of inner poverty, humankind has sought transformation under various forms—salvation, knowledge, liberation. Traditionally, in order to attain a deeper or renewed level of existence or consciousness, cultures and groups have created rites of transition (rites of passage) or new beginnings (*in-itio*) to assist in the process of transformation.

Initiation rituals are a pervasive phenomenon in archaic societies. Besides *rites* of initiation, classical societies also expressed the initiation theme in both mythopoesis (the journey theme and the myth of the hero) and in the higher spiritualities. Mircea Eliade, the great historian of religion, believes that contemporary society is lacking in initiatory forms but that the *instinct* for initiation strongly survives in the human unconscious. Thus initiatory themes can be found in contemporary literature and film. The initiation archetype is therefore, deeply tied to human psychic experience.[14]

Eliade defines initiation as 'a body of rites and oral teachings whose purpose is to produce a decisive *alteration* in the religious and social status of the person to be initiated'.[15] When attained on an intense, deep, and persisting level, this transformation experience is so subjectively powerful that it is felt to be a total rebirth of the personality. Thus in Hinduism those initiated were called the 'twice-born' (*dva-ja*). For the same reason, a new name is conferred in the ceremony of monastic profession. It is the prerogative of the guru to name his disciple. Much of the symbolism that is part of the texture of initiation rituals conveys the theme of death-rebirth, the most drastic of all transformations. Initiation is a *passage* from the old self to the new self.

Mircea Eliade's study of initiation focused on the cultural interpretations of initiation rituals. He found they centered on the theme of death-rebirth. He saw also that the mythopoetic theme of the hero's quest and the journey theme in great myth and literature also deals with a symbolic rite of passage. Furthermore, Eliade realized in his study of yoga that the higher spiritual disciplines of man are a type of *inner* initiation. Eliade asserts, therefore, that there are three basic forms of initiation: tribal puberty rites, secret societies, and mystical religions. Thus initiation rites, the hero myth (journey theme), and the spiritual process are in some sense homologous realities. It is not surprising then that the nature of initiation can throw considerable light on the function of the spiritual guide, for the guide is an *initiator,* an assistant (midwife) of the death-rebirth process.[16]

The classic study of the basis initiation pattern is Arnold Van Gennep's *Rites of Passage* (1909). Van Gennep main-

tained that the initiatory pattern has three phases: withdrawal, liminality, and return. Some describe the same process as separation, marginality, and reincorporation.[17] I suggest that spirituality may follow the same pattern, not in a
simple linear fashion, but in a spiral fashion—a cycle of withdrawal, liminality, and return that is repetitive yet also progressive.[18] It may be the inner moments of marginality,
liminality, are the most creative spiritual moments in our
spiritual life.

Whereas Van Gennep clarified the *structure* of primitive
initiation rituals, Eliade clarified their meaning. Eliade saw
that initiation was an archetypal form of the human search
for transformation. A student of Eliade's, George Weckman,
has made a particularly valuable clarification in the typology
of initiation.[19] In his *Rites and Symbols of Initiation* Eliade
makes a distinction between two types of initiation. The first
type solidifies a person's sense of belonging to the human
community (this is especially true of puberty rites). The
second type gives one a trans-cultural identity, an identity
rooted in something deeper than 'identification' and conformity with mere human symbols and norms. One could say
that the first type is concerned with *formation,* the second
type with *trans-formation.* As Weckman puts it, there are
initiations which usher a person *into* the human realm, and
initiations which take a person *beyond* the human. Both
types of initiation are necessary since the human person has a
dialectical relationship to culture itself. The human person
must stand *within* culture while at the same time being able
to stand *apart* from it. Religion has too frequently remained
only on the first level—the level of behavior, identification,
conformity. Laurence Kohlberg's theory of stages of moral
development and James Fowler's theory of stages of faith
development both assert that at the highest stages of development the most mature religious personality is characterized
by a definite trans-cultural quality.

One of the finest statements of this goal of trans-cultural
identity is Thomas Merton's 'Final Integration: Towards a

350

Monastic Therapy'. Merton borrowed the term 'final integration' from a persian psychiatrist, Dr Reza Arasteh. Arasteh's theory of 'final integration' is itself based on his study of the great persian spiritual guide, Rumi. Merton describes the state of final integration thus:

> Final integration is a state of trans-cultural maturity far beyond mere social adjustment, which always implies partiality and compromise. The man who is 'fully born' has an entirely 'inner experience of life'. He apprehends his life fully and wholly from an inner ground that is at once more universal than the empirical ego and yet entirely his own. He is in a certain sense 'cosmic' and 'universal man'. He has attained a deeper, fuller identity than that of his limited ego-self which is only a fragment of his being. He is in a certain sense identified with everybody; or in the familiar language of the New Testament (which Arasteh evidently has not studied) he is 'all things to all men'. He is able to experience their joys and sufferings as his own, without however becoming dominated by them. He has attained to a deep inner freedom—the Freedom of the Spirit we read of in the New Testament. He is guided not just by will and reason, but by 'spontaneous behaviour subject to dynamic insight'.[20]

Spirituality, seen as inner initiation, leads to a progressively deeper attainment of such a trans-cultural identity. The classic spiritual masters of all traditions undeniably display the qualities mentioned by Merton in the preceding quotation.

The difference between these two distinctive levels of religious realization (formation and transformation) was grasped by Walter Hilton in his *Ladder of Spiritual Perfection.* Hilton says that many Christians live only on the level of 'reformation of faith' (change of behavior), but few live on the level of 'reformation of feeling'. It is a question of how deep transformation goes. Hilton sensed that it included even what we today would term the unconscious—the root of our feeling life. The discovery of 'healing of memories', and so forth, in our own day seems to have the same intuition.

Transformation includes far more than our conscious ego.

Transformation is not attained without a previous *formation*. It seems to me that the spiritual guide works on both levels—formation and transformation. Formation can perhaps easily be attained in a group, an environment, a way of life, through study and assimilation of a tradition. This may be one reason why the monastic tradition has never *demanded* a spiritual 'director' as did some of the post-reformation orders. Transformation, however, in a sense cracks the shell acquired in formation and leads to a re-appropriation of values and beliefs on a deeper level. Transcending formation involves the confusion, pain, and disorientation of inner marginality. But there is a 'homecoming', a return, a reincorporation. Transformation demands a type of 'death' (a leaving behind, a withdrawal) and entrance into an inner liminal phase involving uncertainty and loneliness. For the transition from formation to transformation, the human personal guide seems extremely important and effective, but not indispensible.

From a merely sociological point of view, formation is in one sense a type of 'tribal' initiation and aims at a type of reinforcement of social identity. Culture itself is a guide. It is part of our very humanity. Culture, language, symbols, values, give us our fundamental orientation to the world. Yet this can be shallow, hollow, and even imprisoning. Since Eliade's study of initiation was based largely on anthropological studies of the initiatory rites of primitive tribes, he concluded that the role of the *guide* in initiation is unimportant. Elaide thought it was the group or cultural context that was the most powerful agent of initiation. He was focusing on initiation in the context of 'formation'. His claim about the role of the guide must be reconsidered in the context of 'transformation', that is, when it is a question of the higher forms of initiation. Shamanic initiation may be an archetype of this higher form of initiation. The shaman is definitely an 'outsider', but he is a person of power. And the shaman is initiated by an elder shaman rather than in a group ritual. The shaman is one capable of contacting and exploring realms of spirit not attained by ordinary person.[21]

The sacred person, especially one who functions as a guide, should be an accomplished traveller of the depths and heights potentially accessible to the human spirit. This shamanistic element of the spiritual guide appears in various traditions. Thus the holy man (*iman*) of Shi'ite Islam is described as the 'mystic pole' of the world. A similar image is found in descriptions of the hasidic *zaddik.* The mystic pole is a variation of the symbol of the *axis mundi,* the cosmic tree, which indicates the connection of the realms of being. The *axis mundi* links the horizontal, this-worldly, plane with the underworld of spirits and the transcendent world of the gods. In more sophisticated religious traditions it is common to find the notion of spiritual ascent and the symbol of the ladder. Perhaps something basic to religion is intimated here. Religion (*religare*—to bind) is an experience of the sacred that *connects,* integrates, all experience. Religion is fundamentally that experience which gives coherence to all reality. Nietzsche voiced an archtypal insight when he wrote that 'a tree reaching to heaven must have its roots in the earth'. Holiness—the transforming experience of the sacred—has unfortunately too often been understood to be the building of a type of ascetical superstructure over human existence rather than an experience of wholeness. In jungian terms this danger is referred to as 'inflation'. Inflated persons are hollow, unappealing; the genuinely holy person is 'whole'—a representative of what human nature can be. There is a certain attractive completeness of human nature that characterizes genuinely holy persons of any tradition—especially perhaps the great religious guides. Their experience has gained them a deep knowledge and empathy for the itinerary of the human spirit.

The nature and pattern of initiation provide an important basis of discerning the function of authentic spiritual guidance. First, false spiritual guides and 'guru' cult-figures lead persons to a type of imprisonment in 'formation'—social cohesion in a sub-cultural cacoon, subjection to group pressures, identification with cultural symbols. For many young

Americans, growing up with a type of social anomie, weak family ties and experience, the security of a religious cult becomes a type of addiction. An authentic guide, however, leads one beyond 'identification' to the realization of a trans-cultural identity deeply characterized by freedom. Secondly, part of the valid initiation experience is 'reincorporation'—a deeper assimilation of previously held beliefs and values—and, also, a return to the larger social context. Several of the most authentic eastern spiritual guides popular in America insist that a person return to the religious tradition of his upbringing. The element of return or reincorporation is probably nowhere better portrayed than in the famous zen ox-herding pictures. In the tenth and last picture in the series, the Enlightened person is shown 'entering the market place with helping hands', the commentary adds: ' . . . he strolls into the market; leaning on his staff, he returns *home.* He leads innkeepers and fishmongers in the Way of the Buddha.' It is this element of 'return' that is lacking in the blissed-out disciples of some cults.

In studying the semi-institutionalized traditions of 'master–disciple' over several years, I have been struck with the fact that the great spiritual guides are frequently marginal to a larger tradition. The early christian desert fathers, the sufi sheiks, the hasidic *zaddikim,* all represent a type of 'revitalization' movement within a larger religious tradition. Frequently tension arose between the adherents of these movements gathered around a master and the persons representing mainline, institutionalized orthodoxy. The spiritual masters emphasized direct experience rather than esoteric teaching and conformity.

If a culture or tradition has real vitality, then authentic formation can lead to transformation. Claudio Naranjo, the chilean psychologist, remarks that a true, living, and viable culture need not concern itself with 'transmission'—it transmits itself naturally from person to person, generation to generation. A self-conscious concern with 'formation' may be symptomatic of degeneration and sclerosis in a tradition.

Spiritual masters cannot be turned out on academic assembly lines. The search of so many young people in our time for spiritual masters is perhaps indicative of the failure of our culture, particularly the institutions of religion and education. The quest for spiritual guides in our time arises partly from our cultural crisis. Without strong cultural cohesion and numinous cultural ideals, a situation of anxiety, uncertainty, and restless search prevails. Some turn to the older certainties of neofundamentalism while others turn to forms of neo-gnosticism. It is a time ripe for spiritual fascism, as well as a genuine inner search. So it is all the more important to have a sensitivity to authentic spiritual guides.

Culture, tradition, symbols, rituals are powerful means of formation. They themselves are 'guide'. But they are means; they must be transcended. When a culture or tradition does bear vital religious meaning, then indeed a spiritual guide may in fact simply act as a 're-inforcer' of traditional values. One wonders whether the traditional brahmanic guru is not of this type. His function is primarily to pass-on vedic knowledge. Some feel that the genuine guru in present day India is the guru who leads one into sannyasinhood. The sannyasin is one who renounces society, even external religious symbols. In the ceremony of sannyasinhood, the sannyasin inhales and thus 'internalizes' the sacred fire. The sannyasin becomes a transcultural person.[22]

Frequently the great guides use the gentle iconoclasm of humor as a kind of midwife in itself to lead a person beyond 'formation' to transformation. Many of the great guides were outsiders, marginal to the religious establishment. The zen masters are not so much marginal men at the side of a tradition as marginal men at the heart of a tradition. Zen somehow marvelously incorporated a revitalizing tricksterism in its very substance. The iconoclasm, especially the mocking humor, of the classic Zen masters is a powerful antidote to a mere convention-bound religious formalism.[23] They were experts at a type of healthy iconoclasm that frees one from the canonization of merely cultural forms and concepts.

In sum, authentic spirituality is fundamentally transformation—a deep death/rebirth passage. Initiation is the basic archetype of this passage. The guide is initiator, facilitator of the process, midwife of spiritual rebirth. It is impossible to speak of an authentic spiritual guide without speaking of the authentic nature of the spiritual process itself. Initiation, it seems to me, therefore, provides a very important cross-cultural foundation for criteria of authentic guidance.

A WORD ABOUT MONASTIC SPIRITUAL FATHERHOOD

The monastic spiritual father/mother is more than a midwife; the spiritual guide in this tradition actually *engenders.* I believe this is a valid qualification—though it may be true of other traditions as well. The spiritual 'father' engenders *in the Spirit,* so there is an action of God here that is partly hidden in mystery. From a human point of view though, it seems to me that the spiritual 'father' engenders and midwifes precisely through his fatherly/motherly quality, yet to the more contemporary sensibility 'friendship' may be a more acceptable image of guide than is the image of parent. The metaphor of friend was used by Christ to convey his relation to his disciples: 'And now I call you friends, for I have given you everything I received from my Father'.[24]

The early Desert Fathers took deeply to heart Christ's exhortation 'be perfect as your heavenly Father is perfect'. G. Kittel in his article on 'abba' in the *Theologische Wörterbuch* maintains that the christian tradition gave a new valuation to the notion of fatherhood. Joachim Jeremias calls the notion of God's 'fatherhood' the central message of the New Testament. The context of the phrase 'be ye perfect' reveals something of the New Testament notion of those qualities that constitute God's perfection:

> But I say to you: love your enemies and pray for those
> who persecute you; in this way you will be sons of your
> Father in heaven, for he causes his sun to rise on bad men
> as well as good, and his rain to fall on honest and dishonest
> men alike . . . . You must therefore be perfect just as your

heavenly Father is perfect.[25]
The Desert Fathers strove for these fatherly qualities—
non-judgment, forgiveness, tender mercy. In reading the
Apophthegmata Patrum, I am struck that one of the most
insistent counsels of the desert fathers is non-judgment.

There is a saying in the western esoteric tradition that
'he [she]who does the work becomes his own father'. The
spiritual father, it seems to me, facilitates 'the work of God'
in the disciple.[26] In the letters of Barsanuphius and John one
finds frequently the word *biazathei*—being worked *upon.*

Early monastic guidance is a real communication of life—
life in the Spirit. Dom Odo Casel has said: 'The perfect monk
is essentially an "abba", that is, a pneumataphore, a bearer of
the divine Pneuma or living breath, who is first of all filled
with this form and can in turn communicate it, in such a way
that he becomes a spiritual father who, like St Paul, bears
witness in Jesus Christ.' The spiritual father 'in-spires' in its
deepest sense. St Nil calls the transmission of the Spirit from
master to disciple the 'art of arts'.

'Abba Joseph said to Abba Lot, "You cannot be a monk
unless you become like a consuming fire".'

357

Abba, *The Spiritual Guide*

NOTES

1. Si 6:36.
2. See Giuseppe Tucci, *The Theory and Practice of the Mandala* (New York, 1969). David Miller, 'The Guru as the Center of Sacredness,' unpublished paper delivered at the American Academy of Religion Meeting, 1976. Arthur Green, 'The Zaddiq as Axis Mundi,' *Journal of the American Academy of Religion,* 45 (September 1977) 327-49.
3. See Adolph Guggenbuhl-Craig, *Power in the Helping Professions* (New York, 1971).
4. Swami Abhishiktananda (Dom Henri Le Saux), *Guru and Disciple* (London, 1974) 28-30.
5. Idries Shah, *Reflections: Fables in the Sufi Tradition* (Baltimore, 1972) 146.
6. John McNeill, *A History of the Cure of Souls* (New York, 1951) 307-330, and throughout.
7. See C. G. Jung, *Collected Works* (Princeton, New Jersey) 20 vols.
8. Mary Watkins, *Waking Dreams* (New York, 1976). See also Rix Weaver, *The Old Wise Woman: A Study of Active Imagination* (New York, 1973).
9. Gyomang M. Kubose, *Zen Koans* (Chicago, 1973) 31.
10. See Jacob Needleman and Dennis Lewis (edd.), *Sacred Tradition and Present Need* (New York, 1975). See also, 'The Meaning of Tradition: A Conversation with Huston Smith,' *Parabola: Myth and the Quest for Meaning,* 1 (Winter, 1976) 80-91.
11. See Swami Muktananda, *Guru: Chitshaktivilas—The Play of Consciousness* (New York, 1971) pp. xiv, 13, and throughout. The phenomena of heat and light in such transmission seem to be related to *kundalini;* see Lee Sannella, *Kundalini: Psychosis or Transcendence?* (San Francisco, 1976)
12. Peter Brent, *Godmen of India* (New York, 1972).
13. See James Hillman, *Re-Visioning Psychology* (New York, 1975); also, idem., *The Myth of Analysis: Three Essays in Archetypal*

358

Psychology (New York, 1978).

14. See Eleanor Bertine, 'The Psychological Meaning of Initiation,' chapter 4 in *Jung's Contribution to Our Time: The Collected Papers of Eleanor Bertine* (New York, 1967). Bertine comments: 'The meaning of initiation lies close to the core of the disciplines of both religion and psychology . . . . Anything so nearly universal and felt to be so important must express a deep truth about the nature of man.' See also Joseph L. Henderson, *Thresholds of Initiation* (Middletown, Connecticut, 1967). Henderson, a practicing jungian analyst, considers the archetype of initiation among primitive people and relates it to his findings in his work with his patients. Mircea Eliade belives the instinct for 'initiation' survives in the unconscious of contemporary persons. See also Claus Bleeker (ed.), *Initiation: Study–Conference of the International Association for the History of Religions held at Strasbourg, September 17-22, 1964.*

15. Mircea Eliade, *Rites and Symbols of Initiation: The Mysteries of Birth and Rebirth* (New York, 1958) p. x.

16. Eliade, in *Rites and Symbols of Initiation,* says that the initiator is unimportant. This may be true for tribal puberty rites, etc., but for higher, spiritual initiation the guide–initiator is very important, if not in the case of some traditions a *sine qua non.*

17. See Joseph Campbell, *The Hero With a Thousand Faces* (Princeton, New Jersey, 1968).

18. See Jill Purce, *The Mystic Spiral: Journey of the Soul* (New York, 1974).

19. See George Weckman, 'Understanding Initiation,' *History of Religions,* 10 (August 1970) 62-79, and throughout.

20. Thomas Merton, 'Final Integration: Toward a Monastic Therapy', in *Contemplation in a World of Action* (New York, 1971) 211.

21. Concerning shamanism, see Stephen Larsen, *The Shaman's Doorway: Opening the Mythic Imagination to Contemporary Consciousness* (New York, 1976). Also Mircea Eliade, *Shamanism: Archaic Techniques of Ecstasy* (Princeton, New Jersey, 1964).

22. Swami Abhishaktananda (Dom Henri Le Saux), *The Further Shore* (Delhi, 1975).

23. See Conrad Hyers, *Zen and the Cosmic Spirit* (Philadelphia, 1974).

24. Jn 15:15.

25. Mt 6:45-48.

26. See Irenee Hausherr, SJ, 'Opus Dei', in *Études de Spiritualité Orientale* (Rome, 1969) 121-45.

MONASTIC PARENTHOOD
TWO DISCOVERIES AND SOME RELATED QUESTIONS

David F. K. Steindl-Rast, OSB
The Benedictine Grange

A LLOW ME TO START with a warning: this is strictly a working paper. It will contain more questions than answers. And those questions are intended to stimulate even further questioning. Of course, one might be reminded of the saying that one fool is able to ask more questions than a hundred sages can answer. But, fortunately, it is also said: 'A good question is half the answer'. We may at least hope that there will be a few good ones among the many we are raising. Let me simply set down my two discoveries, then, each followed by a string of questions they occasioned in my mind.

I. *My first discovery* concerns a practice among tibetan buddhist monks. It was related to me in 1973 by the Venerable Lama Samdhong Tulku, Rimpoche, Head of the Institute for Higher Tibetan Studies at the Sanskrit University, Benares. For me personally, the practice described below was certainly a discovery. But it might deserve that designation also in a wider sense, for, up to now, no one seems to have called attention to it in the West.

In some tibetan monasteries a novice receives his training from a team of two monks, rather than from one. These two act out opposite roles and so fulfill complementary functions in the novice's life. One is responsible for confronting the novice with all the stringent demands of monastic life—the *dura et aspera* of St Benedict. His role is that of the father who insists on high standards of achievement. He keeps the novice on his toes. The other one, however, acts the part of the mother whose caring and support does not depend on merit or accomplishment. He always takes the part of the novice, even helps him cut corners here and there, and is available, like St Benedict's *sympaectae,* as someone on whose shoulder the blunderer may cry. This seems all the more important since the little novices there may be mere children.

The full educational impact of this practice emerges only when we consider the following aspects of it: the monk who plays the father role for one novice is put in charge of another one for whom he has to play the role of the mother. By being put in charge of newcomers in this way the elder monks learn to cultivate and balance within themselves *animus* and *anima,* in C. G. Jung's sense. Thus, it may well be that the method in question does as much or more for the psychological balance and spiritual growth of the monks who guide as it does for the ones who are being guided.

In an effort to scan the vistas opened up by Samdhong Tulku's account, one ought to raise a series of questions. I will try to raise them simply, the way an explorer might hoist flags to indicate areas in which the lay of the land needs to be further explored.

1. What are the implicit connotations of the titles 'Father' and 'Mother' in biblical traditions?
2. What does 'spiritual' mean when applied to Fatherhood and Motherhood?
3. Can Fathers be spiritual without being Mothers?
4. Is the model of the spiritual Father in christian traditions God the Father (Mt 23:9), or is it Jesus Christ (Heb 2:13)?
5. Who is to serve as comparable model for the spiritual Mother (Rev 12:2; Gal 4:19; Mt 23:37; Jn 19:27)?
6. Can we speak of God's Fatherhood without equal emphasis on God's Motherhood, even in the biblical tradition?
7. Can Mothers be spiritual without being Fathers?
8. What qualifies a person for spiritual Fatherhood or Motherhood?
9. What are the hidden connotations of the titles 'Father'

361

and 'Mother' in western society?

10. What is the relevance of Gal 3:28 ('In Christ there is no male or female') to monastic parenthood?

11. Are monastics today aware of the extent to which arbitrary social conventions of past ages have formed current monastic notions of spiritual parenthood?

12. What are the assets and liabilities of spiritual parenthood as an institution in our age of tottering male dominance?

13. How can spiritual Mothers go beyong being merely spiritual Fathers with incomplete authority?

14. Are monastics, as representatives of the prophetic element in the Church, willing and ready to bear witness for a spiritual parenthood liberated from conventional distortions?

15. If parenthood is defined with reference to the offspring, what are some of the characteristics which monastic candidates seek today in spiritual Fathers and Mothers?

16. What structures, practices, or methods in our monasteries serve to discover and to train potential spiritual Fathers and Mothers?

As an undercurrent of this whole list, we sense the questionable relationship between a religious and a secular notion of parenthood. Only by distinguishing between those two shall we be able to free ourselves from prejudice. But only by realistically relating one to the other shall we be able to serve both monasticism and society in their joint crisis, which is on many levels a crisis of parenthood.

II. *My second discovery* was at first blurred and indistinct. Only gradually did it come to a sharper focus. It emerged from a variety of encounters with young people, whom, off hand, one might have expected to be candidates for monastic life as we know it. Instead, they are members of what one might broadly designate as counter-culture communities in different parts of this country. Meeting them, one gets the impression of having discovered those missing candidates whom, for some reason or other, our monasteries no longer attract. But the real discovery comes when we realize that these monastic children for whom our spiritual mothers and fathers are waiting in vain are meanwhile following on their own the path of what we might call primordial monasticism.

To illustrate this discovery, it might be helpful to give a brief description of some communities which attract the kind of people who in former times might have become novices in cistercian monasteries. I shall limit myself to a few representative examples with which I am personally well acquainted.

The Lama Foundation, San Cristobal, New Mexico: A commune founded in the early 1960s by men and women open to a variety of spiritual traditions. High in the mountains overlooking the Rio Grande valley, they cleared the land and created an architecture of remarkable beauty, combining adobe brick from their own soil with sophisticated geodesic domes, designed by their own engineers and constructed from their own timber. Living conditions are quite austere. Since the beginning, hundreds of people have come and gone, some spending many years. At present there are some thirty residents, none of them of the founding generation. Government is democratically shared. During the summer months invited gurus from different traditions, including Christians, lead training periods, attended also by outsiders in large numbers. The year-round daily schedule includes manual labor and periods of meditation. In 1976, Sufi influence predominated, but I found Lama truly catholic, in the sense of all-embracing spirituality.

The Abode of the Message, New Lebanon, New York: Only a few years ago, a group of lay people inspired by the teachings of Pir Vilayat Inayat Khan, Head of the Sufi order in the West, acquired an abandoned Shaker village, proceeded to restore the buildings, to rehabilitate the farm, and to develop various crafts to support themselves. Now there are about one hundred residents, ranging from temporary hermits to semi-independent families and to single persons living a strictly cenobitic life. They grow a good part of their own food, have their own doctor and health care, operate a bakery, and run

363

the Winged Heart V.W. Repair Shop in the nearby town. The group is self-governing, but important decisions are submitted to Pir Vilayat Khan. He spends much time on world-wide lecture tours. In order to attract him for longer periods of time, the community has built a house for him and his family. The daily discipline of worship follows a sufi pattern, but incorporates elements of all major traditions. Jewish and christian feasts are solemnized. Close bonds of friendship exist between this community and the Benedictine monks of Weston Priory, Vermont.

The Integral Yoga Institute: many locations throughout the United States, especially Yogaville East, Pomfret Center, Connecticut; and Yogaville West, Santa Barbara, California. Invited to the United States in 1965 by devotees who had met him in India, and pressured to stay here ever since, Swami Satchidananda has become a spiritual father figure for thousands of yoga students, with training centers in many major cities. Communities at those centers differ in size: a handful of residents or ten times that many. After prolonged training, scores of men and women have received formal monastic ordination and form a highly disciplined order in strict obedience to the Swami, who is not tied down to any particular residence. All centers offer yoga instruction to outside students (sometimes in prisons) and provide a typical monastic environment for residents with various degrees of commitment. In addition, larger centers offer such services as a fully equipped clinic, a health food store or restaurant, a kindergarten, a printing press, and a variety of craft shops. All activities are pervaded by a truly contemplative spirit. Although Catholic members cannot easily find time and opportunity to go to church, Swami Satchidananda emphasizes that yoga practice is supportive of any religious path. I have seen as many images of Christ and of the Blessed Virgin on the walls of these yoga institutes as in any convent. Often members feel a close affinity to Catholic contemplatives.

The Children of Carmel, Love Center, Denver, Colorado: In the late sixties, a group of young people in the Denver area gathered around a woman with an outstanding leadership charism, a Third Order Carmelite, married, the mother of small children. The core group organized according to the pattern of a religious community. Both men and women wore habits. The wider community of over one hundred members included others besides Catholics. Understandably, but regrettably, they met with bewilderment and suspicion, both at the parish church they attended and at the Chancery office, although they could have been recognized by their fruits: outstanding and lasting success in rehabilitating alcoholics, drug addicts, ex-convicts, unwed mothers, and other outcasts of society. The prison ministry they did, using a choir and two bands, was highly appreciated by State authorities. But they lost their money when they bought a farm which zoning laws did not permit them to use as a residence for a large group. Apartment living proved too expensive. Efforts to make some empty Church property available, to obtain financial aid, or to get at least a chaplain assigned to so large a group of dedicated young people, all failed. The community bore up under the identity crisis caused by their relationship to the Church, but eventually succumbed to economic pressure and recently disbanded.

San Francisco Zen Center, California: In the mid-sixties, young Americans began to attach themselves to Shunryu Suzuki Roshi, a zen monk in charge of a neighborhood temple in a japanese section of San Francisco. Inevitable tensions arose between the Japanese congregation and the young Americans invading their temple in ever increasing numbers. Eventually, the zen students established their own training center and took the Roshi with them. From the outset the standard of discipline was higher than in many zen monasteries in Japan. Suzuki Roshi assured continuity of tradition by his almost unnoticeable power of guidance and laid the ground for effective cultural adaptation by encouraging his students' creative initiative. In 1974, shortly before his death, he made Richard Baker, a westerner, his successor. Baker Roshi, in turn, has ordained another generation of

fullfledged American zen monks and nuns. The Zen Center, on
Page and Laguna Streets in downtown San Francisco, has
become not only a model monastery with some seventy residents, but the starting point for an impressive urban renewal,
since many more Zen students live and work in the surrounding
area. Zen Center also operates a large ranch (organized like a
monastic grange) at Green Gulch, Marin County, and a mountain center for the intensive monastic training of some forty
students at Tassajara Hot Springs, in Los Padres National
Forest. (Governor Brown goes on retreat there.) Most striking
is the combination of intense monastic observances with a
sense for business and a keen and generous alertness to social
issues like urban renewal and environmental protection.

*Common characteristics of the communities mentioned
above.*
It might be helpful to underscore some characteristics of
the communities mentioned, especially those which have
greater significance in our context. Not all of these distinguishing marks will be equally pronounced in a given case.
But, by and large, these traits, forming a distinct pattern,
seem to be quite typical.

Future-oriented. The outlook of the communities we are
considering is dynamic rather than static, not much concerned
with preserving traditions from the past, but rather with the
realization of an ideal, which is often associated with the idea
of a New Age.

Task-oriented. The community serves a purpose. It is not
seen as an end in itself. Rather, it supports its members in the
personal task of spiritual practice.

Process-oriented. Since spiritual practice is a process, those
whose common task is that practice consider themselves as
fellow seekers, fellow strugglers. The criterion for belonging
to a community of this kind is striving, not accomplishment.

Open. Membership policy is characterized by openness
and flexibility. New members are only gradually admitted to
more intimate degrees of belonging, and not without proving
their sincerity and determination. (Some stories about trials

before admission equal those of the Desert Fathers.) Yet, what counts is faithfulness to one's personal path, not conformity to a predetermined pattern. All will respect this principle. Leaving (and possibly rejoining) the community is, therefore, usually not a great problem.

Non-discriminating. It goes without saying that racial discrimination is virtually unknown in New Age communities. But this non-discrimination is extended also to sexual differences. The communities in question are made up of men and women and tend to give equal status to persons of either sex.

Guru-guided. The role of the guru, or charismatic teacher, may vary, but it is normally an important one. Borderline cases are the first and the last of the communities listed above. In one case the community is nourished by a succession of gurus, one at a time. In the last case, we may be witnessing a transition in which charismatic leadership is being institutionalized. Eventually, the abbot may no longer be expected to be a guru.

Nature-reverent. (Admittedly an awkward word.) The precise adjective would be 'pious', but no one understands that word correctly any more. In Latin, *pietas* means exactly that religiously-tinged awareness of belonging to a family, even in the wider sense of being related to every being in the whole universe. The extent to which this cosmic family feeling shapes the lifestyle of New Age communities can hardly be overestimated. The loving reverence for nature which results may find its expression in non-violence, a vegetarian diet, organic gardening, measures of frugality opposed to consumerism, environmental protection, holistic health care, natural childbirth, care for the aged and the dying, and in many other, seemingly unrelated, areas, down to the choice of title for the Whole Earth Catalog. This cosmic piety may in the beginning be no more than a vague feeling for environmental harmony, but it tends ultimately towards a sense of ecological responsibility with no less than global implications.

Monastic. In our context, this is, of course, the crucial

characteristic, and some might hesitate to find it applicable. What is universally characteristic, however, of monasticism on a worldwide scale is the creation of a controlled environment designed to foster the spiritual transformation of a person. And this, indeed, is a definition applicable to the communities we are considering here—which brings us back to the discovery of primordial monasticism.

Primordial monasticism as latent in New Age communities. The reason I prefer to speak of primordial rather than primitive monasticism is that the word 'primitive' tends to suggest inferiority. We should avoid this connotation. The word 'primordial' is meant to point towards that realm from which the monastic quest takes its origin historically, psychologically, spiritually: the realm of the heart.

When we speak about centering, we speak in contemporary terms about finding that realm which tradition calls the heart. When young people speak about getting themselves together, they speak about the same reality. In fact, a key word for understanding the mystery of the human heart is the word 'together'. When we do get centered, when we find our heart, we reach the realm where we are at long last together with ourselves (and what a task that is for our fragmented existence). But the moment we get ourselves together in that sense, we discover that we are also together with all others. Every one of us knows from experience the paradox: my heart is not only the realm where I am most initimately one with myself, but also with all others—and with God. For in my heart of hearts God is closer to me than I am to myself, as St Augustine discovered long ago, and he was by no means the first one to make that discovery.

When young people want to express high praise, they will say of a person, 'He is really together' or 'She sure is together'. Together with what? With self, with all others, with God (or with ultimate Reality, if we don't want to use the term God). The adverb 'together' has thus become an adjective in recent English usage and characterizes a person who lives from the heart. But to become a person of that kind has been the goal of personal transformation in any monastic tradition, always and everywhere. Monasticism of the heart is the heart of monasticism. That is what primordial monasticism implies.

Members of the communities I have mentioned will not hesitate for one moment to admit that they joined those communities in order to get themselves together in that fullest, deepest sense, in which the opposite of togetherness is alienation—from self, from others, from God. But that is in the last analysis the reason also for joining a cistercian monastery, or any monastic community of any tradition. Here lies the basis for my contention that a genuine monastic core is latent in many of the intentional communities throughout this country and other parts of the world.

This is the reason also for the enthusiasm with which every one of the communities described above, different though they are, have responded to all I have been able to share with them about our own monastic path. And the more basic, central, primordial the matter, the greater their interest. It has made no difference whether they were Buddhist or Hindu or Muslim or Christian in their practice. The key concepts of benedictine monastic life, and even the heart of the christian message, when seen in monastic perspective, has aroused their wholehearted response.

But, given this latent enthusiasm, why do so few of these same young people, and—let us admit it—not always the most promising ones among them, find their way to our monasteries. Perhaps an answer would emerge if we carefully studied the characteristics of New Age communities and checked in what respects they differ from monasteries as we know them. Within the frame of this exploration, I can merely raise some questions which might facilitate this process of comparison. I shall do so, shortly. But first we have to meet a pertinent objection.

If it is true that many respond with enthusiasm to the benedictine expression of primordial monasticism and that possibly only our lifestyle turns them off, should one not expect that, in the midst of all these outlandish forms, one group somewhere would start living christian monasticism in a new style of their own? Yes, one would expect this to happen. For years I have waited for it. In the case of the Children of Carmel it almost came about. When it finally happened, I felt like the astronomer who sighted Pluto through a telescope years after the planet's position in the solar system had been predicted theoretically. Three young men, as typically counter-culture as can be imagined, discovered primordial monasticism, discovered the Rule of St Benedict, discovered the Church (in that sequence). When I came to know of it, the little Community of the Holy Trinity, at Santa Cruz, California, was already living a benedictine life quite as strict and quite as traditional as any other community that follows the Rule of St Benedict. They came to it all on their own. Now they recite the Divine Office seven times a day, but they also meditate together playing on their bongo drums; and I found both experiences truly uplifting. (Yes, they provided me with a small drum, too, so I could join them.) Theirs is a small beginning, to be sure, but it looks fairly solid and is certainly significant. Here again, we might pause to ask questions:

17. How many of the characteristics of New Age communities should apply to our monasteries in following traditional monastic spirituality, and how many do in practice apply?

18. Are there possibly points of contact between the idea of a New Age and the monastic idea of preparing the way for the Lord's coming?

19. On a scale from 1 to 10, how would you rate the degree of dynamic future-orientation in your own monastery?

20. Honestly now, which model is closer to the way we think of our monastic communities (leaving plenty of room for personal humility), 'the Assembly of the Elect' or 'Alcoholics Anonymous' (where the admission that we are in trouble is a condition for membership)?

21. Is it possible that some novices who seem incapable of making a monastic commitment would be quite willing to commit themselves permanently to the monastic quest, if that would not automatically tie them down to one single

pattern of persuing that quest? (And could we offer them alternatives?)

22. To what extent is the exclusion of the opposite sex from our monasteries (and, obviously, we are not questioning celibacy) a help or a hindrance to spiritual maturity?

23. How can charismatic leadership be encouraged and integrated into existing monastic institutions (the way the *startsy*, for example, were part of russian monastic life)?

24. How successfully are we translating our ancient monastic tradition of cosmic piety (based on cosmic Christology) into up-to-date practice?

25. If monastic life is rooted in 'an irradicable instinct of the human heart', as Merton called it, could it be that christian monasticism does not simply happen when we faithfully follow Scripture (Protestants may have a point here), but rather when, in the light of Scripture, we baptize primordial monasticism?

26. Could the baptizing of that primordial monasticism, which springs up around us, possibly become a new form of monastic parenting?

The practical implications of the previous questions may indeed seem staggering. It may appear inconceivable for monastic parents to leave their empty noviciates in order to follow a generation that will not come to them. Yet, there is many a job opening for early retired abbots and abbesses as gurus in quasi-monastic New Age communities. The change of heart on our part for which this would call might well be the change of heart associated with no less monastic a figure than St John the Baptist. Of him it was foretold that he would 'turn the hearts of fathers towards their children' (Lk 1:17). Should we not rather have expected him to turn the hearts of wayward children towards the pure tradition of the fathers?

A painful experience comes to mind in this connection. Two young people from a commune where I stayed one summer went to visit a neighboring monastery. It was a two day trip on foot through the mountains. They left with great expectations and returned with a certain sadness. 'Had they

not been well received,' I asked. 'Oh, very well.' They
described the kindness of the monk who had shown them
around. 'But after a while,' they added, 'we realized that
we felt much closer to him than he felt to us.' They had
recognized their own monasticism in him, but his heart had
not been turned far enough toward them to make this recognition mutual.

If we find it difficult to recognize primordial monasticism
expressed in unfamiliar forms, we should remember that our
own monastic life may appear distorted beyond recognition
when it is seen through the eyes of others. I vividly remember the horror and bewilderment on the face of some young
people when they discovered that certain monks, who had
genuinely impressed them, earned their living by raising
chickens cooped up between two conveyor belts, one that
supplied the feed, and another that carried off the eggs. No
whore-house could have offended my own moral sensibility
as violently as this ecological atrocity offended theirs. Turning the hearts of fathers towards their children will neces-
sitate challenging changes of life style. But, forunately, we
all know the answer to our final question:

27. Does monastic parenthood imply responsibility for the
future of monastic life, or for the perpetuation of our
accustomed way of living it?

COMMUNITY REPORTS

OUR LADY OF GUADALUPE ABBEY
Lafayette, Oregon

To prepare this short report from the Guadalupe Community on the role of the spiritual father in monastic life, we did not hold discussions on the matter or seek to formulate a common statement representing any kind of consensus. Rather, a short questionnaire was issued (to which the majority responded) requesting the brethren to express how they have personally experienced the role of spiritual father or ideally how they *could* experience the role. The results were tabulated, and we have assigned them to three categories: *first,* those wishing to reaffirm the traditional view in western benedictine monasticism of the abbot as the spiritual father, while suggesting certain criticisms of contemporary trends which they see as threatening to undermine this view; the *second* group represents those questioning the traditional view and manifesting personal difficulties experienced under its aegis; the *third* represents a more contemporary position wherein the traditional viewpoint has been modified by a certain modern thinking influenced by sociology, psychology, and other social sciences and certain elements of present-day spirituality.

About half of those answering the questionnaire basically supported the *traditional view* and, as a group, they highlighted those particular and familiar notions: one of the West's primary contributions in the whole area of spiritual fatherhood is the self-revelation of the christian God as Father and, as a consequence, the spiritual father bears his name, not in his own right, but in that of the heavenly Father, as Ephesians 3:15 and Matthew 23:9 indicate: 'All paternity, whether

spiritual or natural, takes its name from the Father in Heaven';
'You must call no one on earth your father. You have only
one Father, and He is in Heaven'. The abbot as spiritual father
is seen as taking the place of Christ in the community with a
mission to nurture this Christ-life, to be a channel of the
Divine Will, and to lead men back to the heavenly Father.
He should be a seasoned, prayerful man of God who exhorts
all to seek divine union under the guidance and asceticism of
the particular application of the Gospel which is the Rule of
St Benedict. His most important gift is seen as spiritual discernment. He should be 'all things to all men', teaching more by
his example than by words. He should remember, too, that he
has undertaken the government of weak souls, including his
own, and should be accordingly, compassionate to both. He
should, particularly in this age of increasing fragmentation,
promote a spirit of unity and peace in the community, striving
to act as its central source and longing to draw all into the
unity for which the Son prayed—'that all may be one'. In an
age of renewal, he should be mindful of the heavenly Father
as the Beginning and Well-spring of all energy. In regard to
temporalities, he must seek first the kingdom of God, trusting
that all else will be added unto them. As spiritual father, the
abbot is considered to be in the best position to know the
minds of the brethren-in-general and best able, therefore,
to advise in matters when their reactions are of key importance. He is also in the most salutary position to implement
whatever needs emerge in the spiritual discernment exercised
in the brethren's regard. The abbot, then, should count both
upon the gift of individual and community spiritual direction
as one of the special graces available to him. Moreover, the
practical experience and insights he gains at General Chapters, Regional Meetings, and the like should be invaluable in
this process.

Concern was expressed that, with the introduction of the
Statute on Unity and Pluralism,* the increase of a democratic

* A declaration of the 1969 General Chapter of the Cistercians of the Strict Observance. The text can be found in an appendix to Geoffrey Moorhouse, *Against
All Reason* (London, 1969; Harmondsworth, 1972).

mindset, the growing lack of discipline evident, and the broader view of obedience, the traditional view of the abbot as a spiritual father was being notably threatened. The importance of unanimity of minds in this whole context was stressed; the more divergent the minds and appetites, the less scope there is for a common spiritual father. The relation of father and son is based on similarity, both in life-in-general and in religious life. The less the similarity, therefore, the less the possibility of genuine paternal/filial relationship. Hence, the current emphasis on pluralism mitigates against an effective spiritual fatherhood, diminishing, as it does, the unanimity of minds and appetites. Diversity in these areas makes for distrust which leads inevitably to failures in charity. Such was held to be a western disease which the true East has probably never known. Moreover, groups of like-minded cliques begin to replace the spiritual father, bolstering, no doubt, their own self-image, but without the necessary theological background or sensitivity to spiritual discernment, they tend to bolster only their own human opinions, often to the detriment of a healthy spirit in the community.

The *second* group, comprising about one fourth of the answers to the questionnaire, was basically critical of the traditional view of spiritual fatherhood, both in theory and because of unfortunate personal experiences in its regard. Is spiritual fatherhood really a viable concept in a post-patriarchal society which has even moved into post-matriarchal structures tending more and more toward a sort of loose, group-management family? Is it viable also in a society whose wry picture of a father includes all too frequently the Archie Bunker or Dagwood Bumstead caricature? Insofar as the abbot seeks to emulate, as he once did, the secular ruler of a former age, to that extent he fails in our day. He can prove successful as a spiritual father, it is insisted, to the degree he refuses to define explicitly the role as such, and proceeds to function unselfconsciously as a modern father of a family seeking to be a good psychological counsellor, team manager, group leader. The question was also raised whether perhaps

377

the same criticism might be directed towards our eastern
brethren who represent a dying patriarchal culture as well.
One of the most mature and experienced monks among us
bore witness that for him personally spiritual fatherhood had
never played an important part in his life, and he conjectured
that such was probably the case with the majority of fellow
religious he knows. He quoted St Thérèse of Lisieux's contention that 'Jesus was her director'. Others in this group
maintained that excessive clericalism, contemporary stress on
personalism, the lack of experienced well-trained, confident
directors all have effected notably the vitality and credibility
of spiritual fatherhood in our day.

The *third* group, representing the remainder of the responses, reflected the influence of the modern social sciences
and present-day spirituality upon their more contemporary
vision of spiritual fatherhood. A typical opinion held the
role of the spiritual father to be that of *liberating* the disciple
from the psychological shackles which prevent him from being
open to his own being and to his God in that being. Empathic
and often silent listening to the frontiers of the disciple's
thought was frequently given high priority as a quality by this
group. The father/son relationship is seen as a phenomeno-
logical experience between two people with the element of
friendship figuring largely. The spiritual father's deepest concern should be to foster the son's God-given personality and
complete individuality, seeking to turn him to God in the
disciple's *own* way rather than attempting to mold him to
another's likeness. The display of confidence by the father in
the son's judgment was esteemed as a key element, whereas
another maintained that the rogerian quality of an 'unconditional positive regard' was the most admirable quality in the
director. The spiritual father, says one more, should be one in
touch with his own self, accepting his own history, deeply
aware of the present reality in and around him, and faithful
to the demands expected of a prophet, a head-watchman of
the *eschaton.*

MOUNT ST MARY'S ABBEY
Wrentham, Massachusetts

The abbess is 'believed to hold the place of Christ in the
monastery'. It would be hard to exaggerate the importance
of her role, which we understand to be the same as that outlined in the *Rule* for the abbot. Others share in her burdens,
but she is the spiritual mother. We see our spiritual mother as
at the very heart of our monastic life, both individually and as
a community. A faith relationship is established between her
and each member who joins the community with the desire of
truly seeking God, faith that God really guides us to himself
by means of this human instrument whom he has specially
chosen for the purpose. An abbess is chosen by the community
in canonical elections, but it would be more exact to say that
election time is a period of discernment and sometimes of deep
purification. Each member opens herself to the Holy Spirit
to know whom He has gifted with the charism of leading this
community and guiding each of its members in the ways of
the spiritual life. Because of canonical structures, this election
process of discernment is repeated quite frequently, and often
reveals a continuity in spiritual motherhood in deep harmony
with the *Rule* of St Benedict.

Spiritual motherhood is a truly paschal grace. A spiritual
mother is a channel of life to her daughters at the price of her
own self-emptying. Her time, energy, thought are drained by
her spiritual children—their problems, trials, their needs, their
growth—and yet she must maintain her own prayer or cease to
be a channel. The result is a really crucified life: crucified
with Jesus and immensely fruitful.

The spiritual direction of all the sisters by means of private
conferences, chapter talks, and dialogues is the special area

in which monastic spiritual motherhood is exercised. However, the abbess' concern extends to the material side of our lives as well, since monastic spirituality (in common with biblical spirituality) sees the person as a whole, frankly recognizing that what touches the body affects the soul. This solicitude expresses itself in concern for work problems, health, and even such things as seeing that the sisters have proper clothing and shoes. Such obvious concern creates a bond between spiritual mother and daughter on which grace and faith can build. This bond facilitates a complete openness with the abbess, even to revealing one's evil thoughts and inclinations. Only then can the spiritual mother help a sister to discern the promptings of the Holy Spirit and so guide her in her quest for purity of heart and continual prayer.

Submission to the judgement and guidance of the spiritual mother is the way outlined by St Benedict throughout the *Rule.* One instance that could be cited is found in Chapter 49, in which 'spiritual father' and 'abbot' are used interchangeably; in it we are told that 'whatever is done without the permission of the spiritual [mother] shall be imputed to presumption and vainglory', and that all should 'be done with the assistance of [her] prayers and with [her] consent'. The abbess herself is reminded in the same *Rule* that she is responsible before God for the spiritual growth of every one of the sisters in the monastery, and that she must constantly be open to the Holy Spirit's light and guidance to know when to reprove, when to encourage. Needless to say, this involves adaptation to a wide variety of characters and intelligences.

We could say that our spiritual mother is a sort of living word of remembrance bound to the forehead and wrist of each daughter—a constant reminder of God's call and a challenge to fulfill it. She is a raised standard to which her nuns may rally in the monastic battle. The role of spiritual mother is a difficult and arduous one, and blessed is the community that has the gift of a good one, Godgiven, supporting her daughters with strong love, and greatly loved in return.

HOLY TRINITY ABBEY
Huntsville, Utah

THE CONCEPT OF SPIRITUAL FATHER

The spiritual father is a person who helps another grow to the degree of holiness ordained for him by God. This relationship is involved to some extent in the encouragement given others through teaching, lectures, homilies, or good example, but it is exercised most clearly and directly in the giving of counsel on a one-to-one basis either in confession or outside it.

Spiritual direction apart from confession does not require that the director be a priest. Increasingly non-priests, both religious and lay, are exercising the role of spiritual director in this way. For this reason the term 'spiritual father' has a connotation that is broader than the office of abbot or superior.

The Rule and its spirituality should guide the relationship between a monk and his spiritual director, even though the monk may draw from other schools of spirituality in his personal piety. The behavioral sciences, although rendering a valuable service in counselling, should not become the primary or sole guide in monastic spiritual direction.

The Rule of St Benedict recognizes different levels of spiritual direction, hence of spiritual paternity. Benedict preferred a system of deaneries whereby capable and exemplary brethren share the authority and responsibilities of the abbot (RB 21). When legislating for monks who commit faults while at work (RB 46), he orders the offenders to confess their public faults to the abbot and community. 'However, should the matter be a secret sin of the soul, let him tell such a thing to the abbot alone, or to a spiritual father (*spiritalibus*

381

senioribus), for they know how to cure both their own wounds and the wounds of others without disclosing and publishing them.' Although the deans would be included among the *spiritalibus senioribus,* there is no indication that they are regarded as the only ones. The point remains that Benedict thought of spiritual direction and paternity in a wider context than that of the abbot and his office. Possibly the whole community could be considered as giving a kind of spiritual direction, because, in fact, each monk receives spiritual direction from several quarters. Novices, for example, receive direction to some degree from confessor, novice masters, and abbot, offices usually held by different individuals.

Differences of circumstances between a monastery of today and one of the past affect the manner of exercising spiritual direction. Today's ready availability of books and audio-visual instruction on prayer and spirituality makes possible a greater degree of self-direction and reduces the need for constant recourse to the spiritual director. Moreover, a good director avoids building up a relationship of dependency between himself and the directed. Rather, he helps the counseled become inner-directed and self-actuating. Good spiritual direction by the spiritual father results in good spiritual self-direction.

Despite the abundance and availability of information on spirituality and prayer, individuals at certain periods in life require the support and objectivity of a personal director, because the spiritual life involves the whole person, not merely his intellect. A living guide is necessary, at least occasionally.

Much of the ordinary spiritual guidance may take place in confession. The two overlap to some extent and are often combined. The fact that the community here sees no rigid division between the two and favors a broad definition of spiritual direction suggests that a sense of freedom prevails among the members in seeking spiritual direction.

THE ABBOT AS SPIRITUAL FATHER

Although most are in agreement that the idea of spiritual fatherhood extends beyond the abbatial office, account must be taken of the special place the abbot holds as spiritual father and guide.

Because the abbot is elected by a majority of the community, it is only logical to suppose that he, best of all, reflects the ideals of that community. Even where he is a compromise candidate, elected because of a division within the community, any weakness he shows will reflect the malaise within that community, for a community gets the kind of abbot it deserves.

The abbot sets the tone for the community, not only because he directs some of the monks personally, but because the other 'spiritual fathers' within the community normally share his ideals. Furthermore, the abbot controls the influences upon the community as a whole, both through his own chapter talks and through the persons he invites to address the community in retreats, courses, and occasional conferences. Thus, indirectly, the abbot influences the spiritual ideals and direction given to all the monks, even those he does not direct personally.

Besides being a spiritual guide, the abbot is also an administrator. The latter function, especially in a large community, precludes the possibility of his acting as immediate spiritual director to each of his monks. Moreover, Canon Law protects the freedom of religious by forbidding superiors to require a manifestation of conscience or to act as ordinary or extraordinary confessors of their subjects. This freedom to select a congenial spiritual guide is seen as beneficial for spiritual direction, but it also involves the danger that an individual will shop around for a guide who merely agrees with him.

Recent changes in society and the abbot's tenure of office have modified the relationship between abbot and community and consequently the abbot's role as spiritual father. Today abbots have the same cultural and educational backgrounds as many of their monks, whereas formerly abbots often were of the nobility and had a greater degree of education than most other members of the community. Today's changed attitudes towards authority, both civil and ecclesiastical, have repercussions within monasteries and are reflected in the growing tendency to limit the abbot's tenure of office.

When a monk realizes that in education he is on a par with his abbot, or even superior to him, and that the abbot is a temporary superior, he may be less inclined to seek out the abbot as his spiritual director. Although these are natural human considerations which ought to be subordinated to faith, they do affect the relationship between members of a community and their abbot.

SANTA RITA ABBEY
Sonita, Arizona

The superior of a house of Trappistines is the spiritual mother, the *Abba;* in fact, all her other roles are subordinated to this one. Not only is it her place to cherish and nourish the growth of each member of the Community, but she can also demand and challenge. Any of these things can be, and often are, done in a non-verbal way.

It takes two to make a spiritual mother: any sister in the community must believe that the superior holds the place of Christ in the monastery (RB 2). This faith is absolutely essential to a genuine spiritual mother–daughter relationship, and it is in this faith that the relationship transcends its analogous counterpart, the family. It follows that a sister's receptivity and submission in all obedience (RB 7) is the highest form of independence, an indication of her spiritual maturity. We expect a sister also to be open to challenge and demand, willing to accept the vulnerability of dwelling in a spirit of obedience, ready, in faith, to leap beyond appearance to the reality of the Lord's presence.

The spiritual mother, for her part, exercises her authority in our midst 'as one who serves' (Lk 22:27), thus giving expression to God's love for her daughters (*Perfectae charitatis* No. 14). She has an ear to listen and a heart to discern. This listening and discerning require of the spiritual mother in a pre-eminent way that *ascesis* of obedience which leads her into the very heart of the paschal mystery of the Lord Jesus.

We feel that these reflections apply in a particular way to our community because of the manner in which our superior mediates the humble presence of Jesus even in her bearing, in her willingness to receive, her desire 'to have an ear and a heart'. May these few lines bear tribute to the gift she makes us of herself.

MONASTERIO LA DEHESA
Chile

That there is a spiritual father in our community seems to
me to be certain, but it is not so easy to identify just who it
is. His role can be described, though this receives relatively
little reflection among us. The role, even though not very
explicitly cultivated, is put into practice in a concrete way in
our monastery. Let us look briefly at three questions.

1. *Who has the role of spiritual father in our community?*
It is interesting to see that in our community the process of
engendering new life in the spirit is exercised by the community as such, more than by one specific person within the
community, though the role is more accentuated in some
members at certain times. It is unthinkable here that the
superior or the novice master or the spiritual director could
effectively engender new life without the close cooperation of
the rest. The affection of spiritual son or spiritual father is not
usually experienced in relation to just one specific person.
Even from the day a candidate arrives, he begins to cooperate
by his own spiritual thrust in the fostering of life in the rest,
though his need to receive life and formation is naturally
greater in the beginning.
For my part, I consider the superior to be the spiritual father
of the whole community by his very office. I also consider
him my own spiritual father personally, because of my attitude toward his office and by my personal choice.
In my last nine years as novice master and a spiritual director, only a few people have told me they feel I am their father
in a way that transcends simple spiritual counseling. The rest
recognize that they receive support through the instrumentality

387

of many. Each member of the community is free, after the novitiate, to choose his spiritual director in the community. The person of his choice is seldom referred to as his spiritual father.

In a word, each one does what he can to cooperate in God's plan, and recognizes that these efforts of all are the channels of God's life to us.

2. *What then is the role of the spiritual father in our community?*
   It is to be a sign or sacrament of the unique and universal paternity of God. A man engenders new life in the spirit to the extent that he mediates the lifegiving act of God. That is why all can and do participate to some extent in the role of spiritual father. The imparting of life is a whole process, not just one simple action. Just as in natural parenthood the role of the father is not terminated with the conception or birth of the child, nor even with his arrival at relative maturity, but only with the son's safe arrival at his eternal destiny (since the process of giving new life can 'miscarry' at any moment until that arrival), so it is too with spiritual fatherhood; the father must sustain his generative effort until his son be *fully* born: 'My little children, with whom I am in labor until Christ be formed in you!'

St Benedict and St Robert [of Molesme] are also our spiritual fathers, for they continue even now to mediate life to us.

The spiritual father must participate in the unique mediation of Christ Jesus the Only Begotten Son, who 'shows' us the Father and makes us sons by incorporating us into Himself. In at least two places (RB 2 and 63) St Benedict refers the name *abbas* to Christ. *Abbas* is Christ's name in the sense that His very Person *is* the essential 'cry', 'Abba!' To be incorporated into Him is to be incorporated into his cry, 'Abba!' The abbot's life must be so completely united with this cry of Christ, that when any brother sees him he too cries, 'Abba!'

3. *Finally, how is this role put into practice in our community?*
I would say, almost unconsciously. No one poses as spiritual father, nor does anyone deny the good of transmitting life in the spirit. But we seem to think that every desire to do God's will and every acceptance of his gift already contributes to giving life to others. Our superior does not ask or desire to be the exclusive spiritual father of any one brother or of the community. Just as St Benedict would have the abbot share his task with others, so our superior readily recognizes that all are cooperating with him in the spiritual effort; it would be impossible clearly to delineate how or to what extent. In practice, our superior exercises a sustained personal communication with many of the brothers. His weekly talks to the community are also of great importance, as well as his constant attitude of humble service. In regard to the newcomers, the superior prefers that they have an intense and unified contact with the novice master, which usually would only be impaired by an intense direct contact with the superior. In fact, as we had occasion to note recently in our report to the regional novice masters' meeting, the personal conversations between each novice and the novice master seem to be one of the most important formative influences in this community. (Equally important is the complete integration of the novices into the *horarium* and life-style of the whole community; only second in importance are the formal instructions offered in classes).
Still in all, spiritual fatherhood in our community is experienced, perhaps strangely so, as a communal reality.

The previous article is only the personal opinion of its author, Brother Lino. Here the same person simply reports the moderate response the article was able to evoke in two days of exposure in the community.
Father Richard, the superior, found occasion to say in community that he liked the article a lot. He reiterated the position that the spiritual father here is not easily identified, and that the vitality of each one fosters life in all.

Brother Placido, a postulant, offers a short quotation from Fr Pierre–Yves Emery, which I shorten even more here. 'There are some men that impress us for the natural gifts they have been able to practise, their way of seeing, hearing, and observing, their capacity to pick up harmonies and connections; . . . also for their warmth of feeling and their sensitive touch . . . . Can't we say that these men are for us initiators, guides, and, at very least, an existential invitation to keep on growing?'

The personal experiences, long and varied, that Brother Edward has had in our monasteries, provided him with a rich basis for writing several pages of reflections on this theme. Negatively, he rejects the notion of spiritual father, and thus does not accept its existence in our community at La Dehesa. Positively, he sees our life in the Spirit (read 'growth', 'change', 'ongoing conversion') as individuals and as community, as a function of brotherhood, community, and leadership. Jesus says, 'Call no man on earth father for one is your Father who is in heaven'. This text is not cited as some kind of a 'proof'. It does, however, when taken in context, indicate Jesus' attitude in regard to the use *of authority. He is not attacking authority; he is attacking—as he does on other occasions—authoritarianism. Christ's prayer in John 17 invites the reflection that we are other Christs, brothers helping brothers to grow ever more deeply in their life with God. The current of brotherly love thus generated in a community having several 'older brothers' serves to inform and stimulate the vocation to this community in those newly called and received. These latter respond by generous cooperation, and their contribution to the dynamism of the community life grows as they themselves grow in this life. Again, it is Christ in all. Leadership is a necessary quality in a superior. Not everyone has this quality to a sufficient degree. In this crucial aspect our community at La Dehesa is favored to have Father Richard as superior.* 'It seems to me that "relationship" is the key element in Richard's exercise of authority. He has fostered a climate of mutual respect and responsiveness that puts the interests of the other—community or another brother—before one's own, and yet without losing sight of one's own real needs. Here indeed is a delicate balance of interpersonal relationships in community. Corollary aspects of this type of leadership are subsidiarity and participation—"we are all in this together". Was it St Augustine who said, "One Christ loving himself"? Now that I have reflected on the subject, I venture to say that it is this quality of leadership [which sets the tone of life at La Dehesa] that is largely responsible for the fact that I am so happy here. The beautiful setting, the wonderful climate just won't do it if one doesn't have a sense of inner freedom and autonomous functioning within the context of this leadership based on relationship . . . . I appreciate . . . gratefully the brotherly fashion in which Richard fosters the growth of the Kingdom in our community and in each of its members.'

Abba, *The Spiritual Guide*

OUR LADY OF MEPKIN ABBEY
Moncks Corner, South Carolina

The 'spiritual father' in our community nowadays is a
mediator, in the sense that his role is to be a transmission
belt, a communicator between a patrimony of monastic
christian truth and the brethren who form the fraternity. It is
a function that cannot be adequately described except through
the concept of *diakonia.* In short, if the abbot is to be at the
head of the monastery, he is to be at the *feet* of his brothers.
His function is one thing: *a call to service.*

To mix a metaphor a bit, the abbot (or abbess), the spiritual
father (or mother), is roughly analogous to the queen bee in
a colony of bees. While she receives special dignity and place
in the life of the hive, this unique headship and deference is
solely so that the fruitful work of the communal life may
move, be genuinely productive, and thus achieve the very
purpose of its existence. A colony simply cannot be unless
there is one who transmits life, one who is (in the inscrutable
or even cunning wisdom of Mother Nature) selected for her
vocation. (And when she is no longer apt for her office, she is
removed from it by the common will of the colony).

This role of the spiritual father–mother (and both *animus*
and *anima* are needed, whatever the person's gender) is one
of responsbility and accountability before God and before
the brethren–'sistren'. While it remains true—as the Holy Rule
instructs us—that the spiritual father takes the place of Christ,
this exalted concept must not be allowed to gloss over the
very human qualities—for weal or for woe—that he possesses.
Indeed, the present-day *tempus definitum* duration in office
tends to underscore the very human limitations of any spiritual father–mother. (I do not believe we have yet had time

392

or experience to perceive the 'ideological' impact of a *father,* an *abba,* being such for a determined period of six years.)

Perhaps in our efforts to understand, to re-evaluate the office of spiritual father, we have been too prone to overlook that before we can penetrate very deeply into the role he plays, we must first come to grips with a theology, a mystique, an articulation of what the community itself is. Too facile, for a number of reasons, is it—presto!—to equate a monastic community with an ordinary family. If there are likenesses, there are perhaps more fundamental unlikenesses. We cannot choose our father-in-the-flesh, nor properly vote him out of office. We can and do do this in the case of the monastic 'parent'. And so on.

The basic quality of our life-style is *faith,* and maybe in no aspect is this so dramatically shown as in the case of the abbot, the spiritual father/mother. For while he is 'voted in' by the community, his right to govern, to serve, to mediate, is not a creature of the voting chapter but a reflection of the power of the Lord operating in a human context. It is a modality of convenantal dependency. When a couple entering the sacrament of matrimony both say 'yes', the bond that results is not *their* creation, but God's. In that sense, the spiritual father/mother does occupy the place of Christ the Bridegroom who is wedded to His Bride because the heavenly Father wills it. The *nexus* shares in the Spirit's love and service and surrender. Perhaps it is time that abbots commence again to wear rings, as espoused to their communities. There is a way in which Christ can be called 'a father'. 'I have been among you as one who serves.'

OUR LADY OF THE MISSISSIPPI ABBEY
Dubuque, Iowa

It is important to distinguish the role of the spiritual
mother in regard to a single disciple and to a community of
disciples. Recently someone told us that authority was composed of three elements, unitive, directive, and corrective. In
her relationship with a single disciple, these three elements
focus on the individual. The spiritual mother guides the
disciple to unity within herself, within her community, with
her God; the mother directs her in ways that she sees specific
to the needs of this individual toward this unity. And she corrects anything that she sees as detrimental to it.

The spiritual mother of a community of disciples hears the
same elements of authority, but in ways that require working
with the group, leading the group, correcting the group. The
methods of doing this will probably entail dialogue, group
dynamics, community gatherings, prayer together.

It is important that the abbess be a spiritual guide and only
secondarily an administrator. In practice, these two functions
flow together, but the leadership of the abbess is primarily a
spiritual leadership and influence. It is through her and under
her direction that God's love and concern, plan and care for
our life is unfolded to us. This is a unique and irreplaceable
relationship. Yet it is not an exclusive one. On the contrary,
it is all inclusive. By this is meant that in the past it was
thought necessary to restrict contact, not only with friends
and visitors, but even with other members of the community.
We certainly learn much from and be influenced by others,
even spiritually (a friendship is a spiritual relationship if it is
anything), but the relationship between a master and a disciple
is so all-encompassing and all-inclusive that it cannot, if

rightly understood, be confused with any other.

In what does this spiritual direction consist? Some of us were impressed with a remark made by Mother Raphael, abbess of Berkel in Holland: 'We must never forget: spiritual life is *life*'. Thus a spiritual guide is a guide to *life*. At every point in her development the disciple appreciates a sympathetic listening and concern for what is happening within her—response to Scripture, in prayer, in feelings, in relationships. The mark of a spiritual director is compassion, and it is this very compassion which directs us to God.

The verbalization of thoughts and strong feelings in an atmosphere of care is a necessity if we are to integrate and direct these inner resources in a positive way, and to open ourselves to the Spirit in these areas. It is good to feel free to bring one's total self to someone who can accept and absorb it.

In regard to the role of the abbess to the community as a whole, we would agree with Henri Nouwen's observation in his account of monastic life, *Genesee Diary,* that the abbot's role is 'crucial . . . much of the mood in a contemplative house seems to depend on his leadership' (p. 10). Thus a concerned, caring, loving community means that there is a concerned, caring, loving abbess in the house. Yet a humble abbess, for no one can give love who has not first learned to receive it—from God, first and above all, from friends, and from her sisters. An abbess, then, might be seen as the primary receiver —only in order to be the primary giver—the sign and symbol of the self-giving of Christ to His people.

We would also briefly suggest the concepts of listener—to the Spirit and the brethren; creator and sustainer of unity; mother—in the sense of the one who brings forth, urges, encourages, nourishes life in each of the members of the community.

ABBEY OF NEW CLAIRVAUX
Vina, California

New Clairvaux's house survey on the spiritual father has
been evaluated in the context of the spiritual father as understood in William of St Thierry, so as to have a concrete point
of reference in dealing with the concept of a spiritual father
within the cistercian tradition and spirituality. William sees
the spiritual father as a very definite, deeply spiritual person.
He, along with God and our conscience, are the three guardians
assisting us through solitude and the Pasch into the experience
of the heavenly Father's goodness. The human spiritual father
encourages us in the pursuit of good (the animal stage), assists
us in developing a healthy monastic discernment and proper
use of reason (the rational stage), and, what is most essential,
receives our 'obedience and charity' (the spiritual stage). By
the obedience of charity the monk confides to his spiritual
father his own personal spirit so that the spiritual father may
direct this spirit to the Holy Spirit also dwelling within the
monk. In practice, this is the folly of obedience or foolishness for the sake of Christ. The spiritual father's effectiveness
is not that of a magnetic personality. Were it to be such, there
would open up the possibility of some foolish act of trust,
commitment, or fidelity—a counterfeit for the true folly for
the sake of Christ.

Ninety per cent of the twenty-two in our community who
offered an opinion consider that they have an individual
person as a spiritual father. The highest rating given the person
fulfilling this role was the abbot, primarily because of his
role in the community. Other persons mentioned were confessors and the master of novices. A minority of ten per cent
does not have a spiritual father as such or uses some other

form of guidance, for example, *lectio divina.*

Those having a spiritual father describe his role in terms that correspond to the animal and rational stages of William's concept. The 'obedience of charity' as such was not expressly mentioned. This is not to say that it is entirely absent from our community. Forty per cent see the role of the spiritual father as also residing in the community as a whole. Shared common life through prayer, work, support, and concern emphasizes the heavenly Father's knowing our needs before we ask.

The communal dimension of the spiritual father is not proper to William's concept. But this dimension does open up some questions we need to ask ourselves:

1. Since William's spirituality could be considered as more individual and solitude oriented, it is to be expected that he would not develop the notion of the community as a spiritual father. But what about the teaching and spirituality proper to Bernard or Aelred regarding the formative aspects of the community?

2. Does not the formative aspect of community (as a source of love and support) savor more of a maternal dimension, and the source of authority that is at the heart of a community more of a paternal dimension?

3. Can the formation given by a community (the Holy Spirit enlivens with his charisms the community and its individual members) adequately supply the paternal aspects of authority which is—in the *Rule* of Benedict—traditionally found in the abbot and the *Rule* (the abbot is also to interpret the *Rule;* the *Rule* is distinct from the community) and other charismatic individuals called to share in the leadership of the abbot and the *Rule?*

We offer no replies to these questions as we hope that the Symposium will give insights into the spiritual father's relationship to the formation given by the community.

VINA
A SUMMARY OF THE SYMPOSIUM

I. *Exploration of the Christian Tradition*
In all of the papers and ensuing discussion, the Symposium participants were striving to discover and elucidate an authentic Christian ideal of spiritual fatherhood/motherhood on which a valid practice could be based. The endeavor made it clear that there are in fact many interpretations of the symbols, spiritual father, spiritual mother.

Our study of spiritual fatherhood in the biblical, desert, monastic, and especially cistercian traditions led to the following clarifications and further questions. The person of Jesus, his actions and teaching, supply the model and source of the idea and practice of spiritual paternity in Christianity. Never calling himself 'father'—a title he reserved exclusively for God—Jesus brought forth children of God, redeemed humanity, thus fulfilling the mission entrusted to him by the Father. Thus it is *as* Son, the perfect Image of the Father, that Jesus became the exemplar for the christian exercise of spiritual fatherhood. Jesus' ministry as spiritual father aims at awakening people to awareness of their grace-given participation in his own being as a child of God.

Under the influence of the Holy Spirit, the idea and practice of spiritual paternity developed in the monastic Near East. Here we find new elements which naturally surfaced as the gospel was applied to the new phenomenon of christian monasticism. The later expression of spiritual fatherhood among the twelfth-century Cistercians had its own particular characteristics. Can the word 'father' adequately express today the richness of experience it symbolized in patristic and medieval usage? Some thought the contemporary devaluation

398

of the father-image made it irrelevant. Others pointed out that the christian ideal of fatherhood is not dependent on imperfect human representation, but that the divine source of all fatherhood reveals to us all what 'father' can mean and ought to mean.

The observation was made that our papers and discussions touched only 'spot samples' taken from the long and complex history of spiritual fatherhood in Christianity. We adverted also to the corrosive power of reflection and to the inadequacy of our language in dealing with the mystery of spiritual fatherhood.

After reviewing spiritual paternity in Rancé, we moved to contemporary experience. The following points emerged. There is a need to emphasize the role of the Holy Spirit in the exercise of spiritual fatherhood. The example of Mary is paramount in this connection; she accepted fecundation by the Spirit and so became the mother of Jesus and the spiritual mother *par excellence.*

We noted the danger, concomitant with the spiritual father-son relationship, of prostituting spiritual methods for non-spiritual purposes. The essential importance for spiritual growth of the ability to 'listen' was underscored, with the corresponding obligation of the father or mother to educate the spiritual child in this art of listening. The question of the role of psychology in spiritual paternity surfaced. It was agreed that spiritual direction is dependent on, and must respect, all psychological laws but is irreducible to them, having its own content. We lack today a theological anthropology capable of bearing the burden of the Good News—the Good News *for everyone,* especially for the poor, the weak, and the sick in mind and body.

Further discussion brought the observation that in most world religions, whenever there is a more than ordinarily intense appropriation of the religious values, there is a corresponding need for spiritual guidance. We listed particular reasons for spiritual guidance for the Christian:

1. because christian life in the pattern of the inner life

of the Trinity is a communion of giving and receiving;

2. because of the sacramental nature of human relationships and of the christian religion;

3. because of the teaching and example of the New Testament, for example, Mary and Elizabeth, Paul and Ananias; and

4. because the Christian shares in the mediatorship of Christ in whom God and man are united.

Study of the reports of the various houses brought out clearly that spiritual fatherhood is understood and practised very diversely depending on the experience, good and bad, in each community. The possible ambivalence of the practice of obedience drew special attention. The opinion prevailed that obedience could lead to freedom or to the abdication of freedom. It also emerged that guidance could come through other means, particularly through friendship, which entails rich possibilities for opening the heart.

II. *Exploration of the Eastern Tradition*

The efforts of this study and discussion were directed toward a sympathetic understanding of the spiritual message of the eastern religions. The prevailing mood was one of eagerness to discover and embrace views and practices of the hindu and zen traditions capable of enriching the christian experience. This naturally led to the question of the limits of compatibility between the great religions of man and Christianity.

Having concluded our review of spiritual fatherhood in the christian tradition, it was appropriate to recall the words of the Second Vatican Council as we began our study of the hindu and zen traditions.

> Thoroughly enriched with the treasures of mysticism adorning the Church's religious tradition, religious communities should strive to give expression to these treasures and to hand them on in a manner harmonious with the nature and the genius of each nation. Let them reflect attentively on how christian religious life may be able to assimilate the ascetic and contemplative traditions whose seeds were sometime already planted by God in ancient

400

cultures prior to the preaching of the gospel.

Decree on the Missionary Activity of the Church, no. 18

After a description of the guru in Indian terms, we had a presentation highlighting the function and vision of the guru in the context of present day America. It was remarked that in India guru is a generic institution covering most teaching roles; anyone from whom anything can be learned may be called a guru. Guruship thus permeates the entire social structure of India. This contrasts sharply with the american scene in which the ersatz guruship of the mass media gives the main line of orientation to american life. Dissatisfied with this situation, many Americans have set out in search for a guru or master in eastern religions. This 'journey to the East' is explicable in the absence or unavailability in western religions of spiritually qualified leaders capable of teaching concrete, practical ways of entering deeply into the inner life. Our discussions evinced the conviction that neither a large scale exodus to the East nor a massive importation of eastern elements by the West provides an adequate solution. More can be hoped for from a mature, mutual encounter of eastern and western traditions which would stimulate the actualization of latent elements in both traditions. In the West today there is a hesitancy on the part of potential spiritual fathers and mothers to accept the burdens of spiritual paternity/maternity. Moreover, contemporary religious structures—especially outside the monastic world—leave insufficient room for the function of spiritual fatherhood and motherhood. As a result, many potential spiritual sons and daughters have not been able to experience this relationship in their lives.

We agreed that while techniques may and ought to be used to facilitate openness to the sanctifying Spirit, holiness cannot be achieved by them alone. A strong caution was given against attempting to take possession of the spiritual riches of the East in a way that debases ways of life to mere techniques. On the other hand, open, respectful meetings between religions of East and West can lead to mutual pollinization. In this light we may ask if it is possible today to have a mature knowledge of one's own spirituality without being exposed to the other religious traditions.

In one session the symposium members had the benefit of an authentic exposition of the zen buddhist roshi–disciple relationship. In the ensuing discussion, attention was given to the many similarities between zen and christian spirituality. Yet the centrality of the person of Christ was held up as a feature Christians cannot give up.

III. *Comparative Studies*

In his opening remarks the chairman emphasized that the essential dialogue is not between East and West, but between the parts of ourselves which we tend to keep separate.

Reports on the 'New Age' communities (for example, the Integral Yoga Institute, San Francisco Zen Center, Lamm Foundation) revealed the following common features: the centrality of community, a unifying goal which leads to the development of a monastic environment which fosters spiritual growth, a dynamic flexibility along with a certain stability, a vision of life as search, and a membership which includes both men and women. The chosen guru or master has been central in most cases.

It was strongly urged that our western monasteries be open to receiving spiritual persons from eastern and 'New Age' communities, even to the extent of introducing a certain flexibility in present structures. A note of caution was added in regard to preparation, selectivity, and periodic review. The need was felt to have a deep exchange between different monks and monastic institutions. A theological and practical reflection on present day structures was called for.

The mutual fecundation among traditions will take time, patience, and continuous effort. The heart as the center of the human being has proved to be a symbol that speaks to most traditions. Thomas Merton, in his holistic view, saw the spiritual father's task as that of facilitating the disciple's return to his own heart so that he might find the freedom to surrender all to God. It is not possible to affirm that the experiences spoken of in different religious traditions actually do refer to the same reality, for experience, properly speaking, has no object. One must look to the transformation which experience produces in one's life to evaluate its worth. The service of the spiritual father is not primarily handing on teaching. He is to guide the disciple to personal experience. Genuine religious formation should lead to transformation and not just be an initiation into established structure.

A Concluding Statement

Man, on his pilgrimage toward his destiny, is not alone. He is called or attracted by the mystery and helped or obstructed by his fellow pilgrims. Human relations are essential to being human. Among these relations, the spiritual relationship between elders and juniors seems to be an essential feature for full humanness. Monastic life has been, down the ages and across cultures and religions, a special place where this spiritual guidance has developed. Because of the impact of modernity on almost all human traditions today, the role of the spiritual master is in crisis and at the same time, for the same reason, appears more relevant than ever. Monastic spirituality, understood as an expression of the human need for vertical transcendence, has a very important role to fulfill both in the encounter of religious traditions and in the deepening development of the nature and function of spiritual masters.

Christian monastic communities are open to the challenge of the times and simultaneously realize their duty to be loyal to their particular traditions. A double travail is seen as imperative: a deepening into and reinterpretation of the foundational and primitive charisms on the one hand and courageous fidelity to the present on the other.

This meeting itself, with its large and varied participation (monks and nuns, active religious and laity, married and single, from some fifteen nations), and the evident mutual trust, openness and quality of dialogue, was experienced as a sign of hope. Its true conclusion will be found in the work of the

SUPPLEMENT

The following significant questions emerged in the course of the Symposium and seemed worthy of noting for future consideration:

☐ At the personal and communal level in the contemporary practice of spiritual fatherhood, can we discern a continuation, degradation, or mutation of ancient tradition? (By mutation is meant actual substitution by other archetypes such as friendship, collective charism, midwife, wounded healer).

☐ Sonship implies obedience. Is it not necessary to distinguish the authentic practice of obedience from immature dependency—this distinction to be made by means of the fruits it produces?

☐ What are the specific opportunities and difficulties in the exercise of spiritual fatherhood in our day?

☐ Patristic literature seems to say that it is more perfect to do the will of another than to follow one's own inclination. Is this a valid concept and mature attitude for today?

☐ What are the distinctive elements in christian theory and practice of spiritual fatherhood vis-à-vis eastern thought and methods?

☐ Are the experiences of enlightenment in East and West ontologically distinct or merely pyschologically diverse?

☐ What are the main consequences for christian spiritual fatherhood of the diversity of interpretation of interior experience in the East and West?

In particular for the Cistercians:

☐ In what way or ways was spiritual paternity thought of and to what extent was it practised among the early Cistercians?

☐ Guerric of Igny witnesses to the traditional concept that

spiritual paternity is a normal development of monastic life. How is this vision realized within present day structures of our cistercian communities?

Abba, *The Spiritual Guide*

Holy Spirit in the heart of each as he responds with a new openness and trust to the call to enter into dialogue and engender new life.

COLUMBA GUARE
RAIMUNDO PANIKKAR
M. BASIL PENNINGTON
WILLIAM WILSON

LIST OF PARTICIPANTS

The Right Reverend Michael Abdo, OCSO
Abbot
Saint Benedict's Abbey
Snowmass, Colorado 81654

The Reverend Francis Acharya
Kurisumala Ashram
Vagamon, 685503, Kottayam
India

The Very Reverend Bruno Barnhart, Cam. OSB
Prior
Immaculate Heart Hermitage
Big Sur, California 93920

The Reverend Joseph Chu-Công, OCSO
St Joseph's Abbey
Spencer, Massachusetts 01562

Sister Donald Corcoran, OSB
Department of Theological Studies
Saint Louis University
Saint Louis, Missouri 63108
[now: Transfiguration Monastery
        RD 2-407A
        Windsor, New York 13865]

Abba, *The Spiritual Guide*

The Reverend Mother Myriam Dardenne, OCSO
Abbess
Redwoods Monastery
Whitethorn, California 95489

The Right Reverend Thomas X. Davis, OCSO
Abbot
Abbey of New Clairvaux
Vina, California 96092

Sister Dorothy Doerner, OSB
628 Mill Street
Excelsior, Minnesota 55331

The Reverend Lino Doerner, OCSO
Monasterio La Dehesa
Casilla 169, Las Condes
Chili

The Reverend Felix Donahue, OCSO
Abbey of Gethsemani
Trappist, Kentucky 40073

Sister Dolores Dowling, OSB
Prioress
The Benedictines of Perpetual Adoration
3888 Paducah Drive
San Diego, California 92117
[now: 2564 Virginia Street, No. 12
        Berkeley, California 94709]

Doctor E. Rozanne Elder
Editorial Director
Cistercian Publications
W.M.U. Station
Kalamazoo, Michigan 49008

List of Participants

Miss Mary T. Edwards
3720 Seven Hills Road
Castro Valley, California 94546

The Reverend Edward Farrell
Sacred Heart Seminary
2701 Chicago Boulevard
Detroit, Michigan 48206

The Reverend Mother Columba Guare, OCSO
Abbess
Our Lady of Mississippi Abbey
Dubuque, Iowa 52001

Mr. David G. Hackett
2451 Ridge Road
Box 107
Berkeley, California 94709

Sister M. Paula Hannah, O.Cist.
Prioress
Cistercian Monastery
Valley of Our Lady
Prairie du Sac, Wisconsin 53578

Sister Jean-Marie Howe, OCSO
[now The Reverend Mother, Abbess]
Abbaye N.-D. de l'Assomption d'Acadie
Rogersville, New Brunswick E0A 2T0
Canada

The Reverend Mother Cecile Jubinville, OCSO
Prioress
Santa Rita Abbey
Box 97
Sonoita, Arizona 85637

The Reverend M. Clement Kong, OCSO
Trappist Monastery
Lantao Island
P.O. Box 5, Peng Chau
Hong Kong

The Reverend Jean Leclercq
Abbaye St. Maurice
Clervaux, Luxembourg

The Right Reverend Dom André Louf, OCSO
Abbot
Abbaye Sainte-Marie-du-Mont
B.P. 3 Godewaersvelde
59270 Bailleul
France

Maezumi Roshi
Zen Center of Los Angeles
927 South Normandie Avenue
Los Angeles, California 90006

Professor Paul Marechal
International Meditation Society
2324 Napoleon Avenue
New Orleans, Louisiana 70115

The Right Reverend Edward McCorkell, OCSO
Abbot [now retired]
Holy Cross Abbey
Berryville, Virginia 22611

The Right Reverend Bernard McVeigh, OCSO
Abbot
Our Lady of Guadalupe Abbey
Lafayette, Oregon 97127

Professor Jacob Needleman
Center for the Study of New Religious Movements
Graduate Theological Union
2465 Le Conte Avenue
Berkeley, California 94709

The Reverend Daniel J. O'Hanlon, SJ
Jesuit School of Theology
1735 Le Roy Avenue
Berkeley, California 94709

Mr. Dennis Overman
St Joseph Church
Kalamazoo, Michigan 49004

Professor Raimundo Panikkar
Department of Religion
University of California at Santa Barbara
Santa Barbara, California 93106

The Reverend M. Basil Pennington, OCSO
St Joseph's Abbey
Spencer, Massachusetts 01562

Sister Miriam Pollard, OCSO
Mount St Mary Abbey
Wrentham, Massachusetts 02093

The Reverend Yves Raguin, SJ
Ricci Institute for Chinese Studies
Hangchow Nan-lu, Section 1
Lane 71, No. 9
Taipai 100
Taiwan, Republic of China

The Right Reverend Dom Benedict Reid, OSB
Abbot
St Gregory's Abbey
Route 3, Box 330
Three Rivers, Michigan 49093

The Right Reverend Monsignor Pietro M. Rossano
Secretario
Secretariato per i non Christiani
Vatican City

Brother Justin Sheehan, OCSO
Abbey of the Genesee
Piffard, New York 14533

Professor John R. Sommerfeldt
Executive Director
Institute of Cistercian Studies
Western Michigan University
Kalamazoo, Michigan 49008
[now: Department of History
       The University of Dallas
       Irving, Texas 75061]

Mrs. Patricia N. Sommerfeldt
Treasurer
Cistercian Publications
Kalamazoo, Michigan 49008
[now: 2809 Warren Circle
       Irving, Texas 75062]

The Most Reverend Dom Ambrose Southey, OCSO
Abbot General
Monte Cistello
Via Laurentina, 289
00142 Roma
Italy

The Right Reverend Emmanuel Spillane, OCSO
Abbot
Holy Trinity Abbey
Huntsville, Utah 84317

Brother David F.K. Steindl-Rast, OSB
Benedictine Grange
West Redding, Connecticut 06896

Tatsugen Sensai
Zen Center of Los Angeles
927 South Normandie Avenue
Los Angeles, California 90006

The Reverend Chrysogonus Waddell, OCSO
Abbey of Gethsemani
Trappist, Kentucky 40073

Brother William Benedict, CHT
Holy Trinity Monastery
3586 Paul Sweet Road
Santa Cruz, California 95065

The Reverend William Wilson, OCSO
New Melleray Abbey
Dubuque, Iowa 52001

LIST OF ABBREVIATIONS

A. **Books of the Bible**

Gn	Genesis	Jr	Jeremiah
Ex	Exodus	Lm	Lamentations
Lv	Leviticus	Ba	Baruch
Nb	Numbers	Ezk	Ezekiel
Dt	Deuteronomy	Dn	Daniel
Jos	Joshua	Ho	Hosea
Jg	Judges	Jl	Joel
Rt	Ruth	Am	Amos
1 S	1 Samuel	Ob	Obadiah
2 S	2 Samuel	Jon	Jonah
1 K	1 Kings	Mi	Micah
2 K	2 Kings	Na	Nahum
1 Ch	1 Chronicles	Hab	Habakkuk
2 Ch	2 Chronicles	Zp	Zephaniah
Ezr	Ezra	Hg	Haggai
Ne	Nehemiah	Zc	Zeckariah
Tb	Tobit	Ml	Malachi
Jdt	Judith		
Est	Esther	Mt	Matthew
1 M	1 Maccabees	Mk	Mark
2 M	2 Maccabees	Lk	Luke
Jb	Job	Jn	John
Ps	Psalms	Ac	Acts
Pr	Proverbs	Rm	Romans
Qo	Ecclesiastes	1 Co	1 Corinthians
Sg	Song of Songs	2 Co	2 Corinthians
Ws	Wisdom	Ga	Galatians
Si	Ecclesiasticus	Ep	Ephesians
Is	Isaiah	Ph	Phillippians

Col	Colossians	Jm	James
1 Th	1 Thessalonians	1 P	1 Peter
2 Th	2 Thessalonians	2 P	2 Peter
1 Tm	1 Timothy	1 Jn	1 John
2 Tm	2 Timothy	2 Jn	2 John
Tt	Titus	3 Jn	3 John
Phm	Philemon	Jude	Jude
Heb	Hebrews	Rv	Revelation

B. Others

CF *Cistercian Fathers* series. Spencer, Massachusetts; Washington, D.C.; Kalamazoo, Michigan, 1970–.

Coll. *Collectania ocr; Collectania cisterciensia.* Rome, Scourmont, 1934–.

CS *Cistercian Studies* series. Spencer, Massachusetts; Washington, D.C.; Kalamazoo, Michigan, 1969–.

CSEL *Corpus scriptorum ecclesiasticorum latinorum.* Vienna, 1866–.

CSt *Cistercian Studies* (periodical). Chimay, Belgium, 1961–.

PG J.-P. Migne (ed.), *Patrologiae cursus completus, series graeca,* 162 volumes. Paris, 1857–1866.

PL J.-P. Migne (ed.), *Patrologiae cursus completus, series latina,* 221 volumes. Paris, 1844–1864.

SBOp Jean Leclercq, H. M. Rochais, C. H. Talbot (edd.), *Sancti Bernardi Opera,* Rome: Editiones Cisterciennes, 1957–.

SC *Sources chrétienne* series. Paris, 1941–.

CISTERCIAN PUBLICATIONS INC.

TITLES LISTING

THE CISTERCIAN FATHERS SERIES

THE CISTERCIAN STUDIES SERIES

Temporarily out of print   †*Forthcoming*